First Workshop on Trolling, Aggression and Cyberbullying (TRAC-2018)

Santa Fe, New Mexico, USA
25 August 2018

ISBN: 978-1-5108-6915-8

COLING 2018

First Workshop on Trolling, Aggression and Cyberbullying (TRAC-2018)

Proceedings of the Workshop

August 25, 2018
Santa Fe, New Mexico, USA

Introduction

In the last few years, we have witnessed a gradual shift from largely static, read-only web to quickly expanding user-generated web. There has been an exponential growth in the availability and use of online platforms where users can post their own content. A major part of these platforms include social media websites and apps, blogs, Q&A forums and several similar platforms. All of these are almost exclusively user-generated websites. In all of these platforms and forums, humongous amount of data is created and circulated every minute. It has been estimated that there has been an increase of approximately 25% in the number of tweets per minutes and 22% increase in the number of Facebook posts per minute in the last 3 years. It is posited that approximately 500 million tweets are sent per day, 4.3 billion Facebook messages are posted and more than 200 million emails are sent each day, and approximately 2 million new blog posts are created daily over the web [1]. There is no such a thing as a 'consolidated figure' of the number of comments and opinion generated on websites worldwide, but it can be safely assumed that such a figure would be staggering.

As the number of people and this interaction over the web has increased, incidents of aggression and related activities like trolling, cyberbullying, flaming, hate speech, etc. have also increased manifold across the globe. The reach and extent of Internet has given such incidents unprecedented power and influence to affect the lives of billions of people. It has been reported that such incidents of online aggression and abuse have not only created mental and psychological health issues for web users, but they have in fact forced many people to change things in their daily lives, spanning deactivating accounts to instances of self-harm and suicide. Thus, incidents of online aggressive behaviour have become a major source of social conflict, with a potential of forming criminal activity. Therefore, it is a timely task for researchers and stakeholders to create preventive measures to safeguard the interests of web users, and to contribute to the maintenance of the civility of the online space in a more general sense.

This workshop focusses on the phenomena of online aggression, trolling, cyberbullying and other related phenomena, in both text (especially social media) and speech. The organisers aim to create a platform for academic discussions on this phenomena, based on previous joint work that they have done as part of a project funded by the British Council. We are particularly interested in promoting conversations dedicated to the automatic detection of aggression in both speech and text, that is, we hope that our workshop will not only be purely academic by nature but it will also generate real-life solutions to tackle the phenomena studied. As such the workshop also includes a shared task on 'Aggression Identification'. The task is to develop a classifier that could make a 3-way classification in between 'Overtly Aggressive', 'Covertly Aggressive' and 'Non-aggressive' text data. We made available a dataset of 15,000 aggression-annotated Facebook Posts and Comments each in Hindi (in both Roman and Devanagari script) and English for training and validation. Additional data for testing was released at a later date.

Both the workshop and the shared task received a very encouraging response from the community. There were more than 130 registrations for the shared task. Out of these, 30 teams submitted their systems. The proceedings include 18 system description papers that were finally submitted by the authors. In addition to this, the workshop also includes 5 regular papers presented in the workshop.

We would like to thank all the authors for their submision and members of the Program Committee for their invaluable efforts in reviewing and providing feedback to all the papers. We would also like to thank all the members of the Organising Comittee who have helped immensely in various aspects of the organisation of the workshop and the shared task.

---

[1] Source: https://www.gwava.com/blog/internet-data-created-daily/

Workshops Chairs

Ritesh Kumar, Dr. Bhimrao Ambedkar University, India
Daniel Kadar, Research Institute for Linguistics, Hungarian Academy of Sciences, Hungary

Organising Committee

Ritesh Kumar, Dr. Bhimrao Ambedkar University, India
Daniel Kadar, Research Institute for Linguistics, Hungarian Academy of Sciences, Hungary
Atul Kr. Ojha, Jawaharlal Nehru University, India
Bornini Lahiri, Jadavpur University, India
Marcos Zampieri, University of Wolverhampton, United Kingdom
Mayank, Jawaharlal Nehru University, India
Shervin Malmasi, Harvard Medical School, United States
Abdul Basit, Dr. Bhimrao Ambedkar University, India
Deepak Alok, Rutgers University, United States

Shared Task Organising Committee

Ritesh Kumar, Dr. Bhimrao Ambedkar University, India
Atul Kr. Ojha, Jawaharlal Nehru University, India
Marcos Zampieri, University of Wolverhampton, United Kingdom
Shervin Malmasi, Harvard Medical School, United States

Editors

Ritesh Kumar, Dr. Bhimrao Ambedkar University, India
Atul Kr. Ojha, Jawaharlal Nehru University, India
Marcos Zampieri, University of Wolverhampton, United Kingdom
Shervin Malmasi, Harvard Medical School, United States

Programme Committee

A. Seza Doğruöz, Tilburg University, Netherlands
Adrián Pastor López Monroy, University of Houston, USA
Amitava Das, IIIT-Sri City, India
Asif Ekbal, IIT-Patna, India
Atul Kr. Ojha, JNU, New Delhi, India
Bruno Emanuel Martins, University of Lisbon, Portugal
Cheng-Te Li, National Cheng Kung University, Taiwan
Chuan-Jie Lin, National Taiwan Ocean University, Taiwan
Claudia Peersman, Lancaster University, UK
Cynthia van Hee, LT3, Ghent University, Belgium
Danilo Croce, University of Roma, Italy
Dennis Tenen, Columbia University, USA
Elizabeth Losh, William and Mary College, USA
Els Lefever, LT3, Ghent University, Belgium
Erik Velldal, University of Oslo, Norway
Eshwar Chandresekharan, Georgia Tech, USA
Fumito Masui, Kitami Institute of Technology, Japan
Girish Nath Jha, Jawaharlal Nehru University, India
Haris Papageorgiou, ATHENA Research and Innovation Center, Greece
Hugo Jair Escalante, INAOE, Mexico
Ingmar Weber, Qatar Computing Research Institute, Qatar
Jen Golbeck, University of Maryland, USA
Jacqueline Wernimont, Arizona State University, USA
Kalika Bali, MSRI Bangalore, India
Lee Gillam, University of Surrey, UK
Liang-Chih Yu, Yuan Ze University, Taiwan
Libby Hemphill, University of Michigan, USA
Lun-Wei Ku, Academia Sinica, Taiwan
Mainack Mondal, University of Chicago, USA
Manuel Montes-y-Gómez, INAOE, Mexico
Marco Guerini, Fondazione Bruno Kessler, Trento
Marcos Zampieri, University of Wolverhampton, UK
Matthew Fuller, University of London, UK
Michael Wiegand, Saarland University, Germany
Michael Paul, University of Colorado Boulder, USA
Min-Yuh Day, Tamkong University, Taiwan
Ming-Feng Tsai, National Chengchi University, Taiwan
Monojit Choudhury, MSRI Bangalore, India
Michal Ptaszynski, Kitami Institute of Technology, Japan
Nemanja Djuric, Uber ATC, USA
Pawan Goyal, IIT-Kharagpur, India
Pete Burnap, Cardiff University, UK
Preslav Nakov, Qatar Computing Research Institute, Qatar
Ritesh Kumar, Dr. B. R. Ambedakar University, India
Roman Klinger, University of Stuttgart, Germany
Ruifeng Xu, Harbin Institute of Technology, China
Saptarshi Ghosh, IIT-Kharagpur, India
Sara E. Garza, Universidad Autónoma de Nuevo León (UANL), Mexico

Shervin Malmasi, Harvard Medical School, USA
Thamar Solorio, University of Houston, USA
Thiago Galery, DBpedia Association and Idio, London, UK
Veronique Hoste, LT3, Ghent University, Belgium
Vladan Radosavljevic, Temple University, USA
William Wang, University of California-Santa Barbara, USA
Xavier Tannier, Université Paris-Sud, LIMSI, CNRS, France
Ye Tian, Amazon Cambridge Development Centre (Alexa), UK
Yelena Mejova, Qatar Computing Research Institute, Qatar
Zeerak Waseem, University of Sheffield, UK
Zhunchen Luo, China Defense Science and Technology Information Center, China

Table of Contents

Conference Program

Saturday August 25, 2018

9:00–10:30   Inaugural Session

9:00–9:10   *Welcome by Workshop Chairs*

9:10–9:30   *Benchmarking Aggression Identification in Social Media*
Ritesh Kumar, Atul Kr. Ojha, Shervin Malmasi and Marcos Zampieri

9:30–10:30   *Keynote Talk*
Rada Mihalcea, University of Michigan, USA

10:30–11:00   *Coffee Break*

11:00–12:30   Poster Session

RiTUAL-UH at TRAC 2018 Shared Task: Aggression Identification
Niloofar Safi Samghabadi, Deepthi Mave, Sudipta Kar and Thamar Solorio

IRIT at TRAC 2018
Faneva Ramiandrisoa and Josiane Mothe

Fully Connected Neural Network with Advance Preprocessor to Identify Aggression over Facebook and Twitter
Kashyap Raiyani, Teresa Gonçalves, Paulo Quaresma and Vitor Beires Nogueira

Cyberbullying Intervention Based on Convolutional Neural Networks
Qianjia Huang, Diana Inkpen, Jianhong Zhang and David Van Bruwaene

LSTMs with Attention for Aggression Detection
Nishant Nikhil, Ramit Pahwa, Mehul Kumar Nirala and Rohan Khilnani

TRAC-1 Shared Task on Aggression Identification: IIT(ISM)@COLING'18
Ritesh Kumar, Guggilla Bhanodai, Rajendra Pamula and Maheshwar Reddy Chennuru

An Ensemble Approach for Aggression Identification in English and Hindi Text
Arjun Roy, Prashant Kapil, KINGSHUK BASAK and Asif Ekbal

Aggression Identification and Multi Lingual Word Embeddings
Thiago Galery and Efstathios Charitos

A K-Competitive Autoencoder for Aggression Detection in Social Media Text
Promita Maitra and Ritesh Sarkhel

Aggression Detection in Social Media: Using Deep Neural Networks, Data Augmentation, and Pseudo Labeling
Segun Taofeek Aroyehun and Alexander Gelbukh

Identifying Aggression and Toxicity in Comments using Capsule Network
Saurabh Srivastava, Prerna Khurana and Vartika Tewari

Degree based Classification of Harmful Speech using Twitter Data
Sanjana Sharma, Saksham Agrawal and Manish Shrivastava

Aggressive Language Identification Using Word Embeddings and Sentiment Features
Constantin Orasan

12:30–13:50   Lunch Break

13:50–15:55   Paper Session I

13:50–14:15   *Aggression Detection in Social Media using Deep Neural Networks*
Sreekanth Madisetty and Maunendra Sankar Desarkar

14:15–14:40   *Merging Datasets for Aggressive Text Identification*
Paula Fortuna, José Ferreira, Luiz Pires, Guilherme Routar and Sérgio Nunes

14:40–15:05   *Cyberbullying Detection Task: the EBSI-LIA-UNAM System (ELU) at COLING'18 TRAC-1*
Ignacio Arroyo-Fernández, Dominic Forest, Juan-Manuel Torres-Moreno, Mauricio Carrasco-Ruiz, Thomas Legeleux and Karen Joannette

15:05–15:30   *Aggression Identification Using Deep Learning and Data Augmentation*
Julian Risch and Ralf Krestel

15:30–15:55   *Cyber-aggression Detection using Cross Segment-and-Concatenate Multi-Task Learning from Text*
Ahmed Husseini Orabi, Mahmoud Husseini Orabi, Qianjia Huang, Diana Inkpen and David Van Bruwaene

15:55–16:20   Coffee Break

Benchmarking Aggression Identification in Social Media

Ritesh Kumar[1], Atul Kr. Ojha[2], Shervin Malmasi[3], Marcos Zampieri[4]
[1]Bhim Rao Ambedkar University, [2]Jawaharlal Nehru University,
[3]Harvard Medical School, [4]University of Wolverhampton,

Abstract

In this paper, we present the report and findings of the Shared Task on Aggression Identification organised as part of the First Workshop on Trolling, Aggression and Cyberbullying (TRAC - 1) at COLING 2018. The task was to develop a classifier that could discriminate between *Overtly Aggressive*, *Covertly Aggressive*, and *Non-aggressive* texts. For this task, the participants were provided with a dataset of 15,000 aggression-annotated Facebook Posts and Comments each in Hindi (in both Roman and Devanagari script) and English for training and validation. For testing, two different sets - one from Facebook and another from a different social media - were provided. A total of 130 teams registered to participate in the task, 30 teams submitted their test runs, and finally 20 teams also sent their system description paper which are included in the TRAC workshop proceedings. The best system obtained a weighted F-score of 0.64 for both Hindi and English on the Facebook test sets, while the best scores on the surprise set were 0.60 and 0.50 for English and Hindi respectively. The results presented in this report depict how challenging the task is. The positive response from the community and the great levels of participation in the first edition of this shared task also highlights the interest in this topic.

1 Introduction

In the last decade, with the emergence of an interactive web and especially popular social networking and social media platforms like Facebook and Twitter, there has been an exponential increase in the user-generated content being made available over the web. Now any information online has the power to reach billions of people within a matter of seconds. This has resulted in not only positive exchange of ideas but has also lead to a widespread dissemination of aggressive and potentially harmful content over the web. While most of the potentially harmful incidents like bullying or hate speech have predated the Internet, the reach and extent of Internet has given these incidents an unprecedented power and influence to affect the lives of billions of people. It has been reported that these incidents have not only created mental and psychological agony to the users of the web but has in fact forced people to deactivate their accounts and in extreme cases also commit suicides (Hinduja and Patchin, 2010). Thus the incidents of aggression and unratified verbal behaviour have not remained a minor nuisance, but have acquired the form of a major criminal activity that affects a large number of people. It is therefore important that preventive measures can be taken to cope with abusive behaviour aggression online.

One of the strategies to cope with aggressive behaviour online is to manually monitor and moderate user-generated content, however, the amount and pace at which new data is being created on the web has rendered manual methods of moderation and intervention almost completely impractical. As such the use (semi-) automatic methods to identify such behaviour has become important and has attracted more attention from the research community in recent years (Davidson et al., 2017; Malmasi and Zampieri, 2017).

Proceedings of the First Workshop on Trolling, Aggression and Cyberbullying, pages 1–11
Santa Fe, USA, August 25, 2018.

This paper reports the results of the first Shared Task on Aggression Identification which was organised jointly with the First Workshop on Trolling, Aggression and Cyberbullying (TRAC - 1) at COLING 2018.

2   Related Work

Verbal aggression *per se* has been rarely explored within the field of Natural Language Processing. However, previous research in the field has been carried out to automatically recognise several related behaviour such as trolling (Cambria et al., 2010; Kumar et al., 2014; Mojica, 2016; Mihaylov et al., 2015) , cyberbullying (Dinakar et al., 2012; Nitta et al., 2013; Dadvar et al., 2013; Dadvar et al., 2014; Hee et al., 2015), flaming / insults (Sax, 2016; Nitin et al., 2012), abusive / offensive language (Chen et al., 2012; Nobata et al., 2016; Waseem et al., 2017), hate speech (Pinkesh Badjatiya and Varma, 2017; Burnap and Williams, 2014; Davidson et al., 2017; Vigna et al., 2017; Djuric et al., 2015; Fortana, 2017; Gitari et al., 2015; Malmasi and Zampieri, 2018; Waseem and Hovy, 2016; Schmidt and Wiegand, 2017), radicalization (Agarwal and Sureka, 2015; Agarwal and Sureka, 2017), racism (Greevy and Smeaton, 2004; Greevy, 2004) and others. In addition to these, there have been some pragmatic studies on behaviour like trolling (Hardaker, 2010; Hardaker, 2013).

This huge interest in the field from different perspectives has created a conglomeration of terminologies as well as understandings of the phenomenon. On the one hand, this provides us with a very rich and extensive insight into the phenomena yet, on the other hand, it has also created a theoretical gap in the understanding of interrelationship among these. Moreover, it has also resulted in duplication of research, to certain extent, and a certain kind of lack of focus and reusability of datasets across different strands of research. In order to make improvements towards solving a complex phenomenon like this, it is of utmost importance that some kind of uniform understanding of problem be achieved so that, at least, standardised datasets and an understanding of different approaches to solving the problem may be developed.

While a large part of the research has focused on any one of these phenomena and their computational processing, it seems there is a significant overlap among these phenomenon in the way they are understood in these studies - and because of this underlying overlap, insights from different studies might prove useful for solving these seemingly different phenomena. All of these behaviours are considered undesirable, aggressive and detrimental for those on the receiving end. So, trolling is intended "to cause disruption and/or to trigger or exacerbate conflict for the purposes of their own amusement" (Hardaker, 2010). Cyberbullying is "humiliating and slandering behavior towards other people" (Nitta et al., 2013). Flaming intends "to offend someone through e-mail, posting, commenting or any statement using insults, swearing and hostile, intense language, trolling, etc." (Krol, 1992).

Waseem et al. (2017) makes an attempt to unify these different trends of research in what may be considered a significantly overlapping field and proposes a 2-way typology for understanding what they call 'abusive language' over the web. They propose 2 scales on which abusive language could be categorised - the target of the abuse (an individual or a group) and the nature of the language (explicit or implicit). Our classification of aggression into overt and covert aggression is largely similar to the explicit-implicit distinction. However, we make a more detailed distinction in relation to the target of the abuse (Kumar et al., 2018b) and it is not made along the axis of individual vs. group. This is so because we noticed in a large number of instances both individuals and groups are simultaneously targeted - in such cases individuals are targeted as members of certain groups or the individuals' actions were considered those of the group and became the locus of attack. As such it was not feasible to distinguish between the individual and group attack in lot of instances while annotating the dataset. The distinction that we made was related to the "locus" of attack and included such targets as gender, religion, caste, country of origin, race, etc. This classification, on the one hand, gave scope for focusing on different kinds of attack (for example, racial attacks or communal attacks) and, on the other hand, each of these targets may actually be attacked using a different set of vocabulary, thereby, making these more natural classes that could be classified using the surface-level linguistic features. Of course, it cannot be denied that these targets are not mutually exclusive and, as such, it makes the problem not just a multi-class classification problem but also multi-label classification problem. In addition to this, we also make use of a different terminology taking into account its use within socio-pragmatics. This was done with an understanding that huge amount of literature within the field of aggression and impoliteness studies might be able to contribute and provide insights to understanding the phenomenon in a better way.

The aim of this shared task was much simpler than the one discussed in the previous para. It only involved classification of the texts into 3 categories - overt aggression, covert aggression and non-aggression. We wanted to use the dataset for experimenting with different approaches to make the most top-level classification of aggression on social media.

3   Task Setup and Schedule

The participants interested in competing in the shared task were required to register using a Google Form. The form gave them an option to participate for either English or Hindi or both the languages. All the registered participants were sent the links to the annotated dataset in the language(s) of their choice, along with a description of the format of the dataset. The participants were allowed to use additional data for training the system, with the condition that the additional dataset should be either publicly available or make available immediately after submission (and well before the submission of the system papers) and this must be mentioned in the submission. Use of non-public additional data for training was not allowed. The participants were given around 6 weeks to experiment and develop the system. However, since more than half of the participants registered after the first release of the data, most of them got less time than this. Initially, the dataset was not released publicly but was emailed only to the registered participants. After the 6 weeks of release of train and dev sets, the test set was released and the participants had 5 days to test and upload their system. The complete timeline of the shared task is given in Table 1. We made use of CodaLab [1] for the evaluation. Each team was allowed to submit up to 3 systems for evaluation. We used the best of the 3 runs for the final ranking and evaluation of the systems.

Date	Event
1 February, 2018	Shared Task Announcement and Start of Registration
13 March, 2018	Release of train and dev sets
25 April, 2018	Release of test set
30 April, 2018	Deadline for Submission of System
2 May, 2018	Declaration of Results
28 May, 2018	Deadline for Submission of System Description Paper

Table 1: Timeline of the Aggression Identification Shared Task at TRAC - 1.

4   Dataset

The participants of the shared task were provided with a dataset of 12,000 randomly sampled Facebook comments for training and 3,000 comments for development and in English and Hindi each, annotated with 3 levels of aggression - Overtly Aggressive (OAG), Covertly Aggressive (CAG) and Non-Aggressive (NAG). For test, 916 English comments and 970 Hindi comments were provided. Additionally, 1,257 English tweets and 1,194 Hindi tweets were given as the surprise test set [2]. The dataset released for the task is a subset of a larger dataset discussed in Kumar et al. (2018b).

4.1   Issues with the Dataset

While most of the participants considered the dataset to be of high quality, two major problems came up during the task -

- **The language issue**: Some of the comments in English dataset contained code-mixed Hindi-English data as well as data from other languages like German. These formed a minuscule proportion of the data but nevertheless these need to be filtered out.

---

[1] https://competitions.codalab.org/

[2] The complete dataset used for the shared task can be downloaded here - http://trac1-dataset.kmiagra.org/

- **The annotation issue**: The second and more serious issue that was raised by some participants is related to the the annotation itself. Several instances of supposedly inaccurate annotation were pointed out. Despite the fact that aggression is a highly subjective phenomenon and different annotators may have different judgments about the same comment, some of the annotation indeed looked highly implausible and consequently it needs further scrutiny and validation.

5   Participants and Approaches

The shared task gave the participants an option to register for either one of the two languages - English or Hindi - or both. A total of 131 participants registered for the shared task, with 73 teams registering to participate only in English track, 2 teams only in Hindi track and 56 teams registered to participate in both the tracks. Out of these, finally a total of 30 teams submitted their systems - 15 teams for both English and Hindi and 30 teams for only English track. All the systems who submitted their system were invited to submit the system description paper, describing the experiments conducted by them. 18 participants submitted the final description paper which are included in the workshop proceedings - it included papers by majority of the top 10 teams. Table 2, lists the participating teams and the language they took part in.

Team	Hindi	English	System Description Paper
saroyehun		✓	(Aroyehun and Gelbukh, 2018)
EBSI-LIA-UNAM		✓	(Arroyo-Fernández et al., 2018)
DA-LD-Hildesheim	✓	✓	(Modha et al., 2018)
TakeLab		✓	(Golem et al., 2018)
sreeIN		✓	(Madisetty and Desarkar, 2018)
Julian	✓	✓	(Risch and Krestel, 2018)
taraka_rama	✓	✓	
uOttawa		✓	(Orabi et al., 2018)
Isistanitos		✓	(Tommasel et al., 2018)
hakuchumu		✓	
DataGeeks	✓	✓	
na14	✓	✓	(Samghabadi et al., 2018)
dinel		✓	(Orasan, 2018)
vista.ue	✓	✓	(Raiyani et al., 2018)
MANITBHOPALINDIA	✓	✓	
IRIT		✓	(Ramiandrisoa and Mothe, 2018)
quine	✓	✓	(Nikhil et al., 2018)
IIIT-Delhi		✓	
PMRS	✓	✓	(Maitra and Sarkhel, 2018)
resham	✓	✓	
IreneR		✓	
Nestor	✓	✓	
UAEMex-UAPT1	✓	✓	
forest_and_trees		✓	(Galery et al., 2018)
groutar		✓	(Fortuna et al., 2018)
Shusrut	✓	✓	(Roy et al., 2018)
malaypramanick		✓	
UAEMex-UAPT-TAC2	✓	✓	
Unito	✓	✓	
bhanodaig		✓	(Kumar et al., 2018a)
Total	**15**	**30**	**18**

Table 2: The teams that participated in the Aggression Identification Shared Task at TRAC - 1.

Next we give a short description of the approach taken by each team for building their system. More details about the approaches could be found in the paper submitted by the respective teams.

- **saroyehun** system gives the best performance with LSTM and they resorted to translation as data augmentation strategy. With the surprise twitter set, a combination of the representations of the RNN and CNN as features, along with additional preprocessing like spelling correction, translation of emoji, and computation of sentiment score gave the best performance. In this case, the dataset was also augmented using translation and pseudolabelled using an external dataset on hate speech.[3] This is the only approach in the competition that performs better on the Twitter dataset, despite being trained the Facebook dataset, thereby, depicting the ability of the approach to generalise across domain.

- **EBSI-LIA-UNAM** system uses a combination of the Passive-Aggressive (PA) and SVM classifiers with character based n-gram (1 - 5 grams) TF-IDF for feature representation.

- **DA-LD-Hildesheim** uses LSTM with pretrained Fasttext vector for embeddings for classifying English Facebook texts. For all other datasets including Twitter data in English and both Facebook and Twitter dataset in Hindi, CNN performs better.

- **TakeLab** uses a Bidirectional LSTM on Glove embeddings to give the best performance.

- **sreeIN** system uses a voting-based ensemble method with 3 classifiers - CNN with 4 layers, LSTM and Bidirectional LSTM.

- **Julian** team uses translation as data augmentation strategy and use an ensemble of TF-IDF based approaches, using character n-grams (2 - 6) and word n-grams (1 - 2) with a bi-directional RNN, using fasttext embeddings, to get the best performance in the task..

- **taraka_rama** uses different systems for different datasets. For English Facebook dataset and Hindi Twitter dataset, the team uses a stacked ensemble classifier that uses a SVM on top of the ensemble of SVM classifiers. The SVMs were trained on 1 - 6 character n-grams and word unigrams. For Hindi Facebook and English Twitter dataset, however, a plain SVM trained using character and word bag-of-n-grams gave the best performance. In this case, the overlapping character and word n-gram features are weigthed with sublinear tf-idf before being used for training and testing. The system is tuned using 5-fold CV on the combined training and develpment sets for maximum number of character and word n-grams included, case normalization, and SVM margin (regularization) parameter C.

- **uOttawa** system is trained using a novel deep-learning architecture for text classification based on Multi-task learning (MTL). The approach, MTL, is evaluated using three neural network models. MultiCNN, multiple convolution structure with a trainable embedding layer, gives the best performance.

- **Isistanitos** system uses a soft voting (average the class probabilities of other models) of two models - a recurrent neural network, and an SVM. The recurrent neural network uses 3 preprocesed set of features. The first set uses an ad-hoc glove model for representing the words, the second is a sentiwornet based model, and the third is a traditional TfIdf plus Vader Sentiment analysis and sentiments associated with the emojis. The SVM model is trained on a TF-IDF of the post stemmed terms, excluding stopwords, and 3 - 5 character n-grams.

- **hakuchumu** system makes use of a Random Forest classifier with some preprocessing including removal of urls and non letter characters and stop words. Along with the bag-of-word, the approach uses multiple occurrences of letters, exclamation marks and question marks in a row and emoticons as binary features.

- **DataGeeks** system uses Logistic Regression classifier with some preprocessing on the data such as removing non-ascii characters, replacing new line with '.', replacing n't with not, removing stopwords and 1 - 3 word n-grams and 2 - 6 character n-grams for training the classifier.

- **na14** also uses Logistic Regression classifier with preprocessing involving replacing URLs, numbers, email addresses and spelling correction. The classifier is trained using word unigrams, tf-idf vectors of word unigram, character 4-gram, character 5-gram and Google news pre-trained word embedding model. For the Hindi dataset, Devanagari texts were transliterated into Roman at the preprocessing stage.

- **dinel** achieves the best accuracy on the Facebook test set using a Random Forest classifier while SVMs performed better for the surprise Twiiter test set. Both the classifiers were trained using 300 semantic features which represent the vector representation of the text, average scores of the top emojis for each of the classes and positive and negative sentiment scores.

- **vista.ue** system is developed using dense neural networks.

- **MANITBHOPALINDIA** system for English is developed using SVM while for English it is trained using deep neural networks.

- **IRIT** system gets the best performance for the English Facebook test set by using a combination of two models - a doc2vec model and a logistic regression classifier. For the Twitter test set, it uses a combination of CNN and LSTM to get the best performance.

- **quine** system is trained using an LSTM with attention and simple embeddings (word to index) instead of pre-trained embeddings.

- **IIIT-Delhi** system uses a Single channel CNN for this task. Bayesian Optimization is used for tuning the parameters.

- **PMRS** system employs a winner-takes- all autoencoder, called Emoti-KATE for Twitter sentiment classification. Each input dimension of Emoti-KATE is a log-normalized, sentiwordnet-score weighted word-count vector. A binary cross-entropy loss function is used to train the network.

- **resham** system for English has been made using an open vocabulary approach and ensemble model of two predictors with soft voting. The first predictor is a Naive Bayes model with CountVectorizer for preprocessing. The second predictor is a recurrent neural network with one embedding layer and two LSTM layers. Pre-trained word vectors have been used for the embedding layer. For Hindi dataset, a Naive Bayes classifier is trained using the dataset augmented with English translations.

- **IreneR** system is based on a Multinomial Naive Bayes classifier that uses unigrams, bigrams, hedging bigrams and trigrams such as 'do you', someone who is','to see that', that potentially signal covert aggressivity, identified with chi-squared test as features. It also includes features from LIWC2015 (list of anger and swear words).

- **Nestor** uses an approach that combines Neural Networks and a new word representation model. The patterns obtained from the word model representation are used for training the back propagation neural network with fix parameters. The length of the post was fixed and the word model representation is language independent, so it was used for both the English and the Hindi tasks.

- **UAEMex-UAPT1** uses the same approach as used by the team Nestor.

- **forest_and_trees** system uses a Pooled Recurrent Unit architecture combined with pre-trained English and Hindi fasttext word embeddings as a representation of the sequence input. In this approach, Hindi and English vectors were aligned using pre-computed SVD matrices that pulls representations from different languages into a single space. This enabled the same model to be used for both the languages, thereby, making data re-utilization and model deployability easier.

- **groutar** system is trained using random forests. The dataset is augmented with an external toxicity dataset [4]. The approach involved understanding the effects of new data on aggression identification.

---

[4] https://www.kaggle.com/c/jigsaw-toxic-comment-classification-challenge

- **Shusrut** system uses an ensemble of CNN 2D with MAXPOOL classifier and a SVM classifier. The ensemble model is passed through 3 dense layers to finally predict the output. Softmax activation is used in the outer layer for classification.

- **malaypramanick** system uses a random forest classifier trained using a set of surface-level features including number of line,s uppercase and lowercase letters, digits, named entities, unicode characters, etc.

- **UAEMex-UAPT-TAC2** system is generated by combination of twelve distance measures, through a K Nearest Neighbors classification algorithm and a canonical genetic algorithm.

- **Unito** is the only unsupervised system submitted in the task. It is based only on a multilingual lexicon of aggressive words. The lexicon is obtained by automatic translation from an handmade lexicon of offensive words in Italian, with minimal human supervision. The original words are expanded into a list of their senses. The senses are manually annotated to filter out senses that are never used in an offensive context. Finally, all the lemmas of the remaining senses are generated with BabelNet in 50+ languages. The words in the lexicon are divided in those translating sense that can be used in an offensive context (but not necessarily are) and words translating senses that are directly offensive. This distinction is mapped to the Overtly Aggressive and Covertly Aggressive classes respectively. The classification of sentences is straightforward: a sentence that does not contain any word from the lexicon is tagged as NAG, a sentence containing more directly offensive words than potentially offensive words is tagged as OAG, and the other cases are tagged as CAG.

- **bhanodaig** system uses a bidirectional LSTM.

6   Results

In this section, we present the results of the experiments carried out by different teams during the shared task. The results of the top 15 teams on English dataset is given in Figure 1 and that on Hindi dataset is in Figure 2.

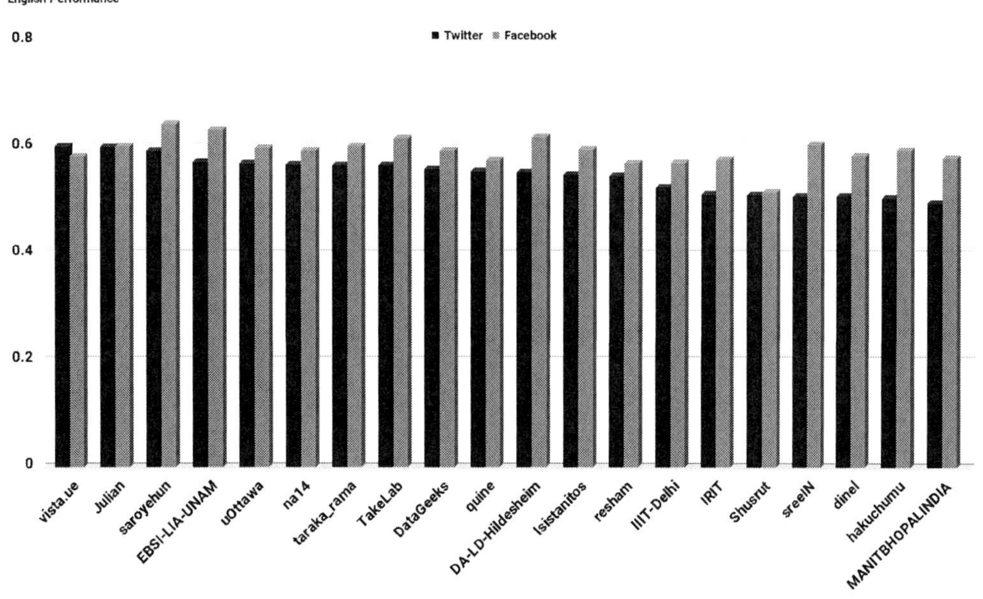

Figure 1: Performance of top 15 teams on English Dataset

The participants were allowed to use other datasets, in addition to the one provided by the organizers of the task. However, because of the lack of similar alternative datasets, all the groups, except 'groutar' and 'saroyehun' team, used only the dataset provided for the task. As we mentioned earlier, the participants were given two kinds of test sets for the final testing of the system - one from Facebook and a surprise test set from Twitter.

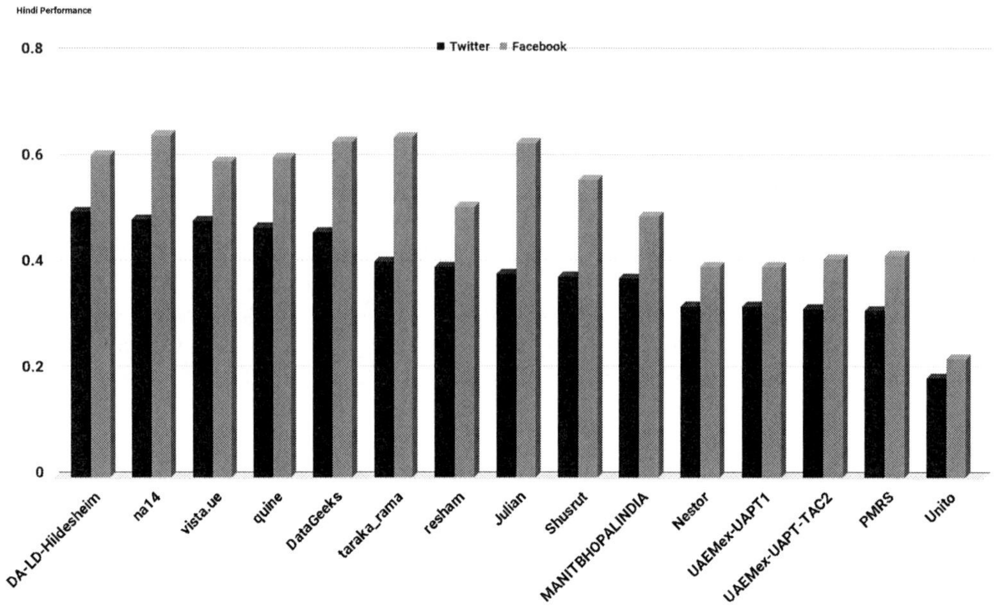

Figure 2: Performance of teams on Hindi Dataset

7 Conclusion

In this paper, we have presented the report of the First Shared task on Aggression Identification organized with the TRAC workshop at COLING 2018. The shared task received a very encouraging response from the community which underlines the relevance and need of the task. More than 100 teams registered and 30 teams finally submitted their system.

The performance of the best systems in the task show that aggression identification is a hard problem to solve. Moreover, the performance of the neural networks-based systems as well as the other approaches do not seem to differ much. If the features are carefully selected then classifiers like SVM and even random forest and logistic regression perform at par with deep neural networks. On the other had, we find quite a few neural networks-based systems not performing quite well in the task. Nonetheless, 14 systems were trained using one or the other architectures of deep neural networks - either solely or as part of an ensemble. Moreover, 8 systems out of the top 15 are trained on neural networks, which shows the efficacy of the approach but at the same time does not rule out the usefulness and relevance of linear models for the task. There was only one system, Unito, that made use of a lexicon-based approach to solve the task. A few participants of the task pointed out the apparent "inconsistencies" in the annotation. It points towards the need to get the annotations validated by multiple human annotators.

Acknowledgements

We would like to thank Microsoft Research India for providing grants to prepare the dataset and to our annotators who worked very hard to finish the annotations within a strict deadline.

We would also like to thank the participants of the Shared Task for their participation and feedback and the TRAC workshop PC members for thoroughly reviewing the shared task papers within a very short span of time.

References

Swati Agarwal and Ashish Sureka. 2015. Using knn and svm based one-class classifier for detecting online radicalization on twitter. In *International Conference on Distributed Computing and Internet Technology*, pages 431 – 442. Springer.

Swati Agarwal and Ashish Sureka. 2017. Characterizing linguistic attributes for automatic classification of intent based racist/radicalized posts on tumblr micro-blogging website.

Segun Taofeek Aroyehun and Alexander Gelbukh. 2018. Aggression detection in social media: Using deep neural networks, data augmentation, and pseudo labeling. In *Proceedings of the First Workshop on Trolling, Aggression and Cyberbullying (TRAC – 1)*, Santa Fe, USA.

Ignacio Arroyo-Fernández, Dominic Forest, Juan-Manuel Torres-Moreno, Mauricio Carrasco-Ruiz, Thomas Legeleux, and Karen Joannette. 2018. Cyber-bullying detection task: the ebsi-lia-unam system (elu) at coling'18 trac-1. In *Proceedings of the First Workshop on Trolling, Aggression and Cyberbullying (TRAC – 1)*, Santa Fe, USA.

Peter Burnap and Matthew L. Williams. 2014. Hate speech, machine classification and statistical modelling of information flows on twitter: Interpretation and communication for policy decision making. In *Proceedings of Internet, Policy & Politics*, pages 1 – 18.

Erik Cambria, Praphul Chandra, Avinash Sharma, and Amir Hussain. 2010. Do not feel the trolls. In *ISWC, Shanghai*.

Ying Chen, Yilu Zhou, Sencun Zhu, and Heng Xu. 2012. Detecting offensive language in social media to protect adolescent online safety. privacy, security, risk and trust (passat). In *International Conference on Social Computing (SocialCom)*, pages 71–80.

Maral Dadvar, Dolf Trieschnigg, Roeland Ordelman, and Franciska de Jong. 2013. Improving cyberbullying detection with user context. In *Advances in Information Retrieval*, pages 693–696. Springer.

Maral Dadvar, Dolf Trieschnigg, and Franciska de Jong. 2014. Experts and machines against bullies: a hybrid approach to detect cyberbullies. In *Advances in Artificial Intelligence*, pages 275–281. Springer, Berlin.

Thomas Davidson, Dana Warmsley, Michael Macy, and Ingmar Weber. 2017. Automated hate speech detection and the problem of offensive language. In *Proceedings of ICWSM*.

Karthik Dinakar, Birago Jones, Catherine Havasi Henry Lieberman, and Rosalind Picard. 2012. Common sense reasoning for detection, prevention, and mitigation of cyberbullying. *ACM Transactions on Interactive Intelligent Systems (TiiS)*, 2(3):18:1–18:30.

Nemanja Djuric, Jing Zhou, Robin Morris, Mihajlo Grbovic, Vladan Radosavljevic, and Narayan Bhamidipati. 2015. Hate speech detection with comment embeddings. In *Proceedings of the 24th International Conference on World Wide Web*, pages 29 – 30.

Paula Fortana. 2017. Automatic detection of hate speech in text: an overview of the topic and dataset annotation with hierarchical classes. Master's thesis, Faculdade de Engenharia da Universidade do Porto.

Paula Fortuna, José Ferreira, Luiz Pires, Guilherme Routar, and Sérgio Nunes. 2018. Merging datasets for aggressive text identification. In *Proceedings of the First Workshop on Trolling, Aggression and Cyberbullying (TRAC – 1)*, Santa Fe, USA.

Thiago Galery, Efstathios Charitos, and Ye Tian. 2018. Aggression identification and multi lingual word embeddings. In *Proceedings of the First Workshop on Trolling, Aggression and Cyberbullying (TRAC – 1)*, Santa Fe, USA.

Njagi Dennis Gitari, Zhang Zuping, Hanyurwimfura Damien, and Jun Long. 2015. A lexicon- based approach for hate speech detection. *International Journal of Multimedia and Ubiquitous Engineering*, 10(4):215 – 230.

Viktor Golem, Mladen Karan, and Jan najder. 2018. Combining traditional machine learning models with deep learning for aggressive text detection. In *Proceedings of the First Workshop on Trolling, Aggression and Cyberbullying (TRAC – 1)*, Santa Fe, USA.

Edel Greevy and Alan F. Smeaton. 2004. Classifying racist texts using a support vector machine. In *Proceedings of the 27th annual international ACM SIGIR conference on Research and development in information retrieval*, pages 468 – 469. ACM.

Edel Greevy. 2004. *Automatic text categorisation of racist webpages*. Ph.D. thesis, Dublin City University.

Claire Hardaker. 2010. Trolling in asynchronous computer-mediated communication: From user discussions to academic definitions. *Journal of Politeness Research. Language, Behaviour, Culture*, 6(2):215–242.

Claire Hardaker. 2013. uh. . . . not to be nitpicky,,,,,but...the past tense of drag is dragged, not drug. an overview of trolling strategies. *Journal of Language Aggression and Conflict*, 1(1):58–86.

Cynthia Van Hee, Els Lefever, Ben Verhoeven, Julie Mennes, Bart Desmet, Guy De Pauw, Walter Daelemans, and Vronique Hoste. 2015. Detection and fine-grained classification of cyberbullying events. In *Proceedings of International Conference Recent Advances in Natural Language Processing (RANLP)*, pages 672–680.

Sameer Hinduja and Justin W Patchin. 2010. Bullying, Cyberbullying, and Suicide. *Archives of suicide research*, 14(3):206–221.

E. Krol. 1992. *The whole internet: User's guide & catalog*. O'Reilly & Associates, Inc., Sebastopol, CA.

Sudhakar Kumar, Francesca Spezzano, and VS Subrahmanian. 2014. Accurately detecting trolls in slashdot zoo via decluttering. In *Proceedings of IEEE/ACM International Conference on Advances in Social Networks Analysis and Mining (ASONAM)*, pages 188–195.

Ritesh Kumar, Guggilla Bhanodai, Rajendra Pamula, and Maheshwar Reddy Chennuru. 2018a. Trac-1 shared task on aggression identification: Iit(ism)@coling18. In *Proceedings of the First Workshop on Trolling, Aggression and Cyberbullying (TRAC – 1)*, Santa Fe, USA.

Ritesh Kumar, Aishwarya N. Reganti, Akshit Bhatia, and Tushar Maheshwari. 2018b. Aggression-annotated corpus of hindi-english code-mixed data. In Nicoletta Calzolari (Conference chair), Khalid Choukri, Christopher Cieri, Thierry Declerck, Sara Goggi, Koiti Hasida, Hitoshi Isahara, Bente Maegaard, Joseph Mariani, Hlne Mazo, Asuncion Moreno, Jan Odijk, Stelios Piperidis, and Takenobu Tokunaga, editors, *Proceedings of the Eleventh International Conference on Language Resources and Evaluation (LREC 2018)*, Paris, France, may. European Language Resources Association (ELRA).

Sreekanth Madisetty and Maunendra Sankar Desarkar. 2018. Aggression detection in social media using deep neural networks. In *Proceedings of the First Workshop on Trolling, Aggression and Cyberbullying (TRAC – 1)*, Santa Fe, USA.

Promita Maitra and Ritesh Sarkhel. 2018. Emoti-kate: a k-competitive autoencoder for aggression detection in social media text. In *Proceedings of the First Workshop on Trolling, Aggression and Cyberbullying (TRAC – 1)*, Santa Fe, USA.

Shervin Malmasi and Marcos Zampieri. 2017. Detecting Hate Speech in Social Media. In *Proceedings of the International Conference Recent Advances in Natural Language Processing (RANLP)*, pages 467–472.

Shervin Malmasi and Marcos Zampieri. 2018. Challenges in discriminating profanity from hate speech. *Journal of Experimental & Theoretical Artificial Intelligence*, 30:1 – 16.

Todor Mihaylov, Georgi D Georgiev, AD Ontotext, and Preslav Nakov. 2015. Finding opinion manipulation trolls in news community forums. In *Proceedings of the Nineteenth Conference on Computational Natural Language Learning, CoNLL*, pages 310–314.

Sandip Modha, Prasenjit Majumder, and Thomas Mandl. 2018. Filtering aggression from multilingual social media feed. In *Proceedings of the First Workshop on Trolling, Aggression and Cyberbullying (TRAC – 1)*, Santa Fe, USA.

Luis G Mojica. 2016. Modeling trolling in social media conversations.

Nishant Nikhil, Ramit Pahwa, Mehul Kumar Nirala, and Rohan Khilnani. 2018. Lstms with attention for aggression detection. In *Proceedings of the First Workshop on Trolling, Aggression and Cyberbullying (TRAC – 1)*, Santa Fe, USA.

Nitin, Ankush Bansal, Siddhartha Mahadev Sharma, Kapil Kumar, Anuj Aggarwal, Sheenu Goyal, Kanika Choudhary, Kunal Chawla, Kunal Jain, and Manav Bhasinar. 2012. Classification of flames in computer mediated communications.

Taisei Nitta, Fumito Masui, Michal Ptaszynski, Yasutomo Kimura, Rafal Rzepka, and Kenji Araki. 2013. Detecting cyberbullying entries on informal school websites based on category relevance maximization. In *Proceedings of IJCNLP*, pages 579–586.

Chikashi Nobata, Joel Tetreault, Achint Thomas, Yashar Mehdad, and Yi Chang. 2016. Abusive Language Detection in Online User Content. In *Proceedings of the 25th International Conference on World Wide Web*, pages 145–153. International World Wide Web Conferences Steering Committee.

Ahmed Husseini Orabi, Mahmoud Husseini Orabi, Qianjia Huang, Diana Inkpen, and David Van Bruwaene. 2018. Cyber-aggression detection using cross segment-and-concatenate multi-task learning from text. In *Proceedings of the First Workshop on Trolling, Aggression and Cyberbullying (TRAC – 1)*, Santa Fe, USA.

Constantin Orasan. 2018. Aggressive Language Identification Using Word Embeddings and Sentiment Features. In *Proceedings of the First Workshop on Trolling, Aggression and Cyberbullying (TRAC – 1)*, Santa Fe, USA.

Manish Gupta Pinkesh Badjatiya, Shashank Gupta and Vasudeva Varma. 2017. Deep learning for hate speech detection in tweets. In *Proceedings of the 26th International Conference on World Wide Web Companion*, pages 759 – 760. International World Wide Web Conferences Steering Committee.

Kashyap Raiyani, Teresa Gonçalves, Paulo Quaresma, and Vitor Beires Nogueira. 2018. Fully connected neural network with advance preprocessor to identify aggression over facebook and twitter. In *Proceedings of the First Workshop on Trolling, Aggression and Cyberbullying (TRAC – 1)*, Santa Fe, USA.

Faneva Ramiandrisoa and Josiane Mothe. 2018. Irit at trac 2018. In *Proceedings of the First Workshop on Trolling, Aggression and Cyberbullying (TRAC – 1)*, Santa Fe, USA.

Julian Risch and Ralf Krestel. 2018. Aggression identification using deep learning and data augmentation. In *Proceedings of the First Workshop on Trolling, Aggression and Cyberbullying (TRAC – 1)*, Santa Fe, USA.

Arjun Roy, Prashant Kapil, Kingshuk Basak, and Asif Ekbal. 2018. An ensemble approach for aggression identification in english and hindi text. In *Proceedings of the First Workshop on Trolling, Aggression and Cyberbullying (TRAC – 1)*, Santa Fe, USA.

Niloofar Safi Samghabadi, Deepthi Mave, Sudipta Kar, and Thamar Solorio. 2018. Ritual-uh at trac 2018 shared task: Aggression identification. In *Proceedings of the First Workshop on Trolling, Aggression and Cyberbullying (TRAC – 1)*, Santa Fe, USA.

Sasha Sax. 2016. Flame Wars: Automatic Insult Detection. Technical report, Stanford University.

Anna Schmidt and Michael Wiegand. 2017. A Survey on Hate Speech Detection Using Natural Language Processing. In *Proceedings of the Fifth International Workshop on Natural Language Processing for Social Media. Association for Computational Linguistics*, pages 1–10, Valencia, Spain.

Antonela Tommasel, Juan Manuel Rodriguez, and Daniela Godoy. 2018. Textual aggression detection through deep learning. In *Proceedings of the First Workshop on Trolling, Aggression and Cyberbullying (TRAC – 1)*, Santa Fe, USA.

Fabio Del Vigna, Andrea Cimino, Felice DellOrletta, Marinella Petrocchi, and Maurizio Tesconi. 2017. Hate me, hate me not: Hate speech detection on facebook. In *Proceedings of the First Italian Conference on Cybersecurity*, pages 86 – 95.

Zeerak Waseem and Dirk Hovy. 2016. Hateful symbols or hateful people? predictive features for hate speech detection on twitter. In *Proceedings of NAACL-HLT*, pages 88 – 93.

Zeerak Waseem, Thomas Davidson, Dana Warmsley, and Ingmar Weber. 2017. Understanding abuse: A typology of abusive language detection subtasks. In *Proceedings of the First Workshop on Abusive Language Online*, pages 78–84. Association for Computational Linguistics.

RiTUAL-UH at TRAC 2018 Shared Task: Aggression Identification

Niloofar Safi Samghabadi   **Deepthi Mave**   **Sudipta Kar**   **Thamar Solorio**
Department of Computer Science
University of Houston
Houston, TX 77204-3010
{nsafisamghabadi, dmave, skar3, tsolorio}@uh.edu

Abstract

This paper presents our system for "TRAC 2018 Shared Task on Aggression Identification". Our best systems for the English dataset use a combination of lexical and semantic features. However, for Hindi data using only lexical features gave us the best results. We obtained weighted F1-measures of 0.5921 for the English Facebook task (ranked 12th), 0.5663 for the English Social Media task (ranked 6th), 0.6292 for the Hindi Facebook task (ranked 1st), and 0.4853 for the Hindi Social Media task (ranked 2nd).

1 Introduction

Users' activities on social media is increasing at a fast rate. Unfortunately, a lot of people misuse these online platforms to harass, threaten, and bully other users. This growing aggression against social media users has caused serious effects on victims, which can even lead them to harm themselves. The TRAC 2018 Shared Task on Aggression Identification (Kumar et al., 2018a) aims at developing a classifier that could make a 3-way classification of a given data instance between "Overtly Aggressive", "Covertly Aggressive", and "Non-aggressive". We present here the different systems we submitted to the shared task, which mainly use lexical and semantic features to distinguish different levels of aggression over multiple datasets from Facebook and other social media that cover both English and Hindi texts.

2 Related Work

In recent years, several studies have been done towards detecting abusive and hateful language in online texts. Some of these works target different online platforms like Twitter (Waseem and Hovy, 2016), Wikipedia (Wulczyn et al., 2016), and ask.fm (Samghabadi et al., 2017) to encourage other research groups to contribute to aggression identification in these sources.

Most of the approaches proposed to detect offensive language in social media make use of multiple types of hand-engineered features. Nobata et al. (2016) use n-grams, linguistic, syntactic and distributional semantic features to build a hate speech detection framework over Yahoo! Finance and News and get an F-score of 81% for a combination of all features. Davidson et al. (2017) combine n-grams, POS-colored n-grams, and sentiment lexicon features to detect hate speech on Twitter data. Van Hee et al. (2015) use word and character n-grams along with sentiment lexicon features to identify nasty posts in ask.fm. Samghabadi et al. (2017) build a model based on lexical, semantic, sentiment, and stylistic features to detect nastiness in ask.fm. They also show the robustness of the model by applying it to the dataset from different other sources.

Based on Malmasi and Zampieri (2018), distinguishing hate speech from profanity is not a trivial task and requires features that capture deeper information from the comments. In this paper, we try different combinations of lexical, semantic, sentiment, and lexicon-based features to identify various levels of aggression in online texts.

Proceedings of the First Workshop on Trolling, Aggression and Cyberbullying, pages 12–18
Santa Fe, USA, August 25, 2018.

3 Methodology and Data

3.1 Data

Data	Training (FB)	Validation (FB)	Test (FB)	Test (SM)
English	12000	3001	916	1257
Hindi	12000	3001	970	1194

Table 1: Data distribution for English and Hindi corpus

The datasets were provided by Kumar et al. (2018b). Table 1 shows the distribution of training, validation and test (Facebook and social media) data for English and Hindi corpora. The data has been labeled with one out of three possible tags:

- **Non-aggressive (NAG):** There is no aggression in the text.

- **Overtly aggressive (OAG):** The text is containing either aggressive lexical items or certain syntactic structures.

- **Covertly aggressive (CAG):** The text is containing an indirect attack against the target using polite expressions in most cases.

3.2 Data Pre-processing

Generally the data from social media resources is noisy, grammar and syntactic errors are common, with a lot of ad-hoc spellings, that make it hard to analyze. Therefore, we first put our efforts to clean and prepare the data to feed it to our systems. For the English dataset, we lowercased the data and removed URLs, Email addresses, and numbers. We also did minor stemming by removing "ing", plural and possessive "s", and replaced a few common abstract grammatical forms with the formal versions.

On manual inspection of the training data for Hindi, we found that some of the instances are Hindi-English code-mixed, some use Roman script for Hindi and others are in Devanagari. Only 26% of the training data is in Devanagari script. We normalize the data by transliterating instances in Devanagari to Roman script. These instances are identified using Unicode pattern matching and are transliterated to Roman script using *indic-trans* transliteration tool[1]. For further analysis, we run an in-house word-level language identification system on the training data (Mave et al., 2018). This CRF system is trained on Facebook posts and has an F1-weighted score of 97%. Approximately 60% of the training data is code-mixed, 39% is only Hindi and 0.42% is only English.

3.3 Features

We make use of the following features:

Lexical: Words are powerful mediums to convey a feeling, describe or express ideas. With this notion, we use word n-grams (n=1, 2, 3), char n-grams (n=3, 4, 5), and k-skip n-grams (k=2, n=2, 3) as features. We weigh each term with its term frequency-inverse document frequency (TF-IDF). We also consider using another weighting scheme by trying binary word n-grams (n=1, 2, 3).

Word Embeddings: The idea behind this approach is to use a vector space model for extracting semantic information from the text (Le and Mikolov, 2014). For the embedding model we use pre-trained vectors trained on part of Google News dataset including about 3 million words[2]. We computed word embeddings feature vectors by averaging the word vector of all the words in each comment. We skip the words which are not in the vocabulary of the pre-trained model. This representation is only used for English data and the coverage of the Google word embedding is 63% for this corpus.

---

[1] https://github.com/libindic/indic-trans
[2] https://code.google.com/archive/p/word2vec/

Sentiment: We use Stanford Sentiment Analysis tool (Socher et al., 2013)[3] to extract fine-grained sentiment distribution of each comment. For every message, we calculate the mean and standard deviation of sentiment distribution over all sentences and use them as feature vector.

LIWC (Linguistic Inquiry and Word Count): LIWC2007 (Pennebaker et al., 2007) includes around 70 word categories to analyze different language dimensions. In our approach, we only use the categories related to positive or negative emotions and self-references. To build the feature vectors in this case, we use a normalized count of words separated by any of the mentioned categories. This feature is only applicable to English data.

Gender Probability: Following the approach in Waseem (2016) we use the Twitter based lexicon presented in Sap et al. (2014) to calculate the probability of gender. We also convert these probabilities to binary gender by considering the positive cases as female and the rest as male. We make the feature vectors with the probability of the gender and binary gender for each message. This feature is not applicable to Hindi corpus.

4 Experiments and Results

4.1 Experimental Settings

For both datasets, we trained several classification models using different combinations of features discussed in 3.3. Since this is a multi-class classification task, we use a one-versus-rest classifier which trains a separate classifier for each class and labels each comment with the class with highest predicted probability across all classifiers. We tried Logistic Regression and linear SVM as the estimator for the classifier. We decided to use Logistic Regression in our final systems, since it works better in the validation phase. We implemented all models using scikit-learn tool[4].

4.2 Results

To build our best systems for both English and Hindi data, we experimented with several models using the different combinations of available features. Table 2 shows the validation results on training and validation sets.

	F1-weighted	
Feature	**English**	**Hindi**
Unigram (U)	0.5804	0.6159
Bigram (B)	0.4637	0.5195
Trigram (T)	0.3846	0.4300
Char 3gram (C3)	0.5694	0.6065
Char 4gram (C4)	0.5794	0.6212
Char 5gram (C5)	0.5758	0.6195
Word Embeddings (W2V)	0.5463	N/A
Sentiment (S)	0.3961	N/A
LIWC	0.4350	N/A
Gender Probability (GP)	0.3440	N/A
BU + U + C4 + C5 + W2V	**0.5875**	N/A
C3 + C4 + C5	0.5494	0.6207
U + C3 + C4 + C5	0.5541	**0.6267**

Table 2: Validation results for different features for the English and Hindi datasets using Logistic Regression model. In this table BU stands for Binary Unigram.

Table 3 shows the results of our three submitted systems for the English Facebook and Social Media data. In all three systems, we used the same set of features as follows: binary unigram, word unigram,

[3]https://nlp.stanford.edu/sentiment/code.html
[4]http://scikit-learn.org/stable/

character n-grams of length 4 and 5, and word embeddings. In the first system, we used both train and validation sets for training our ensemble classifier. In the second system we only used the train data for training the model. The only difference between the second and the third models is that we corrected the misspellings using PyEnchant[5] spell checking tool. Unfortunately, we could not try applying the sentiment and lexicon-based features after spell correction due to the restrictions on the total number of submissions. However, we believe that it can improve the performance of the system.

System	F1 (weighted)	
	FB	**SM**
Random Baseline	0.3535	0.3477
System 1	0.5673	0.5453
System 2	0.5847	0.5391
System 3	**0.5921**	**0.5663**

Table 3: Results for the English test set. FB: Facebook and SM: Social Media.

System	F1 (weighted)	
	FB	**SM**
Random Baseline	0.3571	0.3206
System 1	**0.6451**	**0.4853**
System 2	0.6292	0.4689

Table 4: Results for the Hindi test set. FB: Facebook and SM: Social Media.

Table 4 shows the performance of our systems for the Hindi Facebook and social media data. For the Hindi dataset, the combination of word unigrams, character n-grams of length 3, 4 and 5 gives the best performance over the validation set. These features capture the word usage distribution across classes. Both System 1 and System 2 use these features, trained over training set only and training and validation sets respectively.

4.3 Analysis

Looking at the mislabeled instances at validation phase, we found that there are two main reasons for the classifier mistakes:

1. Perceived level of aggression can be subjective. There are some examples in the validation dataset where the label is CAG but it is more likely to be OAG and vice versa. Table 5 shows some of these examples.

2. There are several typos and misspellings in the data that affect the performance.

Language	Example	Label	
		Actual	**Predicted**
English	What has so far Mr.Yechuri done for this Country. Ask him to shut down his bloody piehole for good or I if given the chance will crap on his mouth hole.	CAG	OAG
	The time you tweeted is around 3 am morning,,which is not at all a namaz time.,As you bollywood carrier is almost finished, you are preparing yourself for politics by these comments.	OAG	CAG
Hindi	ajeeb chutya hai.... kahi se course kiya hai ya paida hee chutya hua tha	CAG	OAG
	Salman aur aamir ki kounsi movie release huyee jo aandhi me dub gaye?? ?Bikau chatukar media	OAG	CAG

Table 5: Misclassified examples in case of the aggression level

---

[5]https://pypi.org/project/pyenchant

Also, it is obvious from Figure 1 that Hindi corpus is more balanced than the English one in case of OAG and CAG instances. That could be a good reason why the performance of the lexical features is better for Hindi data.

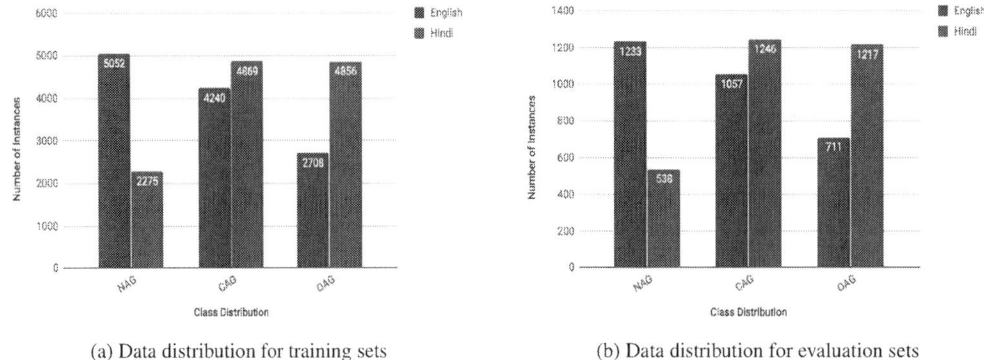

(a) Data distribution for training sets   (b) Data distribution for evaluation sets

Figure 1: Label distribution comparison between training and evaluation sets

Table 6 illustrates the most informative features learned by the classifier for all three classes in Hindi data. We observe that word unigrams and character trigrams are the most important features for the system. From the table, the top features for CAG are mostly swear words in Hindi and character n-grams of the swear words. More English words appear in the top list for NAG than the other two classes. There is no overlap between these features with top features from either CAG or OAG. Our system has difficulty differentiating between OAG and CAG when there is no strong swear word in the comments.

NAG	CAG	OAG
unigram_:	unigram_?	char_tri_gram_kut
unigram_mera	unigram_baki	unigram_bc
unigram_bike	unigram_??	char_tri_gram_cho
unigram_jai	unigram_pm	char_4_gram_ kut
unigram_main	unigram_o	unigram_chutiya
unigram_sahi	char_tri_gram_ ky	unigram_maa
unigram_............	unigram_badla	unigram_mc
unigram_launch	cha_tri_gram_yad	unigram_gand
unigram_jay	char_5_gram_e...	char_tri_gram_tiy
char_tri_gram_mer	unigram_3	char_tri_gram_chu

Table 6: Top 10 features learned by System 1 for each class for the Hindi dataset.

Figure 2a shows the confusion matrix of our best model for all three classes in English Facebook corpus. The most interesting part of this figure is that the classifier mislabeled several NAG instances with CAG label. Since our system is mostly based on lexical features, we can conclude that there are much fewer profanities in CAG instances comparing with the OAG ones, which make it hard to distinguish them from NAG examples without considering the sentiment aspects of the messages. This fact can also be proved by looking at Figure 2b, since it seems that the classifier was also confused to label CAG instances in both cases with and without profanities in English Social Media corpus.

Figure 3a shows that for Hindi Facebook data, the most biggest challenge is to distinguish OAG instances from CAG ones. Since our proposed system, in this case, is completely built on lexical features, it can be inferred from the figure that even indirect aggressive comments in Hindi language contains lots of profanities. However, for the Hindi Social Media corpus, we have the same concern as English data.

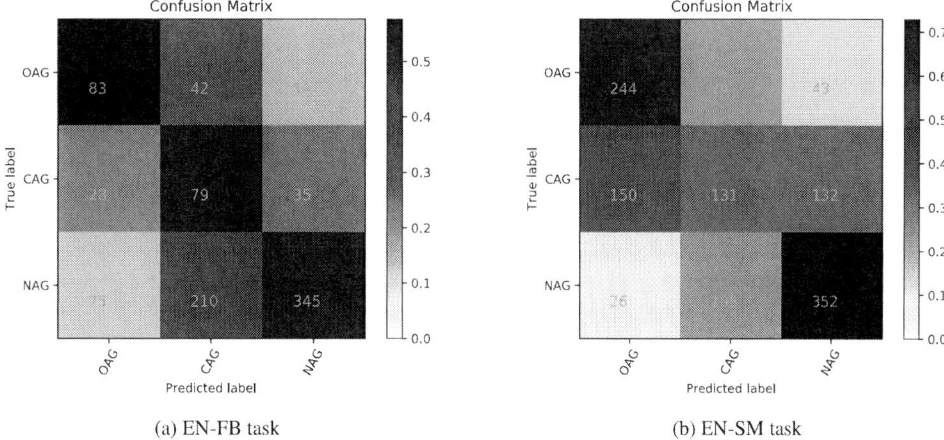

(a) EN-FB task   (b) EN-SM task

Figure 2: plots of confusion matrices of our best performing systems for English Facebook and Social Media data

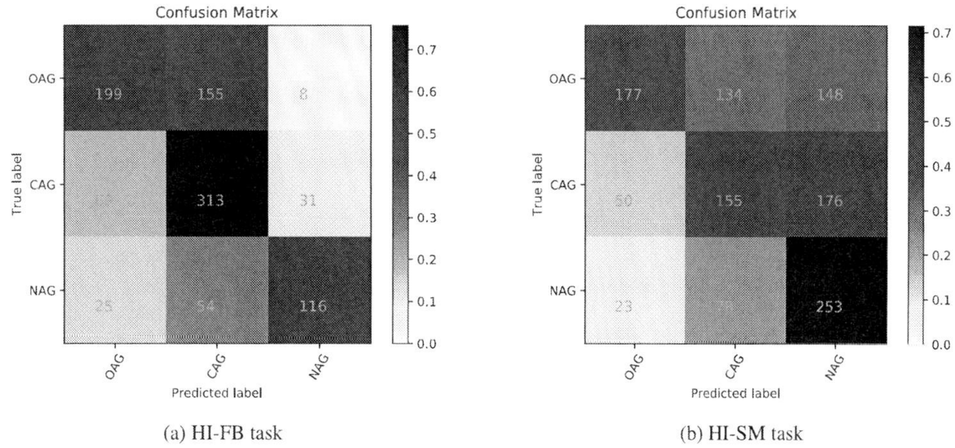

(a) HI-FB task   (b) HI-SM task

Figure 3: Plots of confusion matrices of our best performing systems for Hindi Facebook and Social Media data

5 Conclusion

In this paper, we present our approaches to identify the aggression level in English and Hindi comments in two different datasets, one from Facebook and another from other social media. In our best performing systems, we use a combination of lexical and semantic features for English corpus, and lexical features for Hindi data.

Future work for English data includes exploring more sentiment features to capture implicit hateful comments and adding more pre-processing levels. For instance, non-English character removal can improve the system since our proposed model is mainly based on lexical features, and is likely very sensitive to unknown characters and words. For the Hindi dataset, identifying the Hindi-English code-mixed instances and processing these instances and Hindi monolingual instances separately could be a future direction to explore. As the classification of aggression is subjective in most scenarios, adding sentiment features to the lexical information might help to model performance for Hindi data.

References

Thomas Davidson, Dana Warmsley, Michael Macy, and Ingmar Weber. 2017. Automated Hate Speech Detection and the Problem of Offensive Language. In *Proceedings of ICWSM*.

Ritesh Kumar, Atul Kr. Ojha, Shervin Malmasi, and Marcos Zampieri. 2018a. Benchmarking Aggression Identification in Social Media. In *Proceedings of the First Workshop on Trolling, Aggression and Cyberbulling (TRAC)*, Santa Fe, USA.

Ritesh Kumar, Aishwarya N. Reganti, Akshit Bhatia, and Tushar Maheshwari. 2018b. Aggression-annotated Corpus of Hindi-English Code-mixed Data. In *Proceedings of the 11th Language Resources and Evaluation Conference (LREC)*, Miyazaki, Japan.

Quoc V. Le and Tomas Mikolov. 2014. Distributed representations of sentences and documents. In *ICML*, volume 14, pages 1188–1196.

Shervin Malmasi and Marcos Zampieri. 2018. Challenges in Discriminating Profanity from Hate Speech. *Journal of Experimental & Theoretical Artificial Intelligence*, 30:1–16.

Deepthi Mave, Suraj Maharjan, and Thamar Solorio. 2018. Language Identification and Analysis of Code-Switched Social Media Text. In *Proceedings of the Third Workshop on Computational Approaches to Linguistic Code-Switching*, Melbourne, Australia, July. Association for Computational Linguistics.

Chikashi Nobata, Joel Tetreault, Achint Thomas, Yashar Mehdad, and Yi Chang. 2016. Abusive Language Detection in Online User Content. In *Proceedings of the 25th International Conference on World Wide Web*, pages 145–153. International World Wide Web Conferences Steering Committee.

James W. Pennebaker, Roger J. Booth, and Martha E. Francis. 2007. Liwc2007: Linguistic inquiry and word count. *Austin, Texas: liwc.net*.

Niloofar Safi Samghabadi, Suraj Maharjan, Alan Sprague, Raquel Diaz-Sprague, and Thamar Solorio. 2017. Detecting nastiness in social media. In *Proceedings of the First Workshop on Abusive Language Online*, pages 63–72.

Maarten Sap, Gregory Park, Johannes Eichstaedt, Margaret Kern, David Stillwell, Michal Kosinski, Lyle Ungar, and Hansen Andrew Schwartz. 2014. Developing age and gender predictive lexica over social media. In *Proceedings of the 2014 Conference on Empirical Methods in Natural Language Processing (EMNLP)*, pages 1146–1151.

Richard Socher, Alex Perelygin, Jean Wu, Jason Chuang, Christopher D Manning, Andrew Ng, and Christopher Potts. 2013. Recursive deep models for semantic compositionality over a sentiment treebank. In *Proceedings of the 2013 conference on empirical methods in natural language processing*, pages 1631–1642.

Cynthia Van Hee, Els Lefever, Ben Verhoeven, Julie Mennes, Bart Desmet, Guy De Pauw, Walter Daelemans, and Veronique Hoste. 2015. Detection and fine-grained classification of cyberbullying events. In *Proceedings of the International Conference Recent Advances in Natural Language Processing*, pages 672–680. INCOMA Ltd. Shoumen, Bulgaria.

Zeerak Waseem and Dirk Hovy. 2016. Hateful symbols or hateful people? predictive features for hate speech detection on twitter. In *Proceedings of the NAACL student research workshop*, pages 88–93.

Zeerak Waseem. 2016. Are you a racist or am i seeing things? annotator influence on hate speech detection on twitter. In *Proceedings of the first workshop on NLP and computational social science*, pages 138–142.

Ellery Wulczyn, Nithum Thain, and Lucas Dixon. 2016. Ex machina: Personal attacks seen at scale. *CoRR*, abs/1610.08914.

IRIT at TRAC 2018

Faneva Ramiandrisoa
IRIT, UMR5505, CNRS
Université de Toulouse, France
faneva.ramiandrisoa@irit.fr

Josiane Mothe
IRIT, UMR5505, CNRS
Université de Toulouse, France
ESPE, UT2J
Josiane.Mothe@irit.fr

Abstract

This paper describes the participation of the IRIT team to the TRAC 2018 shared task on Aggression Identification and more precisely to the shared task in English language. The three following methods have been used: a) a combination of machine learning techniques that relies on a set of features and document/text vectorization, b) Convolutional Neural Network (CNN) and c) a combination of Convolutional Neural Network (CNN) and Long Short-Term Memory (LSTM). Best results were obtained when using the method (a) on the English test data from Facebook which ranked our method sixteenth out of thirty teams, and the method (c) on the English test data from other social media, where we obtained the fifteenth rank out of thirty.

1 Introduction

In recent years, the emergence of social media platforms like Facebook, Twitter, etc. changes the way people communicate (Sticca and Perren, 2013).

Although these platforms give many benefits to their users, they can also have several negative impacts where people can be hurt for example by some aggressive texts (Dadvar et al., 2012). The aggression on social media platforms is actually more harmful than traditional bullying for many reasons such as allowing people to hide behind an alias (Sticca and Perren, 2013). Unfortunately, such phenomena of on-line aggression and bullying not only have created psychological and mental health issues for on-line users, but it can end by forcing some of them to change several things in their lives and can even conduct them to suicide according to (Kumar et al., 2018b). The TRAC 2018 workshop has been created in order to study these problems (Kumar et al., 2018a).

The TRAC 2018 workshop aims at providing the framework for evaluatig systems that aim at detecting/identifying aggression, trolling, cyberbullying and other related phenomena in both speech and text from social media (Kumar et al., 2018a). The shared task challenge consists in distinguishing three levels of aggression from text: overtly aggressive, covertly aggressive and non-aggressive. Overtly aggressive means that there is an expression of aggression directly with specific words or keywords. Covertly aggressive expresses aggression subtly such as indirect attack or with more polite expressions. Two different languages are studied independently: English and Hindi.

The shared task was organized into two different stages: training and testing. During the training stage, two datasets of $15,000$ aggression-annotated Facebook posts and comments, one in English and the other in Hindi, were provided. During testing stage, the organizers also included a data set from a second social media platform. Overall, the test data set contains four sub-collections: two from Facebook and two from another social media (not named by the organizers); for each source, one sub-collection is in English while the other is in Hindi.Participants could participate to one or several of the four subtasks which are: (1) English (Facebook) task, (2) Hindi (Facebook) task, (3) English (another social media) task, and (4) Hindi (another social media).

More details about the task can be found in (Kumar et al., 2018a). Our team, IRIT, participated to shared task in English language for both Facebook and the other social media platform: subtask (1) and (3).

Proceedings of the First Workshop on Trolling, Aggression and Cyberbullying, pages 19–27
Santa Fe, USA, August 25, 2018.

In this paper, we report the methods we proposed when participating to the subtasks; we have developed three approaches that we compare in this paper on the problem of aggression identification in texts.

The first method is a combination of two classifiers : *random forest* that relies on features ranging from surface features to more linguistic features and *logistic regression* based on text vectorization. We named this method Trac-RF_LR. The second approach is a deep learning technique widely used in image area and adapted for text classification. It uses a Convolutional Neural Network and we named it Trac-CNN in the rest of the paper. Finally, the third approach is a combination of two deep learning techniques: Convolutional Neural Network (CNN) and Long Short-Term Memory (LSTM). We named this method Trac-CNN_LSTM.

The remaining of this paper is organized as follows: Section 2 is an overview of state-of-the-art approaches for aggression detection. Section 3 details the methods we developed. Section 4 reports the results as well as the data sets and Section 5 concludes this paper.

2   Related Work

Several series of evaluation forums for applications related to social media have been developed in the recent years, such as tweet contextualisation (Ermakova et al., 2017) or e-risk (Losada et al., 2017) in CLEF. TRAC is the first that focus on detecting aggressive text. In the last few years, several studies have been published in which the problem of detecting abusive language in social media has been tackled. Although researchers focused on different aspects of abusive language such as cyberbullying (Dadvar et al., 2013), hate speech (Warner and Hirschberg, 2012), profanity (Sood et al., 2012) and abusive language in general (Chen et al., 2012), most of the approaches are based on supervised approaches (Schmidt and Wiegand, 2017). Generally, the detection of abusive language is considered as a classification problem, mainly as a binary text classification problem (Bosque and Garza, 2014) detecting whether the text contains abusive parts or not.

For text classification problems, approaches based on features are widely used.

Methods are based on simple *surface features* such as unigrams and/or n-grams (Xu et al., 2012; Chen et al., 2012; Waseem and Hovy, 2016; Abdou Malam et al., 2017), key-phrases (Mothe et al., 2018), the frequency of punctuation, capitalized words, Htag, image, URL mentions (Hoang and Mothe, 2017), average length of words, or frequency of words that do not exist in English dictionaries (Chen et al., 2012; Nobata et al., 2016). Other features are: *word generalization* (for example using Latent Dirichlet Allocation (LDA) (Zhong et al., 2016) and word/paragraph embedding (Nobata et al., 2016)), *sentiment analysis* (Xu et al., 2012; Dinakar et al., 2012; Hee et al., 2015); *lexical resources* (Burnap and Williams, 2015; Burnap and Williams, 2016; Gitari et al., 2015; Hoang and Mothe, 2018); *linguistic features* (Xu et al., 2012; Gitari et al., 2015; Burnap and Williams, 2016; Nobata et al., 2016; Abdou Malam et al., 2017); *knowledge-based features* (Dinakar et al., 2012); and *meta-information* (Dadvar et al., 2012; Dadvar et al., 2013; Waseem and Hovy, 2016).

Using these features, supervised classifiers such as Support Vector Machines (SVM) are used in order to classify a text as containing aggressiveness or not (Schmidt and Wiegand, 2017).

In recent years, deep learning has been also employed. For example, (Mehdad and Tetreault, 2016) used Recurrent Neural Network Language Model which is based on Recurrent Neural Networks for the task of abusive language detection. The choice of this type of models is based on the fact that with few training data, they can achieve good results for language models.

In addition of detecting if a text contains something harmful and/or aggressive, another challenge is to distinguish the different aspects of the abusive language. (Malmasi and Zampieri, 2018) try to distinguish general profanity from hate speech, but their results show that it is difficult to differentiate one from the other. Their study also shows that all hate speech, bullying text, cyberbullying and abusive language are not explicit, there are aggressive text written with subtle language and it can be hard to distinguish them. This observation motivated the shared task not only to classify the text as aggressive or not, but also to distinguish two kinds of aggression: overt and covert aggression.

3   Developped methods for the IRIT participation

In this section, we present the three supervised approaches we developed to automatically detect aggression in texts and that we submitted to TRAC 2018 shared task for English.

3.1   Trac-RF_LR: combination of two classifiers

In this model we combine two classifiers namely random forest and logistic regression where the first one is based on different set of features from surface features to more linguistic features and the second one is based on document vectorization. In the following, we first describe each classifier, then we detail the combination method used.

Classifiers description

i) Features - RF Classifier:

This model uses different features, adapted from features used for depression detection in (Abdou Malam et al., 2017), and are computed from the texts to predict the aggression. We represent texts with a vector composed of the features as presented in Table 1.

Name	Hypothesis or tool/resource used
Part-Of-Speech frequency	Normalized frequencies of each tag: adjectives, verbs, nouns and adverbs (four features). The idea behind is to check offensive words used as nouns, verbs, adjectives, or adverbs.
Negation	Normalized frequencies of negative words like: *no, not, didn't, can't, ...* The idea behind is to detect non direct aggressiveness.
Capitalized	The idea behind is that aggressive texts tend to put emphasis on the target they mention. It can indicate feelings or speaking volume.
Punctuation marks	! or ? or any combination of both can emphasize offensiveness of texts.
Emoticons	Another way to express sentiment or feeling.
Sentiment	Use of NRC-Sentiment-Emotion-Lexicons[1] to trace the polarity in text.
Emotions	Frequency of emotions from specific categories: anger, fear, surprise, sadness and disgust. The idea behind is to check the categories related to aggressiveness.
Gunning Fog Index	Estimate of the years of education that a person needs to understand the text at first reading.
Flesch Reading Ease	Measure how difficult to understand a text is.
Linsear Write Formula	Developed for the U.S. Air Force to calculate the readability of their technical manuals[2].
New Dale-Chall Readability	Measure the difficulty of comprehension that persons encounter when reading a text. It is inspired from Flesch Reading Ease measure.
Swear words	The intuition behind is that the texts containing insults are often aggressive.
Lexical analysis with python library *empath*	Empath is a tool for analyzing text across lexical categories. By default, it has 194 lexical categories and each category is considered as feature.

Table 1: List of features used in RF.

Some of these features are used for abusive language detection, hate speech, cyberbullying and the others are used for sentiment or personality analysis that we judged useful for aggression detection.

A random forest classifier was trained on train and validation sets by representing each text with a vector composed by the features we mentioned above. The following parameters were used during the training: class_weight="balanced", max_features="sqrt", n_estimators=60, min_weight_fraction_leaf=0.0, criterion='entropy', random_state=2.

At prediction time, a text from the test set is represented with features and then run the trained model. The output is the estimated probabilities for the three classes (overtly aggressive, covertly aggressive and non-aggressive).

ii) Document vector - LR Classifier:

This model is based on document vectorization using *Doc2vec* (Le and Mikolov, 2014). *Doc2vec* is used to represent sentences, paragraphs, or whole documents as vectors and it can be trained on small corpora, which is case of the task datasets.

Before building the model (LR Classifier), we first trained two separate *Doc2vec* models: a Distributed Bag of Words and a Distributed Memory model (Le and Mikolov, 2014). For the training, we used the same configuration as in (Trotzek et al., 2017) for representing user's text in order to detect if he or she is depressed. The two *Doc2vec models are trained* on English text from the train and validation sets and we used the Python package *gensim*[3](Rehurek and Sojka, 2010). We also concatenated the output vectors of these two models, as done in (Trotzek et al., 2017), resulting in a representation by a 200-dimension vector per text.

Then a logistic regression classifier was trained on the vectors for both the train and validation sets with the following parameters : class_weight="balanced", random_state=1, max_iter=100, solver="liblinear".

At prediction time, the texts from the test set were vectorized by using the two *Doc2vec* models and the 200-dimension vectors were given as input of trained classifier. The output is also a set of class probabilities.

Combination of two classifiers

After the two classifiers (as described in section 3.1) provided their results, the calculated class probabilities obtained from RF classifier and LR Classifier were averaged and finally the class with the highest probability was considered as the class the text belongs to.

3.2 Trac-CNN: Model based on CNN

This model is based on the deep learning technique known as Convolutional Neural Networks (CNN)(LeCun et al., 1998). CNN which is widely used in image analysis (Bhandare et al., 2016) and has been adapted for text classification such as sentiment analysis (Chen et al., 2017). Figure 1 shows the model architecture that we used for TRAC 2018 shared task.

We can see in this figure that before sending the text to the CNN, it is transformed as a matrix where each row is a vector representation[4] of words that compose the text[5] . To perform convolutions on the sentence matrix, we decided to use three sizes of filters[6]: bigrams (height = 2), trigrams (height = 3) and fourgrams (height = 4) filters, each of which has 100 filters (in total we had 300 filters). The result of convolutions is called feature map, a vector with variable-length according to the filter size and we had 300 features map. The 1-max pooling (Boureau et al., 2010), a common strategy, is performed over each

---

[1] `http://saifmohammad.com/WebPages/NRC-Emotion-Lexicon.htm`, Accessed on 2017-02-23

[2] `http://www.streetdirectory.com/travel_guide/15675/writing/how_to_choose_the_best_readability_formula_for_your_document.html`, Accessed on 2018-02-25

[3] `https://radimrehurek.com/gensim/index.html`

[4] We used *word2vec* trained on the training and validation sets. Two models were trained, namely CBOW and Skip-gram (Mikolov et al., 2013), and the final vector is a 200-dimensional vector which is a concatenation of the results from these models.

[5] All the texts need to be the same length in order to have the same matrix size. We used Keras zero-pads at the beginning if a text length is shorter than the maximum length (= length of longer text/document in the datasets).

[6] The width of filters are the same as word vectors (i.e 200) but the heights are different.

feature map. More precisely, the largest number from each feature map is kept and then concatenated to form a concatenated vector, where the dimension is equal to 300. Then we added one fully connected hidden layer to reduce the dimension of the concatenated vector , the dropout is performed on the hidden layer because dropout helps to reduce over fitting (Srivastava et al., 2014). Finally, the latest feature vector is fed through a sigmoid function to generate the final classification.

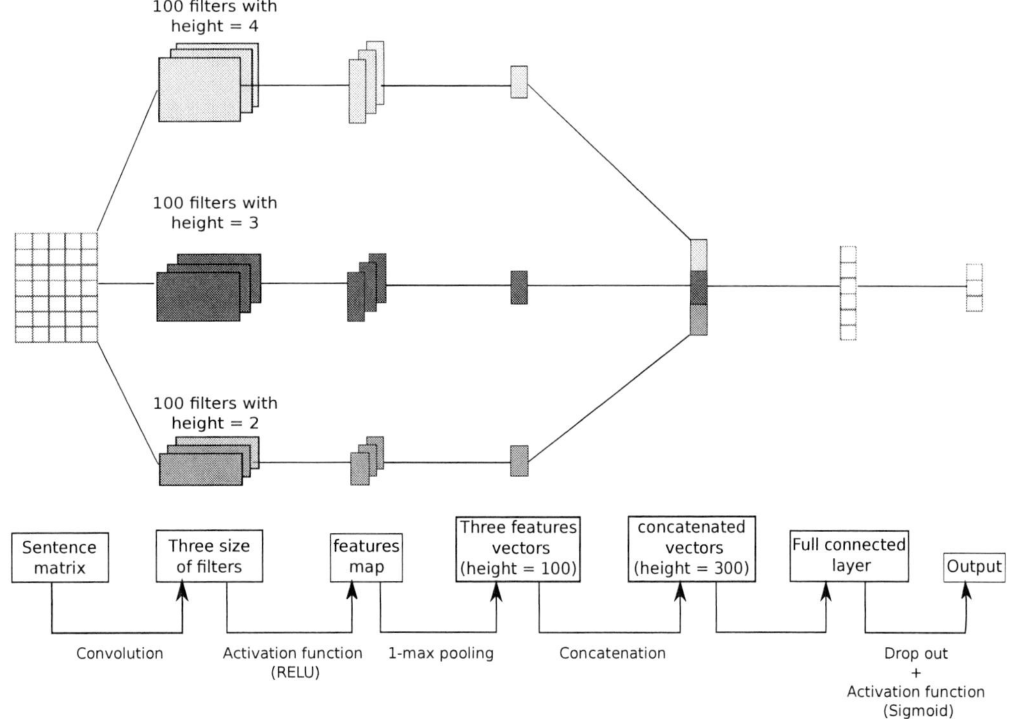

Figure 1: Illustration of a CNN architecture for aggression detection inspired from (Zhang and Wallace, 2015).

3.3 Trac-CNN_LSTM: Combination of CNN and LSTM

This model combines two deep learning techniques: CNN and LSTM. The main idea is to modify the CNN architecture presented in Figure 1 by adding a LSTM layer and change the activation function to softmax for the last classification. The LSTM is inserted after the poling layer and before the fully connected hidden layer. It takes as input the 300-dimension concatenated feature vector and gives as output a 300-dimension vector. Figure 2 presents the architecture of the combination.

4 Results

In this section, we detail the data used for TRAC 2018 shared task and the result we obtained using our different models.

4.1 Data

The way the dataset used in the TRAC 2018 shared task was built is described in (Kumar et al., 2018b).

The dataset in the shared task was divided in three sets: training, validation and test. The training and validation sets were released during the training stage to allow participants to train and built their systems. These two sets are composed of 15,000 aggression-annotated Facebook posts and comments written in English for participants who want to participate in this language and 15,001 aggression-annotated Facebook writen in Hindi for those who prefer to work in this language.

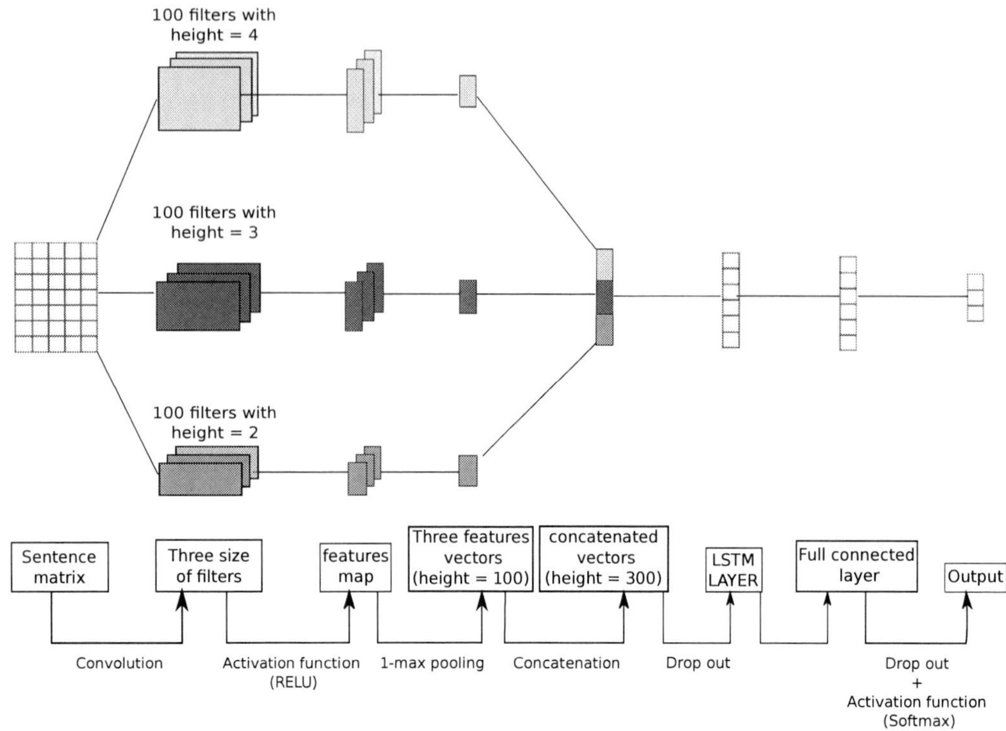

Figure 2: Illustration of a CNN + LSTM architecture for aggression detection inspired from (Zhang and Wallace, 2015).

For the test set, the collection crawled from Facebook is also divided into two languages, 916 posts and comments for the English dataset and 970 for the Hindi dataset. The organizers also included what they called the surprise collection crawled from another social media, also divided into two languages (1,257 posts and comments for English and 1,194 for Hindi). Table 2 describes the datasets used in the shared task, it reports the total number of posts and comments (texts) in each set and the number of texts with overt and covert aggression and texts without aggression. We can see from the Table 2 that the proportion of aggressive text is more important in the Hindi dataset (13,803 texts which correspond to 80.4% of total aggressive text (17,173)) than in the English dataset (9,776 texts which correspond to 56.9% of total aggressive text (17,165)).

Language	Number of	Train	Validation	Test	
				Facebook	other social media
English	texts (=posts+comments)	11,999	3,001	916	1,257
	Overt aggression	2,708	711	144	361
	Covert aggression	4,240	1,057	142	413
	No aggression	5,051	1,233	630	483
Hindi	texts (=posts+comments)	12,000	3,001	970	1,194
	Overt aggression	4,856	1,217	362	459
	Covert aggression	4,869	1,246	413	381
	No aggression	2,275	538	195	354

Table 2: Distribution of training, validation and testing data on TRAC 2018 data collection.

4.2 Models

All submitted models was evaluated using weighted macro-averaged F-scores. This measure is defined by organizers as follow: for each class, the individual F-score was weighted by the proportion of the concerned class in the test set and then the average of these individual weighted F-scores is the final F-score (See (Kumar et al., 2018a)). In order to have a baseline for comparison, the organizers give a random baseline generated by assigning random labels.

Table 3 reports the results we obtained with the three models (see Section 3) we submitted for the shared task and the baseline given by organizers. We can see that all of our models outperform the baseline on both Facebook and the other social media platform. More precisely Trac-RF gives the best results on Facebook and Trac-CNN_LSTM on the other social media.

We can also see that our three models give better results on Facebook, this could be due to the train dataset which is only composed of texts crawled from Facebook.

System	F1 (weighted)	
	Facebook	other social media
Random Baseline	0.354	0.348
Trac-RF_LR	**0.576**	0.405
Trac-CNN	0.562	0.494
Trac-CNN_LSTM	0.559	**0.511**

Table 3: Results for the English (Facebook and other social media) task. Bold value is the best performance.

When compared to other participants, our best model on both social media platforms give encouraging results. We are ranked sixteenth out of thirty teams on Facebook and fifteenth for other social media (see Table 4).

Rank	Team	Facebook
1	saroyehun	0.642
2	EBSI-LIA-UNAM	0.632
3	DA-LD-Hildesheim	0.618
4	TakeLab	0.616
5	sreeIN	0.604
...	...	...
16	**IRIT** (Trac-RF_LR)	0.576

Rank	Team	other social media
1	vista.ue	0.601
2	Julian	0.599
3	saroyehun	0.920
4	EBSI-LIA-UNAM	0.572
5	uOttawa	0.569
...	...	...
15	**IRIT** (Trac-CNN_LSTM)	0.511

Table 4: Results of top 5 teams vs our results which are in Bold.

5   Conclusion and Future Work

In this paper, we presented our participation to TRAC 2018 shared task on aggression identification in English language for both platforms: Facebook and the other social media. We proposed three kinds different methods: (a) a combination of machine learning techniques (classifiers) that relies on a set of features and document vectorization, (b) Convolutional Neural Network (CNN); and (c) combination of CNN and Long Short-Term Memory (LSTM). We obtained encouraging results: sixteenth out of thirty teams with method (a) for Facebook and fifteenth out of thirty for the other social media with method (c).

We can conclude that the model based on features gives the best results if the train dataset is built from the same platform as the test dataset. However a deeper analysis of features is to be done to get stronger conclusions. We can also see that deep learning models perform well even if the train and test datasets are built from different platforms (unlike combined RF and LR models). So these techniques are useful to build systems that can identify aggression on different social media.

For future work, we will analyze what the best features are for aggression detection by analyzing those we alrcady used and/or adding new ones. For example, more linguistic-oriented features such as specific writing or structure of sentences/paragraphs containing aggression could be added and feature like "proportion of aggressive text posted last year". Finally, we would like to improve our model based on deep learning by using different configurations and architectures, by combining it with traditional machine learning algorithms (RF and LR models), and also training a model on large datasets built from different social media platforms.

References

Idriss Abdou Malam, Mohamed Arziki, Mohammed Nezar Bellazrak, Farah Benamara, Assafa El Kaidi, Bouchra Es-Saghir, Zhaolong He, Mouad Housni, Véronique Moriceau, Josiane Mothe, and Faneva Ramiandrisoa. 2017. IRIT at e-Risk (regular paper). In *International Conference of the CLEF Association, CLEF 2017 Labs Working Notes*, volume 1866 of *ISSN 1613-0073*, http://CEUR-WS.org. CEUR Workshop Proceedings.

Ashwin Bhandare, Maithili Bhide, Pranav Gokhale, and Rohan Chandavarkar. 2016. Applications of convolutional neural networks. *International Journal of Computer Science and Information Technologies*, pages 2206–2215.

Laura P. Del Bosque and Sara Elena Garza. 2014. Aggressive text detection for cyberbullying. In *Human-Inspired Computing and Its Applications - 13th Mexican International Conference on Artificial Intelligence, MICAI 2014, Tuxtla Gutiérrez, Mexico, November 16-22, 2014. Proceedings, Part I*, pages 221–232.

Y-Lan Boureau, Jean Ponce, and Yann LeCun. 2010. A theoretical analysis of feature pooling in visual recognition. In *Proceedings of the 27th International Conference on Machine Learning (ICML-10), June 21-24, 2010, Haifa, Israel*, pages 111–118.

Pete Burnap and Matthew L Williams. 2015. Cyber hate speech on twitter: An application of machine classification and statistical modeling for policy and decision making. *Policy & Internet*, 7(2):223–242.

Pete Burnap and Matthew L Williams. 2016. Us and them: identifying cyber hate on twitter across multiple protected characteristics. *EPJ Data Science*, 5(1):11.

Ying Chen, Yilu Zhou, Sencun Zhu, and Heng Xu. 2012. Detecting offensive language in social media to protect adolescent online safety. In *2012 International Conference on Privacy, Security, Risk and Trust, PASSAT 2012, and 2012 International Confernece on Social Computing, SocialCom 2012, Amsterdam, Netherlands, September 3-5, 2012*, pages 71–80.

Tao Chen, Ruifeng Xu, Yulan He, and Xuan Wang. 2017. Improving sentiment analysis via sentence type classification using bilstm-crf and CNN. *Expert Syst. Appl.*, 72:221–230.

Maral Dadvar, de FMG Jong, Roeland Ordelman, and Dolf Trieschnigg. 2012. Improved cyberbullying detection using gender information. In *Proceedings of the Twelfth Dutch-Belgian Information Retrieval Workshop (DIR 2012)*. University of Ghent.

Maral Dadvar, Dolf Trieschnigg, Roeland Ordelman, and Franciska de Jong. 2013. Improving cyberbullying detection with user context. In *Advances in Information Retrieval*, pages 693–696. Springer.

Karthik Dinakar, Birago Jones, Henry Lieberman, Rosalind W. Picard, Carolyn Penstein Rosé, Matthew Thoman, and Roi Reichart. 2012. You too?! mixed-initiative LDA story matching to help teens in distress. In *Proceedings of the Sixth International Conference on Weblogs and Social Media, Dublin, Ireland, June 4-7, 2012*.

Liana Ermakova, Lorraine Goeuriot, Josiane Mothe, Philippe Mulhem, Jian-Yun Nie, and Eric SanJuan. 2017. Clef 2017 microblog cultural contextualization lab overview. In *International Conference of the Cross-Language Evaluation Forum for European Languages*, pages 304–314. Springer.

Njagi Dennis Gitari, Zhang Zuping, Hanyurwimfura Damien, and Jun Long. 2015. A lexicon-based approach for hate speech detection. *International Journal of Multimedia and Ubiquitous Engineering*, 10(4):215–230.

Cynthia Van Hee, Els Lefever, Ben Verhoeven, Julie Mennes, Bart Desmet, Guy De Pauw, Walter Daelemans, and Véronique Hoste. 2015. Detection and fine-grained classification of cyberbullying events. In *Recent Advances in Natural Language Processing, RANLP 2015, 7-9 September, 2015, Hissar, Bulgaria*, pages 672–680.

Thi Bich Ngoc Hoang and Josiane Mothe. 2017. Predicting Information Diffusion on Twitter - Analysis of predictive features. *Journal of Computational Science*, 22, octobre.

Thi Bich Ngoc Hoang and Josiane Mothe. 2018. Location extraction from tweets. *Information Processing & Management*, 54(2):129–144.

Ritesh Kumar, Atul Kr. Ojha, Shervin Malmasi, and Marcos Zampieri. 2018a. Benchmarking Aggression Identification in Social Media. In *Proceedings of the First Workshop on Trolling, Aggression and Cyberbulling (TRAC)*, Santa Fe, USA.

Ritesh Kumar, Aishwarya N. Reganti, Akshit Bhatia, and Tushar Maheshwari. 2018b. Aggression-annotated Corpus of Hindi-English Code-mixed Data. In *Proceedings of the 11th Language Resources and Evaluation Conference (LREC)*, Miyazaki, Japan.

Quoc V. Le and Tomas Mikolov. 2014. Distributed representations of sentences and documents. In *Proceedings of the 31th International Conference on Machine Learning, ICML 2014, Beijing, China, 21-26 June 2014*, pages 1188–1196.

Yann LeCun, Léon Bottou, Yoshua Bengio, and Patrick Haffner. 1998. Gradient-based learning applied to document recognition. *Proceedings of the IEEE*, 86(11):2278–2324.

David E Losada, Fabio Crestani, and Javier Parapar. 2017. erisk 2017: Clef lab on early risk prediction on the internet: Experimental foundations. In *International Conference of the Cross-Language Evaluation Forum for European Languages*, pages 346–360. Springer.

Shervin Malmasi and Marcos Zampieri. 2018. Challenges in Discriminating Profanity from Hate Speech. *Journal of Experimental & Theoretical Artificial Intelligence*, 30:1–16.

Yashar Mehdad and Joel R. Tetreault. 2016. Do characters abuse more than words? In *Proceedings of the SIGDIAL 2016 Conference, The 17th Annual Meeting of the Special Interest Group on Discourse and Dialogue, 13-15 September 2016, Los Angeles, CA, USA*, pages 299–303.

Tomas Mikolov, Kai Chen, Greg Corrado, and Jeffrey Dean. 2013. Efficient estimation of word representations in vector space. *CoRR*, abs/1301.3781.

Josiane Mothe, Faneva Ramiandrisoa, and Michael Rasolomanana. 2018. Automatic Keyphrase Extraction using Graph-based Methods (regular paper). In *ACM Symposium on Applied Computing (SAC), Pau, France, 09/04/2018-13/04/2018*. ACM.

Chikashi Nobata, Joel R. Tetreault, Achint Thomas, Yashar Mehdad, and Yi Chang. 2016. Abusive language detection in online user content. In *Proceedings of the 25th International Conference on World Wide Web, WWW 2016, Montreal, Canada, April 11 - 15, 2016*, pages 145–153.

Radim Rehurek and Petr Sojka. 2010. Software framework for topic modelling with large corpora. In *In Proceedings of the LREC 2010 Workshop on New Challenges for NLP Frameworks*. Citeseer.

Anna Schmidt and Michael Wiegand. 2017. A Survey on Hate Speech Detection Using Natural Language Processing. In *Proceedings of the Fifth International Workshop on Natural Language Processing for Social Media. Association for Computational Linguistics*, pages 1–10, Valencia, Spain.

Sara Owsley Sood, Judd Antin, and Elizabeth F. Churchill. 2012. Using crowdsourcing to improve profanity detection. In *Wisdom of the Crowd, Papers from the 2012 AAAI Spring Symposium, Palo Alto, California, USA, March 26-28, 2012*.

Nitish Srivastava, Geoffrey E. Hinton, Alex Krizhevsky, Ilya Sutskever, and Ruslan Salakhutdinov. 2014. Dropout: a simple way to prevent neural networks from overfitting. *Journal of Machine Learning Research*, 15(1):1929–1958.

Fabio Sticca and Sonja Perren. 2013. Is cyberbullying worse than traditional bullying? examining the differential roles of medium, publicity, and anonymity for the perceived severity of bullying. *Journal of Youth and Adolescence*, 42(5):739–750, May.

Marcel Trotzek, Sven Koitka, and Christoph M. Friedrich. 2017. Linguistic metadata augmented classifiers at the CLEF 2017 task for early detection of depression. In *Working Notes of CLEF 2017 - Conference and Labs of the Evaluation Forum, Dublin, Ireland, September 11-14, 2017*.

William Warner and Julia Hirschberg. 2012. Detecting hate speech on the world wide web. In *Proceedings of the Second Workshop on Language in Social Media*, pages 19–26. Association for Computational Linguistics.

Zeerak Waseem and Dirk Hovy. 2016. Hateful symbols or hateful people? predictive features for hate speech detection on twitter. In *Proceedings of the Student Research Workshop, SRW@HLT-NAACL 2016, The 2016 Conference of the North American Chapter of the Association for Computational Linguistics: Human Language Technologies, San Diego California, USA, June 12-17, 2016*, pages 88–93.

Jun-Ming Xu, Kwang-Sung Jun, Xiaojin Zhu, and Amy Bellmore. 2012. Learning from bullying traces in social media. In *Human Language Technologies: Conference of the North American Chapter of the Association of Computational Linguistics, Proceedings, June 3-8, 2012, Montréal, Canada*, pages 656–666.

Ye Zhang and Byron C. Wallace. 2015. A sensitivity analysis of (and practitioners' guide to) convolutional neural networks for sentence classification. *CoRR*, abs/1510.03820.

Haoti Zhong, Hao Li, Anna Cinzia Squicciarini, Sarah Michele Rajtmajer, Christopher Griffin, David J. Miller, and Cornelia Caragea. 2016. Content-driven detection of cyberbullying on the instagram social network. In *Proceedings of the Twenty-Fifth International Joint Conference on Artificial Intelligence, IJCAI 2016, New York, NY, USA, 9-15 July 2016*, pages 3952–3958.

Fully Connected Neural Network with Advance Preprocessor to Identify Aggression over Facebook and Twitter

Kashyap Raiyani, Teresa Gonçalves, Paulo Quaresma, Vitor Beires Nogueira
{kshyp,tcg,pq,vbn}@uevora.pt
Computer Science Department, University of Évora, Portugal

Abstract

Aggression Identification and Hate Speech detection had become an essential part of cyberharassment and cyberbullying and an automatic aggression identification can lead to the interception of such trolling. Following the same idealization, vista.ue team participated in the workshop which included a shared task on 'Aggression Identification'.

A dataset of 15,000 aggression-annotated Facebook Posts and Comments written in Hindi (in both Roman and Devanagari script) and English languages were made available and different classification models were designed. This paper presents a model that outperforms Facebook FastText (Joulin et al., 2016a) and deep learning models over this dataset. Especially, the English developed system, when used to classify Twitter text, outperforms all the shared task submitted systems.

1 Introduction

A recent article[1] states that on Facebook, every 60 seconds, 510,000 comments are posted and 293,000 statuses are updated. The facebook does have a policy for Violence and Criminal Behavior[2] and with the help of an Automted Aggression Identification system, the posts which violate the official policies can be detected. The TRAC (Trolling, Aggression and Cyberbullying) workshop (Kumar et al., 2018a) is taking a leap in this direction. Here, the task was aimed to develop a system that could make a 3-way classification between 'Overtly Aggressive (OAG)', 'Covertly Aggressive (CAG)' and 'Non-aggressive (NAG)' over text data.

This paper presents the different methodologies developed and tested by the vista.ue team and discusses their results, with the goal of identifying the best possible method for the aggression identification problem in social media. It is organized in the following manner: Section 2 introduces past research over text classification, different open source tools, approaches and presents a brief introduction to text classification and its components; Section 3 describes different methods, data representations, and system modeling and Section 4 discusses the experimental results obtained. Conclusion and future work are highlighted in Section. 5.

2 Related Work

Machine Learning and Deep Learning approaches are been used in a multitude of problems and the text classification is one of them. Many researchers and the companies are working on text classification to get meaningful and relevant information out of text corpora. Next, research published from 2011 to 2018 over aggression, hate speech, offensive, and abusive language identification is presented.

Schmidt and Wiegand (2017) present "A Survey on Hate Speech Detection using Natural Language Processing". Mainly, the authors empathize on features for hate speech detection, namely bag of word including unigram, bigram and trigram word representations and also character level n-gram features.

[1]https://zephoria.com/top-15-valuable-facebook-statistics/
[2]https://www.facebook.com/communitystandards/violence_criminal_behavior/

Proceedings of the First Workshop on Trolling, Aggression and Cyberbullying, pages 28–41
Santa Fe, USA, August 25, 2018.

They report that BoW is most commonly used and character level models perform best. One important concept mentioned is word generalization, meaning that words in test set should also be present in training and validation sets, otherwise systems will not give a correct prediction. One can also resort to doing the sentiment analysis based upon sentiment lexicon where words are grouped (or clustered) according to overtly aggressive, covertly aggressive, non-aggressive and stop words. They also mention the use of Linguistic Features: if two words are syntactically related then, the meaning of the unidentified word can be easily found. They report that the most effective and important features are Knowledge-Based Features and Meta-Information; simple words or vectors do not give meaning to the sentence but rather the context they are in. For example, if the sentence has a sarcastic meaning, n-gram and linguistic features are not able to identify it.

Davidson et al. (2017) discuss "Automated Hate Speech Detection and the Problem of Offensive Language". They mention the difficulty in detecting offensive language and hate speech and empathize that traditional lexical methods that rely on terms fail to differentiate between both (offensive language and hate speech). Their approach uses a crowd-sourced hate speech lexicon enabling to classify between three different categories namely, hate speech, offensive language and none. They show promising results with the conclusion that "Tweets without explicit hate keywords are also more difficult to classify". Therefore, Lexical methods are effective ways to recognize conceivably offensive terms but are fallacious at classifying hate speech.

Similar to the previous work, Malmasi and Zampieri (2017) discuss "Detecting Hate Speech in Social Media". The main difference is that they use supervised classification with character n-grams, word n-grams, and word skip-grams, showing promising results with character 4-grams. They also reached the similar conclusion that "challenge lies in discriminating profanity and hate speech from each other."

A proposal of the typology of abusive language is presented in (Waseem et al., 2017). It summarizes previous work done in similar areas along with their insights on detecting abusive language efficiently. Their typological approach helps in differentiating between Explicit or Implicit in directed & generalized abusive sentence over abusive language. In a nutshell, it gives a vast information about different abusive language usage with reference to Explicit and Implicit abuse.

Kwok and Wang (2013) talk about "Locate the hate: Detecting Tweets Against Blacks". The paper states that Twitter has a large number of black community people and, based upon that, they propose a model that is able to binary classify the text as "racist" or "non-racist". They used a unigram approach to create the vocabulary of offensive words which are related to racism and were able to achieve 86% accuracy in detecting them.

Nobata et al. (2016) talk about the detection of abusive language over web portals. They claim that their model outperforms classical/state-of-art blacklisting, regular expression, and NLP models. For building the model they developed a corpus for abusive language labels and applied a supervised approach using Lexicon, Linguistic, N-grams, Syntactic, word2vec features.

Schofield and Davidson (2017) state three different methods to identify hate speech in the social media. The first approach uses lexicons while the second creates a bags-of-words. The third and final approach mentioned uses Distributional Semantics, a group of methods that summarizes information about word context or co-occurrence.

Fišer et al. (2017) define a framework to detect Socially Unacceptable Discourse (SUD) practices in Slovenia, such as hate speech, threats over social media, use of abusive language and defamation. According to them, Spletno Oko[3] is collecting the biggest and most authoritative database of socially unacceptable online discourse practices in Slovene. With the help of this, they were able to classify target of SUD such as Ethnicity, Race, Sexual orientation, Political affiliation, and Religion. The framework will automatically classify the text based upon the target SUD. The main mission of Spletno oko is in cooperation with Police, Internet Service providers, and other governmental and non-governmental organizations reduce the amount of child sexual abuse images and hate speech online.

Gambäck and Sikdar (2017) propose a "Convolutional Neural Networks to Classify Hate-speech". Using deep learning algorithms like Convolutional Neural Networks and Max Pooling concepts, they

---

[3]http://www.spletno-oko.si/english/

tried to classify racism, sexism, both and nonhate speech using softmax activation. Further, they used features like character 4-grams, word vectors based on semantic information, randomly generated word vectors, and word vectors combined with character n-grams. According to their work, the model with word2vec embeddings outperformed all others. Here, all models were applied to the English Twitter hatespeech dataset created by Waseem and Hovy (2016).

Zhang et al. (2018) report about "Detecting Hate Speech on Twitter Using a Convolution-GRU Based Deep Neural Network". Using deep learning algorithms like Convolutional Neural Networks followed by Gated Recurrent Networks with word-based features, this system is reported to outperform other approaches in 6 out of 7 different datasets. The corpus focuses on hate speech, especially for Muslim and refugees.

Founta et al. (2018) discuss various forms of abusive behavior on Twitter. They intend to cover different types of labeling schemes for various abusive behaviors and made an 80 thousand tweets dataset publicly available for the research purposes. The used labels are Offensive Language, Abusive Language, Hate Speech, Aggressive Behavior, Cyberbullying Behavior, Spam and Normal. Further, they were able to classify whether the state of behavior is Hateful or Normal.

ElSherief et al. (2018) present another great work. It talks about "A Target-based Linguistic Analysis of Hate Speech in Social Media" and they try to focus on the target of the speech, stating that it could be a single entity or a large number of people in a group. According to their observation, direct hate speech tends to be more informal and angrier; on the other side, hate speech towards groups is likely to be targeted for religious hate, political parties dissatisfaction, and social bodies behavior.

Dadvar et al. (2013) talk about the importance of user context in improving cyberbullying and it can give extra features like author profiling. They performed experiments on YouTube comments for detecting cyberbullying and showed promising improvements when user context is taken into account. They looked at the history of user's activities in their dataset and used the averaged content-based features on the users' history to see whether there was a pattern of offensive language usage. They also checked the frequency of profanity in their previous comments and other linguistic characteristics such as a number of pronouns, the average length of the comments and usage of capital letters and the use of emoticons. As the type of words and language structures may vary at different ages, they considered the age of the users as a feature.

Dinakar et al. (2011) empathize with the use of a binary classifier for detecting textual cyberbullying. The idea is to break down textual data into sub-categories until it becomes binary classification. According to authors, binary classification gives better result compared to the multi-label classifier. This enables to retrieve the topic-sensitive classification problem rather bigger picture of cyberbullying. Afterward, Combining all binary classification in to one performs better than multi-label classification in the detection of textual cyberbullying.

Burnap and Williams (2015) present "Cyber hate speech on Twitter: An application of machine classification and statistical modeling for policy and decision making" and focuses on the use of statistical models to forecast the likely spread of cyber hate with the help of different features, like Part-of-Speech (POS), grammatical dependencies and hate speech keyword classification, as input. For model creation standard algorithms like Bayesian Logistic Regression, Support Vector Machine and Random Forest Decision Tree were used. With the help of a voting mechanism, they were able to reduce the number of false positives and false negative and concluded that an "ensemble classification approach is most suitable for classifying cyber hate, given the current feature sets".

A recent discussion on the challenges of identifying profanity vs. hate speech can be found in (Malmasi and Zampieri, 2018). Their results demonstrate that it can be hard to distinguish between overt and covert aggression in social media. Further, it reveals that discriminating hate speech and profanity is not a simple task, which may require features that capture a deeper understanding of the text not always possible with surface n-grams. This is a key motivating factor for this shared task and a highly relevant discussion to include.

3 Data and Methodology

Before proceeding with the methodology, some time was taken to understand the data.

3.1 Data Characteristics

The methods used to compile the shared task dataset is described in (Kumar et al., 2018b). It has 15,000 Facebook Posts/Comments in both English and Hindi. The data has been split into three sets namely, train (9000 samples), validation (3000 samples) and dev (3000 samples). After analyzing them, the following data properties were found:

- Collection Region: India
- Usage of English Stop Words: Low
- Usage of Abbreviation: High
- Emoji Noise Level: Distributed (i.e. emojis are equally distributed among all the classes)
- Language (Hindi-English) Noise: High
- Sentence Length: Highly Fluctuating
- 50 Top Words: Distributed (i.e. the top 50 words are equally distributed over all the classes)
- Class Label Distribution: Imbalanced
- Text Segmentation Level: Moderate (i.e. usage of the hastags or joint words was moderate)

Agarwal et al. (2007) mention that level of noise depends upon the text and discuss which noise to consider and which not on a specific problem. After analyzing the provided dataset, it was noted that most of the data had spelling errors and abbreviations, so it was decided to remove this kind of noise during pre-processing. Like consider two sentences "I am in love with you" and "im in luv wid u". Both the sentences have the same meaning and might be written the same author but the machine will see them as two different representations. The motivation is to reduce the confusion/possibility for the machine learning model. Table 1 presents the preprocessing done over a day to day informal communication abbreviations.

Word	Replaced with
app, wil, im, al, sx, u	application, will, i am, all, sex, you
r, y, hv, c, bcz or coz	are, why, have, see, because
ppl or pepl, nd, hw	people, and, how
bc, fc, mc, wtf, chutiya	fuck

Table 1: Informal Abbreviation Preprocessor

A total of 244 different Emojis were found in the data. From them, 82 were found in CAG data, 68 were found in OAG data and 214 were found in NAG data. Further, the use of emojis was highly overlapped over all the classes, which means that emojis could not serve as a good feature for classification. In day to day social media writing, people often use the symbolic emojis. This step handles such emojies which are not in form of regular emoji. Table 2 shows the replacements done.

Another major consideration was the use of slang/informal abbreviation [4][5]. The slang has a major contribution in classifying the data as stated in (Theodora Chu and Wang, 2016). For example, in many comments, a Hindi informal abbreviation "bc" word was used. It is similar to Engish informal abbreviation "fk" which translate to "fuck". Having such word are likely to be categorized as OAG. So, such Hindi/English words are pre-processed to the actual meaning (refer Table 1). These pre-processing rules (or sets of regular expressions) were defined as a part of the original work. The rules were written after analysing the dataset and the same could be found in the Appendix A.

---

[4]https://blogs.transparent.com/hindi/slang-in-hindi-i/
[5]https://www.paperrater.com/page/british-slang-words

Symbol	Replaced with
:) :) :-) (: (: (-: :')	em_smile
:D : D :-D xD x-D XD X-D	em_laugh
<3 :*	em_love
;-) ;) ;-D ;D (; (-;	em_wink
:-(: (:( ):)-:	em_sad
:,(:'(:"(	em_cry
X(>:-(>:(X-(	em_angry

Table 2: Symbolic Emoji Replacement

Normally, when using TFIDF, most repeated words are ranked lower than rare words, but in this corpus, most repeated words like "BJP", "JNU", "MODI" were a deciding factor of the class. It is impossible to narrow it down manually on the keywords. Though, old papers (Frank et al., 1999) and (Li et al., 2010) talk about the importance of "Domain-Specific Keyphrase Extraction" and "Keyword Extraction for Social Snippets". It shows that we can build a model that does automatic keyphrase extraction but again it depends upon which type of text are you using. On the other hand Zhang and LeCun (2015) claim that without any knowledge of the syntactic or semantic structure of a language, their model can outperform state of art models. Though, it sounds more convenient to present domain-specific keyphrase extraction to training model.

Lastly, the class distribution over the corpus. The provided data for OAG, CAG, and NAG is, 22.30%, 35.40%, and 42.30% for English and 40%, 41%, and 19% for Hindi, respectively. This can be taken into account if basic assumption of statistical machine learning is considered.

In summarization, data property is one of the important factors which need to be counted for high accuracy of the system.

3.2 Methodology

Nowadays there are many technologies for text classification and one of them is FastText (Joulin et al., 2016a). It provides word vectors for 157 languages and supervised models for 8 datasets using a character level n-gram approach (Joulin et al., 2016b). The next sub-section presents the different text data representation the experiments done with them.

3.2.1 Text Representation

The English data representation was done using Tokenizer[6] and GloVe (Pennington et al., 2014) pre-trained word vectors. On another hand, Scikit-Learn API (Buitinck et al., 2013) was used for Tokenizing Hindi data.

A sequential model can be designed for text classification where the text sequence is fed to the machine learning algorithm. Nonetheless, these models only use numerical data and therefore a conversion was needed which involves two subprocesses: Integer Encoding and One-Hot Encoding (Lantz, 2013).

In the Integer Encoding, each unique word/text value is assigned an integer value. For example, "red" is 1, "green" is 2, and "blue" is 3. This process is known as label encoding or an integer encoding and is easily reversible. The idea of one-hot encoding is to replace the integer representation with binary. This means, integer encoded variable is removed and a new binary variable is added for each unique integer value.

3.2.2 Linear Models

Many research works shows that for small datasets people tend to use linear models. Usually, linear models are fed with different word representations like unigram, bigram, and trigram. Hence, a model using Logistic Regression with n-gram(1-3) was created and the results are shown in Figure 1.

From the figure 1, one can see that TFIDF unigram has the highest test accuracy because the dataset has unique tokens like "BJP", "JNU", "MODI", "PAK", etc which are the deciding factor of the class.

---

[6]https://keras.io/preprocessing/text/

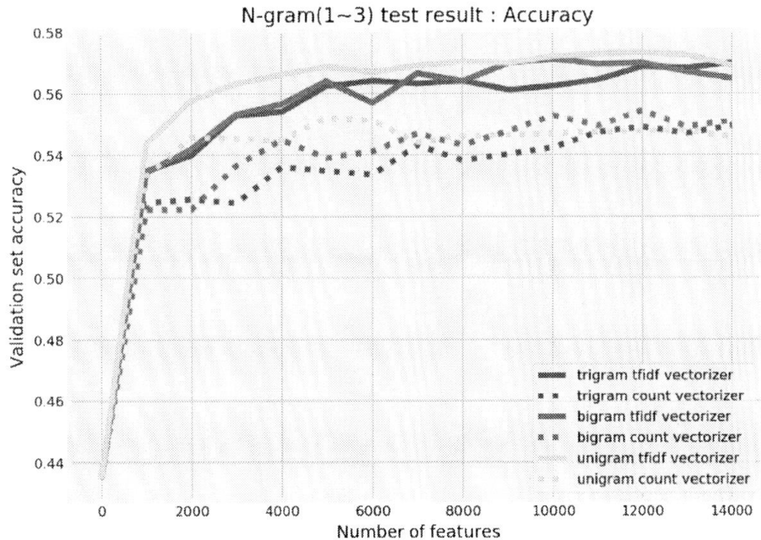

Figure 1: Logistic Regression with N-gram(1-3)

So a TFIDF unigram representation along with sklearn machine learning libraries was used to train the model. Table 3 shows the accuracy results with different sklearn linear models like Logistic Regression, SVC, Multinomial NB, Bernoulli NB, Ridge Classifier, and AdaBoost Classifier. (Here, development set is not equal to the test set.)

Linear Model	Acc on Validation Split	Acc on Development Set
Logistic Regression	57.20	37.45
Linear SVC	54.65	36.61
Linear SVC with L1-based	55.24	36.92
Multinomial NB	56.86	35.41
Bernoulli NB	53.90	36.51
Ridge Classifier	55.36	34.15
AdaBoost Classifier	51.94	33.78

Table 3: Experiment with Sklearn Linear Models: Unigram

3.2.3 Deep Learning Sequential Models

For the research and development, Keras (Chollet and others, 2015) was used as front-end and Tensorflow (Abadi et al., 2016) as back-end.

Generally, a sequential model is designed for text classification where the text sequence is fed to the model for learning and, commonly, the text is pre-processed. As discussed in Section 3.1, a specific language pre-processor was developed. This pre-processor takes care of exempted stop words, regional level abbreviations, emojis, and text segmentation. For segmentation, Ekphrasis (Baziotis et al., 2017) text processing tool was used. After cleaning the data, the text is represented using methods talked in Section 3.2.1 then the model was trained using different algorithms/layers (available in Keras). Table 4 presents the accuracy obtained over English development dataset. The parameters are shown in Appendix B. After analyzing the table 4 results, the general conclusion was that the word representation used for the pre-train word vector was causing this poor results. Therefore, a new model with one-hot representation was formed and discussed in the Section 3.2.4.

33

Method	Acc on Dev (%)
Single layer LSTM	37.93
Multi layer LSTM	39.20
Conv1D & GlobalMaxPooling1D	37.37
Conv1D & MaxPooling1D with Hidden Layer	37.73
Convolutional Layers with LSTM	39.03
Convolutional Layers with Bidirectional LSTM	37.53
Fasttext Text Classification	54.00
Fasttext Text Classification with Skip Gram Model	37.00
Fasttext with Conv1D , MaxPooling1D & Bidirectional LSTM	38.53
Multiple Input RNN with Keras	37.00
Concatenate: 2 Bidirectional	38.00
Concatenate: Bidirectional with Conv1D & MaxPooling1D	37.50

Table 4: Results Using Different Deep Learning Algorithms/Layers

3.2.4 Fully Connected Neural Network with Advance Preprocessor & One-Hot Representation

After experimenting with lots of different methods and algorithms, a simple Dense[7] architecture was used to design the final model for submission. As discussed in Section 3.1, a specific language pre-processor was developed. This pre-processor takes care of exempted stop words, regional level abbreviations, emoji, and text segmentation. Regarding the data representation, a word dictionary was created, in which all the unique words were indexed and the index was used as the word id. These ids were portrayed as a binary matrix with the help of one-hot representation preserving the word orded of the sentences. Consider the figure 2 for better understanding. Assuming the dictionary {"country": 1, "very": 2, "I": 3, "love": 4, "my": 5}.

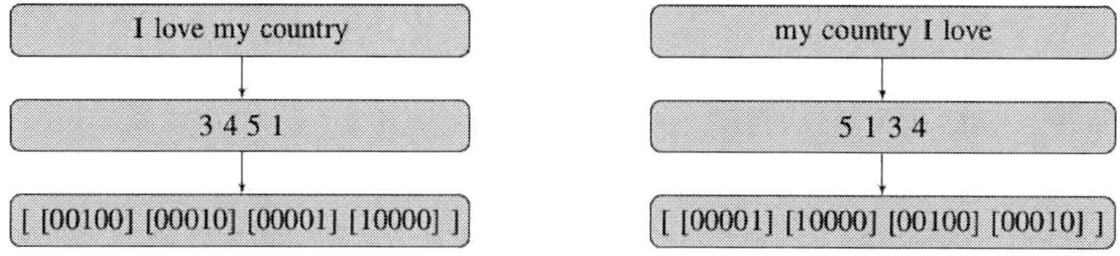

Figure 2: Word Representation

Here, in the figure 2, both sentences use the same words set but their sentence structure is preserved using dictionary index and one-hot representation.

The figure 3 represents the architecture layers of the Dense Neural Network. After several iterations, the number of layers for the architecture was set to three. The 1st hidden layer is having 1024 nodes which take the input from the input layer and the 2nd layer had 512 nodes and the last layer had 256 nodes. Inbetween each layers, mathamatical activation functions like Relu, Sigmoid and Softmax were used. The ordering of this activation function had very high impact on the results. The result of this model is discussed in the section 4.

4 Results and Discussion

Four different test set categories were presented on the shared task: English - Facebook/Twitter and Hindi - Facebook/Twitter

Participants were allowed to submit a maximum of 3 systems for each category and, as such, 3 systems were submitted: Dense, Fasttext and Voting of the two. Tables 5, 6, 7 and 8 show the results, namely the

---

[7]`https://keras.io/layers/core/`

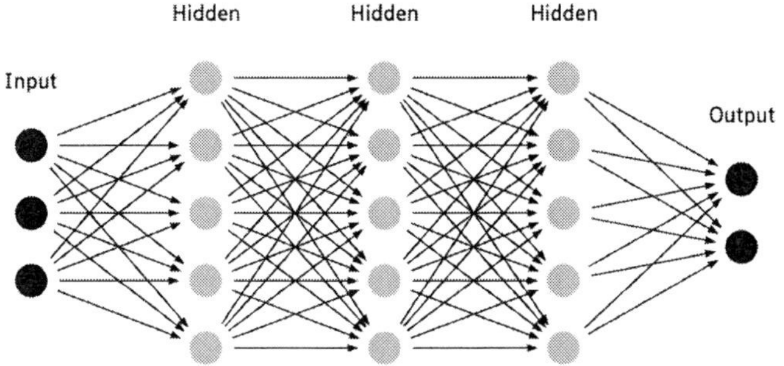

Figure 3: Dense System Architecture

F1 measure, of the 3 systems for each category. These results were given by the organizing committee.

System	F1 (weighted)
Random Baseline	0.3535
Dense	**0.5813**
Fasttext	0.5753
Voting	0.5698

Table 5: English (Facebook) Models.

System	F1 (weighted)
Random Baseline	0.3477
Dense	**0.6009**
Fasttext	0.5544
Voting	0.5324

Table 6: English (Twitter) Models.

System	F1 (weighted)
Random Baseline	0.3571
Dense	**0.5951**
Fasttext	0.5838
Voting	0.5634

Table 7: Hindi (Facebook) Models.

System	F1 (weighted)
Random Baseline	0.3206
Dense	**0.4830**
Fasttext	0.4528
Voting	0.4437

Table 8: Hindi (Twitter) Models.

Tables 9, 10, 11 and 12 present confusion matrix with precision and recall for the Dense model (the best model) in each category.

		Predicted			
		OAG	CAG	NAG	R@1
	OAG	83	38	23	57.64
True	CAG	31	67	44	47.18
	NAG	91	190	349	55.40
	P@1	40.49	22.71	83.89	

Table 9: Confusion matrix of Dense Model - English (Facebook) task.

		Predicted			
		OAG	CAG	NAG	R@1
	OAG	230	113	18	63.71
True	CAG	143	169	101	40.92
	NAG	6	120	357	73.91
	P@1	60.69	42.04	75	

Table 10: Confusion matrix of Dense Model - English (Twitter) task.

The observation from the tables 5–8 is that the Neural Network model is outperforming Fasttext classification model in all categories. Especially, for Twitter classifier.

Table 9 and 11 shows that for OAG class in Facebook (English/Hindi) dataset, precision is varying between 40.49 to 55.96 and the recall is varying between 57.64 to 59.67 and for CAG class, precision is varying between 22.71 to 57.63 and the recall is varying between 47.18 to 65.86.

The table 10 and 12 shows that for OAG class in Twitter (English/Hindi) dataset, precision is varying

		Predicted			
		OAG	CAG	NAG	R@1
	OAG	216	140	6	59.67
True	CAG	125	272	16	65.86
	NAG	45	60	90	46.15
	P@1	55.96	57.63	80.36	

Table 11: Confusion matrix of Dense Model - Hindi (Facebook) task.

		Predicted			
		OAG	CAG	NAG	R@1
	OAG	254	146	59	55.34
True	CAG	143	166	72	43.57
	NAG	76	123	155	43.79
	P@1	53.70	38.16	54.20	

Table 12: Confusion matrix of Dense Model - Hindi (Twitter) task.

between 53.70 to 60.69 and the recall is varying between 55.34 to 63.71 and for CAG class, precision is varying between 38.16 to 42.04 and the recall is varying between 40.92 to 43.57.

In the given context of aggression, hate speech, offensive, and abusive language identification, it is important to identify the aggressive or hate speech keywords. This leads to identifying the OAG and CAG classes with higher recall value. At the same time, it is important to identify contexts in which some words may be hateful. Because simply detecting the words will lead to a lot of false positives even if it does raise the recall.

As mentioned, for a demanding task like aggression identification, the proposed model should not have a lower recall for OAG and CAG classes. Further, it could be identified that systems are suffering from false positive values. This could be overcome by reducing class imbalance or oversampling the positive class (OAG & CAG) or changing the weight of examples.

Below is the official ranking of the models among different categories. This ranking was provided by the organizing committee.

English (Facebook)	English (Twitter)	Hindi (Facebook)	Hindi (Twitter)
14th out of 30	1st out of 30	7th out of 15	3rd out of 15

Table 13: Global Standing of Models: vista.ue

5 Conclusion

After discussing different text classification models, one can surely say that Automatic Aggression Identification is necessary and researchers should put more efforts in making it more robust and precise. From all the experiments and models, the designed model with a Dense architecture performs better than a Fasttext model for all four categories. In fact, the system submitted for English - Twitter stood 1st rank for its category. Between the Facebook and Twitter test dataset contents, the model trained over Facebook dataset can be used for unknown Twitter test set but vice-versa is not true. The main reason for this can be a length of sentence, amounts of hashtags, citation of users (i.e '@' and the amount of retweet).

In this model words that are not found in the dictionary are omitted. As future work, and to address this issue, a neighboring or similar word could be used; here each word would be added to a list from which neighboring/similar word would be founded. This will help in categorizing unseen words to the model. Thus, all the words are included and there is no omission of words. Another line of future work can be to include semantic meaning from the sentences, extracting ontological features either by Part of Speech (POS) tagging or Entity Extraction (EE).

Acknowledgements

The authors would like to thank COMPETE 2020, PORTUGAL 2020 Programs, the European Union, and LISBOA 2020 for supporting this research as part of Agatha Project SI & IDT number 18022 (Intelligent analysis system of open of sources information for surveillance/crime control) made in collaboration with the University of Évora. The colleagues Madhu Agrawal, Silvia Bottura Scardina and Roy Bayot provided insight and expertise that greatly assisted the research.

References

Martín Abadi, Paul Barham, Jianmin Chen, Zhifeng Chen, Andy Davis, Jeffrey Dean, Matthieu Devin, Sanjay Ghemawat, Geoffrey Irving, Michael Isard, Manjunath Kudlur, Josh Levenberg, Rajat Monga, Sherry Moore, Derek G. Murray, Benoit Steiner, Paul Tucker, Vijay Vasudevan, Pete Warden, Martin Wicke, Yuan Yu, and Xiaoqiang Zheng. 2016. Tensorflow: A system for large-scale machine learning. In *Proceedings of the 12th USENIX Conference on Operating Systems Design and Implementation*, OSDI'16, pages 265–283, Berkeley, CA, USA. USENIX Association.

Sumeet Agarwal, Shantanu Godbole, Diwakar Punjani, and Shourya Roy. 2007. How much noise is too much: A study in automatic text classification. *Seventh IEEE International Conference on Data Mining (ICDM 2007)*, pages 3–12.

Christos Baziotis, Nikos Pelekis, and Christos Doulkeridis. 2017. Datastories at semeval-2017 task 4: Deep lstm with attention for message-level and topic-based sentiment analysis. In *Proceedings of the 11th International Workshop on Semantic Evaluation (SemEval-2017)*, pages 747–754, Vancouver, Canada, August. Association for Computational Linguistics.

Lars Buitinck, Gilles Louppe, Mathieu Blondel, Fabian Pedregosa, Andreas Mueller, Olivier Grisel, Vlad Niculae, Peter Prettenhofer, Alexandre Gramfort, Jaques Grobler, Robert Layton, Jake VanderPlas, Arnaud Joly, Brian Holt, and Gaël Varoquaux. 2013. API design for machine learning software: experiences from the scikit-learn project. In *ECML PKDD Workshop: Languages for Data Mining and Machine Learning*, pages 108–122.

Pete Burnap and Matthew L Williams. 2015. Cyber hate speech on twitter: An application of machine classification and statistical modeling for policy and decision making. *Policy & Internet*, 7(2):223–242.

François Chollet et al. 2015. Keras. `https://keras.io`.

Maral Dadvar, Dolf Trieschnigg, Roeland Ordelman, and Franciska de Jong. 2013. Improving cyberbullying detection with user context. In *Advances in Information Retrieval*, pages 693–696. Springer.

Thomas Davidson, Dana Warmsley, Michael Macy, and Ingmar Weber. 2017. Automated Hate Speech Detection and the Problem of Offensive Language. In *Proceedings of ICWSM*.

Karthik Dinakar, Roi Reichart, and Henry Lieberman. 2011. Modeling the detection of textual cyberbullying. In *The Social Mobile Web*, pages 11–17.

Mai ElSherief, Vivek Kulkarni, Dana Nguyen, William Yang Wang, and Elizabeth Belding. 2018. Hate Lingo: A Target-based Linguistic Analysis of Hate Speech in Social Media. *arXiv preprint arXiv:1804.04257*.

Darja Fišer, Tomaž Erjavec, and Nikola Ljubešić. 2017. Legal Framework, Dataset and Annotation Schema for Socially Unacceptable On-line Discourse Practices in Slovene. In *Proceedings of the Workshop Workshop on Abusive Language Online (ALW)*, Vancouver, Canada.

Antigoni-Maria Founta, Constantinos Djouvas, Despoina Chatzakou, Ilias Leontiadis, Jeremy Blackburn, Gianluca Stringhini, Athena Vakali, Michael Sirivianos, and Nicolas Kourtellis. 2018. Large Scale Crowdsourcing and Characterization of Twitter Abusive Behavior. *arXiv preprint arXiv:1802.00393*.

Eibe Frank, Gordon W. Paynter, Ian Witten, Carl Gutwin, and Craig Nevill-Manning. 1999. Domain-specific keyphrase extraction. 07.

Björn Gambäck and Utpal Kumar Sikdar. 2017. Using Convolutional Neural Networks to Classify Hate-speech. In *Proceedings of the First Workshop on Abusive Language Online*, pages 85–90.

Armand Joulin, Edouard Grave, Piotr Bojanowski, and Tomas Mikolov. 2016a. Bag of tricks for efficient text classification. *arXiv preprint arXiv:1607.01759*.

Armand Joulin, Edouard Grave, Piotr Bojanowski, and Tomas Mikolov. 2016b. Bag of tricks for efficient text classification. *CoRR*, abs/1607.01759.

Ritesh Kumar, Atul Kr. Ojha, Shervin Malmasi, and Marcos Zampieri. 2018a. Benchmarking Aggression Identification in Social Media. In *Proceedings of the First Workshop on Trolling, Aggression and Cyberbulling (TRAC)*, Santa Fe, USA.

Ritesh Kumar, Aishwarya N. Reganti, Akshit Bhatia, and Tushar Maheshwari. 2018b. Aggression-annotated Corpus of Hindi-English Code-mixed Data. In *Proceedings of the 11th Language Resources and Evaluation Conference (LREC)*, Miyazaki, Japan.

Irene Kwok and Yuzhou Wang. 2013. Locate the hate: Detecting Tweets Against Blacks. In *Twenty-Seventh AAAI Conference on Artificial Intelligence*.

Brett Lantz. 2013. *Machine Learning with R*. Packt Publishing.

Zhenhui Li, Ding Zhou, Yun-Fang Juan, and Jiawei Han. 2010. Keyword extraction for social snippets. In *Proceedings of the 19th International Conference on World Wide Web*, WWW '10, pages 1143–1144, New York, NY, USA. ACM.

Shervin Malmasi and Marcos Zampieri. 2017. Detecting Hate Speech in Social Media. In *Proceedings of the International Conference Recent Advances in Natural Language Processing (RANLP)*, pages 467–472.

Shervin Malmasi and Marcos Zampieri. 2018. Challenges in Discriminating Profanity from Hate Speech. *Journal of Experimental & Theoretical Artificial Intelligence*, 30:1–16.

Chikashi Nobata, Joel Tetreault, Achint Thomas, Yashar Mehdad, and Yi Chang. 2016. Abusive Language Detection in Online User Content. In *Proceedings of the 25th International Conference on World Wide Web*, pages 145–153. International World Wide Web Conferences Steering Committee.

Jeffrey Pennington, Richard Socher, and Christopher D. Manning. 2014. Glove: Global vectors for word representation. In *Empirical Methods in Natural Language Processing (EMNLP)*, pages 1532–1543.

Anna Schmidt and Michael Wiegand. 2017. A Survey on Hate Speech Detection Using Natural Language Processing. In *Proceedings of the Fifth International Workshop on Natural Language Processing for Social Media. Association for Computational Linguistics*, pages 1–10, Valencia, Spain.

Alexandra Schofield and Thomas Davidson. 2017. Identifying Hate Speech in Social Media. *XRDS: Crossroads, The ACM Magazine for Students*, 24(2):56–59.

Kylie Jue Theodora Chu and Max Wang. 2016. Comment abuse classification with deep learning.

Zeerak Waseem and Dirk Hovy. 2016. Hateful symbols or hateful people? predictive features for hate speech detection on twitter. In *Proceedings of the NAACL Student Research Workshop*, pages 88–93, San Diego, California, June. Association for Computational Linguistics.

Zeerak Waseem, Thomas Davidson, Dana Warmsley, and Ingmar Weber. 2017. Understanding Abuse: A Typology of Abusive Language Detection Subtasks. In *Proceedings of the First Workshop on Abusive Langauge Online*.

Xiang Zhang and Yann LeCun. 2015. Text understanding from scratch. *CoRR*, abs/1502.01710.

Ziqi Zhang, David Robinson, and Jonathan Tepper. 2018. Detecting Hate Speech on Twitter Using a Convolution-GRU Based Deep Neural Network. In *Lecture Notes in Computer Science*. Springer Verlag.

Appendix A   Regional Level Abbreviations

```python
FLAGS = re.MULTILINE | re.DOTALL

def tokenize(text):
    # Different regex parts for smiley faces
    eyes = r"[8:=;]"
    nose = r"['`\-]?"

    # function
    def re_sub(pattern, repl):
        return re.sub(pattern, repl, text, flags=FLAGS)

    text = re_sub(r"https?:\/\/\/\S+\b|www\.(\w+\.)+\S*", " url ")
    # Smile -- :), : ), :-), (:, ( :, (-:, :')
    text = re_sub(r"(:\s?\)|:-\)|\(\s?:|\(-:|:'\))", " em_smile ")
    # Laugh -- :D, : D, :-D, xD, x-D, XD, X-D
    text = re_sub(r"(:\s?D|:-D|x-?D|X-?D)", " em_laugh ")
        # Love -- <3, :*
    text = re_sub(r"(<3|:\*)", " em_love ")
    # Wink -- ;-), ;), ;-D, ;D, (;, (-;
    text = re_sub(r"(;-?\)|;-?D|\(-?;)", " em_wink ")
    # Sad -- :-(, : (, :(, ):, )-:
    text = re_sub(r'(:\s?\(|:-\(|\)\s?:|\)-:)', " em_sad ")
    # Cry -- :,(, :'(, :"(
    text = re_sub(r'(:,\(|:\'\(|:"\()', " em_cry ")
    # remove funnnnny --> funny
    text = re_sub(r"(.)\1+", r"\1\1")
    # remove &
    text = re_sub(r"(-|\')", "")
    text = re_sub(r"@[0-9]+-", " number ")
    text = re_sub(r"{}{}[)dD]+|[)dD]+{}{}".
    format(eyes, nose, nose, eyes), " em_positive ")
    text = re_sub(r"{}{}p+".format(eyes, nose), " em_positive ")
    text = re_sub(r"{}{}\(+|\)+{}{}".
    format(eyes, nose, nose, eyes), " em_negative ")
    text = re_sub(r"{}{}[\/|l*]".
    format(eyes, nose), " em_neutralface ")
    text = re_sub(r'-', r' ')
    text = re_sub(r"([pls?s]){2,}", r"\1")
    text = re_sub(r"([plz?z]){2,}", r"\1")
    text = re_sub(r'\\n', r' ')
    text = re_sub(r" sx ", " sex ")
    text = re_sub(r" u ", " you ")
    text = re_sub(r" r ", " are ")
    text = re_sub(r" y ", " why ")
    text = re_sub(r" Y ", " WHY ")
    text = re_sub(r"Y ", " WHY ")
    text = re_sub(r" hv ", " have ")
    text = re_sub(r" c ", " see ")
    text = re_sub(r" bcz ", " because ")
```

```python
text = re_sub(r" coz ", " because ")
text = re_sub(r" v ", " we ")
text = re_sub(r" ppl ", " people ")
text = re_sub(r" pepl ", " people ")
text = re_sub(r" r b i ", " rbi ")
text = re_sub(r" R B I ", " RBI ")
text = re_sub(r" R b i ", " rbi ")
text = re_sub(r" R ", " ARE ")
text = re_sub(r" hav ", " have ")
text = re_sub(r"R ", " ARE ")
text = re_sub(r" U ", " you ")
text = re_sub(r"U ", " you ")
text = re_sub(r" pls ", " please ")
text = re_sub(r"Pls ", "Please ")
text = re_sub(r"plz ", "please ")
text = re_sub(r"Plz ", "Please ")
text = re_sub(r"PLZ ", "Please ")
text = re_sub(r"Pls", "Please ")
text = re_sub(r"plz", "please ")
text = re_sub(r"Plz", "Please ")
text = re_sub(r"PLZ", "Please ")
text = re_sub(r" thankz ", " thanks ")
text = re_sub(r" thnx ", " thanks ")
text = re_sub(r"fuck\w+ ", " fuck ")
text = re_sub(r"f\*\* ", " fuck ")
text = re_sub(r"\*\*\*k ", " fuck ")
text = re_sub(r"F\*\* ", " fuck ")
text = re_sub(r"mo\*\*\*\*\* ", " fucker ")
text = re_sub(r"b\*\*\*\* ", " blody ")
text = re_sub(r" mc ", " fucker ")
text = re_sub(r" MC ", " fucker ")
text = re_sub(r" wtf ", " fuck ")
text = re_sub(r" ch\*\*\*ya ", " fucker ")
text = re_sub(r" ch\*\*Tya ", " fucker ")
text = re_sub(r" ch\*\*Tia ", " fucker ")
text = re_sub(r" C\*\*\*yas ", " fucker ")
text = re_sub(r"l\*\*\*\* ", "shit ")
text = re_sub(r" A\*\*\*\*\*\*S", " ASSHOLES")
text = re_sub(r" di\*\*\*\*s", " fucker")
text = re_sub(r" nd ", " and ")
text = re_sub(r"Nd ", "and ")
text = re_sub(r"(ind[vs]pak)", " india versus pakistan ")
text = re_sub(r"(pak[vs]ind)", " pakistan versus india ")
text = re_sub(r"(indvsuae)",
" india versus United Arab Emirates ")
text = re_sub(r"[sS]hut[Dd]own[jnuJNU]", " shut down jnu ")
return text
```

Appendix B   Deep Learning Sequential Models

Parameter	Value
Maximum Sequence Length	1000
Maximum Number of Words	20000
Embedding Dimension	200
Validation Split Ratio	0.2
Epochs	7
Batch Size	256
Activation	Softmax
Optimizer	Adam

Table 14: Experiment Parameters

Cyberbullying Intervention Interface Based on Convolutional Neural Networks

Qianjia Huang
Department of Computer Science
University of Ottawa
qhuan035@uottawa.ca

Jianhong Zhang
Department of Computer Science
University of Ottawa
jzhan410@uottawa.ca

Diana Inkpen
Department of Computer Science
University of Ottawa
Diana.Inkpen@uottawa.ca

David Van Bruwaene
SafeToNet Canada
dvanbruwaene@safetonet.com

Abstract

This paper describes the process of building a cyberbullying intervention interface driven by a machine-learning based text-classification service. We make two main contributions. First, we show that cyberbullying can be identified in real-time before it takes place, with available machine learning and natural language processing tools, in particular convolutional neural networks. Second, we present a mechanism that provides individuals with early feedback about how other people would feel about wording choices in their messages before they are sent out. This interface not only gives a chance for the user to revise the text, but also provides a system-level flagging/intervention in a situation related to cyberbullying.

1 Introduction

Cyberbullying, which can be defined as *'when the Internet, cell phones or other devices are used to send or post text or images intended to hurt or embarrass another person'* (Dinakar et al., 2012), has become a pernicious social problem in recent years. This is also worrying, as multiple studies found that cyberbullying victims often have psychiatric and psychosomatic disorders (Beckman et al., 2012), and a British study found that nearly half of suicides among young people were related to bullying (BBC News[1]). These factors underscore an urgent need to understand, detect, and ultimately reduce the prevalence of cyberbullying.

In contrast to traditional bullying (e.g., school bullying), cyberbullying is not limited to a time and place, which makes cyberbullying potentially more prevalent than traditional bullying. Cyberbullying victims may not recognize their experiences as bullying and they may not report them or seek help for associated emotional difficulties. Kowalski and Limber (2007) reported that almost 90% of young cyberbullying victims did not tell their parents or other trusted adults about their online negative experiences. These factors are especially worrying as multiple studies have reported that the victims of cyberbullying often deal with psychiatric and psychosomatic disorders (Beckman et al., 2012; Sourander et al., 2010), and the worst cases are suicides (Tokunaga, 2010).

Given the importance of the problem, content-based cyberbullying detection is becoming a key area of cyberbullying research. Current state-of-the-art methods for cyberbullying detection

[1]http://www.bbc.co.uk/news/10302550

Proceedings of the First Workshop on Trolling, Aggression and Cyberbullying, pages 42–51
Santa Fe, USA, August 25, 2018.

combine contextual and sentiment features (e.g., curse word dictionaries, histories of users activities, grammatical properties, and sentiment features derived from online users content) with text-mining approaches. While performance can be improved by training on text-external features, the scarcity of platform-ubiquitous external features requires a cross-platform new-media text classification algorithm to be trained strictly on text. This reduces the presence of features that are significant in training, but absent from data used in out-of-domain contexts. Hence, we introduce a text-driven model which covers six social media platforms (Facebook, Instagram, Twitter, Pinterest, Tumblr, Youtube), and it could be an ideal solution for this problem.

While presenting their methods for cyberbullying detection7, scholars have also suggested different interfaces for intervention. Dinakar et al. (2012) describe cyberbullying intervention mock-ups for both sender and receiver. With the aid of the text-driven model, this project also implements an Android-based interface which combines and optimizes the mock-ups from Dinakar et al. (2012). For instance, an interface giving the sender a chance to retype/cancel the message (as shown in Figure 1) is considered in our project. This project could be developed into a thrid-party application between users and social media providers for creating a healthy online environment.

Figure 1: Mock-up for delaying and undoing the issuance of messages from Dinakar et al. (Dinakar et al., 2012)

2 Online Cyberbullying Model

2.1 Data Set

This paper uses a dataset that was built for cyberbullying detection. Visr, a predictive wellness company, produced this dataset for use with an application (app) that analyzes online activities and interactions, and then alerts parents to potentially harmful issues their children may be experiencing.[2] Issues that parents are alerted about include bullying, anxiety, and depression. By making parents immediately aware of emerging issues on Instagram, Gmail, Tumblr, YouTube, Facebook, Twitter, and Pinterest, the Visr app aims to help parents address such issues before they grow into thornier problems. The app raises a red flag to warn parents when signs of these issues are detected in a child's online activities, including signs of possible mental health consequences like nascent depression, eating disorders, and self-harm. Visr accesses children's social media content through the API's of these social media channels with the consent of the children who are the account holders. This provides a unique cross-platform dataset with rich information.

---

[2]The app is available at https://app.visr.co, through the Apple App store, or through the Google Play store.

The data was collected by the Visr child safety app from September 2014 to March 2016. Over a half-million online posts were selected from among the social media platforms (Facebook, Instagram, Twitter, Pinterest, Tumblr, Youtube) and Gmail. These posts were randomly chosen among posts that had been viewed, received, or sent by the adolescents (between age 13 to 17). Personally identifying information was removed to ensure the privacy of Visr users. Demographic information such as gender, age, location's time-zone, post time, and the number of likes were recorded as well.

The specific cyberbullying detection dataset is one of Visr's labeled datasets. After combining an enriched selection of those posts with 3,072 'real issues' (posts with issues confirmed by parents), an annotation process was performed by three annotators for the *cyberbullying* label. 1,753 posts were determined to be positive for *cyberbullying*), 304 were labeled as 'unsure', and 12,441 were labeled as negative for *cyberbullying* (Agreement percentage: 95.07%; Cohen's Kappa: 0.805). The posts either labeled as 'unsure' or about which annotators disagreed were removed, leaving a corpus of 14,194.

2.2 Convolutional Neural Networks

Convolutional Neural Networks (CNNs) are known to have good performance on data with high locality, when words get more care weight about the features surrounding them. For our classification problem, we are trying to get high locality in text given their short length and their tendency to focus on cyberbullying.

We used CNNs that received input text in the form of sequences of integer representations of stemmed unigrams. Our character processing included the conversion of emoticons into word representations, and the removal of non-Latin characters. We also removed frequently occurring url components (e.g., names of popular websites), metadata encoded in the main body-text (e.g., 'RT: '), and a variety of social media platform-specific features. Hashtags and @-mentions were reduced to binary features. The text was then lower-cased and tokenized using NLTK's Tweet-Tokenizer[3]. The tokenized text was next encoded using a dictionary of integers, with the original ordering of the tokens preserved. The encoded text was converted into dense vectors of fixed size. This one-dimensional embedding was fed into a single-layer CNN with 200 embedding dimensions, 150 output dimensions, and 200 convolution kernels. The kernels were optimized using Tensorflow's 'adagrad' optimizer (lr=0.001) using categorical cross-entropy as the loss function. The 150 output dimensions were flattened using a sigmoid function into two output nodes whose values are floats between 0 and 1, with 1 representing *bullying* and 0 representing non-bullying.

To test the performance of our model, we took 70% of the dataset as training set, and 30% of it for testing. As suggested by previous research, we also added textual features (total used: 93) from LIWC 2015 [4] to build another model for comparison. We set the threshold which got the best result (here we used highest F-measure to represent the performance). Comparison can be seen in Table 1. We put ZeroR and SVM (Support Vector Machine) models as baselines for comparison. Because the ZeroR model puts everythoing in the majority class, labeling all of the positive instances as negative ones, both the F-measure for the positive class and True

---

[3]http://www.nltk.org/api/nltk.tokenize.html

[4]https://liwc.wpengine.com/

Positive score are 0. Meanwhile, the AUC valus of the ZeroR model is 0.5 and the accuracy measure depends on the distribution of positives and negatives in the dataset. It is obvious that the performance of CNN model is better than that of the SVM model in terms of F-measure, AUC, and True Positive rate. It is also expected that adding LIWC features could help to improve the F-measure and accuracy. However, for other important parameters (i.e., True Positives and AUC value), our original model with NLTK-tokenized features got a better index. Note that all the thresholds are taken as 'optimal' because they lead to the highest F-measure, which is not only influenced by True Positive rate but also by the True Negative rate. However, in real-life, we care more about the true positives than the true negatives; in other words, detecting the normal cases (which is much more frequent than cyberbullying) is not the goal for this project. Hence, we are setting up the thresholds with another method which will be described in section 2.3.

Model name	F-measure	AUC	Accuracy	True Positive
ZeroR	0	0.5	87.6%	0%
SVM	0.517	0.851	87.1%	58.9%
SVM + LIWC	0.585	0.892	90.2%	55.9%
CNN	0.523	0.860	87.1%	60.4%
CNN + LIWC	0.597	0.898	90.0%	60.2%

Table 1: Comparison of the results of the CNN models

2.3 Thresholds Setting

To set up the thresholds of our application, we built an electronic survey which contains 45 cyberbullying posts (being labeled as cyberbullying) from the VISR dataset and there are five posts which did not belong to cyberbullying at all (e.g., non-bullying–'he was a complete ass hole, .. He used 2 tell me that my mom tried to abort me because she didn't want to have another kid', cyberbullying–'Go fuck yourself!'). Then we invited four colleagues (two males and two females, all PhD students) to give feedbacks of their feelings about those cyberbullying-related online posts. The survey goes as follow:

"Assume someone (online, you might know the person or not) is sending you a message via phone/posting a message which @yourid/leaving a comment under your profile, etc. Please give the feedback score about how you feel:
1. It is totally fine;
2. Well, not that comfortable, but there is no need to hide it;
3. Not acceptable, I don't want to see this ever, it should be blocked."

After reviewing the feedback scores from our colleagues to ensure they understand the assumption properly, one survey was deleted as the participant didn't get the whole image and returned the feedback with 47/50 'score 3' ("I suggest to hide every F-word, that's really annoying" the participant wrote in the feedback survey). Thus, three surveys were kept for the threshold setting.

The results from the three participants' feelings and the related bullying index of the chosen text are shown in Figure 2. We averaged the 'feeling score' of the three participants; for instance, the average 'feeling score' 1.67 represents the total score of 5, which means that probably two chose 2 and one chose 1. The cyberbullying index of the selected texts is from 0.0431 to 0.8614. We separated the text with 'feeling score' 1 - 1.33 as 'totally fine' group, 1.67 - 2.33 as 'uncomfortable but not that bad' group, 2.34 - 3 as 'not acceptable' group. With an ANOVA test, we found the 'totally fine' group (mean = 0.17) is significantly different (p = 0.0101) from the other two groups ('uncomfortable but acceptable': 0.40, 'unacceptable': 0.44).

From the results, six messages are mainly considered as 'totally fine' ('feeling score' from 1 to 1.33, similar to the number of not bullying at all) and the average index is 0.17; we set this index as the threshold_1. From our testing document, most of the 'uncomfortable' and 'not acceptable' scores are higher than threshold_1; only three of them would be identified as 'totally fine'. For the threshold_2, we set it with the average index of 'uncomfortable but not that bad' group (0.40); seven of the 'not acceptable' messages get lower index (which would not be sent with warning, as discuss in the following section), but because of the threshold_1, only one of these 'not acceptable' would not be filtered as 'uncomfortable'.

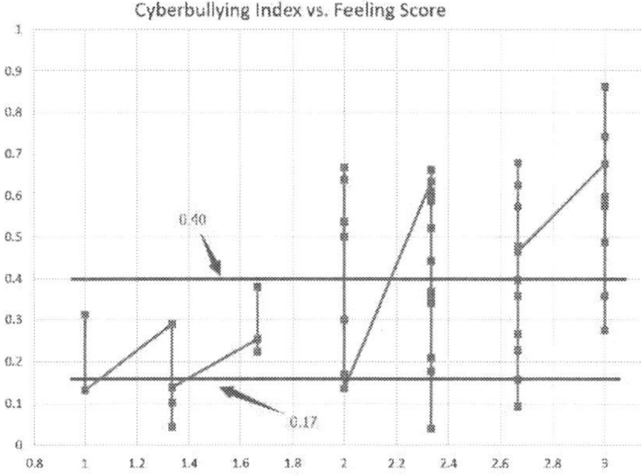

Figure 2: Threshold Setting

3 Application

3.1 Platform and Development Environment

We chose Android OS as our application development platform as it is the most popular mobile OS, and it is an open source, real time operating system which meets our development requirements. We used Android Studio for the development, since it is optimized for all devices, and it provides various APIs and layouts.

3.2   Application Design

3.2.1   Application Subsystem Design

The user interface has a text input field which allows the user to type the message and send it by using the HTTPS to Visr API over the network. This app will extract the cyberbullying index calculated by the Visr API and compare it with the set thresholds. Based on the results of the comparison, a corresponding prompts will be given to the user.

We used HTTPS to transmit data, and we used Volley module to implement the HTTP functions. Volley [5] is a HTTP library developed by Google, it provided us the: 1. Scheduling network request; 2. JSON and images asynchronous downloading; 3. Network request priority handling; 4. Caching; and 5. Powerful APIs.

3.2.2   System Architecture

The system dialog is shown in Figure 3. Regarding users' communication behavior and freedom of speech, the challenges to this interface are presented as follow. On one hand, to build a better online environment, we do not want to miss any of the 'uncomfortable'/'unacceptable' texts and allow them to be sent without filtering. On the other hand, we do not want the users to feel annoying about the intervention; if they really want to send the message, it is not possible to stop them. Hence, we built a win-win solution with the two thresholds and the related interventions.

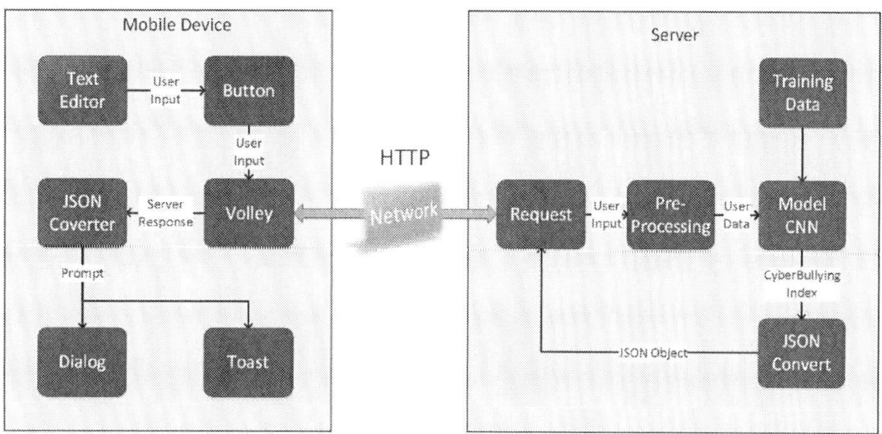

Figure 3: System Diagram

In our interface application, for a text which has index between two thresholds (0.17, 0.40), we send a prompt to the user ('Your message may be aggressive to others, do you really want to send?'). As in this level, the text is not identified as unacceptable; the user could either send it or change it. Similar to figure 1, the prompt is displayed as a delay/chance for user to think about the feelings of the receiver. For the text which has a extremely high index (>0.40) of cyberbullying, the app will first send a prompt as 'Your message may make others feel uncomfortable, please change the tone.' and stay on the same page for the sender to modify the message. If the user

---

[5]https://developer.android.com/training/volley/index.html

changes it (or not) and the index is still high (above 0.40), the app will send another prompt as 'Your message may make others feel uncomfortable, do you really want to send with warnings?'. This second step comes as we do not want to infringe on users' freedom of speech and we respect the users' communication behavior as well. The only idea is to give advice to the writer about how other people would feel when reading the message. The system flow chart is shown in Figure 4.

4   Examples of the interface

To understand the system better, here are examples of situations with different outputs from the Visr API.

Imagine a user typed a message which receives the cyberbullying index as 0.20 which belongs to the 'uncomfortable but acceptable' level; the prompt would pop us as 'Alert: Your message may be aggressive to others, do you really want to send?' If the user clicks 'yes', it will send the message immediately; if user clicks 'no', there would be a chance to change the message.

For the 'extremely high index' message, such as 'what's your opinion for this fucking shit? You are retard!', the system will display the prompt as shown in figure 5. Please note there is no way to submit this message at the first time. No matter whether the user changes the content or not, if the second time the submitted text's index is still higher than threshold_2, a prompt which is similar to 'uncomfortable but acceptable' would pop up. This prompt is shown in figure 6. If the user wants to send it anyways, there will be warnings with this message, interventions such as hiding the message or sending the message with a warning could be applied at the receiver's end.

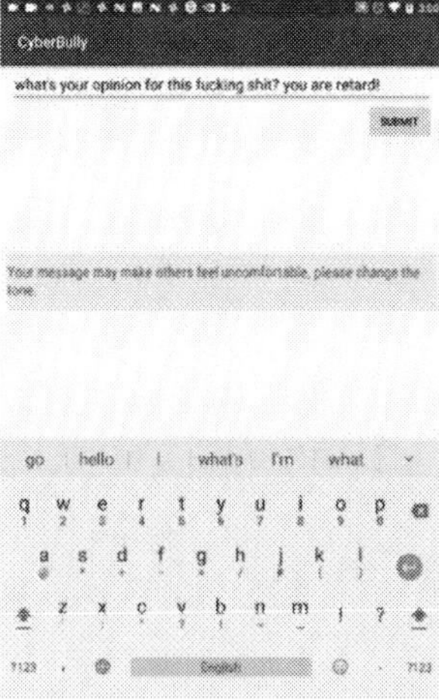

Figure 5: 'Extremely high index' message

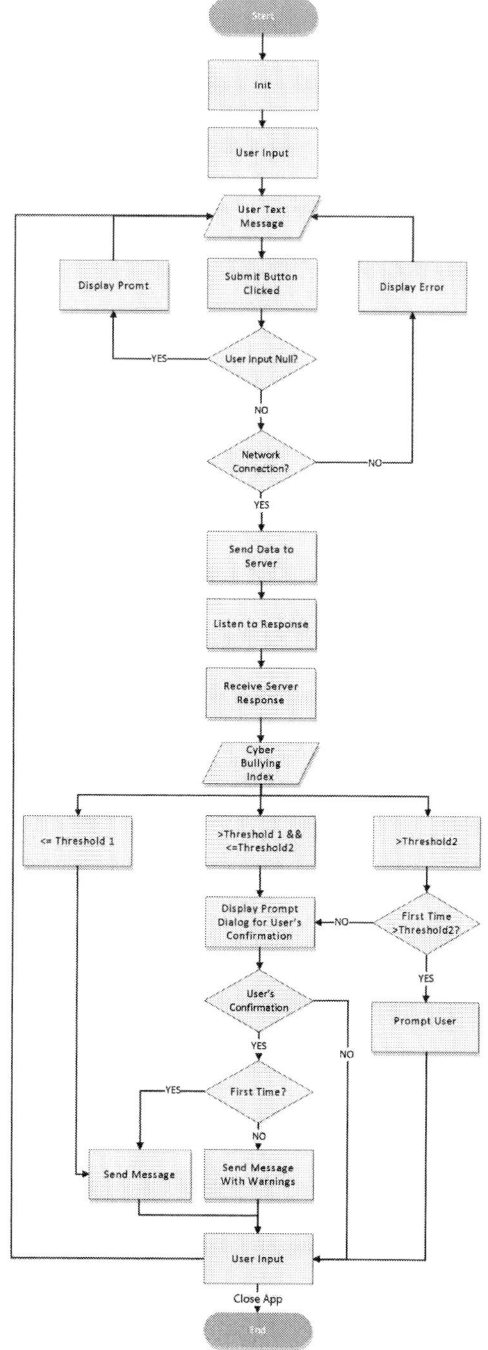

Figure 4: Flow Chart

Figure 6: The second time 'extremely high' index of the message

5 Conclusion and Future Work

This paper described the process of creating a cyberbullying intervention application based on a convolutional neural network learning model trained on a multi-platform dataset. The model is then used to compute a cyberbullying index for any new message.

For setting the two thresholds based on the feedbacks of the participants, different interventions could be taken for different levels of the cyberbullying index. Finally, as discussed, this project could be seen as the first step towards a framework of building an effective cyberbullying intervention application for online applications. Social media platforms could use the textual cyberbullying index and our proposed thresholds in order to make interventions to safeguard users from cyberbullying.

Several possible optimizations for future work are as follow:

- Word embeddings, such as GloVe[6] or Word2Vec[7] could be utilized to initialize our CNN models, which might lead to better results.

- As sending images and videos is becoming popular among adolescents (Singh et al., 2017), image/video processing would be another important area for cyberbullying detection.

- The user interface designed in this project takes the user's input directly. In the future, it can be designed as a background running application, which can collect user's input from different applications (while respecting privacy and security issues).

- A complete social network relationship graph (Huang et al., 2014) (for example, whether this conversation is between two good friends or not) could be taken into consideration for improving the cyberbullying identification.

---

[6]https://nlp.stanford.edu/projects/glove/
[7]https://code.google.com/archive/p/word2vec/

References

Linda Beckman, Curt Hagquist, and Lisa Hellström. 2012. Does the association with psychosomatic health problems differ between cyberbullying and traditional bullying? *Emotional and behavioural difficulties*, 17(3-4):421–434.

Karthik Dinakar, Birago Jones, Catherine Havasi, Henry Lieberman, and Rosalind Picard. 2012. Common sense reasoning for detection, prevention, and mitigation of cyberbullying. *ACM Transactions on Interactive Intelligent Systems (TiiS)*, 2(3):18.

Qianjia Huang, Vivek Kumar Singh, and Pradeep Kumar Atrey. 2014. Cyber bullying detection using social and textual analysis. In *Proceedings of the 3rd International Workshop on Socially-Aware Multimedia*, pages 3–6. ACM.

Robin M Kowalski and Susan P Limber. 2007. Electronic bullying among middle school students. *Journal of adolescent health*, 41(6):S22–S30.

Vivek K Singh, Marie L Radford, Qianjia Huang, and Susan Furrer. 2017. " they basically like destroyed the school one day": On newer app features and cyberbullying in schools. In *CSCW*, pages 1210–1216.

Andre Sourander, Anat Brunstein Klomek, Maria Ikonen, Jarna Lindroos, Terhi Luntamo, Merja Koskelainen, Terja Ristkari, and Hans Helenius. 2010. Psychosocial risk factors associated with cyberbullying among adolescents: A population-based study. *Archives of general psychiatry*, 67(7):720–728.

Robert S Tokunaga. 2010. Following you home from school: A critical review and synthesis of research on cyberbullying victimization. *Computers in human behavior*, 26(3):277–287.

LSTMs with Attention for Aggression Detection

Nishant Nikhil
IIT Kharagpur
Kharagpur India
nishantnikhil@iitkgp.ac.in

Ramit Pahwa
IIT Kharagpur
Kharagpur India
ramitpahwa123@iitkgp.ac.in

Mehul Kumar Nirala
IIT Kharagpur
Kharagpur India
mehulkumarnirala@iitkgp.ac.in

Rohan Khilnani
IIT Kharagpur
Kharagpur India
rkhilnani9@iitkgp.ac.in

Abstract

In this paper, we describe the system submitted for the shared task on Aggression Identification in Facebook posts and comments by the team Nishnik. Previous works demonstrate that LSTMs have achieved remarkable performance in natural language processing tasks. We deploy an LSTM model with an attention unit over it. Our system ranks 6th and 4th in the Hindi subtask for Facebook comments and subtask for generalized social media data respectively. And it ranks 17th and 10th in the corresponding English subtasks.

1 Introduction

In recent years, there has been a rapid growth in social media usage. Interactions over the web and social media have seen an exponential increase. While usage of social media helps users stay connected; incidents of aggression, trolling, cyberbullying, flaming, and hate speech are more prevalent now than ever.

Recent works on aggression classification include the use of logistic regression classifier (Davidson et al., 2017). They create a bunch of hand-crafted features like binary and count indicators for hashtags, lexicon based sentiment scores for each tweet, unigram, bigram, and trigram features. They use two logistic regression models, the first one to reduce dimensionality of the features and the second one to make classification. Kwok and Wang (2013) train a binary classifier to label tweets into 'racist' and 'non-racist'. They deploy Naive Bayes classifier on unigram features. Neural language model was used in Djuric et al. (2015). First they learn embedding of the text passages using paragraph2vec (Le and Mikolov, 2014). Then, they train a logistic regression classifier over those embeddings to classify into hateful and clean comments. Schmidt and Wiegand (2017) surveys the recent development in this field.

The first shared task on aggression identification (Kumar et al., 2018a) was held at the first workshop on Trolling, Aggression and Cyberbullying (TRAC). The goal was to classify social media posts into one of three labels (Overtly aggressive, Covertly aggressive, Non-aggressive).

The major contribution of the work can be summarized as a neural network based model which has LSTM units followed by an attention unit to embed the given social media post and training a classifier to detect aggression. We discuss our methods in section 2. Section 3 contains the details about the experiments and training data. In Section 4, we discuss the results and Section 5 concludes the paper with closing remarks.

2 Methodology

We hypothesize that aggression identification requires processing of the words of a sentence in a sequential manner. The positioning of a particular word at different places can alter the aggressiveness of the sentence. Example:

Proceedings of the First Workshop on Trolling, Aggression and Cyberbullying, pages 52–57
Santa Fe, USA, August 25, 2018.

These aliens are filthy, but they live in a good neighbourhood. (Aggressive)
These aliens are good, but they live in a filthy neighbourhood. (Less aggressive)

Recurrent Neural Networks (Mikolov et al., 2010) are good at handling sequential data and have achieved good results in natural language processing tasks. As RNNs share parameters across time, they are capable of conditioning the model on all previous words of a sentence. Although theoretically it is correct that RNNs can retain information from all previous words of a sentence, but practically they fail at handling long-term dependencies. Also, RNNs are prone to the vanishing and exploding gradient problems when dealing with long sequences. Long Short-Term Memory networks (Hochreiter and Schmidhuber, 1997), a special kind of RNN architecture, were designed to address these problems.

2.1 Long Short-Term Memory networks

LSTMs use special units in addition to standard RNN units. These units include a 'memory cell' which can maintain its state for long periods of time. A set of non-linear gates is used to control when information enters the memory(Input gate), when it's outputted (Output gate), and when it's forgotten (Forget gate). The equations for the LSTM memory blocks are given as follows:

$$f_t = \sigma_g(W_f x_t + U_f h_{t-1} + b_f) \tag{1}$$

$$i_t = \sigma_g(W_i x_t + U_i h_{t-1} + b_i) \tag{2}$$

$$o_t = \sigma_g(W_o x_t + U_o h_{t-1} + b_o) \tag{3}$$

$$c_t = f_t \circ c_{t-1} + i_t \circ \sigma_c(W_c x_t + U_c h_{t-1} + b_c) \tag{4}$$

$$h_t = o_t \circ \sigma_h(c_t) \tag{5}$$

In these equations, x_t is the input vector to the LSTM unit, f_t is the forget gate's activation vector, i_t is the input gate's activation vector, o_t is the output gate's activation vector, h_t is the output vector of the LSTM unit and c_t is the cell state vector. w, u, B are the parameters of weight matrices and bias vectors which are learned during the training.

2.2 Attention

Here, the attention module is inspired by (Bahdanau et al., 2014). We deploy it after the LSTM unit. It helps the model decide the importance of each word for the classification task. It scales the representation of the words by a learned weighing factor, as determined by these equations:

$$e_t = h_t w_a \tag{6}$$

$$a_t = \frac{exp(e_t)}{\sum_{i=1}^{T} exp(e_i)} \tag{7}$$

$$v = \sum_{i=1}^{T} a_i h_i \tag{8}$$

In these equations, h_t is the hidden representation of a word at a time step t, w_a is the weight matrix for the attention layer, a_t is the attention score for the word at time t, and v is the final representation of the sentence obtained by taking a weighted summation over all time steps.

3 Experiments

3.1 Datasets

The training datasets for the English and Hindi sub-tasks are constructed by 11,999 and 12,000 Facebook posts and comments, respectively. The testing set includes 3,001 and 3,000 respectively. These are collected and manually annotated by the organizers. Most of the datum has an id and is classified into one of the three classes: OAG (Overtly aggressive), CAG (Covertly aggressive), NAG (Non-aggressive).

The distribution of the classes in the training dataset for English and Hindi are shown in Table 1. The organizers released a modified version of the data where they remove the rows without specific id. As the id is not important for prediction, we decided to work on the initially released dataset. The data collection methods used to compile the dataset for the shared task are described in Kumar et al. (2018b).

Class	Train (English)	Test (English)	Train (Hindi)	Test (Hindi)
Non-aggressive	5,051	1,233	2,275	538
Covertly aggressive	4,240	1,057	4,869	1,246
Overtly aggressive	2,708	711	4,856	1,217

Table 1: Class distribution in train and test sets

3.2 Preprocessing

Before feeding the Facebook comments to the LSTM classifier, we performed the following operations on the text:

1. We used the ekphrasis toolkit (Baziotis et al., 2017) for normalizing the occurrence of the following in the comments: URL, E-mail, percent, money, phone, user, time, date, and number. For example, URLs are replaced by <url>, and all occurrences of @someone are replaced by <user>.

2. We then passed the normalized text through the Social tokenizer. Unlike normal tokenizers, the Social tokenizer is specifically aimed at the unstructured social media content. It understands and parses complex emoticons, emojis and other unstructured expressions like dates, times, phone numbers etc.

3. Then, we removed the punctuations and used ekphrasis's inbuilt spell corrector on the text.

4. Lastly, we used NLTK's WordNet lemmatizer (Loper and Bird, 2002) to lemmatize the words to their roots.

3.3 Parameters

Our model uses an embedding layer of 100 dimensions to project each word into a vector space. We place a dropout (Srivastava et al., 2014) layer after this. To capture the context of the words passed from the dropout layer we use an LSTM layer having 100 hidden dimensions. As the LSTM cells already have non-linear activation functions, it helps the model capture non-linear semantics from the data. The output from the LSTM is then passed through an attention module. The attention module helps the model determine which word to give more importance to. The weighted output from attention module is passed through a fully-connected layer. To get the probabilities of each class, softmax function is applied to the output. We use the cross-entropy function to calculate the loss between the predicted and the target value. Adam optimizer is used with a learning rate of 0.001 to learn the weights of the model. The dropout rate was either 0.2 or 0.3 and is discussed in the Results section.

Although many machine learning classifiers like Naive Bayes, Decision Tree, Support Vector Machine or Random Forest could be used as a baseline classifier for this task. Due to constraint of time we have only used a Random Forest classifier. We train the classifier on a set of hand-crafted features. The features used are as follows:

1. Number of words with positive sentiment.

2. Number of words with negative sentiment.

3. Number of punctuations.

4. Total number of words.

5. Inverse of the 2nd feature.

6. Natural logarithm of the 2nd feature.

We use the lists made available by Hu and Liu (2004) for extracting positive and negative words.

4 Results

Due to a mistake on our side, we first submitted a model which considered only the first 45 words of the post/comment and used a dropout rate of 0.2, we denote this model as Eng-A in the tables. In Eng-B, we use dropout rate of 0.3 and considered all the words. RF baseline is the random forest classifier based model baseline of hand-crafted features.

System	F1 (weighted)
Random Baseline	0.3535
EF-A	0.5533
EF-B	**0.5746**

Table 2: Results for the English (Facebook) task.

System	F1 (weighted)
Random Baseline	0.3477
RF Baseline	0.3888
Eng-A	0.5304
Eng-B	**0.5548**

Table 3: Results for the English (Social Media) task.

For both the Hindi sub-tasks, we used the LSTM classifier with dropout probability of 0.3. We denote the model as Hi-A in the tables.

System	F1 (weighted)
Random Baseline	0.3571
Hi-A	**0.6032**

Table 4: Results for the Hindi (Facebook) task.

System	F1 (weighted)
Random Baseline	0.3206
Hi-A	**0.4703**

Table 5: Results for the Hindi (Social Media) task.

Looking at the confusion matrices of the English subtasks, it is clear that the model is performing well at classifying the non-aggressive comments from the aggressive or covertly aggressive comments. But it performs poorly and classifies a lot of over-aggressive and non-aggressive comments to covertly aggressive. The results in Malmasi and Zampieri (2018) also convey the same message.

5 Conclusion

In this paper, we present an LSTM network with an attention based classifier for aggression detection. It gives competitive results while relying only on the dataset provided. The performance reported in this paper could be further boosted by utilizing transfer learning methods from larger datasets, like using pre-trained word embeddings. Furthermore, the model tends to over-fit on the training data. Better generalization techniques, like the use of an increased dropout rate, might help in increasing the performance of the model.

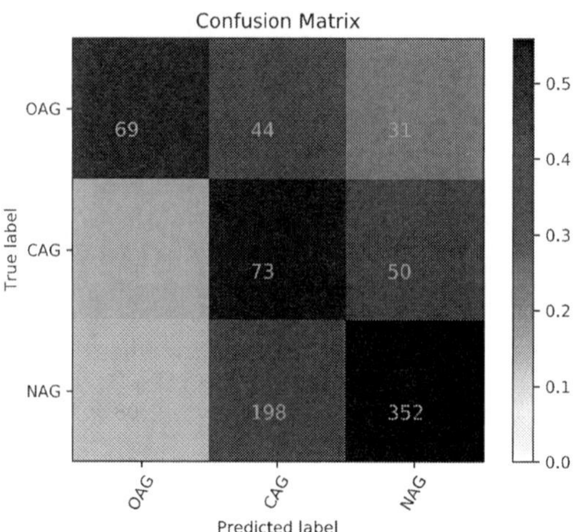

Figure 1: Confusion matrix for English (Facebook) task.

References

Dzmitry Bahdanau, Kyunghyun Cho, and Yoshua Bengio. 2014. Neural machine translation by jointly learning to align and translate. *CoRR*, abs/1409.0473.

Christos Baziotis, Nikos Pelekis, and Christos Doulkeridis. 2017. Datastories at semeval-2017 task 4: Deep lstm with attention for message-level and topic-based sentiment analysis. In *Proceedings of the 11th International Workshop on Semantic Evaluation (SemEval-2017)*, pages 747–754. Association for Computational Linguistics.

Thomas Davidson, Dana Warmsley, Michael Macy, and Ingmar Weber. 2017. Automated Hate Speech Detection and the Problem of Offensive Language. In *Proceedings of ICWSM*.

Nemanja Djuric, Jing Zhou, Robin Morris, Mihajlo Grbovic, Vladan Radosavljevic, and Narayan Bhamidipati. 2015. Hate speech detection with comment embeddings. In *Proceedings of the 24th International Conference on World Wide Web Companion*, pages 29–30. International World Wide Web Conferences Steering Committee.

Sepp Hochreiter and Jürgen Schmidhuber. 1997. Long short-term memory. *Neural Comput.*, 9(8):1735–1780, November.

Minqing Hu and Bing Liu. 2004. Mining and summarizing customer reviews. In *Proceedings of the Tenth ACM SIGKDD International Conference on Knowledge Discovery and Data Mining*, KDD '04, pages 168–177, New York, NY, USA. ACM.

Ritesh Kumar, Atul Kr. Ojha, Shervin Malmasi, and Marcos Zampieri. 2018a. Benchmarking Aggression Identification in Social Media. In *Proceedings of the First Workshop on Trolling, Aggression and Cyberbulling (TRAC)*, Santa Fe, USA.

Ritesh Kumar, Aishwarya N. Reganti, Akshit Bhatia, and Tushar Maheshwari. 2018b. Aggression-annotated Corpus of Hindi-English Code-mixed Data. In *Proceedings of the 11th Language Resources and Evaluation Conference (LREC)*, Miyazaki, Japan.

Irene Kwok and Yuzhou Wang. 2013. Locate the hate: Detecting Tweets Against Blacks. In *Twenty-Seventh AAAI Conference on Artificial Intelligence*.

Quoc Le and Tomas Mikolov. 2014. Distributed representations of sentences and documents. In *Proceedings of the 31st International Conference on International Conference on Machine Learning - Volume 32*, ICML'14, pages II–1188–II–1196. JMLR.org.

Edward Loper and Steven Bird. 2002. Nltk: The natural language toolkit. In *Proceedings of the ACL-02 Workshop on Effective Tools and Methodologies for Teaching Natural Language Processing and Computational Linguistics - Volume 1*, ETMTNLP '02, pages 63–70, Stroudsburg, PA, USA. Association for Computational Linguistics.

Shervin Malmasi and Marcos Zampieri. 2018. Challenges in Discriminating Profanity from Hate Speech. *Journal of Experimental & Theoretical Artificial Intelligence*, 30:1–16.

Tomáš Mikolov, Martin Karafiát, Lukáš Burget, Jan Černocký, and Sanjeev Khudanpur. 2010. Recurrent neural network based language model. In *Eleventh Annual Conference of the International Speech Communication Association*.

Anna Schmidt and Michael Wiegand. 2017. A Survey on Hate Speech Detection Using Natural Language Processing. In *Proceedings of the Fifth International Workshop on Natural Language Processing for Social Media. Association for Computational Linguistics*, pages 1–10, Valencia, Spain.

Nitish Srivastava, Geoffrey Hinton, Alex Krizhevsky, Ilya Sutskever, and Ruslan Salakhutdinov. 2014. Dropout: A simple way to prevent neural networks from overfitting. *J. Mach. Learn. Res.*, 15(1):1929–1958, January.

TRAC-1 Shared Task on Aggression Identification:
IIT(ISM)@COLING'18

Ritesh Kumar
Department of CSE
IIT(ISM) Dhanbad
India, 826004
ritesh4rmrvs@gmail.com

Guggilla Bhanodai
Department of CSE
IIT(ISM) Dhanbad
India, 826004
bhanodaig@gmail.com

Rajendra Pamula
Department of CSE
IIT(ISM) Dhanbad
India, 826004
rajendra@iitism.ac.in

M. R. Chennuru
Department of CSE
IIT(ISM) Dhanbad
India, 826004
cmr.mahesh@gmail.com

Abstract

This paper describes the work that our team **bhanodaig** did at Indian Institute of Technology (ISM) towards TRAC-1 Shared Task on Aggression Identification in Social Media for COLING 2018. In this paper we label aggression identification into three categories: Overtly Aggressive, Covertly Aggressive and Non-aggressive. We train a model to differentiate between these categories and then analyze the results in order to better understand how we can distinguish between them. We participated in two different tasks named as *English (Facebook) task* and *English (Social Media) task*. For *English (Facebook) task* **System 05** was our best run (i.e. 0.3572) above the random Baseline (i.e. 0.3535). For *English (Social Media) task* our **system 02** got the value (i.e. 0.1960) below the Random Bseline (i.e. 0.3477). For all of our runs we used Long Short-Term Memory model. Overall, our performance is not satisfactory. However, as new entrant to the field, our scores are encouraging enough to work for better results in future.

1 Introduction

In the last few years, there is exponential growth in social media and user generated contents. The online platforms like blogs, Q&A forums, online discussion forum and so on helps user to post their comments and to reply other user's comment. These comments may be of various forms like lovable, aggressive, hate speech, offensive languages etc. As the number of people and this interaction over the web has increased, incidents of aggression and related activities like trolling, cyberbullying, flaming, hate speech, etc. have also increased manifold across the globe. Thus, incidents of online aggressive behaviour have become a major source of social conflict, with a potential of forming criminal activity.

A key challenge for aggression identification on social media is to classify it from offensive or vitriolic languages. Some of the task has been performed in this area but still it is a hot topic among researchers. Keeping it in mind, we develop a system to discriminate between Overtly Aggressive (OAG), Covertly Aggressive (CAG), and Non-aggressive (NAG) content in texts. In the paper (Kumar et al., 2018a) the relevant task description is defined in detail.

In this paper, we used the fact that emojis serve as a proxy for the emotional contents of a text. Therefore, pre-training on the classification task of predicting which emoji were initially part of a text can improve performance on the target task. We used word embeddings that were trained on the classification task. Then we used simple transfer learning approach, *chain-thaw* that sequentially unfreezes and fine-tunes a single layer at a time. This approach increases accuracy on the target task at the expense of extra computational power needed for the fine-tuning. By training each layer separately the model is able to adjust the individual patterns across the network with a reduced risk of overfitting.

Organization of rest of the paper is as follows. We describe Related Work in Section 2. Section 3 describes Methodology and Dataset and Section 4 analyse our Results. Finally, we conclude in Section 5 with directions for future work.

Proceedings of the First Workshop on Trolling, Aggression and Cyberbullying, pages 58–65
Santa Fe, USA, August 25, 2018.

2   Related Work

The interest in identifying trolling, aggression, cyber-bullying and hate speech, particularly on social media, has been growing in recent years. This topic has attracted attention from researchers interested in linguistic and sociological features of aggression, and from engineers interested in developing tools to deal with aggression on social media platforms. In this section we review a number of studies and briefly discuss their findings. For a recent and more comprehensive survey on hate speech detection we recommend (Schmidt and Wiegand, 2017).

Prior work has used theories of emotion such as Ekmans six basic emotions and Plutchiks eight basic emotions(Suttles and Ide, 2013) and (Mohammad, 2012). The heterogeneous NLP tasks are bounded by dearth of manually annotated data. Therefore, emotional expression plays significant role to gauge the mood of users. (Deriu et al., 2016) and (Tang et al., 2014) tried to see the effect of positive/negative emoticons for training their models. Similarly, (Mohammad, 2012) mapped hashtags such as #anger, #joy, #happytweet, #ugh, #yuck and #fml into emotional categories for emotion analysis.

(Davidson et al., 2017) used crowd-sourced hate speech lexicon to collect tweets containing hate speech keywords. They used crowd-sourcing to label a sample of these tweets into three categories: those containing hate speech, only offensive language, and those with neither. They found that Tweets without explicit hate keywords were also more difficult to classify.

(Xu et al., 2012) proposed sentiment analysis to detect bullying roles in tweets. For this they used Latent Dirichlet Allocation to find out relevant topics in bullying texts.They classified the texts either they are bullying or not.

(Dadvar et al., 2013) presented the results of a study on the detection of cyberbullying in YouTube comments. They used a combination of content-based, cyberbullying-specific and user-based features. their results showed that incorporation of context in the form of users activity histories improves cyber-bullying detection accuracy.

(Kwok and Wang, 2013) detected tweets against blacks. They used unigram model and supervised learning for their approach. (Djuric et al., 2015) used binary classification to detect hate speech. For this they used word embeddings that performed better than bag-of-words model.

(Burnap and Williams, 2015) studied cyber hate speech in twitter. They showed that the production of a machine classifier that can be developed into a technical solution for use by policymakers as part of an existing evidence-based decision-making process.

(Nobata et al., 2016) studied the abusive language detection in online user content. They used different syntactic features as well as different embedding features. They found that combining these features with the features of NLP can boost F-score.

(Waseem and Hovy, 2016) presented a list of criteria based in critical race theory to identify racist and sexist slurs. They used n-grams model for their approach. The dataset footnote[1] used for this criteria is freely available for users.

presenting the Hate Speech Detection dataset used in (Malmasi and Zampieri, 2017) and a few other recent papers on the topic. A proposal of typology of abusive language sub-tasks is presented in (Waseem et al., 2017). A recent discussion on the challenges of identifying profanity vs. hate speech can be found in (Malmasi and Zampieri, 2018).

Most of the study,including ours, to discriminate between hate speech and abusive language are in english due to its well annotation. However, few recent studies have also been published in some other languages. Examples are (Mubarak et al., 2017) studied abusive language detection on Arabic Language. (Su et al., 2017) rephrased profanity in Chinese language. (Tulkens et al., 2016) studied racism detection in Dutch social media.

The results demonstrated that it can be hard to distinguish between overt and covert aggression in social media.This is a key motivating factor for this shared task and a highly relevant discussion to include.

---

[1] https://github.com/zeerakw/hatespeech

Table 1: Results for the English (Facebook) task.

System	F1 (weighted)
Random Baseline	0.3535
LSTM-01	0.3160
LSTM-04	0.3160
LSTM-05	**0.3572**

3 Data

The data collection methods used to compile the dataset used in the shared task is described in (Kumar et al., 2018b). The *Aggression Identification* dataset is composed of 15,000 aggression-annotated Facebook Posts and Comments each in Hindi (in both Roman and Devanagari script) and English for training and validation. The users were asked to develop a system that could make three-way classification in between Overtly Aggressive, Covertly Aggressive and Non-aggressive text data.

4 Methodology

4.1 Preprocessing

We preprocessed the texts firstly. Punctuation symbols, unicode, urls and emoji were removed from data. All the tokens were also lowercased. For generalization proper tokenization is important. We tokenized all tweets on the basis of word-by-word. Words that contain two or more repeated characters were shortened to the same token (e.g. *fool* and *fooool* were tokenized such a way that could be treated as same). After the tokenization, we included these in training set i.e. in the FB/Tweet that contains 1 token (not a punctuation symbol), special token [2].

For all of our runs we used Long-Short-Term-Memory (LSTM) model that performed successfully in many NLP tasks (Sutskever et al., 2014) and (Hochreiter and Schmidhuber, 1997). Moreover, for the word representation we have used deepmoji and *chain-thaw* method similar manner as in (Felbo et al., 2017) to sequentially unfreezes and fine-tunes a single layer at a time. Please see Figure1 for illustration.

4.2 Model

Our model uses an embedding layer of 256 dimensions to project each word into a vector space. We used pretrained embeddings from deepmoji. To capture context of each word we use a bidirectional LSTM layer with 50 hidden units each layer. Then to capture higher level features we used one-dimensional global max pooling. Then in next layer we use 50 hidden units with ReLU as an activation function. In the next layer to avoid over-fitting we set dropout to 0.1. Finally, we used softmax layer with 3 units, each corresponding to one of three given classes. We used categorical cross-entropy as loss function and Adam optimization algorithm for optimization. Please refer Figure2 for illustration.

Our model is implemented using Theano (Team et al., 2016). We also implemented easy-to-use version available in Keras (Chollet, 2016).

Table 2: Results for the English (Social Media) task.

System	F1 (weighted)
Random Baseline	0.3477
LSTM-02	0.1960

5 Results

The scores obtained by us are shown in Table 1 and Table2. The official evaluation measures is *F1* measure. We used random baseline for sake of comparison. Table 1 contains results for English (facebook) task. For English (Facebook) task we submitted three runs. In this paper, we have just named

---

[2] https://github.com/bfelbo/DeepMoji

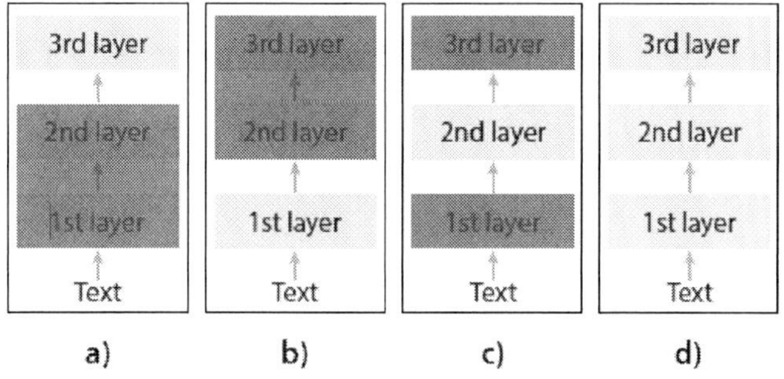

Figure 1: Illustration of the chain-thaw transfer learning approach, where each layer is fine-tuned separately. Layers covered with a blue rectangle are frozen. Step a) tunes any new layers, b) then tunes the 1st layer and c) the next layer until all layers have been fine-tuned individually. Lastly, in step d) all layers are fine-tuned together.

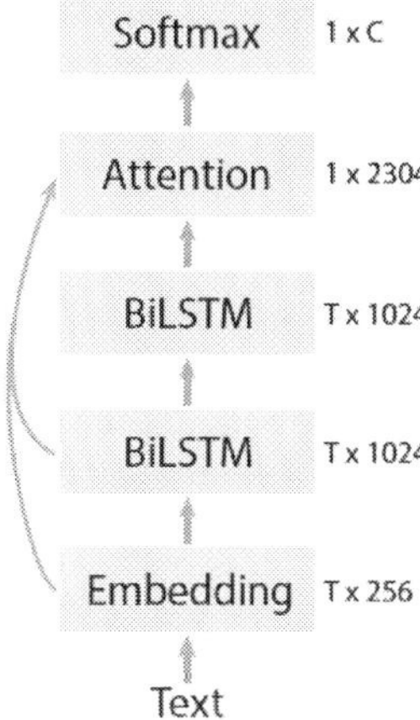

Figure 2: Illustration of the DeepMoji model with T being text length and C the number of classes.

our run as LSTM-01, LSTM-02, LSTM-03, LSTM-04 and LSTM-05. Here, **LSTM-05** performs better than LSTM-01 and LSTM-04. We just obtained slightly better score (i.e 0.3572) comparative to random baseline (i.e. 0.3535). Table2 contains the results for English (Social Media) task. Here, we get the score (i.e. 0.1960) for LSTM-02 that is much lower than random baseline.

The confusion matrix for EN-FB task and EN-TW task is shown in Figure3 and Figure4 respectively. In Figure3 we see that maximum number of 'NAG' comment is correctly predicted. 'CAG' comment is predicted after 'NAG'. The lowest prediction is of 'OAG' Comment. 'OAG' class is little bit confused with 'CAG' class.

Similarly, in Figure4 we see that 71 number of 'NAG' comment is correctly predicted. There is large difference between the class 'OAG' and 'CAG'.

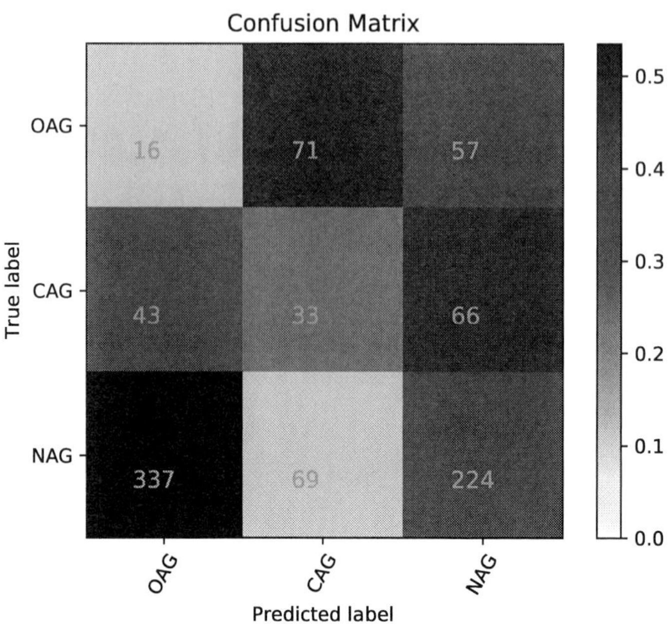

Figure 3: Confusion Matrix for EN-FB task for our 3-classes,

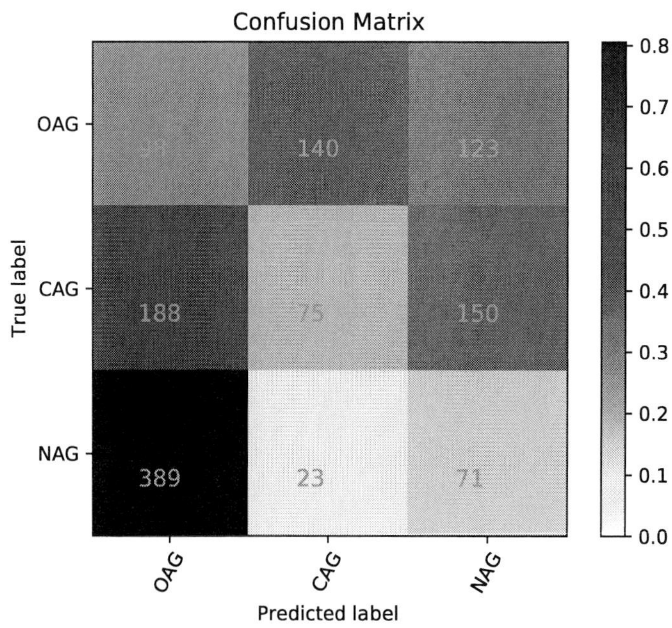

Figure 4: Confusion Matrix for EN-TW task for our 3-classes

6 Conclusion

This year we participated in TRAC-1 Shared Task on Aggression Identification in Social Media. We tried to develop 3-way classification in between 'OAG', 'CAG' and 'NAG'. Our system performs better on English (Facebook) task in comparison with English (Social Media) task. We have experimented using Deepmoji word embeddings which couldn't capture sub categories of aggression like 'OAG' or 'CAG'. While there can be no denial of the fact that our overall performance is dismal, initial results are suggestive as to what should be done next. We need to consult another model like SVM model, Ensemble model etc. for classification. Also, it will be interesting to use char CNN to extract character level features and then to use Random forest as a classifier. We shall explore some of these models in the coming days.

References

Pete Burnap and Matthew L Williams. 2015. Cyber hate speech on twitter: An ap-plication of machine classification and statistical modeling for policy and decision making. Policy & Internet, 7(2):223–242.

Franc¸ois Chollet. 2016. Xception: Deep learning with depthwise separable convolutions. arXiv preprint.

Maral Dadvar, Dolf Trieschnigg, Roeland Ordelman, and Franciska de Jong. 2013. Improving cyberbullying detection with user context. In Advances in Information Retrieval, pages 693–696. Springer.

Thomas Davidson, Dana Warmsley, Michael Macy, and Ingmar Weber. 2017. Automated Hate Speech Detection and the Problem of Offensive Language. In Proceedings of ICWSM.

Jan Deriu, Maurice Gonzenbach, Fatih Uzdilli, Aurelien Lucchi, Valeria De Luca, and Martin Jaggi. 2016. Swisscheese at semeval-2016 task 4: Sentiment classification using an ensemble of convolutional neural networks with distant supervision. In Proceedings of the 10th International Workshop on Semantic Evaluation, number EPFL-CONF-229234, pages 1124–1128.

Nemanja Djuric, Jing Zhou, Robin Morris, Mihajlo Grbovic, Vladan Radosavljevic, and Narayan Bhamidipati. 2015. Hate speech detection with comment embeddings. In Proceedings of the 24th International Conference on World Wide Web Companion, pages 29–30. International World Wide Web Con-ferences Steering Committee.

Bjarke Felbo, Alan Mislove, Anders Søgaard, Iyad Rahwan, and Sune Lehmann. 2017. Using millions of emoji occurrences to learn any-domain representations for detecting sentiment, emotion and sarcasm. arXiv preprint arXiv:1708.00524.

Sepp Hochreiter and Jurgen¨ Schmidhuber. 1997. Long short-term memory. Neural computation, 9(8):1735–1780.

Ritesh Kumar, Atul Kr. Ojha, Shervin Malmasi, and Marcos Zampieri. 2018a. Benchmarking Aggression Identification in Social Media. In Proceedings of the First Workshop on Trolling, Aggression and Cyberbulling (TRAC), Santa Fe, USA.

Ritesh Kumar, Aishwarya N. Reganti, Akshit Bhatia, and Tushar Maheshwari. 2018b. Aggression-annotated Corpus of Hindi-English Code-mixed Data. In Proceedings of the 11th Language Re-sources and Evaluation Conference (LREC), Miyazaki, Japan.

Irene Kwok and Yuzhou Wang. 2013. Locate the hate: Detecting Tweets Against Blacks. In Twenty-Seventh AAAI Conference on Artificial Intelligence.

Shervin Malmasi and Marcos Zampieri. 2017. Detecting Hate Speech in Social Media. In Proceedings of the International Conference Recent Advances in Natural Language Processing (RANLP), pages 467–472.

Shervin Malmasi and Marcos Zampieri. 2018. Challenges in Discriminating Profan-ity from Hate Speech. Journal of Experimental & Theoretical Artificial Intelligence, 30:1–16.

Saif M Mohammad. 2012. # emotional tweets. In Proceedings of the First Joint Conference on Lexical and Computational Semantics-Volume 1: Proceedings of the main conference and the shared task, and Volume 2: Proceedings of the Sixth International Workshop on Semantic Evaluation, pages 246–255. Associa-tion for Computational Linguistics.

Hamdy Mubarak, Kareem Darwish, and Walid Magdy. 2017. Abusive language detection on arabic social media. In Proceedings of the First Workshop on Abusive Language Online, pages 52–56.

Chikashi Nobata, Joel Tetreault, Achint Thomas, Yashar Mehdad, and Yi Chang. 2016. Abu-sive Language Detection in Online User Content. In Proceedings of the 25th International Conference on World Wide Web, pages 145–153. International World Wide Web Conferences Steering Committee.

Anna Schmidt and Michael Wiegand. 2017. A Survey on Hate Speech Detection Using Natural Language Processing. In Proceedings of the Fifth International Workshop on Natural Language Processing for Social Media. Association for Computational Linguistics, pages 1–10, Valencia, Spain.

Hui-Po Su, Zhen-Jie Huang, Hao-Tsung Chang, and Chuan-Jie Lin. 2017. Rephrasing profanity in chinese text. In Proceedings of the First Workshop on Abusive Language Online, pages 18–24.

Ilya Sutskever, Oriol Vinyals, and Quoc V Le. 2014. Sequence to sequence learning with neural networks. In Advances in neural information processing systems, pages 3104–3112.

Jared Suttles and Nancy Ide. 2013. Distant supervision for emotion classification with dis-crete binary values. In International Conference on Intelligent Text Processing and Computational Linguistics, pages 121–136. Springer.

Duyu Tang, Furu Wei, Nan Yang, Ming Zhou, Ting Liu, and Bing Qin. 2014. Learning sentiment-specific word embedding for twitter sentiment classification. In Proceedings of the 52nd Annual Meeting of the Association for Computational Linguistics (Volume 1: Long Papers), volume 1, pages 1555–1565.

The Theano Development Team, Rami Al-Rfou, Guillaume Alain, Amjad Almahairi, Christof Angermueller, Dzmitry Bahdanau, Nicolas Ballas, Fred´eric´ Bastien, Justin Bayer, Anatoly Belikov, et al. 2016. Theano: A python framework for fast computation of mathematical expressions. arXiv preprint arXiv:1605.02688.

Stephan´ Tulkens, Lisa Hilte, Elise Lodewyckx, Ben Verhoeven, and Walter Daelemans. 2016. A Dictionary-based Approach to Racism Detection in Dutch Social Media. In Proceedings of the Workshop Text Analytics for Cybersecurity and Online Safety (TA-COS), Portoroz, Slovenia.

Zeerak Waseem and Dirk Hovy. 2016. Hateful symbols or hateful people? predictive features for hate speech detection on twitter. In Proceedings of the NAACL student research workshop, pages 88–93.

Zeerak Waseem, Thomas Davidson, Dana Warmsley, and Ingmar Weber. 2017. Understand-ing Abuse: A Typology of Abusive Language Detection Subtasks. In Proceedings of the First Workshop on Abusive Langauge Online.

Jun-Ming Xu, Kwang-Sung Jun, Xiaojin Zhu, and Amy Bellmore. 2012. Learning from bullying traces in social media. In Proceedings of the 2012 conference of the North American chapter of the association for computational linguistics: Human language technologies, pages 656–666. Association for Computational Linguistics.

An Ensemble approach for Aggression Identification in English and Hindi Text

Arjun Roy, Prashant Kapil, Kingshuk Basak, Asif Ekbal
Department of Computer Science
and Engineering
Indian Institute of Technology Patna, India
`(arjun.mtmc17, prashant.pcs17, kingshuk.mtcs16, asif) @iitp.ac.in`

Abstract

In this paper we describe our system that we develop as part of our participation in the shared task at COLING 2018 **TRAC-1: Aggression Identification**. The objective of this task was to predict online aggression spread through online textual post or comment. The datasets were released in two languages, one for English and the other for Hindi. For each of these languages we submitted one system. Both of our systems are based on an ensemble architecture where the individual models are based on Convoluted Neural Network (CNN) and Support Vector Machine (SVM). Our system on English facebook and social media post obtains the F1 scores of 0.5151 and 0.5099, respectively where evaluation on Hindi facebook and social media obtains F1 score of 0.5599 and 0.3790, respectively.

1 Introduction

In our modern world Internet has become a very powerful tool to convey and spread our feelings, voices and intentions to a large section of people in a very short span of time. There has been a phenomenal growth in web contents due to the emergence of numerous social media networking platforms, blogs, review sites etc. There is also a growing rate of misusing these social media and other sources against individuals, groups, organization etc. by targeting them directly or indirectly. There has not been much literature that focus on machine learning applications towards building intelligent systems that could detect aggression, cyberbullying, hate speech, profanity etc. which often have overlapping characteristics. The task is more difficult when the contents are mixed with more than one language, the phenomenon which is very well-known as code mixing.

The task defined in the shared task was related to detecting aggression in two languages, namely Hindi and English. (Baron and Richardson, 1994) defined aggression as a behavior that is intended to harm another individual who does not wish to be harmed.(Buss, 1961) distinguished between physical aggression (e.g. hitting,kicking etc.), verbal aggression (e.g. yelling, screaming etc.) and relational aggression. The datasets provided in the shared task were labeled with three classes, namely "Overtly","Covertly" and "Non- aggressive".

2 Related Works

Aggression, Trolling, Cyberbullying, etc. are the problems that have attracted attention to the various stakeholders (common people, governments, researchers) as these are some of the severe issues that need urgent attention due to the abundance of information generated daily from the various social media sources. Although not much of drafted works can be found on developing an automated system to address these problems, a few works are available on the problem domains that are very closely related, such as the detection of offensive languages and hate speech. (Potapova and Gordeev, 2016) studied verbal expression of aggression and they found

Proceedings of the First Workshop on Trolling, Aggression and Cyberbullying, pages 66–73
Santa Fe, USA, August 25, 2018.

that detection of such contents using machine learning techniques such as Random Forest (RF) and Convolutional Neural Network (CNN) combined with Part-of-Speech (PoS) information can produce good results. (Chu et al., 2017)showed that character embedding performed better than word embedding for CNN in classifying the contents into two classes: personal attack and not-personal attack. (Chen et al., 2012) proposed the Lexical Syntactic Feature (LSF) architecture to detect offensive content and identify the potential offensive users in social media. (Gao and Huang, 2017) proposed two types of hate speech detection models that incorporate context information, a logistic regression model with context features and a neural network model with learning components for context. Their evaluation showed that both the models outperform a strong baseline by around 3% to 4% in F1 score and combining these two models further improved the performance by another 7% in F1 score. (Nobata et al., 2016) divided their feature set into 4 classes as N-grams, linguistic, syntactic and distributional semantics to distinguish between clean and abusive post. The abusive posts were further fine-grained into hate, derogatory and profanity. Their character n-grams based approach also outperformed some word-based deep learning models. (Davidson et al., 2017) discussed the problems in distinguishing the hate speech from the offensive instances. They observed that lexical methods are inaccurate at identifying hate speech and emphasized to take care of social biases into context.

Although there are works available for English in these related domains, we did not find any such work on Hindi. However, there is a considerable increase in the volume of Indian language social media contents, especially in Hindi. Hence detecting trolling, cyberbullying in such languages have a very high relevance in today's scenarios. In this paper we develop an ensemble based architecture for aggression identification which tries to solve the problem in two languages, *viz.* English and Hindi.

3 Problem Definition

The problem of the shared task was on Aggression Identification. The goal is to classify the text into three classes, namely overtly, covertly and non-aggressive.
We first define aggression, and then put forward the different classes of aggression mentioned in the task with examples.

1. **Aggression:** It is a human behavior intended to harm another by verbally, physically and psychologically. **Overtly Aggressive (OAG):** This class includes the following cases.

   (a) Aggression shown openly with verbal attack directly pointed towards any group or individuals.
   (b) Attack commenced using abusive words or calling names or comparing in a derogatory manner.
   (c) By supporting false attack or supporting others comment.
   (d) Sometimes these texts also contain indirect references.

2. **Covertly Aggressive (CAG):** In these attacks aggression is generally hidden and contains sarcastic negative emotions due to its indirect nature. It can be summarized as follows.

   (a) By using metaphorical words to attack an individual,nation,religion.
   (b) Praising someone by criticizing group irrespective of being right or wrong.
   (c) Sometimes these texts also contain direct references.

3. **Non Aggressive (NAG):** These statements generally lack the intention to be aggressive and mostly used while referring to the correct facts, wishing or supporting individuals or groups on social issues.

Table 1 shows a few examples of each class.

Class	Sentence
Overtly Aggressive	1.We want to get rid of u Indians......why don't u hear our loud cries
	2.I support his speech, RSS is divider of country, they do not want to stay peace.
	3.The U S Government of Donald Trump will do nothing
	4."गटर के कीड़े" ।
	5.एस कुत्ते को जेल मे दाल दो .देश द्रोही हैं ।
Covertly Aggressive	1.Modi ji, all the Pain & no Real Gain
	2.udhav has shown bjp its place,bravo shivsena
	3.Reservation is like another form of terrorism
	4.दंगाई के कुसी में बैठ जाने से चरित्र नही सुधरता ।
	5.दोनों दलाल है और इन दोनों का दलाल मिडिया है ।
Non-Aggressive	1.Sorry sir I forgot.
	2.When is work on NH-8 getting completed? Particluarly Hero Honda Chowk??
	3.I want to upgrade from my 180 CC to 400CC
	4.विदिशा से बीजेपी की सुषमा स्वराज आगे ।
	5.जन्म दिन की हार्दिक बधाई महाशया ।

Table 1: **Some examples from English and Hindi data**

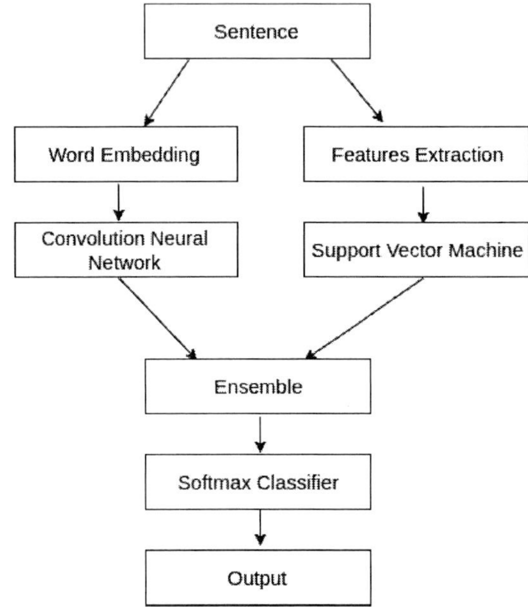

Figure 1: Block Diagram of our System

4   System Overview

We adopt an Ensemble architecture to solve the problem of offensive language detection. The base models are based on CNN and SVM. A block diagram of the system is shown in Figure 1.

4.1   Preprocessing

As the dataset was collected from social media platforms, it contains URLs, emoticons, hashtag, smiley, etc. It also includes a lot of inconsistencies in the form of typos and abbreviations. So the first step that we perform is the removal of URLs for the convenience of preprocessing. The only '#' hash signs are removed from #soldmedia, #Bhagwa,#शव etc. to preserve the meaning. After that for further preprocessing we remove punctuations and apostrophe words. These steps are performed for both Hindi and English datasets. Detailed examples are given in Table 2. The Hindi dataset further posed an additional challenge. The data has sentences mixed with actual

Hindi words, transliterated Hindi words and actual English words- commonly known as code-mixed social media text. To handle this, we convert the transliterated Hindi words and actual English words into actual Hindi words using Indic-Trans api.

1	Before	#shameonjournalism #soldmedia
	After	Shame on journalism sold media
2	Before	Which one is the best example of #Bhagwa terrorism.
	After	Which one is the best example of bhagwa terrorism
3	Before	goons and #presstitutes
	After	goons and presstitutes
4	Before	दोनों शहीदों के #शव के साथ बर्बरता
	After	दोनों शहीदों के शव के साथ बर्बरता

Table 2: **Preprocessing example**

4.2 Word Embedding

In order to fit textual data into Neural Network we need vectorization of texts. This provides useful evidence in capturing semantic property of a word. For Hindi we use the pre-trained model of Wikipedia (Bojanowski et al., 2016). Each word is represented as a vector of 300 dimension. For English, we use the pre-trained Glove(Pennington et al., 2014) vectors. After preprocessing the data, the English dataset has an average sentence length of 20 words with maximum sentence length of 50 words, while the Hindi dataset has an average sentence length of 21 words with maximum sentence length of 50 words [1]. We consider maximum length of a sentence to be 50-words. We use padding with zeros if the sentence length is less than 50, and prune from the last if length of the sentence is greater than 50.

4.3 Features

To train any statistical machine learning model we need a set of features to be extracted from the dataset. The features that we use to train the SVM model are:

- **Uni-grams:** An n-gram of size 1 is referred to as a "unigram". Unigrams helps us to identify which words in the corpus are important to which particular class. Top 1000 unigrams in the corpus are taken as one of the features for training our system.

- **Tf-Idf vectors:** We compute the Term Frequency-Inverse Document Frequency (TF-IDF) and use as feature. Term Frequency refers to how many times a particular word appears in a particular class, whereas Inverse document frequency refers to how much relevant the word is to any particular class, whether the word is common or rare across all.

4.4 Methodology

In this section we describe our proposed methodologies, which are based on SVM and CNN.

- **Support Vector Machines:** Support Vector Machine (SVM) is a popular algorithm used for solving many classification problems.(Vapnik, 2013)demonstrates that abstract learning theory established conditions for generalization and understanding these conditions inspired new algorithm approach to function estimation problems. He explained the generalization ability of learning machine depends on capacity concepts. In our model we use Support Vector Machine as one of the individual model used to form the ensemble system. In particular we use an SVM trained using John Platt's sequential minimal optimization algorithm[2] to solve the quadratic programming problem.

---

[1] while calculating max and avg sentence for both the English and Hindi dataset we consider all the sentences of training and development dataset

[2] http://weka.sourceforge.net/doc.dev/weka/classifiers/functions/SMO.html

- **Convolutional Neural Network:** In the recent times it has been seen that the convolution and pooling functions of CNN can be successfully used in text classification problems. A convolution layer of $n \times m$ kernel size is used (where m-size of word embedding) to look at n-grams of word at a time and then a Max-pooling layer selects the largest from the convoluted inputs. In our system the convolutional layer is constructed with filter size 64 and ReLU as activation function. We capture the bi-gram features from this layer by taking kernel size as $2 \times EmbeddingSize$. In Max-pooling layer we have used pool size of 1×2.

- **Ensemble:** Classifier ensemble[3] aims at combining the predictions of different classifiers. Ensembles (Florian et al., 2003; Ekbal and Bandyopadhyay, 2008) are often seen to be much more accurate than the individual classifiers that make them up. In the system being discussed output of the max-pooling layer of CNN classifier goes to a flatten layer and then to a dense layer with ReLU activation. On the other hand output of SVM is passed through a dense layer with ReLU activation. Output tensor form both CNN and SVM are then concatenated and passed through a dense layer and a Dropout layer with hyper-parameter of 0.5. This is finally inputted to the output layer with *Softmax* as an activation function. We use *Adam* as an optimizer and *Categorical Cross Entropy* for loss function.

5 Data set

The **Hindi** (Roman and Devanagari) training dataset consists of 15000 annotated (6072 as OAG, 6115 as CAG and 2812 as NAG) instances, while the **English** training dataset consists of 12000 annotated (2708 as OAG, 4240 as CAG and 5052 as NAG) instances of Facebook posts and comments. For tuning the system, validation set of 3000 instances of annotated (1216 as OAG, 1246 as CAG and 538 as NAG) Hindi data and 3000 instances of annotated (711 as OAG, 1056 as CAG and 1233 as NAG) English data were provided. The test data has two different sets which were prepared from two different sources-one from facebook (English: 1515, Hindi: 970) and the another one from other social media (English: 1257, Hindi: 1194) posts and comments which helped in determining generic performance ability of our system. Some details are depicted in Table 4 for Hindi, and in Table 3 for English.

Class	Train	Dev	Test FB	Test SM
CAG	4240	1056		
NAG	5052	1233	1515	1257
OAG	2708	711		

Table 3: **English data description**

Class	Train	Dev	Test FB	Test SM
CAG	4869	1246		
NAG	2275	538	970	1194
OAG	4856	1216		

Table 4: **Hindi data description**

6 Experiments and Results

We perform all the experiments in Python 3 and Java Jdk8 environment. We use the following packages: Keras, NLTK, Numpy and Weka.

---

[3]"ensemble classifier", "classifier ensemble" and "ensemble system" are used interchangeably referring to the same system.

We use F1-score as the evaluation metric, and use development data to fine-tune the system. We first conduct our experiments with a DT (Decision Tree) model using unigrams as features. The DT model performed on the development data with a weighted F1-score of 0.4593 on Hindi data and 0.470 for English. Thereafter we conduct our experiments using a SVM model with unigrams as features. We obtain the F1-score of 0.4986 and 0.5030 for Hindi and English, respectively. We then performed experiments on the same SVM model using bigrams as features. To our surprise, the performance of the model deteriorated to a weighted F1-score of 0.3858 on Hindi data and 0.404 on English data, and predicted almost two third of the instances as NAG for both the datasets. We then used unigrams and tf-idf vectors as features and conducted our experiments on the SVM model. Performance of the model increased to the weighted F1-score of 0.5457 for Hindi and 0.556 for English. To achieve better performance, we then looked into some deep learning strategies. First, we performed our experiments using an LSTM model. The weighted F1-score given by the model is 0.4061 on Hindi data and 0.4142 on English data. Thereafter we used a CNN model that captures unigram features. The weighted F1-score of the model is 0.5422 on Hindi data and 0.5431 on English data. Then on increasing the kernel size to capture bigram features, the CNN model yields the weighted F1-score of 0.5663 for Hindi and 0.578 for English. The weighted F1-score of the final ensemble system, using CNN with kernel size $2 \times EmbeddingSize$ and SVM with unigrams and tf-idf features, on Hindi development data is **0.5987** while that on English development data is **0.6273**. Evaluation on the test data shows the F1-score of **0.5151** on English facebook data and F1-score of **0.5599** on Hindi facebook data. We obtain the F1-score of **0.5099** on English social media data and F1-score of **0.3790** on Hindi social media data. These results are depicted in details in Table 5 for English Facebook data and other social media data. Similarly, in Table 6 we report for Hindi Facebook data and the Hindi other social media data.

Class	English-FB			English-SM		
	Precision	Recall	F1-Score	Precision	Recall	F1-Score
CAG	0.2178	0.6197		0.3900	0.4165	
NAG	0.8612	0.4333	0.5151	0.5906	0.7764	0.5099
OAG	0.3795	0.5139		0.6243	0.3130	

Table 5: Result: English test data

Class	Hindi-FB			Hindi-SM		
	Precision	Recall	F1-Score	Precision	Recall	F1-Score
CAG	0.5180	0.7676		0.3415	0.4777	
NAG	0.6280	0.5282	0.5599	0.4393	0.5113	0.3790
OAG	0.4137	0.3729		0.6243	0.2244	

Table 6: Result: Hindi test data

6.1 Error analysis

For analysis we study confusion matrix for each of the test sets. It is observed that for the Hindi-FB test data depicted in Table 9, data originally labeled as OAG gets mostly confused with the class CAG, where as data originally labeled as CAG gets mostly confused with the class NAG. This pattern is also seen in case of test set for Hindi-SM (i.e. social media Hindi) data as depicted in Table 10 and in case of test set for English-SM data as depicted in Table 8. In case of English-FB test data as depicted in Table 7, OAG class gets mostly confused with CAG, NAG class also gets confused with CAG but the data originally labeled as CAG gets confused with both OAG and NAG classes almost equally. The reason for OAG getting converted to CAG was a lot of common keywords present in both the classes like killed, terrorist etc. The reason for misclassification of CAG to NAG was because of indirect mentions and good words used in a very sarcastic way. Due to this system could not capture the exact feeling behind those sentences. The system performs better for classifying the CAG and NAG classes for all the test datasets in comparison to the classification of OAG. Some of the misclassified examples are shown in Table 11.

Class	OAG	CAG	NAG
OAG	74	51	19
CAG	29	88	25
NAG	92	265	273

Table 7: **Confusion matrix:English-FB**

Class	OAG	CAG	NAG
OAG	113	180	68
CAG	49	172	192
NAG	19	89	375

Table 8: **Confusion matrix:English-SM**

Class	OAG	CAG	NAG
OAG	135	215	12
CAG	47	317	49
NAG	12	80	103

Table 9: **Confusion matrix:Hindi-FB**

Class	OAG	CAG	NAG
OAG	103	240	116
CAG	84	182	115
NAG	62	111	181

Table 10: **Confusion matrix:Hindi-SM**

Original	Predicted	Sentence
CAG	OAG	I told you wait.7 pak killed within hours of their cowardice act.Go and weep for them .
OAG	CAG	yes we remember you are biggest terrorist country in the world you will do anything against humanity
CAG	NAG	Just get new currency to people and we will be happy
OAG	NAG	late night party enjoying life and now once he woke up he start complaining
CAG	OAG	अबे साले वह हमारे सैनिक को मार रहे हैं और तुम सब कड़ी निंदा ही कर रहे हो ।
OAG	CAG	चोरो की सरकार से आज़ादी मिल गया ।

Table 11: **Example of Sentence predicted to different class**

7 Conclusion

In this paper, we have presented the system that we developed as part of our participation in the shared task. We have developed a supervised ensemble approach for detecting the aggression. As base classification algorithm we use CNN and SVM. We evaluate the algorithms for two languages, namely English and Hindi. Datasets of two different kinds of domains were considered: textual posts and the comments made on social media platforms. Since the LSTM model did not perform well in our experiments, it would be interesting to see how the network fares when an attention mechanism will be deployed. As in many of the overtly and covertly aggressive instances named entity is often seen especially with '#hashtags', it would also be interesting to see that extracting NER feature from the data whether having any significant impact. In future, we would like to explore some other relevant linguistic features and hybrid machine learning architectures to improve the performance of the system further.

References

Robert A Baron and Deborah R Richardson. 1994. Human aggression: Perspectives in social psychology. *Nova Iorque: Plenum Press.*

Piotr Bojanowski, Edouard Grave, Armand Joulin, and Tomas Mikolov. 2016. Enriching word vectors with subword information. *arXiv preprint arXiv:1607.04606.*

Arnold H Buss. 1961. *The psychology of aggression.* Wiley.

Ying Chen, Yilu Zhou, Sencun Zhu, and Heng Xu. 2012. Detecting offensive language in social media to protect adolescent online safety. In *Privacy, Security, Risk and Trust (PASSAT), 2012 International Conference on and 2012 International Confernece on Social Computing (SocialCom)*, pages 71–80. IEEE.

Theodora Chu, Kylie Jue, and Max Wang. 2017. Comment abuse classification with deep learning.

Thomas Davidson, Dana Warmsley, Michael Macy, and Ingmar Weber. 2017. Automated hate speech detection and the problem of offensive language. *arXiv preprint arXiv:1703.04009*.

Asif Ekbal and Sivaji Bandyopadhyay. 2008. Bengali named entity recognition using support vector machine. In *Proceedings of the IJCNLP-08 Workshop on Named Entity Recognition for South and South East Asian Languages*.

Radu Florian, Abe Ittycheriah, Hongyan Jing, and Tong Zhang. 2003. Named entity recognition through classifier combination. In *Proceedings of the seventh conference on Natural language learning at HLT-NAACL 2003-Volume 4*, pages 168–171. Association for Computational Linguistics.

Lei Gao and Ruihong Huang. 2017. Detecting online hate speech using context aware models. *arXiv preprint arXiv:1710.07395*.

Chikashi Nobata, Joel Tetreault, Achint Thomas, Yashar Mehdad, and Yi Chang. 2016. Abusive language detection in online user content. In *Proceedings of the 25th international conference on world wide web*, pages 145–153. International World Wide Web Conferences Steering Committee.

Jeffrey Pennington, Richard Socher, and Christopher D. Manning. 2014. Glove: Global vectors for word representation. In *Empirical Methods in Natural Language Processing (EMNLP)*, pages 1532–1543.

Rodmonga Potapova and Denis Gordeev. 2016. Detecting state of aggression in sentences using cnn. *arXiv preprint arXiv:1604.06650*.

Vladimir Vapnik. 2013. *The nature of statistical learning theory*. Springer science & business media.

Aggression Identification and Multi-Lingual Word Embeddings

Thiago Galery
Idio Ltd / The Cursitor,
London,
WC2A1EN
thiago.galery@idio.ai

Efstathios Charitos
Idio Ltd / The Cursitor,
London,
WC2A1EN
stathis.charitos@idio.ai

Abstract

The system presented here took part in the 2018 *Trolling, Aggression and Cyberbullying* shared task (Forest and Trees team) and uses a Gated Recurrent Neural Network architecture (Cho et al., 2014) in an attempt to assess whether combining pre-trained English and Hindi *fastText* (Mikolov et al., 2018) word embeddings as a representation of the sequence input would improve classification performance. The motivation for this comes from the fact that the shared task data for English contained many Hindi tokens and therefore some users might be doing *code-switching*: the alternation between two or more languages in communication. To test this hypothesis, we also aligned Hindi and English vectors using pre-computed SVD matrices that pulls representations from different languages into a common space (Smith et al., 2017). Two conditions were tested: (i) one with standard pre-trained fastText word embeddings where each Hindi word is treated as an OOV token, and (ii) another where word embeddings for Hindi and English are loaded in a common vector space, so Hindi tokens can be assigned a meaningful representation. We submitted the second (i.e., multilingual) system and obtained the scores of 0.531 weighted F1 for the EN-FB dataset and 0.438 weighted F1 for the EN-TW dataset.

1 Introduction

This paper details a system demonstration for the 2018 *Trolling, Aggression and Cyberbullying* shared task (Kumar et al., 2018). The challenge was to provide a system capable of predicting the true class of a social media post which would be either one of (i) *Non-Aggression* (NOAG), (ii) *Covert Aggression* (CAG), or (iii) *Overt Aggression* (a multi-class but not a multi-label text classification problem). The shared task had two datasets available, one in English and another in Hindi, that were split into test / validation subsets. Systems were benchmarked against two datasets, one sourced from facebook (FB) and another from twitter (TW) for each language (EN or HI).

Despite the fact that data was divided by language, we noticed that some Hindi vocabulary appeared in the English data. This raised an interesting question. Could such vocabulary be conveying information regarding the aggressive or polite nature of the content? Considering words from other languages as mere noise could have unwanted consequences, as they could be instances of *code-switching*: situations in which terms from two or more languages are used in a message to better convey the speaker's intent. For example, by mixing Spanish and English, a speaker who says 'La onda is to fight y jambar' means something similar to 'The in-thing is to fight and steal' (Woolford, 1983). In these cases, understanding the switched word (in this case, 'fight') is essential to understand the sentence's meaning.

Against this background, we have decided to test the following hypothesis. Does the inclusion of word representations from other languages (say, Hindi) increase the classification score of a given shared task's dataset? Although this is applicable to both English and Hindi datasets, we decided to focus our experiments on the English one. This is partially due to time / effort reasons and logistics around the registration for having access to the data.

To test our hypothesis, we used a classification pipeline that would run two conditions. In the *single language condition* we simply regarded foreign (Hindi) words as OOV tokens. In the *multi language condition*, we aligned English and Hindi *fastText* (Mikolov et al., 2018) vectors via SVD matrices that

Proceedings of the First Workshop on Trolling, Aggression and Cyberbullying, pages 74–79
Santa Fe, USA, August 25, 2018.

pull representations from different languages into a common space (Smith et al., 2017). We will discuss some of the background behind these decisions in the next section.[1]

2   Related Work

2.1   Out-of-Vocabulary information

The idea behind using the meaning of words from different languages to improve classification results is somewhat similar to the motivation for capturing emoticons and misspellings in text classification tasks.

The use of emoticons in text classification has been extensively discussed in sentiment analysis (Hogenboom et al., 2013; Hu et al., 2013; Mozetič et al., 2016; Novak et al., 2015; Thelwall et al., 2010; Zhao et al., 2012). Some have defended that the use of emoticons as a cue for sentiment analysis of tweets results in better accuracy compared to using the linguistic text alone (Hogenboom et al., 2013; Hu et al., 2013). Although emoticons tend to be a better indicator for an overall negative tweet than a positive one, their meaning depends on the context, therefore they do not always act as a direct indicator of emotions (Tian et al., 2017).

Building on this literature, we assumed that emoticons could be indicators of the aggression level of a specific social media post. Borrowing from previous work (Eisner et al., 2016), we have generated embeddings for emoticons based on their unicode descriptions and used these representations (Emoji2Vec) in our classification pipeline.

These are not the only out-of-vocabulary signal that might improve classification results discussed by the literature. Given that online abuse unfortunately happens frequently, companies that manage message boards started employing automatic detection methods in order to prevent abuse from happening in message boards and social media platforms. Because these detection mechanisms initially relied on a list of offensive words that would ban posts to be published, many users have changed their writing style in order to bypass such forms of abuse prevention. For example, a message containing 'kill yourself asshole' would be changed into 'kill yrslef a$$hole'. Given that this type of intentional misspelling is very hard to predict or blacklist and yet fundamental to the abusive nature of the message, our system needs to be robust against this kind of stylistic variation (Nobata et al., 2016).

Dense word embeddings, such as *Word2Vec* (Mikolov et al., 2013b) and *Glove* (Pennington et al., 2014), have been used as the *de facto* representations for the meaning of words in complex NLP pipelines. However, these representations do not incorporate information about meaning at the sub-word level, which means that we either get the vector for a word if it exists in the vocabulary, or some random (or zero based) representation. As a consequence, using pre-trained Word2Vec or Glove representations would not allow to capture the kind of creative misspelling just mentioned (e.g. 'a$$hole' would be considered an OOV token). To bridge this gap, a new type of representation has been motivated, namely *fastText* (Mikolov et al., 2018). The main advantage of this type of model is that it allows the retrieval of vectors for character n-grams in a way similar to word lookups. This means that we can devise a method for retrieving the vector of a systematically misspelled word by exploring its character level embeddings.

In conclusion, the discussion in this section motivates a better treatment of two forms of OOV tokens: (i) emoticons and (ii) systematically misspelled words. We will discuss how both are captured in our system when defining the classification pipeline.

2.2   Text Classification Architecture

In order to solve the classification challenge set out by the shared task, we need to employ some supervised machine learning model. Recurrent Neural Networks have been considered a natural match for sequence modelling because they output a probability distribution over the next element of the sequence given the current one) (hence a candidate for capturing sentence meaning). Despite of this, some (Bengio et al., 1994) have showed that they are difficult to train because their gradients tend to vanish or explode.

In order to avoid these problems, Cho et al (Cho et al., 2014) proposed a unit whose activation employs gating functions that determine whether the hidden states should be updated or reset. This allows the network to adaptively 'forget' irrelevant aspects of the data and 'remember' long term information.

---

[1]The implementation of this experiment is available at `https://github.com/tgalery/geiger`, see *notebooks*.

They proposed this technique in the context of machine translation, but they also showed that the projected embeddings learned by the network captured semantic and syntactic relationships of phrases and sentences (Van Der Maaten, 2013). Therefore, we decided to employ a GRU network for text classification, as the target class might depend on phrasal-like aspects of meaning (for example, an aggressive word's meaning could be neutralised under the scope of negation).

3 Methodology and Data

3.1 Classification pipeline

Our general classification pipeline is defined as follows. After tokenization and preprocessing, the token sequence would be passed to a token identifier, which would determine whether the token is (i) an emoticon, (ii) a foreign (Hindi) token, or (iii) a standard (English) token.

Emoticons would be assigned a vector by averaging the vectors of the tokens of its unicode description. The treatment of foreign tokens would be split into two conditions: (i) an OOV vector (*Single Language Condition*), (ii) aligned fastText vector (*Multi Language Condition*, to be detailed below). Finally, standard (English) tokens would be processed as follows. If a embedding could not be found for a word, we would generate character trigrams from it and average the character-level vectors. In summary, the processing pipeline would look like this.

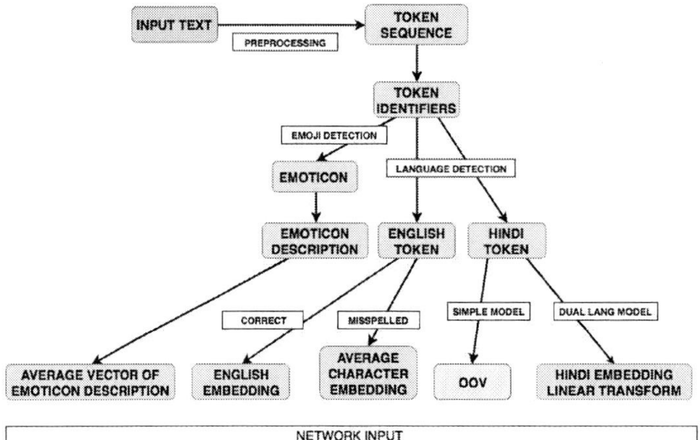

Figure 1: Text Pipeline

The token sequence would then be padded and clipped to maximum length of 200 tokens. Then, each token would be then mapped to its corresponding word embedding given the details above (Embedding Layer). This layer is followed by a 1D spatial dropout layer (value is 0.2), which is then piped into a Bidirectional Gated Recurrent Unit layer. This layer is then followed by a pooling layer that concatenates an 1D global average pooling and global max pooling. This would then be finally fed into a Dense layer whose dimensionality corresponds to the number of classes defined by the task: Non-Aggression, Covert-Aggression, and Overt-Aggression and whose activation is softmax. We selected the class with the maximum probability as the output. The model used categorical cross-entropy and Adam as an optimizer and was trained for 10 epochs. Schematically, we have:

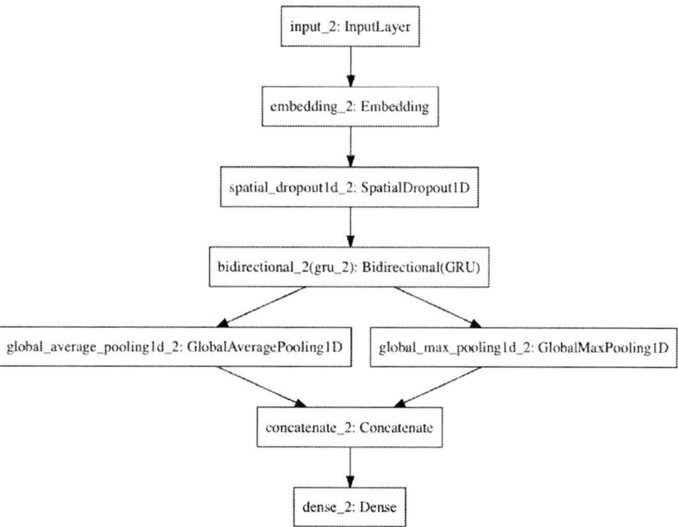

Figure 2: Network Architecture

3.2 Aligning Multi Lingual Vectors

At this point, it is important to discuss the alignment process to embed pre-trained English and Hindi embeddings within a single space. Combining pre-trained fastText word embeddings from English and Hindi generates a problem. Since they were trained by different corpora, the word distribution in each model does not necessarily align with the word distribution of similar words in the other model. In our previous example of code-switching, 'La onda is to fight y jambar.', we would like for the word embedding corresponding of 'fight' to be very similar to the word embedding of its Spanish counterpart (namely, 'luchar'), but that is not something that is guaranteed by our use of the pre-trained vectors.

To bridge this gap, we have borrowed from a technique that uses a Singular Value Decomposition (SVD) to learn a linear transformation capable of aligning difference vector spaces (Smith et al., 2017). This 'offline' way to project word embeddings contrasts the 'online' way in which embeddings from multiple languages are learnt together via bilingual corpora of aligned sentences (Mikolov et al., 2013a).

Building on previous work (Xing et al., 2015), Smith et al. (2017) argue that Mikolov's linear transformation is an orthogonal matrix (mapping a vector from *source* to *target* language should allow you to map that target vector back and obtain the original representation). To infer the orthogonal matrix, they form two ordered matrices X_D and Y_D from a bilingual dictionary (obtained via google translate), such that the ith row of both matrices corresponds to the source and target language word vectors of the ith pair in the dictionary. This allows SVD to be applied to both matrices (multiplying the transpose of one by the other) maximising the cosine similarity of translation pairs in the dictionary.

This somehow makes the meaning of 'fight' and 'luchar' in our example above to be more similar than they otherwise would be. We did not learn the orthogonal transform ourselves, but instead relied on a pre-learned representation built on top of *fastText* embeddings made available by Babylon.[2]. Thus, for the *multi language* condition, the fastText embeddings for English and Hindi were aligned after being loaded, making our embedding matrix consistent for both languages.

4   Results

With regards to our hypothesis, we did not find any striking difference between multi (weighted F1 0.58) and single language conditions(weighted F1 0.554) using validation data as a benchmark.

---

[2]Obtained through `https://github.com/Babylonpartners/fastText_multilingual`

There are multiple reasons for this. First, it could be that the foreign (Hindi) tokens were not indicative of the aggressive nature of the content. Another possibility is that the SVD method for aligning the geometry of embeddings in different languages did not provide good enough representations. In hindsight, we realized that the number of Hindi tokens that occur as part of the English dataset is too low, suggesting that *code switching* in not a deep characteristic of the data.

We were curious to see how our system would perform against others in the shared task, so we submitted results from the multi lingual version, taking the 24th place in the shared task's leaderboard. The results (and confusion matrices) were the following:

System	F1 (weighted) EN-FB	F1 (weighted) EN-TW
Random Baseline	0.3535	0.3477
Multi Lingual Pooled GRU	**0.5315**	**0.4389**

Table 1: Results for the English (Facebook) task and English (Social Media) task.

Table 2: Datasets confusion matrices
EN-FB   EN-TW

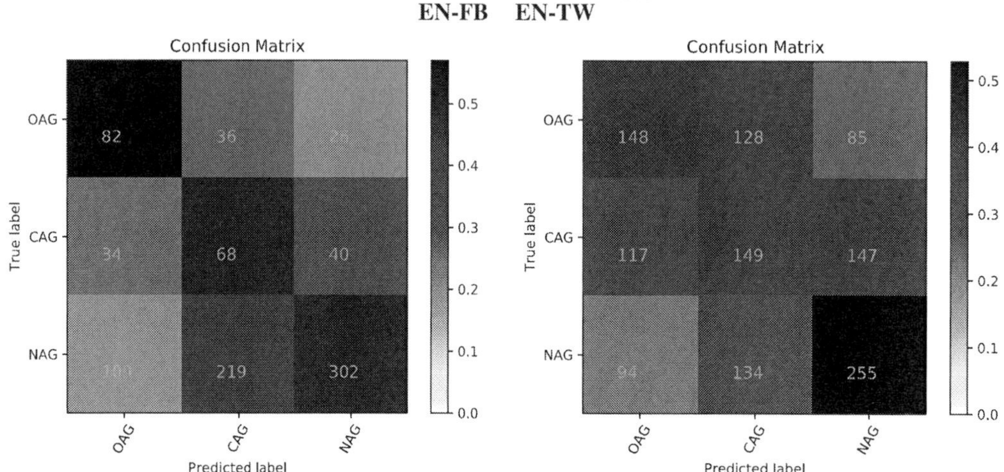

For the facebook dataset it seems that the system provides much better answers than a random baseline. Looking at the confusion matrix it seems that our classifier is more comfortable with overt aggression and fairs worse with distinguishing covert aggression from non aggressive content.

5   Conclusion

It seems that for the shared task's dataset, the use of aligned multi lingual vocabulary did not improve the classification results. We do feel that our hypothesis has not been completely invalidated though. It would be interesting to test it against a dataset with more systematic forms of code-switching in order to draw better conclusions.

With regards to the architecture, we felt that the model had a problem when distinguishing between overt aggression and non aggression. Given this limitation, a better solution would involve a combination of two binary classifiers: (i) one distinguishing aggressive from non aggressive content and (ii) another distinguishing covert from overt types of aggression.

References

Yoshua Bengio, Patrice Simard, and Paolo Frasconi. 1994. Learning long-term dependencies with gradient descent is difficult. *IEEE transactions on neural networks*, 5(2):157–166.

Kyunghyun Cho, Bart Van Merriënboer, Caglar Gulcehre, Dzmitry Bahdanau, Fethi Bougares, Holger Schwenk, and Yoshua Bengio. 2014. Learning phrase representations using rnn encoder-decoder for statistical machine translation. *arXiv preprint arXiv:1406.1078*.

Ben Eisner, Tim Rocktäschel, Isabelle Augenstein, Matko Bošnjak, and Sebastian Riedel. 2016. emoji2vec: Learning emoji representations from their description. *arXiv preprint arXiv:1609.08359*.

Alexander Hogenboom, Daniella Bal, Flavius Frasincar, Malissa Bal, Franciska de Jong, and Uzay Kaymak. 2013. Exploiting emoticons in sentiment analysis. In *Proceedings of the 28th Annual ACM Symposium on Applied Computing*, pages 703–710. ACM.

Xia Hu, Jiliang Tang, Huiji Gao, and Huan Liu. 2013. Unsupervised sentiment analysis with emotional signals. In *Proceedings of the 22nd international conference on World Wide Web*, pages 607–618. ACM.

Ritesh Kumar, Atul Kr. Ojha, Shervin Malmasi, and Marcos Zampieri. 2018. Benchmarking Aggression Identification in Social Media. In *Proceedings of the First Workshop on Trolling, Aggression and Cyberbulling (TRAC)*, Santa Fe, USA.

Tomas Mikolov, Quoc V Le, and Ilya Sutskever. 2013a. Exploiting similarities among languages for machine translation. *arXiv preprint arXiv:1309.4168*.

Tomas Mikolov, Ilya Sutskever, Kai Chen, Greg S Corrado, and Jeff Dean. 2013b. Distributed representations of words and phrases and their compositionality. In *Advances in neural information processing systems*, pages 3111–3119.

Tomas Mikolov, Edouard Grave, Piotr Bojanowski, Christian Puhrsch, and Armand Joulin. 2018. Advances in pre-training distributed word representations. In *Proceedings of the International Conference on Language Resources and Evaluation (LREC 2018)*.

Igor Mozetič, Miha Grčar, and Jasmina Smailović. 2016. Multilingual twitter sentiment classification: The role of human annotators. *PloS one*, 11(5):e0155036.

Chikashi Nobata, Joel Tetreault, Achint Thomas, Yashar Mehdad, and Yi Chang. 2016. Abusive Language Detection in Online User Content. In *Proceedings of the 25th International Conference on World Wide Web*, pages 145–153. International World Wide Web Conferences Steering Committee.

Petra Kralj Novak, Jasmina Smailović, Borut Sluban, and Igor Mozetič. 2015. Sentiment of emojis. *PloS one*, 10(12):e0144296.

Jeffrey Pennington, Richard Socher, and Christopher Manning. 2014. Glove: Global vectors for word representation. In *Proceedings of the 2014 conference on empirical methods in natural language processing (EMNLP)*, pages 1532–1543.

Samuel L Smith, David HP Turban, Steven Hamblin, and Nils Y Hammerla. 2017. Offline bilingual word vectors, orthogonal transformations and the inverted softmax. *arXiv preprint arXiv:1702.03859*.

Mike Thelwall, Kevan Buckley, Georgios Paltoglou, Di Cai, and Arvid Kappas. 2010. Sentiment strength detection in short informal text. *Journal of the Association for Information Science and Technology*, 61(12):2544–2558.

Ye Tian, Thiago Galery, Giulio Dulcinati, Emilia Molimpakis, and Chao Sun. 2017. Facebook sentiment: Reactions and emojis. In *Proceedings of the Fifth International Workshop on Natural Language Processing for Social Media*, pages 11–16.

Laurens Van Der Maaten. 2013. Barnes-hut-sne. *arXiv preprint arXiv:1301.3342*.

Ellen Woolford. 1983. Bilingual code-switching and syntactic theory. *Linguistic inquiry*, 14(3):520–536.

Chao Xing, Dong Wang, Chao Liu, and Yiye Lin. 2015. Normalized word embedding and orthogonal transform for bilingual word translation. In *Proceedings of the 2015 Conference of the North American Chapter of the Association for Computational Linguistics: Human Language Technologies*, pages 1006–1011.

Jichang Zhao, Li Dong, Junjie Wu, and Ke Xu. 2012. Moodlens: an emoticon-based sentiment analysis system for chinese tweets. In *Proceedings of the 18th ACM SIGKDD international conference on Knowledge discovery and data mining*, pages 1528–1531. ACM.

A K-Competitive Autoencoder for Aggression Detection in Social Media text

Promita Maitra
Mumbai, India
promita.maitra@gmail.com

Ritesh Sarkhel
Ohio State University
Columbus, Ohio
sarkhel.5@osu.edu

Abstract

We present an approach to detect aggression from social media text in this work. A winner-takes-all autoencoder, called Emoti-KATE is proposed for this purpose. Using a log-normalized, weighted word-count vector at input dimensions, the autoencoder simulates a competition between neurons in the hidden layer to minimize the reconstruction loss between the input and final output layers. We have evaluated the performance of our system on the datasets provided by the organizers of TRAC workshop, 2018. Using the encoding generated by Emoti-KATE, a 3-way classification is performed for every social media text in the dataset. Each data point is classified as 'Overtly Aggressive', 'Covertly Aggressive' or 'Non-aggressive'. Results show that our proposed method is able to achieve promising results on some of these datasets. In this paper, we have described the effects of introducing an winner-takes-all autoencoder for the task of aggression detection, reported its performance on four different datasets, analyzed some of its limitations and how to improve its performance in future works.

1 Introduction

With the rapid growth of unregulated social media platforms, a major problem coming to surface is the aggressive nature of text used by people while interacting in these mediums. Manual monitoring or filtering of this user generated data is a challenging task due to its sheer scale. Therefore, automatic detection of aggressive text is the logical first step to combat the issue. There has been an increased interest among contemporary researchers to propose an acceptable solution of this problem in recent years. However, proposing an automated solution for this problem has some inherent obstacles. One of the most challenging obstacles among this to annotate these texts with an appropriate sentiment score. Social media texts are almost always short in length, and exhibit ambiguous grammatical syntax including abbreviated forms, typo errors, repeated alphabets to emphasize intentions as well as coinage of new words. Additionally, detecting aggression on social media posts or comments is especially challenging due to its lack of context. Almost all of these posts are provide very little to no context. Detecting common 'hate-words' using a bag-of-words analysis does not work in these cases as conventionally non-aggressive words can be deemed aggressive when used sarcastically.

In this paper we have proposed Emoti-KATE, a winner-takes-all autoencoder for representing social media text. Performance of our autoencoder is evaluated on a downstream task of classifying the text based on its aggression level. We have broadly categorized a social media post or comment into one of three categories: *Overtly Aggressive*, *Covertly Aggressive* and *Non-Aggressive*. In recent times, researchers (Socher et al., 2011b; Hermann and Blunsom, 2013; Chen and Zaki, 2017) have established that autoencoders can be effectively used to learn representations of document text for various applications. However, they have some inherent limitations. As Chen et al. (Chen and Zaki, 2017) has pointed out, in a traditional autoencoder, contributions of most of the hidden neurons in reconstructing the input vector are often redundant. They have shown that introducing competition among these hidden neurons can help get rid of these redundancies. The output vectors generated by such winner-takes-all approach

Proceedings of the First Workshop on Trolling, Aggression and Cyberbullying, pages 80–89
Santa Fe, USA, August 25, 2018.

outperform most of the popular, contemporary document representation techniques as well. Inspired by their success, we have taken a similar approach in this work. Emoti-KATE introduces a K-competition layer between the input and output layers to generate the vector representation of each social media text. We have evaluated the performance of our approach on a dataset of 15,000 aggression-annotated Facebook posts and comments each in Hindi (in both Roman and Devanagari script) and English. After basic preprocessing on the raw data[1], the winner-takes-all autoencoder is deployed with a log-normalized vector at its input dimensions. Results show that while our system's performance is promising in case of English texts (weighted F1 score of 0.5694), the classifier has much scope of improvement for Hindi texts (weighted F1 score of 0.4189). The main contribution of this work is an exhaustive investigation into the performance of K-competitive autoencoders (Chen and Zaki, 2017) in identifying aggression level in short, sparsely contexualized social media posts and comments. Our experimental result suggests that introducing a competitive hidden layer in a autoencoder framework improves the performance of aggression detection in sparse social media texts. A complete pseudocode of our system is presented in Algorithm 1.

The rest of the paper is organized as follows: Section 2 gives a brief overview of the work already done in this field. Section 3 describes the details of the dataset, preprocessing steps and the system we have used to address the problem. Section 4 presents the analysis of results and finally, the conclusion and future scopes are discussed in Section 5.

2   Related Work

Automatically detecting cyber-bullying and use of hate speech from textual analysis has gained momentum with the rise of increasing amount of user-generated content on web. Most of the research works have considered this to be a binary classification problem, i.e. aggressive or non-aggressive. The set of features that has been widely used by contemporary researchers Schmidt and Wiegand (2017) includes various word-level and character-level features including n-grams, usage of punctuations, capitalization, and token-length. Some recent approaches have also proposed sentiment polarity detection, using lexical resources available in web along with bag-of-words, and linguistic features such as POS tagging, dependency parsing, knowledge-based feature extraction using ontology information etc. for this purpose. To solve the problem of context sparsity, researchers have proposed some word clustering techniques as well as meta-data analysis including user-profile analysis, and user-activity history analysis etc. However, most of these existing works have some strong assumptions inherent to their systems. For example, in Dinakar et al. (2011) the authors assumed that an aggressive post in social media can primarily be about one of the few topics, which include physical appearance, sexuality, race and culture, and intelligence. They trained a multi-class classifier for identifying texts on these topics and individual binary classifiers to subsequently classify whether the text covered one of the topics mentioned above. Features such as TF-IDF, presence of swear words, frequent bigrams, and topic-specific n-grams were used to train the classifiers. Dadvar et al. (2013) followed a similar approach and introduced user-profile specific meta-data (separate classifiers based on user gender), which helped them to improve the precision of their system. Nahar et al. (2012) extracted semantic features using Latent Dirichlet Allocation (LDA) along with lexicon features, TF-IDF values and second-person pronouns to train a Support Vector Machine for classification purposes. Sentiment analysis technique was leveraged to detect cyberbullying in a Twitter dataset by Xu et al. (2012). They used Latent Dirichlet Allocation to identify the most frequent topics in tweets that exhibited signs of bullying. Semi-supervised approaches with bootstrapping have also been proposed in recent years (Schmidt and Wiegand, 2017). While there have been many significant research contributions in this area, most of them considered the problem of aggression detection as a binary classification task, i.e., each text was to be classified either as aggressive or non-aggressive. Malmasi and Zampieri (2018) is one of the early works that has taken a different approach. In their work, every social media text is classified into three categories, hate speech, aggressive text and neutral. They argued that as general profanity is an unavoidable part of social media posts due to their unregulated nature, our efforts

---

[1]we observed that 'hashtags' carry significant information in social media text and the segmentation improved our prediction score on validation set by 3% to 5%

should focus on distinguishing profanity from hate speech that targets an individual or a group. They have used a single as well as ensemble classifiers with stacked generalization for this purpose. Their feature set includes n-grams, skip-grams and clustering-based word representations.

With the evolution of deep neural network (DNN) based models for natural language analysis, there has been some works using leveraged DNN models for this purpose as well. For example, Mehdad and Tetreault (2016) have proposed a Recurrent Neural Network based Language Model approach with character n-gram feature for this task to overcome the challenge of scarcity of large-scale dataset. Zhao et al. (Zhao and Mao, 2017) have recently proposed a semantically enhanced marginalised denoising autoencoder for detecting cyberbullying on social media text. In this work, they have extended a stacked denoising autoencoder with semantic dropout noise and sparsity constraints. Contrary to these methods, we have used a shallow autoencoder in Emoti-KATE. Following the work of Chen and Zaki (2017), we have introduced a K-competition layer in our framework to tackle the problem of data sparsity and little contextual information in these texts. This layer reduces the redundancy of reconstructed input patterns in the respective contributions of hidden neurons to the final output layer. The main contribution of our work is an exhaustive investigation of winner-takes-all autoencoder framework in detecting aggression level in sparse social media texts. Our model has been evaluated on datasets collected from Facebook and Twitter, in both Hindi and English languages.

Algorithm 1: K-competitive Autoencoder

Input: Training set (D_{train}), Test set (D_{test})
Output: Feature vectors (V_{test}) of D_{test}

Initialize $O_{test} \leftarrow \Phi$ $\triangleright$ O_{test} $\leftarrow$ Autoencoder output vectors for D_{test}

        for *each document $d \in \{D_{train} \cup D_{test}\}$* **do**
| Compute input vector v_d
        end
$W' \leftarrow \texttt{training}(V_{train})$
$O_{test} \leftarrow \tanh(W' V_{test} + b)$ $\triangleright$ $V_{test} \leftarrow$ Input vectors of D_{test}
return O_{test}

procedure $\texttt{training}$: $\triangleright$ $V_{train} \leftarrow$ Input vectors for D_{train}
        Forward propagate $z = \tanh(W V_{train} + b)$
        Apply K-competition on activations $z' = \texttt{K-compete}(z)$
        Compute error, back-propagate and iterate until convergence
        return W;

---

3   Methodology and Dataset

A K-competitive autoencoder for aggression detection in social media text is proposed in this work. A detailed description of the dataset, some of its interesting characteristics and our approach towards this task will be presented in this section.

3.1   Description of the dataset

The aggression-annotated dataset used in this shared task(Kumar et al., 2018a) has been collected and prepaed by Kumar et al. (2018b). Collecting approximately 18k tweets and 21k facebook comments from social media users in India, they used Crowdflower, a crowd-sourced platform to annotate the entire dataset.[2] This dataset is code-mixed i.e., it contains text in English and Hindi (written in both Roman and Devanagari script). A total of 3 top-level and 10 level-2 tags were assigned to the entire dataset. In this shared task, we have only considered the top-level tags, which are as follows: 'Overtly Aggressive', 'Covertly Aggressive', and 'Non-aggressive'. The organizers of TRAC 2018 have divided

---

[2]Interested readers can find more details about the data collection methods used to compile this dataset in Kumar et al. (2018b).

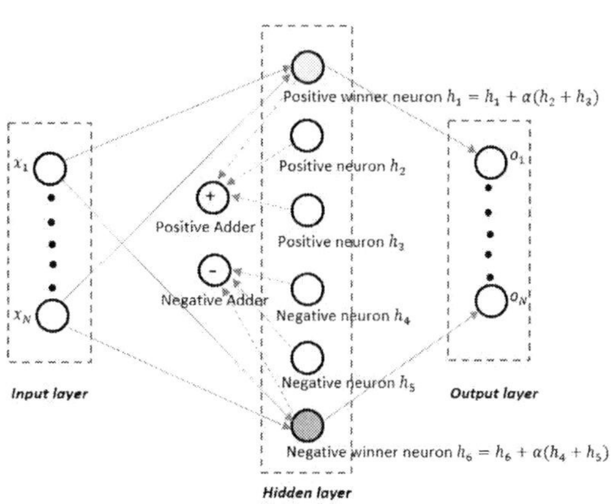

Figure 1: **An illustration of competition among the hidden neurons in Emoti-KATE; The hidden layer shows only one of each positive and negative neurons are selected as the winners out of the six neurons competing to contribute to the output layer; All of the neurons in input, hidden and output layers are fully connected but not shown in this figure for ease of interpretation**

this dataset into a number of smaller datasets based on their origin (social media platform from where it was collected) and language. This resulted in 4 different datasets for this task, which are as follows, *English-Facebook* dataset, *English-Social Media* dataset, *Hindi-Facebook* dataset, and *Hindi-Social Media* dataset. We have evaluated and reported the performance of *Emoti-KATE* in Section 4, for each of these datasets.

3.2 Preprocessing steps

Depending on the dataset, each document undergoes a number of preprocessing steps. The stopwords were removed first. Then, the documents were stemmed using Porter Stemmer. We have used the NLTK library for both of these steps. Next, each document representing a post in Twitter was further processed as the 'hashtags' used along the normal text were further segmented into meaningful words. For example, *"#savethegirlchild"* is segmented into four distinct words *"save"*, *"the"*, *"girl"*, and *"child"* at the end of this step. If there are multiple such meaningful segmentations possible, all of these combinations are generated. The segmented words generated by this process is then appended to the rest of the text in the document, in the order they appeared in the original 'hashtag' itself. We have used data-driven exhaustive search within the Brown corpus (Marcus et al., 1993) for this purpose. Split points are decided by iteratively searching for every possible combination of meaningful words within the corpus. The split points that produced the highest percentage of meaningful words are considered to be a possible segmentation of the 'hashtag'. We observe that although this strategy of handling 'hashtags' provides the highest recall, it is very slow. Additionally, for social media platforms such as Twitter where the maximum number of characters is limited and a significant number of posts use code-mixed data, this strategy do not work very well.

3.3 Description of Emoti-KATE

Autoencoders (Vincent et al., 2008) are neural networks tasked to reconstruct an input vector by minimizing the loss between the input and the final output layer. In recent years, it has been successfully used to extract features encoding text data (Socher et al., 2011a; Li et al., 2015; Yang et al., 2017). We have used a K-competitive autoencoder, called *Emoti-KATE* in this work. Contrary to a traditional shallow autoencoder, a K-competitive autoencoder (Chen and Zaki, 2017), introduces a competition layer among the hidden neurons. It has been shown in Chen and Zaki (2017), when encoding a sparse text document, this competition among hidden neurons helps get rid of the redundancy contributed by some of the hidden neurons in the final encoding. In the K-competitive layer, neurons compete among themselves for the right to respond to the input vector, therefore focusing more on unique and important patterns in the input data. Complete pseudo-code of the K-competitive encoder used in this work is presented in Algorithm 1. Emoti-KATE is a shallow autoencoder, with a single competitive hidden layer. Let, $x \in \text{Re}^d$ denotes the d-dimensional input vector of the autoencoder. The objective of this autoencoder is to reconstruct x at the output layer. Let, $h_1, h_2, ...h_n$ denotes the neurons at the hidden layer. The weights between the input-to-hidden layers and hidden-to-output layers are tied together. Therefore, if $W \in \text{Re}^{d \times n}$ represents the input-to-hidden layer weight matrix, $W^T \in \text{Re}^{n \times d}$ will denote the weight matrix between hidden-to-output layer. We have used $\tanh(x) = \frac{e^{2x}-1}{e^{2x}+1}$ as the activation function between the input-to-hidden layer and sigmoid function $f(x) = \frac{1}{1+e^{-x}}$ as the activation function between hidden-to-output layer in our implementation.

Input vector	Description
X_1	Word-counts weighted by sentiment-score
X_2	X_1 augmented with character-case information
X_3	X_2 with 'hashtags'-segmented into unique words

Table 1: **A brief overview of the input vectors used in our implementation**

In this work, we have experimented with three different input vectors. A brief overview of how these input vectors are computed is presented in Table 1. As mentioned, the first representation (X_1) denotes a weighted word-count vector of the document. Each word count is weighted by the sentiment score for that word. We have used the sentiment analysis module embedded in *nltk*[3] for this purpose. The second input vector representation (X_2) appends X_1 with character-case statistics of the document. More specifically, X_1 is appended with a vector $C = c_1c_2c_3$ of length 3, where c_1, c_2 and c_3 denote the number of lower, upper, and camel case words in the document. Finally, the last input vector (X_3) follows the same steps as X_2, except one preprocessing step. The main difference between X_2 and X_3 is based on how they process 'hashtags' in a document. In case of both X_1 and X_2 they are treated as distinct, individual words, whereas X_3 takes a different approach. Each 'hashtag' in the document is segmented into distinct meaningful words. The steps followed for this purpose has been described in Section 3.2. Following the implementation by Chen et al. (Chen and Zaki, 2017), each input vector was log-normalized before it is fed into the autoencoder. The training and encoding steps of Emoti-KATE have been shown in Algorithm 1. We have used cross-entropy loss to compute the backpropagation error in our implementation.

The main difference of a K-competitive autoencoder from a traditional shallow autoencoder is a K-competition hidden layer. As mentioned before, we have used a single K-competitive layer in this work. In a K-competitive layer with n neurons, say $h_1, h_2, ...h_n$, gradients flowing through only the top-K neurons obtain the right to contribute to the output layer. In Emoti-KATE, this selection of K neurons is performed based on the activation values of the hidden neurons. We select the top $\lceil \frac{K}{2} \rceil$ positive neurons and the lowest $\lfloor \frac{K}{2} \rfloor$ negative neurons during each feedforward step. The rest of the $n - K$ loser neurons are zeroed out. To compensate for the loss of these neurons as well as to amplify the competition among the neurons, the winner neurons are then rewarded. This means reallocating the loss of activations of the loser neurons to the winners therefore amplifying them in the process. We have illustrated the workflow of the K-competition layer in Fig 1. Activations from the hidden neurons with positive activations i.e., h_2 and h_3 are suppressed and their activations are reallocated to h_1, essentially amplifying its contribution to the output neurons. Therefore, the only positive neuron that contributes to the output layer in Fig. 1 is h_1, as $h_2, h_3 \to 0$. α is called the amplification factor. It decides how much of the loser activations flow through the winners. For example, if $\alpha > \frac{2}{K}$, gradients flowing through loser neurons are amplified, whereas if $\alpha = 0$, they are completely suppressed and Emoti-KATE effectively (Chen and Zaki, 2017) turns into a K-sparse autoencoder (Makhzani and Frey, 2013). The same process is repeated for the negative neurons too. Hidden neurons h_4 and h_5 are zeroed out and their activations are reallocated to

---

[3]https://www.nltk.org/api/nltk.sentiment.html

Dataset	Input Vector	Description	F1 (weighted)
English-FB	X_1	wordcount (WC) + sentiment score (SC)	0.5431
	X_2	WC + SC + capitalization feature (CF)	0.5285
	X_3	WC + SC + CF + hashtag analyzer (HA)	0.5694
		Random Baseline	0.3535
English-Social Media	X_1	wordcount (WC) + sentiment score (SC)	0.3379
	X_2	WC + SC + capitalization feature (CF)	0.2884
	X_3	WC + SC + CF + hashtag analyzer (HA)	0.3191
		Random Baseline	0.3477
Hindi-FB	X_1	wordcount (WC) + sentiment score (SC)	0.3969
	X_2	WC + SC + capitalization feature (CF)	0.3911
	X_3	WC + SC + CF + hashtag analyzer (HA)	0.4189
		Random Baseline	0.3571
Hindi-Social Media	X_1	wordcount (WC) + sentiment score (SC)	0.2668
	X_2	WC + SC + capitalization feature (CF)	0.3143
	X_3	WC + SC + CF + hashtag analyzer (HA)	0.3142
		Random Baseline	0.3206

Table 2: **Results of Emoti-KATE on experimental datasets**

the negative winner neuron h_6 with α amplification. As a result, h_6 is the only negative neuron that contributes to the output layer.

4 Results

In this section, we will evaluate Emoti-KATE in learning meaningful representations of social media text in detecting aggression in four different social media datasets. All of our experiments were performed on a 2.80 GHz Intel i7 with 32GB RAM. We have used Keras[4], a high level neural network library for implementing the autoencoder. In our implementation for Emoti-KATE, we have closely followed the design choices by Chen et al.[5] (Chen and Zaki, 2017).

The system was evaluated on the basis of weighted macro-averaged F-scores. The individual F-score achieved for class i.e., Overtly Aggressive (OAG), Covertly Aggressive (CAG) and Non-Aggressive (NAG) was weighted by the proportion of the concerned class in the test set and the final F-score is the average of these individual F-scores of each class. Our system achieved best result for English Facebook texts and the lowest score was in Hindi Twitter data. A detailed description of the results for each dataset has been provided below. The best performance achieved by Emoti-KATE for each of these datasets has been highlighted in the respective tables. The best performance achieved by randomly assigning class labels (random baseline) for each of the datasets have also been reported.

4.1 Results on the English-Facebook dataset

Our system performed best in English Facebook texts with a weighted F1 score of 0.5694 for the input vector X_3, i.e., the input vector that considered Sentiment Score weighted Word Count vector augmented with capitalization feature and 'hashtag' analyzer. The primary reason of our system performing better on this particular dataset is the length of the texts. Typically, texts present in this dataset were longer offering more context, resulting in a less sparse vector which ultimately improved the performance of the classifier. Performance of Emoti-KATE on this dataset, for three different variations of input vectors is presented in Table 2. We have also reported a class wise performance analysis for the best performance (X_3) of our system in Table 3. A heatmap representing the confusion matrix of this run is presented in Fig. 2.

---

[4]https://github.com/keras-team/keras
[5]https://github.com/hugochan/KATE

Class	Precision	Recall
OAG	39.216	39.216
CAG	33.803	22.967
NAG	72.063	80.639

Table 3: **Class-wise distribution of Precision and Recall for the best result observed** (X_3)

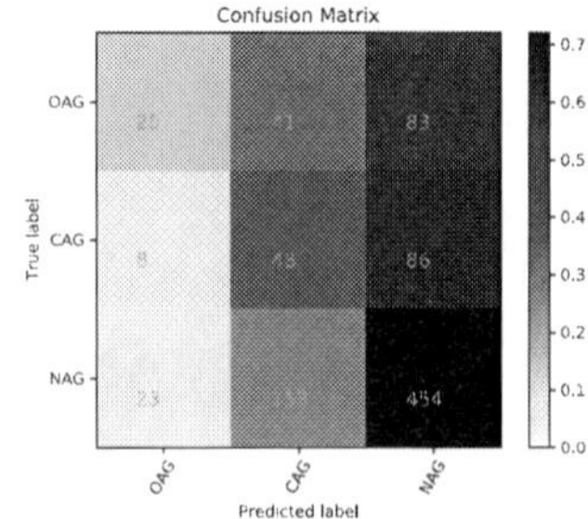

Figure 2: **Heatmap of the confusion matrix for our best result observed** (X_3)

4.2 Results on the English-Social Media dataset

Even though our approach achieved promising score in one of the English datasets, for the English social media (Twitter) dataset, it has significant scope of improvement. The best run for this dataset could only achieve a weighted F1 score of 0.3379. Two main reasons for this are as follows: (1) social media texts, specially tweets consists of a lot of abbreviated forms, repeating characters in a word, newly coined terms etc. which was not efficiently normalized, therefore not present during the training of the classifier, and (2) length of the texts in this dataset was also very short which eventually resulted in sparse vectors. Performance of our system for three different variations of input vectors has been described in Table 2. We have also reported a class wise performance analysis for the best performance (X_1) of our system in Table 4. The heatmap representing a confusion matrix for this run is presented in Fig. 3.

For both the datasets in English, one interesting observation that came up from the confusion matrix is that the system is biased towards the class NAG and this resulted in achieving higher recall in that particular class (highest 80.639%).

4.3 Results on the Hindi-Facebook dataset

Similar to English, our system performs better in classifying Hindi Facebook texts than the social media dataset (Twitter) by achieving a weighted F1 score of 0.4189, which is higher than the random baseline. However, this dataset failed to score at par with the English dataset mainly due to the lack of good quality sentiment lexicon resource in Hindi.

Performance of Emoti-KATE on this dataset, for three different variations of input vectors is presented in Table 2. We have also reported a class wise performance analysis for the best performance (X_3) of our system in Table 5. A heatmap representing the confusion matrix of this run is presented in Fig. 4.

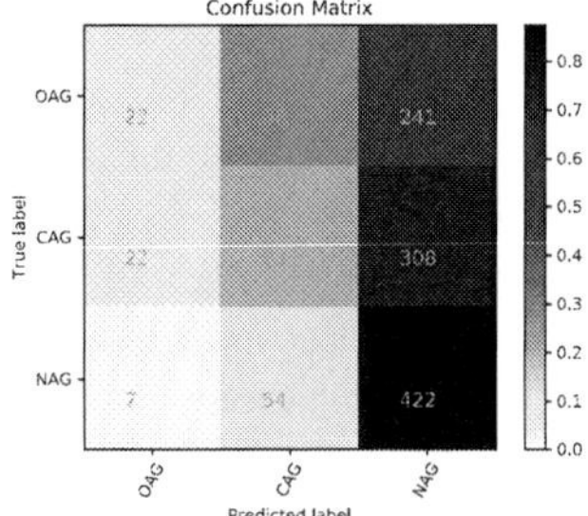

Class	Precision	Recall
OAG	43.137	6.094
CAG	35.319	20.097
NAG	43.46	87.371

Table 4: **Class-wise distribution of Precision and Recall for the best result observed** (X_1)

Figure 3: **Heatmap of the confusion matrix for our best result observed** (X_1)

Class	Precision	Recall
OAG	46.988	32.32
CAG	46.379	72.881
NAG	31.944	11.795

Table 5: **Class-wise distribution of Precision and Recall for the best result observed** (X_3)

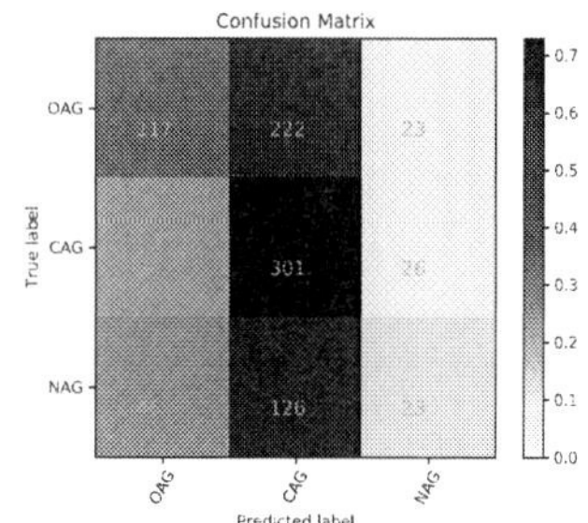

Figure 4: **Heatmap of the confusion matrix for our best result observed** (X_3)

4.4 Results on the Hindi-Social Media dataset

Similar to English-Social Media dataset, there is a lot of scope to improve the performance of our system on the Hindi-Social Media dataset. We observed that unlike the English dataset, the inclusion of the 'hashtag' analyzer module did not improve the performance of this particular dataset. This is because (1) 'hashtags' only consisted about 10 to 30 percent of the entire text on average which was not enough to offset the performance for the entire text content, and (2) the 'hashtag' segmentation module did not leverage a code mixed corpus to generate all possible unique segmentations for this dataset. Training Emoti-KATE on sufficiently large code mixed corpus for 'hashtag' analysis as well as feature vector generation mark some of the most significant future scopes of research. Performance of our system on this dataset, for three different variations of input vectors is presented in Table 2. Similar to the rest of the datasets, We have reported a class wise performance analysis for the best performance (X_2) of our system in Table 6 for this dataset also. A heatmap representing the confusion matrix of this run is also presented in Fig. 5. We observe that our system is biased towards the class CAG in Hindi datasets. Interestingly, highest recall values were obtained for the class CAG for both of the Hindi datasets in our experimental setup.

We have compared our performance against two traditional approaches, a word2vec-based input vector, and an LDA-based input vector. We noticed an average improvement of 13.62% and 16.25% respectively for Word2vec and LDA for all of our training datasets. To investigate the contribution of the competitive hidden layer for the aggression detection task, we have also compared our performance against a traditional variational autoencoder. We observed an average improvement of 19.47% across all datasets. This boost in performance stems from the removal of redundant, confounding contributions made by some of the hidden nodes which were removed by the competitive hidden layer. The differences between output vectors reconstructed by a traditional autoencoder and Emoti-KATE has been illustrated

Class	Precision	Recall
OAG	37.586	23.747
CAG	33.424	64.829
NAG	32.727	15.254

Table 6: **Class-wise distribution of Precision and Recall for the best result observed** (X_2)

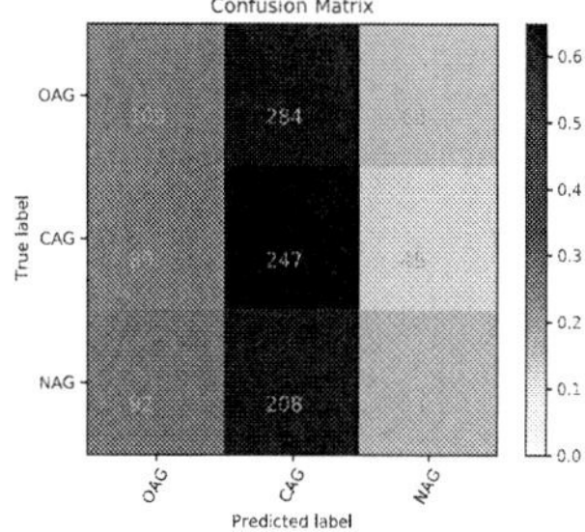

Figure 5: **Heatmap of the confusion matrix for our best result observed** (X_2)

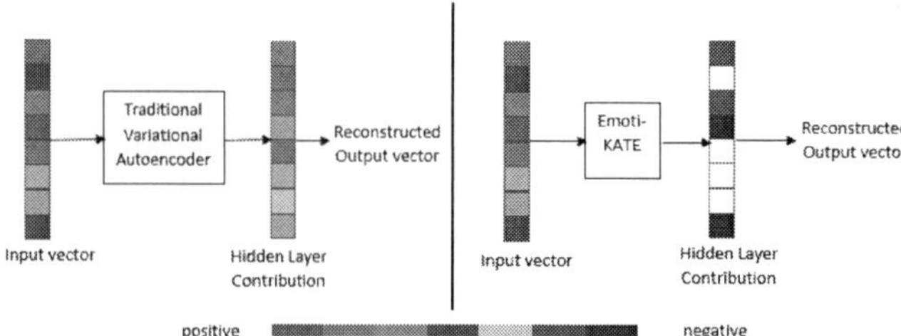

Figure 6: **An illustration of the differences between reconstructed output vectors by a traditional Variational Autoencoder and Emoti-KATE**

in Fig. 6 for better understanding. Additionally, downstream effects of this competitive layer is more pronounced in our results due to the short length nature and contextual sparsity, often observed in social media texts.

It was observed that the system failed to identify a few aggressive sentences mainly due to the absence of a few words in our training vocabulary which contributed to the aggression score. To cite one example, our system predicted the sentence *"Saala darpok. When he comes to south he comes with full security. He makes early morning visit and runs away from backdoor :D"* to be 'NAG', while the correct classification is 'CAG'. For English texts, we trained our system with standard dictionary words and common english slangs, but code-mixed nature of dataset resulted in a decline in performance.

On the other hand, one can notice from the dataset specific precision-recall tables, that we achieved promising result in case of texts which are covertly aggressive, such as *"I have seen rajamouli and his brahman uncle cleaning toilet... and a dalit is head priest in tirupati...lol mahismati. .. this flim also brahmanwadi agenda...bahubali got poonool..99.99% PRAJA are shudra. .."* or *"Or hum ne 1971 se 2017 tak 90k se zeyada tumaray soldiers mar diye"*. Even though these sentences do not explicitly contain any word which can generally be tagged as aggressive, our system was able to detect the sense unlike the traditional autoencoder which tagged these as non-aggressive. While the traditional variational autoencoder failed to capture this category of texts successfully, the introduction of competitive hidden layer helped us achieve a better precision for 'CAG' tagged texts across all domains owing to the removal of loser neurons' contribution as shown in 6.

5 Conclusion

We have proposed an approach for aggression detection from social media text in this work. Using the feature vectors generated by Emoti-KATE, a shallow winner-takes-all autoencoder, a 3-way classification was performed on the experimental datasets, classifying each data point as 'Overtly Aggressive' (OAG), or 'Covertly Aggressive' (CAG) or 'Non-aggressive' (NAG). One of the main challenges of this task was identifying Covertly Aggressive texts. We observed that distinguishing CAG from the rest of the categories (especially NAG) is a difficult task. Handling code switch and transliteration in the Hindi datasets as well as presence of out-of-domain test data in the Social Media datasets made this task more challenging. Results show that our method is a little biased towards the class NAG for English datasets, and the class CAG for the Hindi ones. We also observed that NAG and CAG classes formed the largest set of accurately[6] classified categories in English and Hindi datasets respectively. Although we have achieved promising results for the English datasets, the performance on Hindi datasets can be significantly improved in future works. Using appropriate Hindi corpus for sentiment scoring, training our model on English-Hindi code-mixed data as well as readily available out-of-domain datasets may help achieve better performance than the present system. Additionally, instead of a shallow autoencoder like Emoti-KATE, investigating the performance of competitive stacked denoising autoencoders is also an exciting future endeavor.

---

[6]based on both precision and recall

References

Yu Chen and Mohammed J Zaki. 2017. Kate: K-competitive autoencoder for text. In *Proceedings of the 23rd ACM SIGKDD International Conference on Knowledge Discovery and Data Mining*, pages 85–94. ACM.

Maral Dadvar, Dolf Trieschnigg, Roeland Ordelman, and Franciska de Jong. 2013. Improving cyberbullying detection with user context. In *Advances in Information Retrieval*, pages 693–696. Springer.

Karthik Dinakar, Roi Reichart, and Henry Lieberman. 2011. Modeling the detection of textual cyberbullying. In *The Social Mobile Web*, pages 11–17.

Karl Moritz Hermann and Phil Blunsom. 2013. The role of syntax in vector space models of compositional semantics. In *Proceedings of the 51st Annual Meeting of the Association for Computational Linguistics (Volume 1: Long Papers)*, volume 1, pages 894–904.

Ritesh Kumar, Atul Kr. Ojha, Shervin Malmasi, and Marcos Zampieri. 2018a. Benchmarking Aggression Identification in Social Media. In *Proceedings of the First Workshop on Trolling, Aggression and Cyberbulling (TRAC)*, Santa Fe, USA.

Ritesh Kumar, Aishwarya N. Reganti, Akshit Bhatia, and Tushar Maheshwari. 2018b. Aggression-annotated Corpus of Hindi-English Code-mixed Data. In *Proceedings of the 11th Language Resources and Evaluation Conference (LREC)*, Miyazaki, Japan.

Jiwei Li, Minh-Thang Luong, and Dan Jurafsky. 2015. A hierarchical neural autoencoder for paragraphs and documents. *arXiv preprint arXiv:1506.01057*.

Alireza Makhzani and Brendan Frey. 2013. K-sparse autoencoders. *arXiv preprint arXiv:1312.5663*.

Shervin Malmasi and Marcos Zampieri. 2018. Challenges in Discriminating Profanity from Hate Speech. *Journal of Experimental & Theoretical Artificial Intelligence*, 30:1–16.

Mitchell P Marcus, Mary Ann Marcinkiewicz, and Beatrice Santorini. 1993. Building a large annotated corpus of english: The penn treebank. *Computational linguistics*, 19(2):313–330.

Yashar Mehdad and Joel Tetreault. 2016. Do characters abuse more than words? In *17th Annual Meeting of the Special Interest Group on Discourse and Dialogue*, pages 299–303, Los Angeles, CA, USA.

Vinita Nahar, Li Xue, and Pang ChaoyiXu. 2012. An effective approach for cyberbullying detection. In *Communications in Information Science and Management Engineering*.

Anna Schmidt and Michael Wiegand. 2017. A Survey on Hate Speech Detection Using Natural Language Processing. In *Proceedings of the Fifth International Workshop on Natural Language Processing for Social Media. Association for Computational Linguistics*, pages 1–10, Valencia, Spain.

Richard Socher, Eric H Huang, Jeffrey Pennin, Christopher D Manning, and Andrew Y Ng. 2011a. Dynamic pooling and unfolding recursive autoencoders for paraphrase detection. In *Advances in neural information processing systems*, pages 801–809.

Richard Socher, Jeffrey Pennington, Eric H Huang, Andrew Y Ng, and Christopher D Manning. 2011b. Semi-supervised recursive autoencoders for predicting sentiment distributions. In *Proceedings of the conference on empirical methods in natural language processing*, pages 151–161. Association for Computational Linguistics.

Pascal Vincent, Hugo Larochelle, Yoshua Bengio, and Pierre-Antoine Manzagol. 2008. Extracting and composing robust features with denoising autoencoders. In *Proceedings of the 25th international conference on Machine learning*, pages 1096–1103. ACM.

Jun-Ming Xu, Kwang-Sung Jun, Xiaojin Zhu, and Amy Bellmore. 2012. Learning from bullying traces in social media. In *Proceedings of the 2012 conference of the North American chapter of the association for computational linguistics: Human language technologies*, pages 656–666. Association for Computational Linguistics.

Zichao Yang, Zhiting Hu, Ruslan Salakhutdinov, and Taylor Berg-Kirkpatrick. 2017. Improved variational autoencoders for text modeling using dilated convolutions. *arXiv preprint arXiv:1702.08139*.

Rui Zhao and Kezhi Mao. 2017. Cyberbullying detection based on semantic-enhanced marginalized denoising auto-encoder. *IEEE Transactions on Affective Computing*, 8(3):328–339.

Aggression Detection in Social Media: Using Deep Neural Networks, Data Augmentation, and Pseudo Labeling

Segun Taofeek Aroyehun
CIC, Instituto Politécnico Nacional
Mexico City, Mexico
aroyehun.segun@gmail.com

Alexander Gelbukh
CIC, Instituto Politécnico Nacional
Mexico City, Mexico
www.gelbukh.com

Abstract

With the advent of the read-write web which facilitates social interactions in online spaces, the rise of anti-social behaviour in online spaces has attracted the attention of researchers. In this paper, we address the challenge of automatically identifying aggression in social media posts. Our team, *saroyehun*, participated in the English track of the Aggression Detection in Social Media Shared Task. On this task, we investigate the efficacy of deep neural network models of varying complexity. Our results reveal that deep neural network models require more data points to do better than an NBSVM linear baseline based on character n-grams. Our improved deep neural network models were trained on augmented data and pseudo labeled examples. Our LSTM classifier receives a weighted macro-F1 score of *0.6425* to rank *first* overall on the Facebook sub-task of the shared task. On the social media sub-task, our CNN-LSTM model records a weighted macro-F1 score of *0.5920* to place *third* overall.

1 Introduction

The read-write web has enabled user-generated content on several online platforms. A major part of these platforms is the social media websites. These websites facilitate social interactions by way of posting comments and replying to comments submitted by other users. As with offline interactions, interactions taking place online are subject to anti-social behaviours such as trolling, flaming, abuse, bullying, and hate speech. With globally increasing internet penetration, which has enabled unprecedented access to the web, the illusion of 'invisibility' by web users has given rise to growing anti-social behaviour in online spaces. Consequently, web users are exposed to mental, psychological, and emotional distress if such behaviour goes unchecked.

In an attempt to make the web more civil, the automatic detection of content that contains or could have the effect of abuse, aggression or hate speech on social media platforms has being an important task. However, most accessible (with publicly available datasets) studies on automatic hate speech detection has focused on Twitter. The shared task on aggression detection (Kumar et al., 2018a) aims to benchmark classifiers developed for the automatic identification aggression in social media platforms by making annotated data collected from Facebook available. The task is to develop a multi-class classifier that could make subtle distinction among texts that belong to one of three categories: overtly aggressive, non-aggressive and covertly aggressive.

Motivated by existing work that applies machine learning to the task of automatic hate speech detection, we investigate the effectiveness of models that rely on little or no feature engineering. The presence of noisy content such as misspellings, acronyms, code-mixing, and incorrect grammar in social media posts makes the extraction of linguistic features using Natural Language Processing (NLP) tools highly error-prone. As a result, we experimented with linear (NBSVM with n-grams) and deep learning models (CNN, LSTM, BiLSTM, and combinations thereof). The linear model serves as our baseline (hard to beat) while we refine our deep learning models for this task. We aim to examine (1) the relationship between model complexity and effectiveness and (2) the dataset requirements in order to accurately detect aggression in social media posts.

Proceedings of the First Workshop on Trolling, Aggression and Cyberbullying, pages 90–97
Santa Fe, USA, August 25, 2018.

In the rest of this paper, Section 2 outlines related work. Sections 3 and 4 present the data and our methodology respectively. The results of our experiments are in Section 5 and we conclude in Section 6.

2   Related Work

The task of aggression detection in social media can be considered as a document classification task. This task can also be sub-divided into binary classification or multi-class classification. In the context of detection of aggressiveness, the binary classification would imply the presence or absence of some anti-social phenomena such as abuse (Nobata et al., 2016) in a given example (abusive or not abusive). Whereas in the multi-class scenario, specific types of anti-social behaviour are of interest (Waseem et al., 2017) such as racism, sexism, hate speech, and bullying. It has been observed that contents which contain anti-social phenomena are rare in a collection of social media posts. This usually leads to imbalanced datasets where posts which lack the phenomena of interest are overwhelming. This problem is even more pronounced in the multi-class scenario which leads to difficulty in learning discriminative features by classifiers. In (Malmasi and Zampieri, 2018), it was concluded that subtle distinction between types of anti-social behaviour: profanity and hate speech is a difficult task for machine learning classifiers. By extension, it will be difficult to differentiate between overt and covert aggression. Also, (Davidson et al., 2017) submits that posts that does not contain explicit aggressive words are likely to be difficult to identify. This would be likely applicable to the covertly aggressive class in this study.

Acknowledging the cost of annotating data for hateful comments in social media, (Gao et al., 2017) proposed a system that leverages the availability of unlabeled data. Their result shows improvement over systems that rely only on manually annotated data. This approach is most related to our work.

The identification of aggression in social media is closely related to existing studies in hate speech, abuse, and cyberbullying detection. Methods used to tackle these tasks as supervised classification broadly falls into two. One approach is based on manual feature engineering. With the feature engineering approach, extracted features serve as input to classic machine learning algorithms such as naive bayes, logistic regression, support vector machines, and random forest (Schmidt and Wiegand, 2017; Malmasi and Zampieri, 2017). The other approach is based on deep neural networks that automatically learn features from input data. (Gambäck and Sikdar, 2017) employed convolutional neural networks to classify hate speech and (Zhang et al., 2018) used a combination of convolutional neural network and gated recurrent unit (GRU) for the same task.

Rather than rely only on the textual content of social media posts in identifying hate speech, (Qian et al., 2018; Founta et al., 2018) investigated the use of metadata about the users or the posts. However, the metadata may not be readily available from the social media platforms. In addition, this approach may breakdown where a social media platform allows anonymous posting.

3   Data

In this section, we describe the datasets used in this work and the data augmentation strategy. Also, the details of the pseudo labeling approach is presented.

Dataset   We used the annotated data provided by the task organizers. The details of the annotation procedure is in (Kumar et al., 2018b). The dataset consists of posts collected from Facebook. The posts are related to entities (organizations, individuals or issues) in India. The dataset covers both English and Hindi. We used the English part in this work. The dataset provides three high-level tagsets namely: covertly aggressive, non-aggressive, and overtly aggressive. Each post is annotated with one of these tagsets. The English dataset consists of 12000 training examples, 3001 development examples, 916 test examples from Facebook, and 1257 examples from an undisclosed social media platform. On the training set, the number of examples per class is unbalanced. The covertly aggressive class is approximately 34% of the training examples; non-aggressive class is approximately 42% of the training examples and overtly aggressive class is approximately 24% of the training examples. The minimum and maximum number of tokens on the training set are 1 and 1200 respectively. We observed that the training set contains redundant posts: different post ID but duplicate content.

Data Preprocessing   We used well-formed texts in our experiments. We lowercased all alphabetic characters. We removed punctuation, digits, URL, repeated characters, non-English characters, alphanumerics, and usernames. In addition, we decoded emoji(emoticons) into their text equivalents and transformed hashtags into their constituent tokens where possible. To address misspellings, we used a spell-checker.

Data Augmentation and Pseudo Labeling   A common technique to improve model generalization in computer vision is to enlarge the dataset using label-preserving transformation(s) (Simard et al., 2003). This is usually achieved via known invariant operations such as rotation and scaling of images in the training set. Inspired by this technique, we simulate transformations by translating each example to an intermediate language and back to English. We translated into four intermediate languages: French, Spanish, German, and Hindi. We observed marginal increase in model performance using the four languages. Machine translation is known to yield conceptually equivalent output in a target language. We used the Google Translate API for the translation. We rely on a weak notion of label-preserving transformation for text by translating the original training text to an intermediate language and backtranslate to English. We hypothesize that the translation into several intermediate languages will help diversify our augmented training set in terms of different lexical choice using each of the intermediate languages as a source language and English as the target language in the backtranslation phase. Even though the process of translation and backtranslation is error prone, this procedure increases the size of our training set by a factor of 5. The resulting augmented training set is highly interdependent. With this technique, our DNN models outperform the linear baseline model.

One of the test sets provided by the shared task organizers for evaluation is data collected from an undisclosed social media platform. In order to diversify our training examples, we used a related dataset collected from Twitter for hate speech detection which is publicly available [1]. There are two datasets with a total of 22075 tweets (subject to change based on availability on the Twitter platform). We hypothesize that the dataset contains the phenomenon we are interested in. So, we used the model with the highest performance on the development dataset to label the Twitter dataset. The examples with the pseudo labels were added to the original training dataset and our deep learning models were retrained.

4   Methodology

Our approach was to develop a baseline model and a number of deep neural network models. The models as well as our submissions are presented in this section.

Baseline Model   A support vector machine (SVM) model that uses naive bayes (NB) log-count ratio features (NBSVM) is proposed in (Wang and Manning, 2012). NBSVM demonstrates consistent performance across text classification tasks. We used the logistic regression classifier in place of the SVM. We consider this model a strong linear baseline. We implemented two variants of the NBSVM model. One based on word n-grams and the other based on character n-grams. We found the model based on character n-grams superior on the development dataset for aggression detection. The character n-grams NBSVM serves as our baseline based on which we compare our deep neural network models during our experiments.

Input Representation   The representation of inputs to the deep neural network models is the embedding layer. The embedding layer encode each word in the vocabulary used in the model. We experimented with different pre-trained word vectors for the embedding layer including word2vec, Glove, SSWE, and fastText. We observed that the coverage of the pre-trained embeddings are limited. FastText has the highest vocabulary coverage in our experiment (with about 5000 missing entires). Thus, instead of using a pre-trained word vector file to look up the vector representation for each word, we used the fastText pre-trained model (Mikolov et al., 2018) to infer the vector representation for each word in the vocabulary of our model. This allows us to use the sub-word level information to derive vector representation for words not in the vocabulary of the corpus (Wikipedia) on which the fastText model was pre-trained. This facility is especially important for social media posts which usually contains typos and

---

[1] https://github.com/ZeeraKW/hatespeech

abbreviations. In addition, we used a randomly initialized embedding which is trained with the network to learn task-specific word representation. So, the input representation to our deep neural network models is a concatenation of 300 dimensional word vectors derived from fastText model and a 50 dimensional task-specific word vector.

Deep Neural Network Models We experimented with seven deep learning models for aggression detection: CNN, LSTM, BiLSTM, CNN-LSTM, LSTM-CNN, CNN-BiLSTM, and BiLSTM-CNN. The models are of varying complexity, with the combination of BiLSTM and CNN: CNN-BiLSTM and BiLSTM-CNN being the most complex neural architecture. CNNs have being used for text classification (Kim, 2014). CNN is able to learn features from words or phrases in different positions in the text. LSTMs model long-term dependencies in text and has been found to be useful for text classification . BiLSTMs consists of two LSTMs. One encode information in a sequence in the forward direction and the other in the backward direction. The past and future information is available to the model in making classification decisions. CNNs and (Bi)LSTMs are complementary in their modeling capabilities. Each of CNNs and (Bi)LSTMs capture information at different scales. As such, we explored whether there could be potential improvements in combining multiple information at different scales for aggression detection. We explored passing the input representation into the CNN and feed the local features learnt by the CNN into the (Bi)LSTM in the CNN-(Bi)LSTM model. Conversely, we also passed the input representation into the (Bi)LSTM and fed the long-term features learnt by the (Bi)LSTM into the CNN in the (Bi)LSTM-CNN model. The representations learnt by the CNN, (Bi)LSTM, and combinations thereof serve as input to the fully-connected layer. The output of the fully-connected layer is a softmax output (probability) which indicates the chance of belonging to each of the three classes. The class with the highest probability is the predicted class.

In training our deep neural network models, we used the sparse categorical cross-entropy as our objective function. We chose the RMSprop optimizer to minimize the loss function through backpropagation within 5 epochs. We used feature dropout and earlystopping as regularization mechanisms to avoid overfitting. A spatial dropout (Tompson et al., 2015) probability of 0.2 was applied to the embedding layer.

Submissions Our team, 'saroyehun' submitted three systems for evaluation on the unseen test dataset. Our first submission is the predictions obtained from the LSTM model. This model was trained using the augmented dataset. The second submission uses the representations learnt by the CNN and LSTM in the CNN-LSTM set-up. This submission was trained on the larger training set consisting of augmented and pseudo labeled examples. In addition, we computed sentiment score for each example and used the score as an additional feature to the representations learnt by the CNN-LSTM layers before making predictions. The third submission is an ensemble of the predictions made by our deep neural network models trained on (1) augmented data and (2) combination of augmented and pseudo labeled data, and sentiment score for each post. The final predictions was obtained by majority voting.

System	F1 (weighted)	F1 (weighted)[+]	F1 (weighted)[++]
NBSVM	**0.5116**	0.5135	–
CNN	0.4989	0.5520	0.5741
LSTM	0.4940	**0.5679**	0.5561
BiLSTM	0.4714	0.5274	0.5776
CNN-LSTM	0.4702	0.5296	**0.5822**
LSTM-CNN	0.3679	0.5624	0.5729
CNN-BiLSTM	0.3839	0.5272	0.5573
BiLSTM-CNN	0.4836	0.5523	0.5440

Table 1: Weighted Macro-F1 Scores on the English Development set
[+]: Data Augmentation
[++]: Data Augmentation and Pseudo Labeling

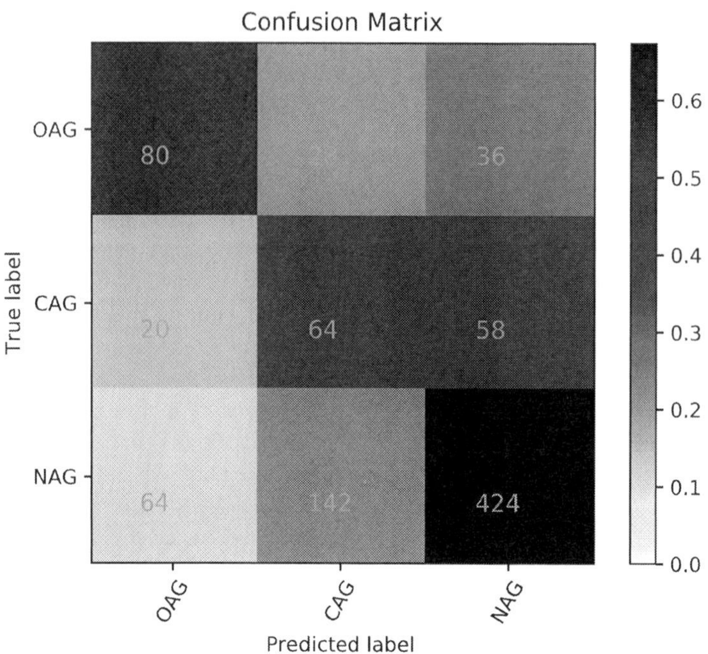

Figure 1: Confusion Matrix of the LSTM Predictions on the English (Facebook) Test Set

5   Results

This section shows the results obtained on the English development and the test datasets (Facebook and Social Media) in terms of weighted macro-F1 scores.

In Table 1, the performance of the baseline model (NBSVM) and the DNN models are presented. Using the training dataset as given for training, the NBSVM model achieves the highest performance. The table shows the impact of data augmentation and pseudo labeling on the models. It can be observed that using data augmentation, the performance gain on the NBSVM is very minimal (0.0019) compared to the DNN models where the maximum performance gain of 0.1433 is observed on the LSTM model. The combination of data augmentation and pseudo labeling results in slight performance improvement on the DNN models except for the LSTM model. Overall, data augmentation results in approximately 5% weighted macro-F1 improvement on the development set over the NBSVM baseline model. Also, the combination of data augmentation and pseudo labeling yields about 7% weighted macro-F1 gain over the linear baseline model. Pseudo labeling gives a marginal improvement of about 2%. The substantial gain in performance (about 5%) is from the introduction of data augmentation. These gains demonstrate the effectiveness of the data augmentation approach and complementarity of pseudo labeling in our approach. In addition, we experimented with and without the sentiment score as a feature. However, we did not observe any substantial gain in performance.

Table 2 shows the performance of the outputs of the three systems we submitted for evaluation on the Facebook test set. All our submissions are better than the random baseline score provided by the task organizers. All our systems exhibit comparable performance; they are all within 0.05 F1 score of each other. The LSTM model trained on the augmented training set achieved the best weighted macro-F1 score of **0.6425**. This score ranks **first** on the shared task which attracted **30** submissions. It is clear that a complex model (CNN-LSTM) does not necessarily give the best result. Figure 1 shows the confusion matrix for our best system, the LSTM model. From the confusion matrix, one can see that the most mistakes made by the model is on the non-aggressive class (NAG) in absolute terms; the model predicts covertly aggressive (CAG) when the true label is NAG. However, in relative terms, the most difficult

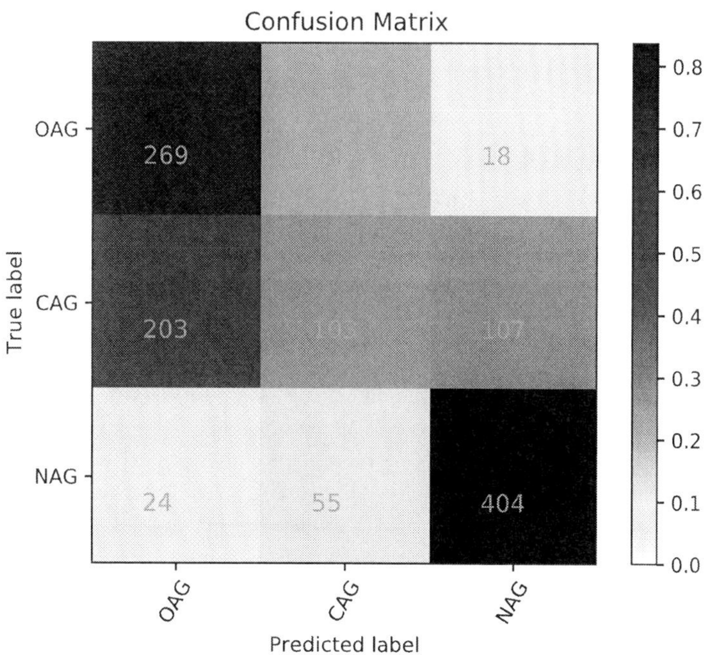

Figure 2: Confusion Matrix of the CNN-LSTM Predictions on the English (Social Media) Test Set

class for the model is the CAG. Here, the most mistakes result from the model predicting NAG where the true labels are CAG. In addition, one can see that the model performs best on the NAG class followed by the overtly aggressive class (OAG) and the least performance is recorded on the CAG class.

System	F1 (weighted)
Random Baseline	0.3535
LSTM	**0.6425**
CNN-LSTM	0.6058
Ensemble	0.5897

Table 2: Weighted Macro-F1 Scores on the English (Facebook) Test set

Table 3 outlines the scores achieved by our systems on the surprise test dataset collected from an unnamed social media platform. On this dataset, our CNN-LSTM model trained on the combination of the augmented training data, and pseudo labeled Twitter data as well as sentiment score as a feature received our best weighted macro-F1 score of **0.5920**. This score places the system on an overall ranking of **third** among 30 systems that participated in this track. In this case, a complex model aided by an out-of-domain data is superior. In figure 2, the confusion matrix gives us an insight into how the CNN-LSTM model performs on each class. It can be observed that the model made the most mistakes on the CAG class; predicting OAG when the true class is CAG. The model performs best on the NAG class followed by the OAG class and records the least performance on the CAG class.

Going by the performance trend observed in our results, the performance of our best model for each track seems to reflect the distribution of examples per class in the original training set. One can see that our models show better performance on classes with more training examples compared with classes having lesser training examples. Also, it is unsurprising that even though the OAG class has the least number of examples, the performance of our models on the OAG class is better than on the CAG class which has more examples. The performance of the OAG class validates a previous finding that a post which explicitly contains aggressive word(s) is easy to classify. Given our result, it is obvious that the

System	F1 (weighted)
Random Baseline	0.3477
LSTM	0.5400
CNN-LSTM	**0.5920**
Ensemble	0.5682

Table 3: Weighted Macro-F1 Scores on the English (Social Media) Test set

finding is true even when the category containing explicit word(s) is the minority class.

6 Conclusion

In this paper, we address the challenge of automatically detecting aggression in social media posts. We developed a linear baseline classifier using NBSVM with character n-grams as features. We conducted experiments with deep neural network (DNN) models of varying complexity ranging from CNN, LSTM, BiLSTM, CNN-LSTM, LSTM-CNN, CNN-BiLSTM to BiLSTM-CNN. In order to do better than our linear baseline using deep neural networks, we experimented with data augmentation, pseudo labeling, and sentiment score as a feature. We observed the greatest improvement from our data augmentation strategy. The improved DNN models were better than the linear baseline model on the development set. Hence, for this task the DNN models require more data points than a non-DNN model (in this case NBSVM). As our results show, a complex model does not necessarily bring performance improvement on this task. The classifier based on LSTM received the best weighted macro-F1 score on the English Facebook task. With a score of 0.6425 on the Facebook test set we rank first out of 30 submissions. The CNN-LSTM classifier receives a weighted macro-F1 score of 0.5920 on the social media test set. With this score, we achieved an overall ranking of third out of 30 teams that participated in the social media track.

The performance trend of our models on the three classes shows that for both tracks, our models performed best on the NAG class and least on the CAG class. This is consistent with previous work on the nature of implicit offensive language. The trend reflects the distribution of examples per class in the training set provided for this task. We see a better performance on classes with more training examples and lower performance otherwise. A natural avenue for future work is the investigation of approaches to improve performance on classes with minimal number of training examples.

Acknowledgement

The last author acknowledges the support of the Mexican government via CONACYT (SNI) and the Instituto Politécnico Nacional grant SIP-20181792.

References

Thomas Davidson, Dana Warmsley, Michael Macy, and Ingmar Weber. 2017. Automated Hate Speech Detection and the Problem of Offensive Language. In *Proceedings of ICWSM*.

Antigoni-Maria Founta, Despoina Chatzakou, Nicolas Kourtellis, Jeremy Blackburn, Athena Vakali, and Ilias Leontiadis. 2018. A unified deep learning architecture for abuse detection. *CoRR*, abs/1802.00385.

Björn Gambäck and Utpal Kumar Sikdar. 2017. Using convolutional neural networks to classify hate-speech. In *Proceedings of the First Workshop on Abusive Language Online*, pages 85–90.

Lei Gao, Alexis Kuppersmith, and Ruihong Huang. 2017. Recognizing explicit and implicit hate speech using a weakly supervised two-path bootstrapping approach. In *Proceedings of the Eighth International Joint Conference on Natural Language Processing (Volume 1: Long Papers)*, volume 1, pages 774–782, Taipei, Taiwan.

Yoon Kim. 2014. Convolutional neural networks for sentence classification. In *Proceedings of the 2014 Conference on Empirical Methods in Natural Language Processing (EMNLP)*, pages 1746–1751, Doha, Qatar.

Ritesh Kumar, Atul Kr. Ojha, Shervin Malmasi, and Marcos Zampieri. 2018a. Benchmarking Aggression Identification in Social Media. In *Proceedings of the First Workshop on Trolling, Aggression and Cyberbulling (TRAC)*, Santa Fe, USA.

Ritesh Kumar, Aishwarya N. Reganti, Akshit Bhatia, and Tushar Maheshwari. 2018b. Aggression-annotated Corpus of Hindi-English Code-mixed Data. In *Proceedings of the 11th Language Resources and Evaluation Conference (LREC)*, Miyazaki, Japan.

Shervin Malmasi and Marcos Zampieri. 2017. Detecting Hate Speech in Social Media. In *Proceedings of the International Conference Recent Advances in Natural Language Processing (RANLP)*, pages 467–472.

Shervin Malmasi and Marcos Zampieri. 2018. Challenges in Discriminating Profanity from Hate Speech. *Journal of Experimental & Theoretical Artificial Intelligence*, 30:1–16.

Tomas Mikolov, Edouard Grave, Piotr Bojanowski, Christian Puhrsch, and Armand Joulin. 2018. Advances in pre-training distributed word representations. In *Proceedings of the International Conference on Language Resources and Evaluation (LREC 2018)*.

Chikashi Nobata, Joel Tetreault, Achint Thomas, Yashar Mehdad, and Yi Chang. 2016. Abusive Language Detection in Online User Content. In *Proceedings of the 25th International Conference on World Wide Web*, pages 145–153. International World Wide Web Conferences Steering Committee.

Jing Qian, Mai ElSherief, Elizabeth M Belding, and William Yang Wang. 2018. Leveraging intra-user and inter-user representation learning for automated hate speech detection. *arXiv preprint arXiv:1804.03124*.

Anna Schmidt and Michael Wiegand. 2017. A Survey on Hate Speech Detection Using Natural Language Processing. In *Proceedings of the Fifth International Workshop on Natural Language Processing for Social Media. Association for Computational Linguistics*, pages 1–10, Valencia, Spain.

Patrice Y Simard, David Steinkraus, John C Platt, et al. 2003. Best practices for convolutional neural networks applied to visual document analysis. In *ICDAR*, volume 3, pages 958–962.

Jonathan Tompson, Ross Goroshin, Arjun Jain, Yann LeCun, and Christoph Bregler. 2015. Efficient object localization using convolutional networks. In *Proceedings of the IEEE Conference on Computer Vision and Pattern Recognition*, pages 648–656.

Sida Wang and Christopher D Manning. 2012. Baselines and bigrams: Simple, good sentiment and topic classification. In *Proceedings of the 50th Annual Meeting of the Association for Computational Linguistics: Short Papers-Volume 2*, pages 90–94. Association for Computational Linguistics.

Zeerak Waseem, Thomas Davidson, Dana Warmsley, and Ingmar Weber. 2017. Understanding Abuse: A Typology of Abusive Language Detection Subtasks. In *Proceedings of the First Workshop on Abusive Langauge Online*.

Ziqi Zhang, David Robinson, and Jonathan Tepper. 2018. Detecting Hate Speech on Twitter Using a Convolution-GRU Based Deep Neural Network. In *Lecture Notes in Computer Science*. Springer Verlag.

Identifying Aggression and Toxicity in Comments using Capsule Network

Saurabh Srivastava   **Prerna Khurana**   **Vartika Tewari**
TCS Research
{sriv.saurabh,prerna.khurana2,vartika.tewari}@tcs.com

Abstract

Aggression and related activities like trolling, hate speech etc. involve toxic comments in various forms. These are common scenarios in today's time and websites react by shutting down their comment sections. To tackle this, an algorithmic solution is preferred to human moderation which is slow and expensive. In this paper, we propose a single model capsule network with focal loss to achieve this task which is suitable for production environment. Our model achieves competitive results over other strong baseline methods, which show its effectiveness and that focal loss exhibits significant improvement in such cases where class imbalance is a regular issue. Additionally, we show that the problem of extensive data preprocessing, data augmentation can be tackled by capsule networks implicitly. We achieve an overall ROC AUC of 98.46 on Kaggle-toxic comment dataset and show that it beats other architectures by a good margin. As comments tend to be written in more than one language, and transliteration is a common problem, we further show that our model handles this effectively by applying our model on TRAC shared task dataset which contains comments in code-mixed Hindi-English.

1 Introduction

In today's time, with an ever increasing penetration of social media, news portals, blogs, QnA forums, and other websites that allow user interaction, users often end up inviting comments that are nasty, harrasing, insulting, toxic etc. This can have adverse effects on users, who then become victims of cyberbullying or online harrasment. An online survey carried out by the Pew Research Centre in 2017 states that 4 in 10 Americans have personally experienced online harrasment. Strikingly, 1 in 5 Americans have witnessed severe form of online harrasment like physical threats, stalking, sexual harrasment etc. There are several challenges associated with solving this kind of problem. First being the problem of class imbalance found in the dataset. Since such type of comments are sparse in nature, they introduce skewness in the dataset. There are several ways to handle this problem, however, we choose a more recent technique which modifies the standard cross entropy loss function known as Focal Loss (Lin et al., 2017). We will briefly describe how it helps in improving classifier performance. The next problem we want to address is that of data preprocessing. This is the most time consuming task and requires a good understanding of the data. However, we wish to minimise this process so as to have a good model with minimal preprocessing of the data.

Another frequently observed challenge is transliteration, which is often observed, especially, when we are working with text data from social networking websites. Users tend to speak in more than one language in the same statement. This leads to several *out of vocabulary* or OOV words for which the model would not have any word embedding. We use randomly initialised word embeddings in such a case and show how they can be trained during model training procedure such that it results in clusters of OOV words which have similar meaning in Hindi. We propose to tackle all the above described challenges using a single model as opposed to ensemble of several other models, which is a common practice in such competitive challenges. We also show that our proposed model can converge really quickly, hence the model can be trained in lesser time. This is essential when the model has to be deployed in a production environment where it requires retraining periodically.

98

Proceedings of the First Workshop on Trolling, Aggression and Cyberbullying, pages 98–105
Santa Fe, USA, August 25, 2018.

2   Related Work

Early works in automated detection of abusive language made use of basic machine learning like Tf-Idf (Yin et al., 2009), SVM (Warner and Hirschberg, 2012), Naive Bayes, random forests, or logistic regression over a bag-of-ngrams and achieved limited success. Newer approaches include solving problems using deep learning architectures like CNNs (Kim, 2014; Zhang et al., 2015; Conneau et al., 2017b; Park and Fung, 2017) which just focus on spatial patterns or LSTMs which treat text as sequences (Tai et al., 2015; Mousa and Schuller, 2017). Another popular approach completely ignores the order of words but focuses on their compositions as a collection, like probabilistic topic modeling (Blei et al., 2003; Mcauliffe and Blei, 2008) and Earth Movers Distance based modeling (Kusner et al., 2015; Ye et al., 2017).

Recently Capsule Network (Sabour et al., 2017) has been used in text classification (Zhao et al., 2018).It makes use of the dynamic routing process to alleviate the disturbance of some noise capsules which may contain background information such as stop words and words that are unrelated to specific categories and show that capsule networks achieves significant improvement over strong baseline methods. As we focus to solve the problem of toxic comments and cyberbullying, we are confronted with the issue of large class imbalance. We use focal loss (Lin et al., 2017) to tackle it as it prevents the vast number of easy negatives from overwhelming the detector during training. Also, in the online space people tend to talk using different languages in the same comment and often use transliteration. We show that our model is suitable for such data as well.

3   Capsule Net for Classification

Proposed Model: The model proposed in (Zhao et al., 2018) has been used for the experimentation with an inclusion of Focal Loss (Lin et al., 2017) as a loss function to address the class imbalance problem. In our experiments we have compared performances of CNNs and RNNs as feature extractors and found that sentence representation obtained from RNNs performs better than representations obtained after applying convolution operation, although CNNs tends to perform better on short texts. The model consists of four layers:

(i) ***Word Embedding Layer:*** We represent every comment x_i, as a sequence of one-hot encoding of its words, $x_i = (w_1, w_2, ...w_n)$ of length n_{max}, which is the maximum length of the comment, with zero padding. Such a sequence becomes the input to the embedding layer. To represent word tokens several ideas like sparse representation or dense representation (Collobert and Weston, 2008; Bengio et al., 2003) have been proposed.

(ii) ***Feature Extraction Layer:*** This layer has been used to extract either n-grams feature at different position of a sentence through different filters (CNNs) or long term temporal dependencies within the sentence (RNNs). We use RNNs as feature extractors in our final model.

(iii) ***Capsule Layer:*** The Capsule layer is primarily composed of two sub-layers *Primary Capsule Layer* and *Convolutional Capsule Layer*. The primary capsule layer is supposed to capture the instantiated parameters of the inputs, for example, in case of texts local order of words and their semantic representation. Suppose we have $\hat{e}$ number of feature extractors, then the input to the Primary capsule layer will be $Z \in \mathbb{R}^{n \times \hat{e}}$ (where n is the number of timesteps in RNNs). The primary capsules transform a scalar-output feature detector to vector-valued capsules to capture the instantiated features. Let d be the dimension of each capsule, then for each capsule $p_i \in \mathbb{R}^d$, where p denotes instantiated parameters set of a capsule (Sabour et al., 2017), we have $p_i = \mathbf{g}\left(W Z_i + \mathbf{b}\right)$, where Z_i is captured by RNNs in the feature extractor layer. Here, $\mathbf{g}$ is the nonlinear squash function which shrinks the small vectors to around 0 and large vectors around 1.

(iv) ***The Convolutional Capsule:*** The Conv layers capsules output a local grid of vectors to capsules in earlier layers using different transformation matrices for each capsule and grids member (Sabour et al., 2017).Capsule networks are trained using a dynamic routing algorithm that overlooks words that are not important or unrelated in the text, like stopwords and name mentions.

Model_Name	Kaggle-toxic comment classification (ROC-AUC)	TRAC - 1 (English-FB) (Weighted F1)	TRAC - 1 (English-TW) (Weighted F1)
CNN-multifilter	95.16	55.43	53.41
CNN-LSTM	96.85	62.20	47.68
Bi-directional LSTM with maxpool	97.35	59.79	51.146
FeedForward Attention Networks	97.42	57.43	55.49
Hierarchical ConvNets	97.95	51.38	50.43
Bi-LSTM, Logistic Regression	98.17	57.17	52.1
Bi-LSTM, xgboosted	98.19	57.33	52.31
Bi-LSTM with skip connections	98.20	61.78	51.98
Pre-trained LSTMs	98.25	60.18	58.7
CapsuleNet without Focal Loss	98.21	62.032	58.600
CapsuleNet with Focal Loss	**98.46**	**63.43**	**59.41**

Table 1: Comparison of several deep learning approaches with Capsule Net on the three datasets

Focal Loss: To handle the class imbalance problem, we have used Focal Loss which is given by the following formula :

$$FL(p_t) = -\alpha_t(1 - p_t)^\gamma \log(p_t), \text{ where } p_t = \{ \begin{array}{ll} p & if \ y = 1 \\ 1 - p & else \end{array}$$

γ is the focusing parameter which smoothens the rate at which easy examples are down weighted and, α is the weight assigned to the rare class.

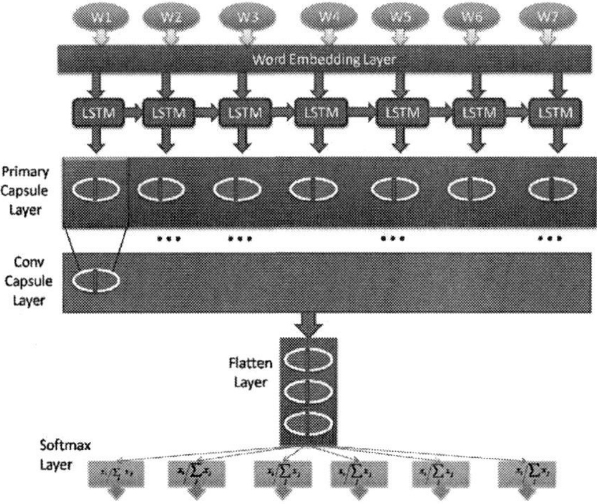

Figure 1: CapsNet with LSTMs as feature extractor

4 Experiments

In this section we attempt to describe different models that we have used for the classification process. We seek to answer the following questions: (1) Is combination of Capsules and focal loss the new apotheosis for toxic comment classification problems? (2) Can capsules solve the problem of OOV and transliteration implicitly ?

4.1 Datasets

4.1.1 Kaggle Toxic Comment Classification:

Recently, Kaggle hosted a competition named Toxic Comment Classification. This dataset has been contributed by Conversation AI, which is a research initiative founded by Jigsaw and Google. The task was comprised of calculating the log-likelihood of a sentence for the six classes, i.e., given a sentence calculate the probability of it belonging to six classes. The six different classes were toxic, severe toxic, obscene, threat, insult and identity hate.

4.1.2 TRAC dataset:

"First Shared Task on Aggression Identification" released a dataset for Aggression Identification. The task was to classify the comments into one of the three different classes Overtly Aggressive, Covertly Aggressive, and Non-aggressive. The train data was given in English and Hindi, where some of the comments in Hindi dataset were transliterated to English.

4.2 Data Preprocessing

For all our experiments, to show efficacy of our approach we kept the preprocessing as minimal as possible. Apart from word lowerization, tokenization, and punctuation removal we didn't perform any other activity.

4.3 Baseline Algorithms

We evaluate and compare our model with several strong baseline methods including: LSTM with Max-pool (Lai et al., 2015), Attention networks (Raffel and Ellis, 2015), Pre-trained LSTMs (Dai and Le, 2015), Hierarchical ConvNet (Conneau et al., 2017a), Bi-LSTM with Skip-connections, variation of CNN-LSTM (Wang et al., 2016), CNN-multifilter (Kim, 2014), Bi-LSTM with xgboost and logistic regression. We experiment with these models on three datasets. The models were first evaluated on Kaggle competition for Toxic Comment Classification. All the model parameters and attributes were decided on the basis of our best performing model, and were kept same for the rest of experimentations and datasets.

4.4 Model Training

For all our experiments we have used pre-trained embeddings for each word token obtained from (Joulin et al., 2016). We have also exploited (Pennington et al., 2014), (Mikolov et al., 2013), random and manually trained embeddings for initialization. After experimentation, fasttext embeddings with dimension of 300 were found to perform better than rest of the initialization process. In our experiments we observed that RMSProp (Tieleman and Hinton, 2012) and Adam (Kingma and Ba, 2014) as an optimizer works well for training RNNs and CNNs respectively and used this throughout. The learning rate was kept between [.1 and .001]. For CNNs, number of Kernels was chosen from the range [128, 256, 512] and the LSTM units were selected from the range [128, 256]. In all of our experiments with the proposed model only a single layer for feature extraction was used. Number of capsules was varied from [8, 10, 16], the vector length of 8 for each capsule was found to be the best, and the dropout values for RNNs were taken as per suggestions from (Zaremba et al., 2014). The α and γ values in focal loss were experimented for [1.5, 2, 2.5, 3, 3.5] and [.2, .25, .3] and finally $\alpha = 2$ and $\gamma = 0.25$ were taken.

5 Results and Discussions

The proposed CapsNet architecture was able to beat other strong baseline algorithms with reasonable difference in accuracies with minimal preprocessing. We demonstrated that using focal loss along with CapsNet gave us .25 raise in the ROC-AUC for Kaggle's toxic comment classification and 1.39 and .80 gain in F1 scores on TRAC shared task dataset in English, from Facebook and Twitter comments respectively. All of our experiments were performed on NVIDIA Quadro M1200 4096 MB GPU system with 32 GB RAM and Intel i7 processor. The model took almost 33 minutes for an epoch to train which was faster in comparison with other models, with exception to the models using CNNs as feature extractors. For example, the second best performing model, which uses Pre-trained LSTM embeddings takes more than a day for the autoencoder to train and further 39+ minutes for each epoch. Hence, we can say that our model is viable for production environment.

We have tested the capability of the architecture to handle the OOV words or misspelled words. For this we used TRAC shared dataset, initialised the word embeddings randomly and trained the model for classification process. Next, we enabled the embeddings to be changed during training process which is mentioned as dynamic channel in (Kim, 2014) to let the model learn new embeddings. After training, we took the weights of embedding layer and plotted these embeddings using Tensorboard (Abadi et al., 2015). From figure 2 we can see that the model is able to minimise the distance between the misspelled word

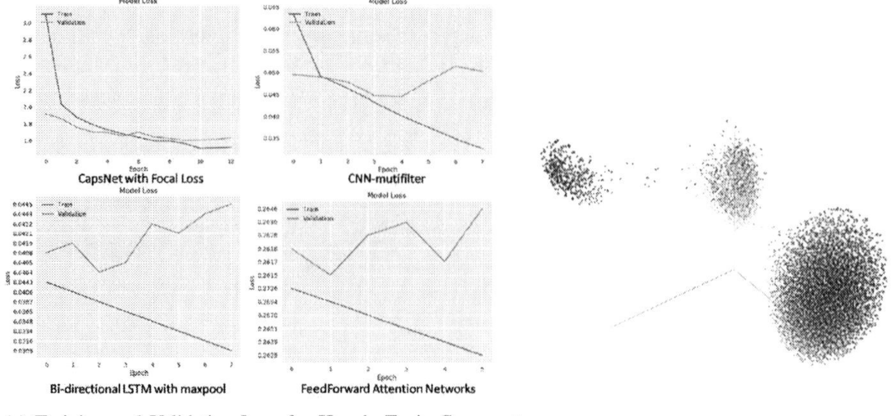

(a) Training and Validation Loss for Kaggle Toxic Comment Classification Dataset   (b) Clusters for word obtained after training

Figure 2

and is able to capture the relationship between transliterated words as in Table:2. We found that total of 3 clusters were formed after the experiment as shown in Fig:2b. We investigated these clusters and found that some of the highly used words in the comments belonged to certain classes. For example, one of the cluster contained more of neutral words, another cluster contained highly aggressive and abusive words, and the third cluster contained some toxic words along with place and country names related to one's origin which were used in some foul comments.

We show the capability of our model to tackle the problem of overfitting, as observed during training we see the model to have comparatively lower difference in training and validation loss than other models. Same can be seen from Fig:2a the loss margin difference doesn't change . We have shown that, not only our model has performed well on the classification task, it also has ability to generalise well and can learn good representation for word tokens.

NN to "politics"	NN to "bharat"	NN to "kut*e"(Hindi)
politic	bharatiya	chu**ya
politican	bhar	sa*le
politico	mahabharata	tere
politicize	bharti	g**d
politician	bhaskar	ma***rc**d

Table 2: Example of handling misspelt words and transliteration. NN : Nearest Neighbour

6   Conclusion and Future Work

In this work, we have proposed to automatically detect toxicity and aggression in comments, we show that with minimal preprocessing techniques we are able to achieve a good model performance and demonstrated how OOV words and semantic sense are learnt implicitly with random initialisation. We show the effectiveness of our proposed model against strong benchmark algorithms and that it outperforms others.

In this work, we did basic preprocessing of the data, however in future we intend to explore more preprocessing techniques for the dataset, like data augmentation using translation approaches and methods to deal with mispelled words. We further would examine the results of capsule net by visualising which words or phrases does the model correctly recognises for classification as opposed to benchmark algorithms. Also, we would like to examine the usage of focal loss with the rest of the baseline models.

References

Martín Abadi, Ashish Agarwal, Paul Barham, Eugene Brevdo, Zhifeng Chen, Craig Citro, Greg S. Corrado, Andy Davis, Jeffrey Dean, Matthieu Devin, Sanjay Ghemawat, Ian Goodfellow, Andrew Harp, Geoffrey Irving, Michael Isard, Yangqing Jia, Rafal Jozefowicz, Lukasz Kaiser, Manjunath Kudlur, Josh Levenberg, Dandelion Mané, Rajat Monga, Sherry Moore, Derek Murray, Chris Olah, Mike Schuster, Jonathon Shlens, Benoit Steiner, Ilya Sutskever, Kunal Talwar, Paul Tucker, Vincent Vanhoucke, Vijay Vasudevan, Fernanda Viégas, Oriol Vinyals, Pete Warden, Martin Wattenberg, Martin Wicke, Yuan Yu, and Xiaoqiang Zheng. 2015. TensorFlow: Large-scale machine learning on heterogeneous systems. Software available from tensorflow.org.

Yoshua Bengio, Réjean Ducharme, Pascal Vincent, and Christian Jauvin. 2003. A neural probabilistic language model. *Journal of machine learning research*, 3(Feb):1137–1155.

David M Blei, Andrew Y Ng, and Michael I Jordan. 2003. Latent dirichlet allocation. *Journal of machine Learning research*, 3(Jan):993–1022.

Ronan Collobert and Jason Weston. 2008. A unified architecture for natural language processing: Deep neural networks with multitask learning. In *Proceedings of the 25th international conference on Machine learning*, pages 160–167. ACM.

Alexis Conneau, Douwe Kiela, Holger Schwenk, Loic Barrault, and Antoine Bordes. 2017a. Supervised learning of universal sentence representations from natural language inference data. *arXiv preprint arXiv:1705.02364*.

Alexis Conneau, Holger Schwenk, Loïc Barrault, and Yann Lecun. 2017b. Very deep convolutional networks for text classification. In *Proceedings of the 15th Conference of the European Chapter of the Association for Computational Linguistics: Volume 1, Long Papers*, volume 1, pages 1107–1116.

Andrew M Dai and Quoc V Le. 2015. Semi-supervised sequence learning. In *Advances in Neural Information Processing Systems*, pages 3079–3087.

Armand Joulin, Edouard Grave, Piotr Bojanowski, and Tomas Mikolov. 2016. Bag of tricks for efficient text classification. *arXiv preprint arXiv:1607.01759*.

Yoon Kim. 2014. Convolutional neural networks for sentence classification. *arXiv preprint arXiv:1408.5882*.

Diederik P Kingma and Jimmy Ba. 2014. Adam: A method for stochastic optimization. *arXiv preprint arXiv:1412.6980*.

Matt Kusner, Yu Sun, Nicholas Kolkin, and Kilian Weinberger. 2015. From word embeddings to document distances. In *International Conference on Machine Learning*, pages 957–966.

Siwei Lai, Liheng Xu, Kang Liu, and Jun Zhao. 2015. Recurrent convolutional neural networks for text classification. In *AAAI*, volume 333, pages 2267–2273.

Tsung-Yi Lin, Priya Goyal, Ross B. Girshick, Kaiming He, and Piotr Dollár. 2017. Focal loss for dense object detection. In *IEEE International Conference on Computer Vision, ICCV 2017, Venice, Italy, October 22-29, 2017*, pages 2999–3007.

Jon D Mcauliffe and David M Blei. 2008. Supervised topic models. In *Advances in neural information processing systems*, pages 121–128.

Tomas Mikolov, Ilya Sutskever, Kai Chen, Greg S Corrado, and Jeff Dean. 2013. Distributed representations of words and phrases and their compositionality. In *Advances in neural information processing systems*.

Amr Mousa and Björn Schuller. 2017. Contextual bidirectional long short-term memory recurrent neural network language models: A generative approach to sentiment analysis. In *Proceedings of the 15th Conference of the European Chapter of the Association for Computational Linguistics: Volume 1, Long Papers*, volume 1, pages 1023–1032.

Ji Ho Park and Pascale Fung. 2017. One-step and two-step classification for abusive language detection on twitter. *arXiv preprint arXiv:1706.01206*.

Jeffrey Pennington, Richard Socher, and Christopher Manning. 2014. Global vectors for word representation. In *Empirical Methods in Natural Language Processing*, EMNLP.

Colin Raffel and Daniel PW Ellis. 2015. Feed-forward networks with attention can solve some long-term memory problems. *arXiv preprint arXiv:1512.08756*.

Sara Sabour, Nicholas Frosst, and Geoffrey E Hinton. 2017. Dynamic routing between capsules. In I. Guyon, U. V. Luxburg, S. Bengio, H. Wallach, R. Fergus, S. Vishwanathan, and R. Garnett, editors, *Advances in Neural Information Processing Systems 30*, pages 3856–3866. Curran Associates, Inc.

Kai Sheng Tai, Richard Socher, and Christopher D Manning. 2015. Improved semantic representations from tree-structured long short-term memory networks. *arXiv preprint arXiv:1503.00075*.

Tijmen Tieleman and Geoffrey Hinton. 2012. Lecture 6.5-rmsprop: Divide the gradient by a running average of its recent magnitude. *COURSERA: Neural networks for machine learning*, 4(2):26–31.

Xingyou Wang, Weijie Jiang, and Zhiyong Luo. 2016. Combination of convolutional and recurrent neural network for sentiment analysis of short texts. In *Proceedings of COLING 2016, the 26th International Conference on Computational Linguistics: Technical Papers*, pages 2428–2437.

William Warner and Julia Hirschberg. 2012. Detecting hate speech on the world wide web. In *Proceedings of the Second Workshop on Language in Social Media*, LSM '12. Association for Computational Linguistics.

Ellery Wulczyn, Nithum Thain, and Lucas Dixon. 2017. Ex machina: Personal attacks seen at scale. In *Proceedings of the 26th International Conference on World Wide Web*, pages 1391–1399. International World Wide Web Conferences Steering Committee.

Jianbo Ye, Yanran Li, Zhaohui Wu, James Z Wang, Wenjie Li, and Jia Li. 2017. Determining gains acquired from word embedding quantitatively using discrete distribution clustering. In *Proceedings of the 55th Annual Meeting of the Association for Computational Linguistics (Volume 1: Long Papers)*, volume 1, pages 1847–1856.

Dawei Yin, Brian D. Davison, Zhenzhen Xue, Liangjie Hong, April Kontostathis, and Lynne Edwards. 2009. Detection of harassment on web 2.0.

Wenpeng Yin, Katharina Kann, Mo Yu, and Hinrich Schütze. 2017. Comparative study of cnn and rnn for natural language processing. *arXiv preprint arXiv:1702.01923*.

Wojciech Zaremba, Ilya Sutskever, and Oriol Vinyals. 2014. Recurrent neural network regularization. *arXiv preprint arXiv:1409.2329*.

Xiang Zhang, Junbo Zhao, and Yann LeCun. 2015. Character-level convolutional networks for text classification. In *Advances in neural information processing systems*, pages 649–657.

Wei Zhao, Jianbo Ye, Min Yang, Zeyang Lei, Suofei Zhang, and Zhou Zhao. 2018. Investigating capsule networks with dynamic routing for text classification. *arXiv preprint arXiv:1804.00538*.

A   Baseline Algorithm Descriptions

A.1   CNN Multifiter

The idea of applying CNNs for text classification was proposed in (Kim, 2014), where authors applied filters of different length to extract N-gram features from text. The authors tried static and dynamic embedding channels and concluded that the model with combination of both outperformed others. For our setting we found that filters of length [2, 3, 4] have outperformed other filter sizes, we tried various combinations from range [2, 5]. For activations we used Leaky ReLU, and performed Batch Normalization to stablize the data.

A.2   CNN LSTM

A joint architecture of CNNs and RNNs were proposed in (Wang et al., 2016), where the authors tried combination of CNNs with different RNNs like GRUs and LSTMs. In our experiment, we again used Leaky ReLU for CNNs activations, filter size of 3 was fixed for the experiments to decide the dropout values and other hyperparameters tuning.

A.3   Bi-directional LSTM with maxpool

In (Lai et al., 2015), authors took Max Over Time on the RNN representation of the input. Their model RNN outperformed other models in 3 out of 4 datasets. In our experiments, we fixed LSTM units to be 51, and rest of the parameters were decided on the basis of validation-data experiments.

A.4 Hierarchical ConvNets

Convolutional Neural Networks are known to perform well on short texts (Yin et al., 2017), in (Conneau et al., 2017a) authors proposed to concatenate representation at different levels of input sentence. The model was claimed to capture hierarchical abstractions of the input sentence. For our experiments, we fixed 128 kernels of size 2, 3, 4, 4 at 4 different levels. These values were decided after the experiments with different number of kernels and their sizes.

A.5 Bi-LSTMS with skip connections

In one of our experiments, the summary vector obtained from LSTMs was concatenated with the vector obtained after appying Max Over Time on the hidden state representation of the input. The intuition behind this was that, by passing most relevant features along with summary of the input to the softmax layer may enhance the clasification process. From the experiments we obtained competetive results using this model.

A.6 Pre-trained LSTMs

In (Dai and Le, 2015), authors claimed that by pretraining LSTMs on some related task as Auto-Encoder or as a Language Model, could optimize the stability of the LSTMs training process. The authors reported improvenemt in error rates by good margin in many tasks like, text classification on 20 Newsgroup, IMDB etc. For our experiments we gathered many related datasets like all of Wikimedia datasets (Wulczyn et al., 2017), TRAC shared dataset, IMDB movie reviews dataset. An autoencoder was trained on these datasets and the LSTMs from the encoder part were extracted and used in the classifcation task.

Degree based Classification of Harmful Speech using Twitter Data

Sanjana Sharma
LTRC, KCIS
IIIT Hyderabad, India
sanjana.sharma
@research.iiit.ac.in

Saksham Agrawal
IIIT Hyderabad, India
saksham.agrawal
@research.iiit.ac.in

Manish Shrivastava
LTRC, KCIS
IIIT Hyderabad, India
m.shrivastava
@iiit.ac.in

Abstract

Harmful speech has various forms and it has been plaguing the social media in different ways. If we need to crackdown different degrees of hate speech and abusive behavior amongst it, the classification needs to be based on complex ramifications which needs to be defined and hold accountable for, other than racist, sexist or against some particular group and community. This paper primarily describes how we created an ontological classification of harmful speech based on degree of hateful intent, and used it to annotate twitter data accordingly. The key contribution of this paper is the new dataset of tweets we created based on ontological classes and degrees of harmful speech found in the text. We also propose supervised classification system for recognizing these respective harmful speech classes in the texts hence. This serves as a preliminary work to lay down foundation on defining different classes of harmful speech and subsequent work will be done in making it's automatic detection more robust and efficient.

1 Introduction

Hate, as a simple standalone word is easily understood by everyone. But as a concept, hate is vast, complex and has multiple themes and extensions. The issue of harmful speech has been widely debated and analyzed by scholars in multiple fields of knowledge. If youve been on social media lately, chances are good that you stumbled across something that might be classified as harmful speech online. Perhaps you would have read a tweet that used offensive language to describe its recipient, or maybe you saw a Facebook post that was designed to demean a particular group of people.

Modern artificial intelligence has proven useful in detecting patterns, whether that be in images for facial recognition or audio for speech regulation. But language is fluid, and as Mark Zuckerberg also recently noted in his testimony[1] before the US Congress that harmful speech can be heavily dependent on the context around the hateful words used and intent of the speaker. Some terms found in hate speech are slang, and hence not part of the common vernacular used to train AI. Other pressing issues remain determining different ways of expression of hate and the degree to which it affects people and communities, trying to make a fine line differentiating freedom of speech with hate speech, with making guidelines in defining hate speech (Sellars, 2016). Harmful speech has many manifestations, in speeches, prose, literature, real like conversations; and thus it does define it's own certain form in online discourse. It's important for us to understand the amplifications and extensions of harmful speech online, plaguing the social media primarily (Ashar et al., 2016).

Twitter is also actively in an ongoing process to enforce new guidelines related to how it handles hateful conduct and abusive behavior, by users, taking place on its platform. In addition to threatening violence or physical harm, they also want to look for accounts affiliated with certain respective groups that promote violence against citizens to move further in their hateful intentions. Any content that glorifies violence or the perpetrators of a violent act will also be incorporated in violation of Twitters new guidelines to combat hate speech. All these new developments in tackling hate speech in online discourse

[1] https://www.nytimes.com/2018/04/10/us/politics/mark-zuckerberg-testimony.html

Proceedings of the First Workshop on Trolling, Aggression and Cyberbullying, pages 106–112
Santa Fe, USA, August 25, 2018.

with a spectrum showcasing various degrees and ways (sarcasm, troll, profanity, violent threats etc) manifests a need to studying "Harmful speech online" in detail. This motivated us to develop a classification based on an ontological view of harmful speech, taking inspiration from philosophical and social point of view of hate speech, the intent of speakers involved, affiliation of recipient to an ideology/group or individuality , and deduce them into classes marking some difference in degree of hateful intent.

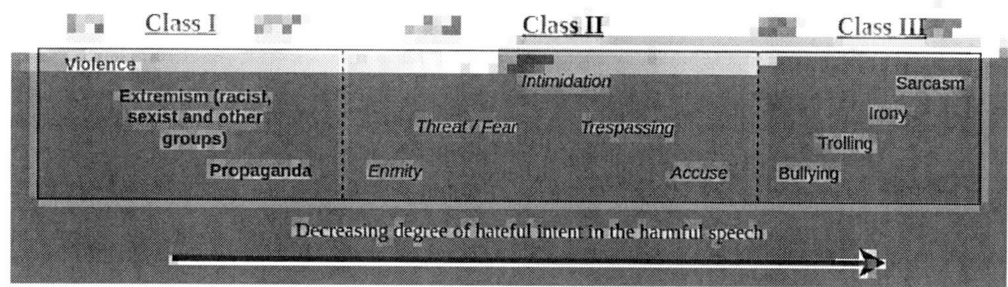

Figure 1: Spectrum showing degree based classes of harmful speech

2 Background and Related Work

Research on harmful speech has been happening for some time now, but the datasets which are publicly available only classify the text as offensive or not, with a small percentage identifying racist or sexist content. The manual way of filtering out harmful tweets is not scalable, hence it has motivated researchers to identify automated ways. The problem of defining a classification of a tweet and formulating context dependent bad language examples makes the task quite challenging, due to the inherent complexity of the natural language constructs different forms of hatred, different kinds of targets, different ways of representing the same meaning.

Combining psychology of hatred with context based classification of hateful speech can prove to reduce the entropy of subjectivity of detection of harmful speech. There are some publicly available datasets that are annotated with degree of hate speech, like [2] which includes toxic, severe toxic etc as labels. The Kaggle data has around 150k Tweets out of which 16k are toxic, which is around twice the hate speech present in the collected data. But it has classified the degree of hatred into only two distinct classes, severe toxic and toxic, without any granularity like we present in our spectrum classification. To the best of our knowledge, we are the first ones to work on conceptualizing, identifying and classifying ontological classes of harmful speech based on understanding degree of harmful content, intent of the speaker and how it affects people on social media.

(Hovy and Waseem, 2016) provided a Hate Speech dataset and the respective annotation procedure in which an initial manual search was conducted in Twitter in order to collect common slurs and terms pertaining to religious, sexual, gender, and ethnic minorities. The main researcher of the article, together with a gender studies student, manually annotated the dataset of 16,918 tweets in categories as racist, sexist and neither of the two. Another article

(Chang et al., 2016) describes a dataset where messages are classified in the general class abusive language, and within the subclasses hate speech, derogatory and profanity. The authors sampled 2,000 comments posted on Yahoo! Finance and News, and noticed that Fleisss Kappa value dropped to 0.213 when using the fine-grained three classes (hate speech, derogatory and profanity) as compared to 0.401 for binary classification (only with the class abusive language).

The majority of the studies that we found for hate speech were conducted for English. However, some other languages were considered. (Cabrera et al., 2017) is an example of a dataset collection and annotation in German, in the specific topic of hate speech against refugees. The results of this study pointed out that hate speech is a vague concept that requires definitions and guidelines in order

---

Degree	Some examples
Class I	1. "I fucking hate feminists and they should all be raped and burned to death. #sluts" 2. "All muslims are faggots & should be slaughtered like pigs." 3. "Now that Trump is president, I'm going to shoot you and all the blacks I can find."
Class II	1. "You're just an attention whore with no self esteem." 2. "You are so tan. Ugly dirty bitch. #LOL" 3. "Shove your opinion up your arse and dance like a monkey."
Class III	1. "I hope you all have a great weekend. Except you, Lisa Kudrow. #CantStandHer" 2. "If you find Benedict Cumberbatch attractive, I'm guessing you'd also quite enjoy staring directly at poop." 3. "Going to Africa. Hope I don't get AIDS. I am white. #JustKidding"

Table 1: List of examples for categories of Harmful Speech

for having reliable annotations. They also provided solutions for improving this classification task by annotating multiple labels for each tweet, which can be an advantage. Moreover, the authors also note that considering hate speech detection as a regression problem, instead of a binary classification task, can also improve the classifiers performance.

The most recent paper in hate speech dataset annotation is (Davidson et al., 2017). This paper presents data collected using the CrowdFlower platform using hate speech lexicon compiled by Hatebase.org in English. They were instructed that the presence of a particular word, despite being offensive, did not necessarily indicate a tweet is hate speech. They have used the majority decision in CrowdFlower for each tweet to assign a label (Hateful, Offensive or Neither). The intercoder-agreement score provided by CrowdFlower was 92% and a total percentage of only 5% of tweets were coded as hate speech by the majority of coders. Consistent with previous work, this study pointed out that certain terms are particularly useful for distinguishing between hate speech and offensive language. Besides, the results also illustrate how hate speech can be used in different ways: it can be directly sent to a person or group of people targeted; it can be espoused to nobody in particular; and it can be used in conversation between people.

The current Facebook Community Standards also segregates different types and targets of people using harmful speech, though our classification on the usage and basis of harmful speech is not inspired by the guidelines laid by them.

3 Categorization of Hate Speech

For classifying harmful speech with it's ontological implications, we looked at the philosophical point of view to understand the emotion and verb : hate. Karin Sternberg's theory of hate [3] observed hate as an emotion, a feeling; from an erudite perspective which inspired to form extended nominal categories of hatred. The harmful speech can be molded into a spectrum showing gradient of hate and harm, with some distinguishing characteristics to particular classes and their degrees. The classes have been defined on their decreasing degree of hateful intent from the speaker's perspective, with three classes (Class I, Class II and Class III) showcasing various categories of different types and examples of harmful speech found in social media (like extremism, threatening someone or trolling), as shown in figure 1. As we have devised a spectrum, not a discrete classification, the classes do have an overlapping in their definitions and examples, but in a linear way.

Some of the guidelines used to distinguish the classes are given below. Annotators were asked to keep them in mind along with common sense to classify the respective tweets. Table 1 shows some examples of the three classes thus defined, classified by the annotators subsequently.

Class I :

---

[3]http://www.robertjsternberg.com/hate/

- Incites violent actions beyond the speech itself.

- Is either public or directed at a particular group, mostly with no redeeming purpose. We considered hatred and violent behavior projected to a group to be of more degree than individual accusation and violence. This is an assumption made from the psychological point of view and by seeing various examples that adhere to it.

- The context makes it evident that the speaker wants to intend hurting sentiments of certain isms (extremism) for a violent response to be possible in return.

Class II :

- Cyber banter (accusing, threatening and using aggressive/provocative language for disagreeing etc.) and verbal dueling constitutes.

- The violent characteristic is less than the degree in which Class I operates, which hurts sentiments but not to the degree to invoke a violent response.

- Correlates between linguistic violence and non-linguistic/demographic intimidating and trespassing someone in an online space. Can be highly provocative when addressing an individual rather than some ideology or community/group.

Class III :

- Mildly provocative in nature, mostly given to an individual entity, not necessarily targeting a group or community .

- Uses more profane and filthy words not directed or having context from the speaker to the recipient to form a coherent remark. Context mainly revolves around trolling, ironic and sarcastic tone.

- Indirect or covert linguistically hurt sentiments, least degree of hateful intent shown in the categories.

4 Corpus Creation and Annotation

We constructed the corpus using the tweets posted online from Twitter. We had mined tweets with querying for profane slang words and harmful words that we compiled from searching synonyms and various parts of speech extensions of common words that can be used in hateful context. We scraped tweets with hashtags focused on three groups who are often the target of abuse: African Americans (black people), overweight people and women. Some examples of keywords and hashtags handled are : #IfMyDaughterBroughtHomeABlack, Nigger(s), White Trash, #IfIWereANazi or the tweets in response to #MakeAMovieAFatty. Certain hashtags and keywords from recent events surrounding politics, public protests, riots, etc., which have a good propensity for the presence of harmful speech were also used. Certain example of above case can be attributed to the #GamerGate fiasco, where trolls and haters decided to occupy and corrupt the #TakeBackTheTech and #ImagineAFeministInternet hashtags by posting thousands of anti-feminist and misogynistic tweets and memes. We also used resources from Hatebase.org[4] to narrow down slangs and hate speech used against the group who are a target of abuse. We retrieved a total of 15,438 tweets from Twitter in json format, which consists of information such as timestamp, URL, text, user, re-tweets, replies, full name, id and likes. A random sampling of the tweets containing respective hashtags and an extensive processing was carried out to remove same tweets (certain reposts of tweets). As a result of manual filtering, a dataset of **14,906** tweets was created.

---

[4] https://www.hatebase.org/

Categories	No. of tweets
Class I	2138
Class II	3924
Class III	3002
All	**9064**

Table 2: Twitter harmful speech dataset statistics

4.1 Annotation

For the annotation purpose, there were 3 annotators selected, who were very well versed with english language as well had a fair amount of experience with witnessing harmful speech online that we deal with on a day-to-day basis on social media.

Harmful Speech or Normal Speech : A lot of tweets in the dataset collected had occurrence of words which can be used in harmful perspective but didn't evoke any hateful context in the respective tweet at all. Hence, it was required to filter out such normal speech to get a rich dataset of harmful speech only. The initial task in hand was to annotate each tweet with one of the two tags (Harmful Speech or Normal Speech). Harmful speech was detected in **9064** tweets. Remaining 5842 tweets in the dataset comprised of normal speech, having no context of intent of harm at all, and were of no use for our experiment.

The annotators were provided with a definition along with a detailed guidelines of all the classes and respective categories and examples. Annotators were asked to think about the contextual implications of a tweet, more importantly from the speaker's intent perspective, rather than lexical based judgment of the text, as a syntactic extension of harmful words can not necessarily indicate a tweet inciting hate. It could very well be, plainly stating facts and truth with no intention of hurting sentiments of the recipients. For borderline cases and overlapping examples; sub categories inside the classes (propaganda, enmity, sarcasm etc) their definitions were used, along with measuring relative degree of hateful intent and context, to classify the tweet into a respective class (I, II and III). Annotation of the corpus was carried out as follows:

Categories of Harmful Speech : All the 9064 harmful tweets were then manually annotated according to the guidelines mentioned, for classes of harmful speech (Class I, Class II and Class III). The dataset then consisted of **2138** Class I, **3924** Class II and **3002** Class III harmful tweets, after successful annotation. The annotated dataset (consisting of tweet ids and respective tag of harmful class) with the classification system will be made available online later. All the dataset statistics are shown in Table 2 itself.

4.2 Inter Annotator Agreement

In order to validate the quality of annotation, subsequent iterations of annotation was carried out by, in total, 2 human annotators. We calculated the inter-annotator agreement between the two iterations of annotation using Cohens Kappa coefficient (Cohen, 1960). Kappa score was **0.689** which indicates that the quality of the annotation and presented schema is substantially effective, given how subjective it is to determine the new classification and tuning the degree of harmful content.

5 Pre-processing of the tweets

Given a tweet, we started by applying a light pre-processing procedure based on that reported in (**?**). A Twitter-python API[5] was used to pre process the tweets as described below :

1. **Removal of URLs and User Names:** All the URLs and links do not contribute towards any kind of sentiment in the text for the tweets. Also, the mentions which are directed to certain users hold no value, hence were also removed.

---

[5]https://pypi.python.org/pypi/tweet-preprocessor/0.4.0

Classifiers	Accuracy
Naive Bayes	73.42%
Support Vector Machines	71.71%
Random Forest	76.42%

Table 3: Accuracy of classification using respective classifiers

2. **Normalising Hashtags:** Furthermore, we also normalised hashtags into words, so #killthemuslims became kill the muslims. This is because such hashtags are often used to compose sentences, and we require full words instead, for our method to not miss on the context derived from hashtags too. We used dictionary based look up to split such hashtags, which were made of coherent and correct usage of words.

3. **Removal of Special Characters :** All the punctuation marks and special characters (: , ; & ! ? \) in a tweet are also removed.

6 Experiment and Results

In this section, we presented our machine learning models which are trained and tested on the respective dataset described in the previous sections. We performed experiments with three different classifiers for multi-class classification namely Support Vector Machines with linear function kernel, Naive Bayes method and Random Forest Classifier. For training our system classifier, we have used Scikit-learn (Blondel et al., 2011). In all the experiments, we carried out 10-fold cross validation. Table 3 describe the accuracy of each model used, in the case of Naive Bayes, Support vector machine and Random forest classifier respectively. The feature set used for SVM and Naive Bayes methods included tf-idf method, and for Random Forest classifier, we used bag of words. Random forest classifier performed the best out of the three and gave a highest accuracy of 76.42%, while the other two models also gave relevant accuracy with Naive Bayes with 73.42% and SVM with linear function kernel with 71.71%.

7 Conclusion and Future Work

Through this paper, we tried to get the ontological grasp of the hate expression and how it perpetuates it's existence in social media. Harmful speech online is a very subjective domain and has different structures in the social media outreach, from website comments sections to chat sessions in online games. In this paper, we presented an annotated corpus of tweets categorized over various degrees of hate, consisting of tweet ids and the corresponding annotations, in which we tried to give a viable ontological classification model to distinguish harmful speech. We also presented the supervised system used for detection of the class of harmful speech (Class I, Class II and Class III) in the twitter dataset, based on our linear classification skeleton of harmful speech. The corpus consists of 9064 harmful speech tweets annotated with all three classes (degrees) of harmful speech. Best accuracy of 76.42% was achieved when bag of words approach was used in the feature vector using Random Forest as the classification system.

As a part of future work, the supervised methods can be carried out on specific feature set like character n-grams, word n-grams, punctuation, negation words and hate lexicon which can give more insight in detailed account of accuracy for each method.

The class-based labeling of tweets makes the task in hand very one dimensional, it can be further improved. If the annotation is done by giving scores to each tweet based on degree of hateful intent and other designated characteristics of hate speech in general, the classification problem for automated harmful speech detection and recognition of respective degrees will be considered as a regression model (Davidson et al., 2017) as compared to a mere classification task to conceptualize linear degree of hateful intent of the text. Various deep learning methods can also be tried and tested on the respective classification to automate the process to some extent.

Our future work includes enlarging and enriching our datasets from social media outlets other than Twitter (example : Reddit) and to work on computationally automatic methods for classifying different forms of harmful speech with subsequent degrees with different methods and this framework a viable scale to distinguish different harmful speech online. All these major subsequent tasks makes this work defined as in-progress hence.

References

Amar Ashar, Robert Faris, Urs Gasser, and Daisy Joo. 2016. Understanding harmful speech online. *Berkman Klein Center Research Publication No. 2016-21.*

Mathieu Blondel, Vincent Dubourg, Alexandre Gramfort, Olivier Grisel, Vincent Michel, Fabian Pedregosa, Peter Prettenhofer, Bertrand Thirion, Gaël Varoquaux, Ron Weiss, and Others. 2011. Scikit-learn: Machine learning in python. *Journal of machine learning research*, 12(Oct):2825–2830.

Benjamin Cabrera, Guillermo Carbonell, Nils Kurowsky, Michael Rist, Bjrn Ross, and Michael Wojatzki. 2017. Measuring the reliability of hate speech annotations: The case of the european refugee crisis. In *Proceedings of NLP4CMC III: 3rd Workshop on Natural Language Processing for Computer-Mediated Communication (Bochum).*

Yi Chang, Yashar Mehdad, Chikashi Nobata, Joel Tetreault, and Achint Thomas. 2016. Abusive language detection in online user content. In *Proceedings of the 25th International Conference on World Wide Web*, pages 145–153. International World Wide Web Conferences Steering Committee.

Jacob Cohen. 1960. A coefficient of agreement for nominal scales. *Educational and Psychological Measurement*, 20(1):37–46.

Thomas Davidson, Michael W. Macy, Dana Warmsley, and Ingmar Weber. 2017. Automated hate speech detection and the problem of offensive language. *CoRR*, abs/1703.04009.

Dirk Hovy and Zeerak Waseem. 2016. Hateful symbols or hateful people? predictive features for hate speech detection on twitter. In *Proceedings of NAACL-HLT*, pages 88–93.

Andrew Sellars. 2016. Defining hate speech. *Berkman Klein Center Research Publication No. 2016-20.*

Aggressive language identification using word embeddings and sentiment features

Constantin Orăsan
Research Group in Computational Linguistics
University of Wolverhampton, UK
C.Orasan@wlv.ac.uk

Abstract

This paper describes our participation in the First Shared Task on Aggression Identification. The method proposed relies on machine learning to identify social media texts which contain aggression. The main features employed by our method are information extracted from word embeddings and the output of a sentiment analyser. Several machine learning methods and different combinations of features were tried. The official submissions used Support Vector Machines and Random Forests. The official evaluation showed that for texts similar to the ones in the training dataset Random Forests work best, whilst for texts which are different SVMs are a better choice. The evaluation also showed that despite its simplicity the method performs well when compared with more elaborated methods.

1 Introduction

Social media has become a normal medium of communication for people these days as it provides the convenience of sending messages fast from a variety of devices. Unfortunately, social networks also provide the means for distributing abusive and aggressive content. Given the amount of information generated every day on social media, it is not possible for humans to identify and remove such messages manually, instead it is necessary to employ automatic methods. In an attempt to boost the research in this area, the First Workshop on Trolling, Aggression and Cyberbullying[1] has organised the First Shared Task on Aggression Identification.[2] The purpose of this shared task was to encourage the development of methods capable of classifying messages from social media (in the case of this task Facebook and Twitter) into three categories *Overtly Aggressive* (OAG), *Covertly Aggressive* (CAG) and *Non-aggressive* (NAG). The task was organised for English and Hindi. For each of the languages, the organisers prepared a training dataset containing texts and comments from Facebook. Participants were able to test their systems on two datasets. The first one was a dataset which contained text from Facebook and therefore it was similar to the training set. The second dataset consisted of tweets and gave the opportunity to test the systems on a dataset which was quite different than the training data. The systems were evaluated using a weighted macro-averaged F-measure. A detailed description of the task, the data used and an overview of the results can be found in (Kumar et al., 2018a).

Recent years have seen an increase in the number of papers attempting to detect hate speech, offensive and abusive language. A high number of papers published in this area are from researchers who attempt to tackle the problem of cyberbullying (Dinakar et al., 2011; Xu et al., 2012; Dadvar et al., 2013). As is the case with many other fields in Natural Language Processing, the vast majority of the existing methods rely on machine learning. (Burnap and Williams, 2015) uses Support Vector Machines, Random Forests and a meta-classifier to distinguish between hateful and non-hateful messages. More recent papers focus on using Deep Learning for this task:(Gambäck and Sikdar, 2017) train several classifiers based on convolutional networks and (Zhang et al., 2018) combine convolutional and gated recurrent networks to detect hate speech in tweets. A survey of recent research in the field is presented in (Schmidt and Wiegand, 2017) and the current challenges are discussed in (Malmasi and Zampieri, 2018)

---

[1]https://sites.google.com/view/trac1/home
[2]https://sites.google.com/view/trac1/shared-task

Proceedings of the First Workshop on Trolling, Aggression and Cyberbullying, pages 113–119
Santa Fe, USA, August 25, 2018.

This paper presents a machine learning method which combines information from word embeddings, features derived from emoticos and information from a sentiment analyser to identify texts which contain aggression. The structure of the remainder of the paper is as follows: Section 2 describes the methodology used to train the machine learning methods and how the features were calculated. Section 3 presents the evaluation results, followed by conclusions in Section 4. The code corresponding to the research presented in this paper is available at `https://github.com/dinel/aggression_identification`.

2 Methodology

The approach used in this research relies on machine learning to distinguish between the three categories of texts used in this shared task. The features used to train our algorithm are presented in Section 2.1, followed by a discussion of the machine learning algorithms employed in Section 2.2. They were applied to the data set provided by the organisers. The data collection methods used to compile the dataset used for training, development and testing are described in (Kumar et al., 2018b).

2.1 Features used

The approach explored in this research relies on three sources of information for extracting the features corresponding to a text: word embeddings, emoticons and the sentiment expressed in the text. In order to extract these features, our pipeline relies at the preprocessing stage only on NLTK[3] to tokenise the texts. Analysis of the output of the tokeniser showed that it is not robust enough to deal with some of the data it had to process. This is particularly true in the case of Twitter data. Therefore, one way to improve the results reported in Section 3 could be to use a more accurate tokeniser. The reminder of this section describes the way each type of feature is determined.

2.1.1 Word embeddings

The main purpose of the method proposed here was to investigate to what extent the semantic information encoded by word embeddings can be used to identify texts that contain aggression. For this reason, we used GloVe vectors (Pennington et al., 2014) to extract the vector representation of words. For the experiments presented in this paper, we used the pretrained word vectors obtained from the Common Crawl corpus containing 840 billion tokens and 2.2 million vocabulary entries. Each word was represented using a vector with 300 elements.[4] We experimented with other versions of the word vectors which were trained on less data or had smaller dimensions, but they did not lead to better results. However, we did not experiment with word embeddings generated from Tweets. Given the significantly lower results obtained on the Social media data (see section 3) it would be interesting to train the system using these word embeddings and compare the results.

In order to obtain the embedding features associated with a text, we add all the vectors corresponding to words in the text and divide them by the number of words in the text. The words which are not present in the GloVe vectors are ignored and not used for weighting the overall vector.

Analysis of the data revealed that 12552 words from the training data and 3119 words from the development data do not appear in the GloVe vectors we used. In addition, 1499 words from the Facebook testing dataset and 3823 from the Twitter dataset are not present in the GloVe vectors. In most of the cases these words appear only once. The majority of these words are not English words or are badly tokenised words. Overall, the numbers reported above are small given the size of the data which makes us believe that the missing words had little influence on the performance of the system.

2.1.2 Emoticons

In addition to word vectors, the proposed method also uses the emoticons in the training data to determine an 'emoticon score' for each of the classes to be predicted. The assumption is that some emoticons are more likely to indicate a type of aggression or the lack of aggression than others. To this end, we use the training data to calculate the TF*IDF score for each of the emoticons with respect to each class. This

---

[3] http://nltk.org
[4] This file can be downloaded from `http://nlp.stanford.edu/data/glove.840B.300d.zip`

is achieved by calculating the frequency of each emoticon in a class and the number of classes in which the emoticon appears. After that, we apply a slightly modified TF*IDF formula to calculate the score where we consider that we have a total of four classes rather than three. In this way we do not end up with lots of emoticons with a score of zero. This was decided after initial experiments where the score was calculated considering three classes led to worse results. Table 1 presents the top 5 emoticons for each class as determined by our method. As can be seen in the table, some of the emoticons are highly ambiguous, with *:face_with_tears_of_joy:* appearing in top 5 of all three classes.

Class	CAG	NAG	OAG
1	:face_with_tears_of_joy:	:heart_suit:	:face_with_tears_of_joy:
2	:grinning_face:	:cross_mark:	:hatching_chick:
3	:clapping_hands:	:anger_symbol:	:cross_mark:
4	:smiling_face_with_horns:	:face_with_tears_of_joy:	:pouting_face:
5	:OK_hand:	:hushed_face:	:joker:

Table 1: Top emoticons for each class

For each new text we calculate three features, each corresponding to one of the classes to be predicted. The values of the features are the sum of the emoticons scores appearing in the text for the corresponding class. The values of these three features are normalised by the number of emoticons in the text.

The emoticons are converted to their corresponding strings description using *emoji* library.[5] This step was not really necessary this particular research, but was introduced in order to accommodate future extension of the proposed method in which we may try to group emoticons together on the basis of their meaning. One possible way of doing this is by using information from EmojiNet.[6]

2.1.3 Sentiment features

The third type of features used by our method are sentiment features as determined by SentiStrength[7] (Thelwall et al., 2010). In contrast with other methods for sentiment analysis which indicate whether a text is positive or negative, or give a number corresponding to rating, SentiStrength returns two scores between 1 and 5 indicating the amount of positive and negative sentiments in a text. The intuition behind including this feature is that texts containing aggression are more likely to be negative. These features were not used in all the runs.

2.2 Machine learning algorithms

The approach used to determine whether a text contains aggression or not relies on machine learning. Several machine learning methods were evaluated during the development stage of the competition and Support Vector Machines (Vapnik, 1995) and Random Forests (Breiman, 2001) proved to be the most appropriate for the task.

2.2.1 Support Vector Machines

Support Vector Machines (SVMs) are a class of supervised machine learning algorithms that can be used for both classification and regression, and proved very useful in NLP applications. When used as a classification method, as is the case in this research, SVMs learn from the training data the parameters of a hyperplane which separates the data in the best way. When data is not linearly separable, a kernel function is employed in order to project the data in a different space which may make the data linearly separable. There are several kernel functions available such as the radial basis function (RBF), sigmoid function and the polynomial function. Experiments carried out during the development stage showed that the best results are obtained using the RBF kernel.[8]

---

[5] https://pypi.org/project/emoji/

[6] http://emojinet.knoesis.org/

[7] http://sentistrength.wlv.ac.uk/

[8] https://en.wikipedia.org/wiki/Radial_basis_function_kernel

The accuracy of SVMs is influenced by the soft margin parameter C which determines the penalty of wrongly classifying an instance. In addition, the RBF kernel also has the γ parameter which is the inverse standard deviation of the RBF function. A grid search was performed in order to determine the best values of the C and γ parameters. The best results on the development dataset were obtained using $C = 2$ and $\gamma = 0.5$ when no sentiment features were used, and $C = 5$ and $\gamma = 0.5$ in the setting where the sentiment features were employed.

2.2.2 Random Forests

Random Forests classifiers are ensembles of decision trees trained on random splits of the training data and which are used together to classify new instances. Random Forests also proved useful in NLP largely due to their ability to avoid overfitting. In contrast to SVMs, random forests have fewer parameters to estimate. In the case of this research, a grid search was performed to determine the number of trees used and their maximum depth. The best results on the development data set were obtained when 160 trees were considered with a maximum depth of 10.

3 Results

We participated in the shared task with three systems in order to test the performance of different combinations of machine learning methods and sets of features. These are:

1. **SVM-no-sentiment**: in this setting we used SVM as a classifier and we did not include the sentiment features. The parameters used were $C = 2$ and $\gamma = 0.5$

2. **SVM-with-sentiment**: in this setting we used SVM as a classifier and we included the sentiment features. The parameters used were $C = 5$ and $\gamma = 0.5$

3. **RF-with-sentiment**: in this setting we used random forests as a classifier and we included the sentiment features. The parameters used were 160 for the number of trees and 10 for the maximum depth.

Tables 2 and 3 present the performance of the three systems on the unseen test data. The figures reported in the table are **F1 (weighted)**, the official evaluation metric, **Accuracy** (on the test data) and **Accuracy on dev**, which is the accuracy of the method on the development dataset and which was used as reference when comparing various method during the development phase. The best performing setting on the Facebook dataset (RF-with-sentiment) ranked 13th out of 30 participants, whilst the best on the Twitter dataset (SVM-with-sentiment) ranked 18th out of 30 systems.

As can be seen, for the Facebook dataset the best result is obtained by the Random Forest classifier, whereas for the Twitter data the best result is obtained by the SVM classifier. In both cases sentiment features are used. The performance of the three systems submitted is quite similar on the Facebook data. On the social media data, the performance of the system which uses random forests as a classifier is significantly lower than the other two. This is particularly surprising given that it led to the best results on the Facebook data and indicates that the system which uses random forests overfits to the domain and cannot be easily ported to a new domain.

System	F1 (weighted)	Accuracy	Accuracy on dev
Random Baseline	0.3535	-	-
SVM-no-sentiment	0.5717	0.5295	0.5768
SVM-with-sentiment	0.5672	0.5251	0.5591
RF-with-sentiment	**0.5830**	0.5579	0.5459

Table 2: Results for the English (Facebook) task.

Figures 1 and 2 present the confusion matrices for the best system. As can be seen, in the case of the Facebook data, the most problematic class to identify is OAG with an F-score of 0.2692, followed by CAG with an F-score of 0.3353. Figure 1 shows that a large number of OAG are misclassified as CAG,

System	F1 (weighted)	Accuracy	Accuracy on dev
Random Baseline	0.3477	-	-
SVM-no-sentiment	0.4956	0.5441	0.5768
SVM-with-sentiment	**0.5074**	0.5529	0.5591
RF-with-sentiment	0.3892	0.4749	0.5459

Table 3: Results for the English (Twitter) task.

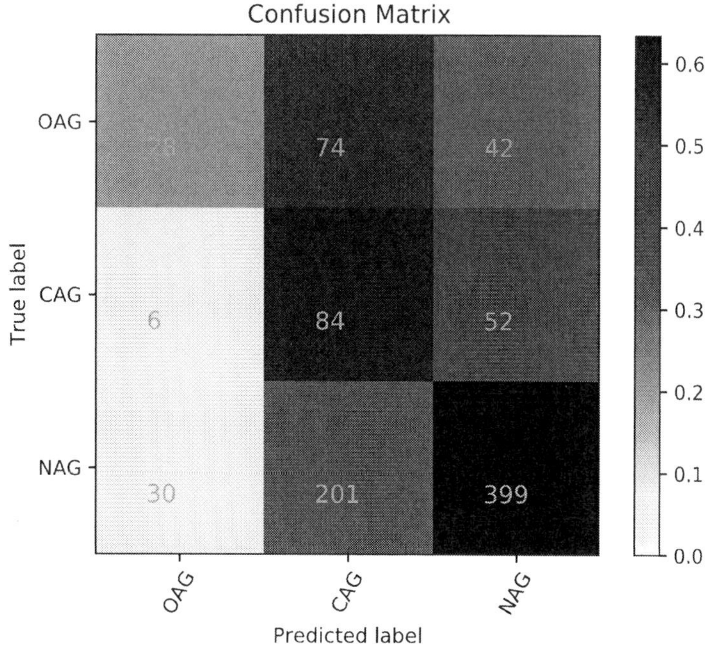

Figure 1: Confusion matrix for the SVM-with-sentiment system on the English (Facebook) task

and most of the misclassifications of CAG are as NAG. The latter is to be expected given the difficulties of identifying covert aggression. Despite the large number of NAG instances misclassified, this class has the highest f-score: 0.7106.

The picture is different for the Twitter data. The class with the lowest f-score is CAG (0.3247) followed by OAG (f-score 0.4424) and NAG (f-score 0.7122). Interestingly enough, the proposed method has over 97% recall on the NAG class, but only 56% precision. The same method had only 56% recall and 82% precision on the NAG class on the facebook data.

4 Conclusion

This paper has briefly presented our participation in the Aggression Identification Shared Task. Several systems were developed and the code corresponding to these systems was made available at `https://github.com/dinel/aggression_identification`. When testing on a dataset similar to the one used for training (i.e. Facebook data) the best system is one which uses Random Forests as a classifier. On a dataset which contains tweets, and therefore is different from the training data, the best classifier is the one which uses Support Vector Machines. The features used by the two systems are the same. In both cases the inclusion of features which capture the sentiment of the texts helped. The core of the methods is the use of features extracted from word embeddings. Despite their simplicity the methods performed well ranking 13th out of 30 participants on the Facebook dataset and 18th out of 30 systems on the Twitter dataset. Analysis of the pipeline used in this research revealed several avenues to

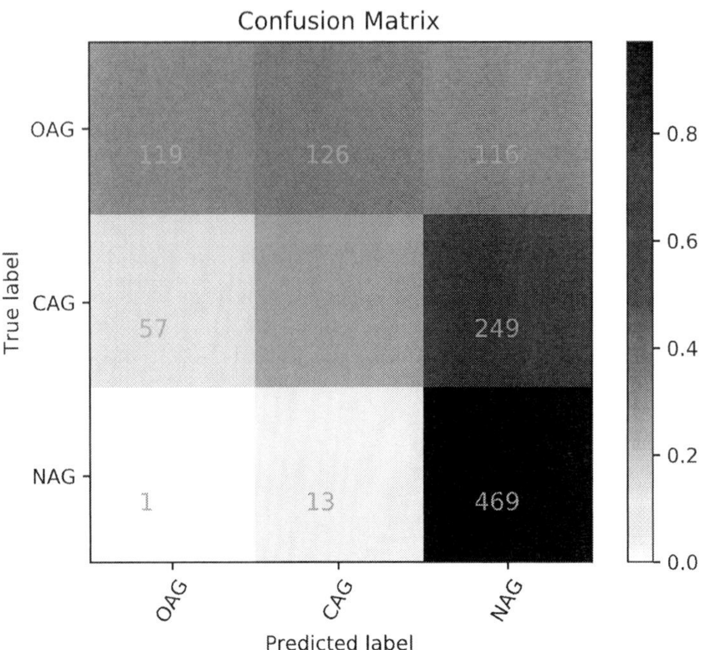

Figure 2: Confusion matrix for the SVM-with-sentiment system on the English (Twitter) task

improve its performance. This includes better tokenisation of the texts and use of domain specific word embeddings. However, the most likely way to improve significantly the results is to use more powerful learning architectures (e.g. use neural networks) and more informative features.

References

Leo Breiman. 2001. Random forests. *Machine Learning*, 45(1):5–32, October.

Pete Burnap and Matthew L Williams. 2015. Cyber hate speech on twitter: An application of machine classification and statistical modeling for policy and decision making. *Policy & Internet*, 7(2):223–242.

Maral Dadvar, Dolf Trieschnigg, Roeland Ordelman, and Franciska de Jong. 2013. Improving cyberbullying detection with user context. In *Advances in Information Retrieval*, pages 693–696. Springer.

Karthik Dinakar, Roi Reichart, and Henry Lieberman. 2011. Modeling the detection of textual cyberbullying. In *The Social Mobile Web*, pages 11–17.

Björn Gambäck and Utpal Kumar Sikdar. 2017. Using Convolutional Neural Networks to Classify Hate-speech. In *Proceedings of the First Workshop on Abusive Language Online*, pages 85–90.

Ritesh Kumar, Atul Kr. Ojha, Shervin Malmasi, and Marcos Zampieri. 2018a. Benchmarking Aggression Identification in Social Media. In *Proceedings of the First Workshop on Trolling, Aggression and Cyberbulling (TRAC)*, Santa Fe, USA.

Ritesh Kumar, Aishwarya N. Reganti, Akshit Bhatia, and Tushar Maheshwari. 2018b. Aggression-annotated Corpus of Hindi-English Code-mixed Data. In *Proceedings of the 11th Language Resources and Evaluation Conference (LREC)*, Miyazaki, Japan.

Shervin Malmasi and Marcos Zampieri. 2018. Challenges in Discriminating Profanity from Hate Speech. *Journal of Experimental & Theoretical Artificial Intelligence*, 30:1–16.

Jeffrey Pennington, Richard Socher, and Christopher D. Manning. 2014. Glove: Global vectors for word representation. In *Empirical Methods in Natural Language Processing (EMNLP)*, pages 1532–1543.

Anna Schmidt and Michael Wiegand. 2017. A Survey on Hate Speech Detection Using Natural Language Processing. In *Proceedings of the Fifth International Workshop on Natural Language Processing for Social Media. Association for Computational Linguistics*, pages 1–10, Valencia, Spain.

Mike Thelwall, Kevan Buckley, Georgios Paltoglou, Di Cai, and Arvid Kappas. 2010. Sentiment in short strength detection informal text. *Journal of the American Society for Information Science and Technology*, 61(12):2544–2558, December.

Vladimir N. Vapnik. 1995. *The Nature of Statistical Learning Theory*. Springer-Verlag, Berlin, Heidelberg.

Jun-Ming Xu, Kwang-Sung Jun, Xiaojin Zhu, and Amy Bellmore. 2012. Learning from bullying traces in social media. In *Proceedings of the 2012 conference of the North American chapter of the association for computational linguistics: Human language technologies*, pages 656–666. Association for Computational Linguistics.

Ziqi Zhang, David Robinson, and Jonathan Tepper. 2018. Detecting Hate Speech on Twitter Using a Convolution-GRU Based Deep Neural Network. In *Lecture Notes in Computer Science. ESWC 2018*, Heraklion, Greece.

Aggression Detection in Social Media using Deep Neural Networks

Sreekanth Madisetty
Department of CSE
IIT Hyderabad
Hyderabad, India
cs15resch11006@iith.ac.in

Maunendra Sankar Desarkar
Department of CSE
IIT Hyderabad
Hyderabad, India
maunendra@iith.ac.in

Abstract

With the rise of user-generated content in social media coupled with almost non-existent moderation in many such systems, aggressive contents have been observed to rise in such forums. In this paper, we work on the problem of aggression detection in social media. Aggression can sometimes be expressed directly or overtly or it can be hidden or covert in the text. On the other hand, most of the content in social media is non-aggressive in nature. We propose an ensemble based system to classify an input post into one of three classes, namely, *Overtly Aggressive*, *Covertly Aggressive*, and *Non-aggressive*. Our approach uses three deep learning methods, namely, Convolutional Neural Networks (CNN) with five layers (input, convolution, pooling, hidden, and output), Long Short Term Memory networks (LSTM), and Bi-directional Long Short Term Memory networks (Bi-LSTM). A majority voting based ensemble method is used to combine these classifiers (CNN, LSTM, and Bi-LSTM). We trained our method on Facebook comments dataset and tested on Facebook comments (in-domain) and other social media posts (cross-domain). Our system achieves the F1-score (weighted) of 0.604 for Facebook posts and 0.508 for social media posts.

1 Introduction

In recent years, a plethora of data is posted on the web. The data is in the form of text, images, audio, video, memes, etc. Facebook, Twitter are some of the popular social networking sites where a lot of data is posted. This data (tweets or posts) contains the opinions, feelings expressed by the users on various topics or incidents that are happening across the world or about their personal life. Along with a large increase of user-generated content in social networks, the amount of aggression related content is also increasing (Kumar et al., 2018b).

Aggression in social media is targeted to a particular person or group to damage the identity and lower their status and prestige (Culpeper, 2011). Aggression is often expressed in two ways: directly expressed or hidden in the posts. According to (Kumar et al., 2018a), aggression in social media can be broadly classified into three classes: *Overtly Aggressive (OAG)*, *Covertly Aggressive (CAG)*, and *Non-aggressive (NAG)*. Aggression is expressed directly in the overtly aggressive text. It can be expressed either through lexical features or lexical items or certain syntactic structure. Any text in which the aggression is not expressed directly is said to be covertly aggressive text. Aggression is hidden here. It is very hard to distinguish between overtly aggressive text and covertly aggressive text (Malmasi and Zampieri, 2018). In this paper, we develop a classifier for the problem of aggression detection in social media. Table 1 contains some examples of *Overtly Aggressive*, *Covertly Aggressive*, and *Non-aggressive* posts, from the dataset (Kumar et al., 2018b).

Aggression also contains hate speech. Hate speech is generally defined as any communication that defames a person or group on the basis of some characteristic such as color, gender, race, sexual orientation, ethnicity, nationality, religion, or other characteristic (Nockleby, 2000). We proposed a voting based ensemble classifier using deep learning methods in the ensemble for detecting the aggression in

Proceedings of the First Workshop on Trolling, Aggression and Cyberbullying, pages 120–127
Santa Fe, USA, August 25, 2018.

Table 1: Example Facebook posts showing different categories of aggression

Id	Text	Category
101	Pakistan is comprised of fake muslims who does not know the meaning of unity and imposes their thoughts on others.....all the rascals have gathered there...	Overtly Aggressive
102	Communist parties killed lacks of opponents in WB in 35 years ruling????? ?	Overtly Aggressive
103	For tht those hv more thn 2 flats or 2 land is legal rest has to surrender properties to govt	Covertly Aggressive
104	In government office implement the online transactions... also all parties should show off their account transaction for running their elections in RTI.	Covertly Aggressive
105	Hi Anuj brought divis to days at 710 what to do and Tata motor dvr 275 any target	Non-aggressive
106	please advice about Bank nifty & how the NPA will benefit for PSU Banks ?	Non-aggressive

social media posts. The deep learning methods used in the ensemble are CNN, LSTM, and Bi-LSTM. First, we apply CNN on the training data. Next, we apply LSTM and Bi-LSTM on the same training data. Finally, we use majority voting ensemble method to predict the final label for the given post.

Rest of the paper is organized as follows. Related literature for current work is described in Section 2. Next in Section 3, problem statement of our work is defined and details of the proposed method are presented. Experimental evaluation of the method is described in Section 4. We conclude the work by providing directions for future research in Section 5.

2   Related Work

In this section, we describe the literature work in the areas of aggression, hate speech, offensive, and abusive language detection. Hate speech and cyberbullying are often considered as same.

Detection of cyberbullying is modeled in (Dinakar et al., 2011). The authors found that cyberbullying in the text can be automatically detected by building topic-sensitive classifiers. Binary classifiers outperform multiclass classifiers. Bullying traces in social media is studied in (Xu et al., 2012). The authors formulated several NLP tasks with the bullying traces in social media. NLP tasks used here are text categorization, role labeling, sentiment analysis, and latent topic modeling. However, only a few baseline solutions were studied in the context of this problem. (Dadvar et al., 2013) proposed a method to improve the cyberbullying detection by taking user context into account. Here user context is the past (six months) comments of each user. Three types of features are used: content based features, cyberbullying features, and user based features. A method is developed to detect the tweets against blacks in (Kwok and Wang, 2013). The authors applied a simple Naive Bayes classifier with unigrams as features. They built a dataset with class labels: racist and non-racist. However, only unigrams may not be sufficient to differentiate the tweets of racist and non-racist.

An approach to detect hate speech with comment embeddings is developed in (Djuric et al., 2015). The authors have used two phase approach. In step 1, *paragraph2vec* is used to learn the embeddings of comments and words. In step 2, a binary classifier is applied on the learned embeddings. They have used Yahoo finance dataset with 56,280 hate speech comments and 895,456 clean comments. A dictionary-based approach to detect racism in Dutch social media is proposed in (Tulkens et al., 2016). The authors have used three dictionaries. The first dictionary was created by taking the racist terms from the training data. The second dictionary was created through automatic expansion using word2vec. The last dictionary was created by manually filtering incorrect expansions. A method is developed for abusive language detection in online user content in (Nobata et al., 2016). The authors have used the following features: N-gram features, linguistic features, syntactic features, distributional semantic

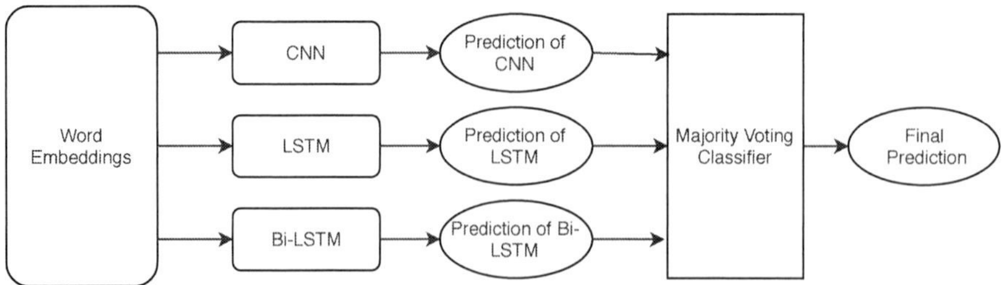

Figure 1: An overview of our proposed method.

features. They have used Vowpal Wabbits regression model [1]. Recently a survey on hate speech detection using natural language processing is done in (Schmidt and Wiegand, 2017). An automated method to detect hate speech and offensive language is developed in (Davidson et al., 2017). The authors have used the following features: TF-IDF (Unigram, Bigram, and Trigram), POS (Unigram, Bigram, and Trigram), Flesch-Kincaid Grade Level, Flesch Reading Ease scores, sentiment lexicon, and some content based features. They have used the classes: hate speech, only offensive language, and neither.

A method to detect abusive language on Arabic social media is proposed in (Mubarak et al., 2017). The authors have created a list of obscene words and hashtags. They also expand the list of obscene words using this classification. Obscene, offensive and clean are the classes used. A rule based approach to rephrase profanity in Chinese text is developed in (Su et al., 2017). The authors have framed 29 rephrasing rules. The proposed system will provide rephrased text with less offensive content. However, these rules are handcrafted. Convolutional Neural Networks are used to classify hate speech in (Gambäck and Sikdar, 2017). The authors have used four CNNs: character 4-grams, word vectors based on semantic information built using word2vec, randomly generated word vectors, and word vectors combined with characters.

A recent discussion on the challenges of identifying profanity vs. hate speech can be found in (Malmasi and Zampieri, 2018). The results demonstrated that it can be hard to distinguish between overt and covert aggression in social media.

3 Methodology and Data

In this section, we describe the methodology used for the problem of aggression detection in social media. First, we describe the CNN architecture used in our approach. Next, we describe the LSTM and Bi-LSTM architectures. Finally, we explain our voting based ensemble classifier used in this paper. An overview of our proposed method is shown in Figure 1.

3.1 Convolutional Neural Networks (CNN)

Recently, CNNs have been achieving excellent results in various NLP tasks. Our CNN model is inspired from (Kim, 2014). There are two channels in CNN architecture: static and non-static. In static channel, the word vectors are static and are not changed whereas in non-static channel, the word vectors are tuned according to the task. Word vectors are low dimensional dense representations of one hot vectors. These word vectors or word embeddings can be treated as universal feature extractors i.e., they can be applied to any task and achieve comparable performance.

Our CNN architecture contains five layers: Input layer, convolution layer, pooling layer, hidden dense layer, and output layer. Let $w_i \in \mathbb{R}^d$ be the d-dimensional word vector corresponding to ith word in the sentence. Let the sentence be comprised of sequence of tokens: $\{t_1, t_2, t_3, ... t_n\}$. The sentence vector can be obtained by the following equation.

$$w_{1:n} = w_1 \circ w_2 \circ w_3 ... \circ w_n \tag{1}$$

---

[1] https://github.com/JohnLangford/vowpal_wabbit

where $\circ$ is concatenation operator, w_i is the corresponding word vector of t_i. Sentence matrix of length $s \times d$ is given as input to the input layer, where s is the number of tokens in the sentence and d is the dimension size. As part of convolution operation, a filter ft is applied to a window of h words to produce a new feature. Similarly, all the convolution features are calculated for all the possible windows of h words. Multiple filters can also be used. After finding the convolution features, these are given as input to the pooling layer. The purpose of pooling layer is to get most important activation. In this architecture, we use max pooling for this purpose. Next, features which are obtained by applying max pooling are given as input to hidden dense layer and then finally softmax activation function is used to get the prediction for the given text or sentence. We also use dropout parameter to reduce the problem of overfitting.

3.2 Long Short Term Memory networks (LSTM)

In conventional neural networks, we assume that all inputs are independent of each other. However, this assumption may not be valid for several problems where the input is inherently sequential, or there are explicit dependencies between the input segments. For example, to predict a next word in a sentence, it is better to know the previous words in the sentence. Recurrent Neural Networks (RNN) can predict the next word in the sentence based on the previous words which come before it. RNNs work well if the context is short. If the context is long RNNs may not work properly because they can not remember the long dependencies and also because of *vanishing gradient* problem. To overcome the drawbacks of RNNs, Long Short Term Memory networks (LSTM) were introduced. These are special kind of RNNs which are capable of learning long-term dependencies and long contexts.

LSTMs have the capability to add or remove the information to the cell state C_t with the help of structured gates. The first component of LSTM is *forget gate*. The function of *forget gate* is to decide which information to remember and which information to forget. Sigmoid activation function is used in this layer. So, it will output 1 if the information needs to be remembered otherwise 0. It can be computed by looking at previous state h_{t-1} and current state x_t as follows.

$$f_t = \sigma(W_f.[h_{t-1}, x_t] + b_f) \tag{2}$$

where $[h_{t-1}, x_t]$ is the concatenated vector of h_{t-1} and x_t, b_f is the bias term, W_f is a weight vector. Next, LSTM choose what new information to be stored by the cell state. It can be done in two parts. In the first part, *input gate* decides what values to update.

$$i_t = \sigma(W_i.[h_{t-1}, x_t] + b_i) \tag{3}$$

In the second part, a vector of new candidate values $\tilde{C}_t$ that could be added to the cell state is generated by applying *tanh* activation function.

$$\tilde{C}_t = \sigma(W_C.[h_{t-1}, x_t] + b_C) \tag{4}$$

Now, the new cell state is computed by the following equation.

$$C_t = f_t * C_{t-1} + i_t * \tilde{C}_t \tag{5}$$

Final gate is *output gate*. It is computed as follows.

$$o_t = \sigma(W_o.[h_{t-1}, x_t] + b_o) \tag{6}$$

$$h_t = o_t * tanh(C_t) \tag{7}$$

Output is calculated by the o_t. h_t is calculated by applying *tanh* activation to the cell state C_t and by multiplying with o_t. This will decide which information should be passed to the next state.

Table 2: The number of instances in the aggression dataset

Aggression	Train	Dev	Test 1 (Facebook posts)	Test 2 (Social media posts)	All
Overtly Aggression (OAG)	2708	711	144	361	4532
Covertly Aggression (CAG)	4240	1057	142	413	5852
Non-aggressive (NAG)	5052	1233	630	483	6790
All	12000	3001	916	1257	17174

3.3 Bi-directional Long Short Term Memory networks (Bi-LSTM)

Bi-directional Long Short Term Memory networks (Bi-LSTM) use two LSTMs instead of one LSTM for training. The first LSTM is applied on the normal sentence and the second LSTM is applied on the reversed copy of the given input sentence. This can provide faster learning and additional context for better training. In all the above deep learning methods, we use Glove word embeddings (Pennington et al., 2014) with dimension size 200.

3.4 Voting Based Ensemble Classifier

There are different ensemble methods such as bootstrap aggregating (bagging), boosting, stacking, simple averaging, majority voting, etc. to combine the classifiers. In bagging ensemble method, each classifier is trained on random sub-samples which are drawn from the original dataset using bootstrap sampling method. In boosting, each classifier is trained on the same samples but the weights of the instances are adjusted according to the error of the last prediction. In stacking, the classifiers are combined using another machine learning algorithm. In simple averaging, the predictions of classifiers are averaged to get the final predictions. Finally, in majority voting ensemble method, for each test instance, the final prediction is the one which is predicted by the majority of classifiers.

Generally, the performance of the ensemble method is often better than the performances of individual methods in the ensemble. We use majority voting based ensemble method for our problem. The methods used in the ensemble are CNN, LSTM, and Bi-LSTM.

Data

The number of instances for each of the aggression categories in training and validation set are presented in Table 2. For testing, we use two datasets. One dataset is from Facebook posts with 916 instances and another one is from social media posts with 1257 instances. The data collection methods used to compile the dataset used in the task is described in Kumar et al. (2018b).

4 Results

In this section, we describe the results obtained by applying our proposed method.

Evaluation Metrics

Let tp denotes the true positives, fn denotes the false negatives, fp denotes the false positives, and tn denotes the true negatives. The following are the evaluation metrics used in this paper.

- *Precision*: Precision is computed as follows.

$$Precision(P) = \frac{tp}{tp + fp} \tag{8}$$

- *Recall*: Recall is computed as follows.

$$Recall(R) = \frac{tp}{tp + fn} \tag{9}$$

124

Table 3: Evaluation results of Facebook posts

Aggression	Precision	Recall	F1-score	#Samples
OAG	0.4938	0.5556	0.5229	144
CAG	0.2360	0.5634	0.3326	142
NAG	0.8602	0.5667	0.6833	630
Avg/Total	0.7059	0.5644	0.6037	916

Table 4: Evaluation results of Social Media posts

Aggression	Precision	Recall	F1-score	#Samples
OAG	0.5032	0.4294	0.4634	361
CAG	0.3953	0.4116	0.4033	413
NAG	0.6089	0.6542	0.6307	483
Avg/Total	0.5084	0.5099	0.5080	1257

- *F1-score*: F1-score (weighted) is calculated as follows.

$$F1\text{-}score = \frac{2PR}{P+R} \tag{10}$$

Weighted F1-score calculate metrics for each class label, and find their average, weighted by support (the number of true instances for each label).

The evaluation results with Facebook posts by applying our proposed method are shown in Table 3. It can be observed that precision, recall, and F1-score of *Non-aggressive* class are higher than other two classes. Similarly, for the *Covertly Aggressive* class all these metrics are lower than other classes. This is because aggression is hidden in *CAG* class posts and it is very difficult to identify that type of posts. For *CAG* class our proposed method is not doing well. However, overall precision, recall, and F1-score values are good.

The evaluation results with social media posts by applying our proposed method are shown in Table 4. The evaluation metrics are behaving in a similar manner as the results of applying our method to Facebook posts i.e., *NAG* class values are better and *CAG* class values are worse than remaining two classes. However, overall values are less compared to the results of Facebook posts. This is because, in the first case, the training and testing are done from the same domain (Facebook) whereas in the second case, the training is done on one domain (Facebook) and testing is done on other domain (other social networking site).

Table 5: Comparison of our proposed method results for Facebook posts.

System	F1 (weighted)
Random Baseline	0.3535
Proposed method	**0.6037**

Table 6: Comparison of our proposed method results for social media posts.

System	F1 (weighted)
Random Baseline	0.3477
Proposed method	**0.5080**

The comparison of our proposed method with random baseline method for Facebook posts is shown in Table 5. In random baseline method, class labels are assigned randomly to each post and F1-score is calculated. It can be observed that our proposed ensemble method outperforms the random baseline

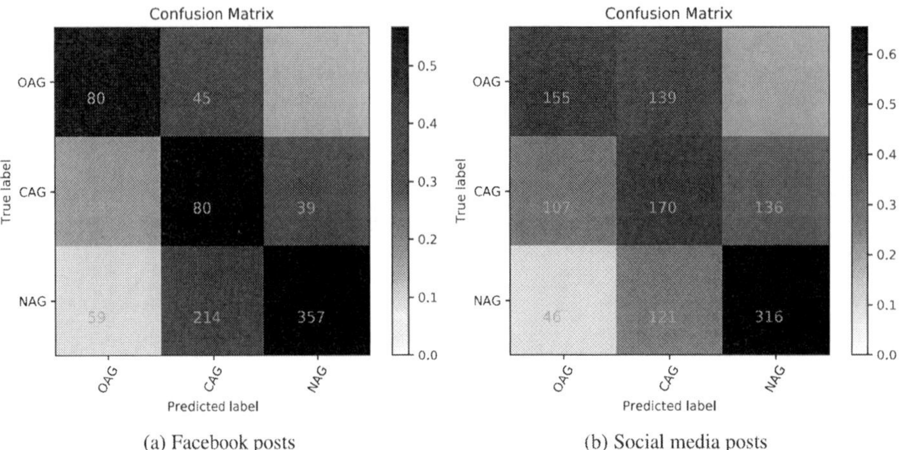

(a) Facebook posts   (b) Social media posts

Figure 2: Confusion matrix of the proposed ensemble model for the three classes. The heat map represents the fraction of correctly classified examples in each class. The raw numbers are also presented in each cell.

method. This shows the effectiveness of our proposed method. Similarly, the comparison of our proposed approach for social media posts is shown in Table 6. Our proposed approach is performing better than the random baseline method.

The confusion matrix of our proposed method for Facebook posts is shown in Figure 2a. This shows there is the maximum confusion between *NAG* and *CAG*, with *Non-aggressive* frequently being confused for *Covertly Aggressive* content. A considerable amount of *Non-aggressive* content is misclassified as being *Covertly Aggressive*. The *Non-aggressive* class achieves the best result, with a huge majority of instances being correctly classified. The confusion matrix of our proposed method for social media posts is shown in Figure 2b. This figure shows there is a large amount of confusion between *OAG* and *CAG*, with *Overtly Aggressive* being confused for *Covertly Aggressive*. Similarly, there is a substantial amount of confusion between *CAG* and *NAG*, with *Covertly Aggressive* content is being misclassified as *Non-aggressive* and vice-versa. In this case also, the *Non-aggressive* class achieves best result, with a large number of instances being correctly classified.

5   Conclusion

We developed an ensemble method for aggression detection in social media with three deep learning methods in the ensemble. Ensemble method performance is better than the performance of individual methods in the ensemble. We observed that our approach is achieving good performance on cross-domain also. Our proposed method outperforms the random baseline method. It is very difficult to differentiate between *Covertly Aggressive* posts and *Non-aggressive* posts in social media. There is a scope to improve our method because some of the classes (*CAG* and *OAG*) have lower precision values. For future work, we want to include both feature based and deep learning methods in the ensemble.

References

Jonathan Culpeper. 2011. *Impoliteness: Using language to cause offence*, volume 28. Cambridge University Press.

Maral Dadvar, Dolf Trieschnigg, Roeland Ordelman, and Franciska de Jong. 2013. Improving cyberbullying detection with user context. In *Advances in Information Retrieval*, pages 693–696. Springer.

Thomas Davidson, Dana Warmsley, Michael Macy, and Ingmar Weber. 2017. Automated Hate Speech Detection and the Problem of Offensive Language. In *Proceedings of ICWSM*.

Karthik Dinakar, Roi Reichart, and Henry Lieberman. 2011. Modeling the detection of textual cyberbullying. In *The Social Mobile Web*, pages 11–17.

Nemanja Djuric, Jing Zhou, Robin Morris, Mihajlo Grbovic, Vladan Radosavljevic, and Narayan Bhamidipati. 2015. Hate speech detection with comment embeddings. In *Proceedings of the 24th International Conference on World Wide Web Companion*, pages 29–30. International World Wide Web Conferences Steering Committee.

Björn Gambäck and Utpal Kumar Sikdar. 2017. Using Convolutional Neural Networks to Classify Hate-speech. In *Proceedings of the First Workshop on Abusive Language Online*, pages 85–90.

Yoon Kim. 2014. Convolutional neural networks for sentence classification. *arXiv preprint arXiv:1408.5882*.

Ritesh Kumar, Atul Kr. Ojha, Shervin Malmasi, and Marcos Zampieri. 2018a. Benchmarking Aggression Identification in Social Media. In *Proceedings of the First Workshop on Trolling, Aggression and Cyberbulling (TRAC)*, Santa Fe, USA.

Ritesh Kumar, Aishwarya N. Reganti, Akshit Bhatia, and Tushar Maheshwari. 2018b. Aggression-annotated Corpus of Hindi-English Code-mixed Data. In *Proceedings of the 11th Language Resources and Evaluation Conference (LREC)*, Miyazaki, Japan.

Irene Kwok and Yuzhou Wang. 2013. Locate the hate: Detecting Tweets Against Blacks. In *Twenty-Seventh AAAI Conference on Artificial Intelligence*.

Shervin Malmasi and Marcos Zampieri. 2018. Challenges in Discriminating Profanity from Hate Speech. *Journal of Experimental & Theoretical Artificial Intelligence*, 30:1–16.

Hamdy Mubarak, Darwish Kareem, and Magdy Walid. 2017. Abusive Language Detection on Arabic Social Media. In *Proceedings of the Workshop on Abusive Language Online (ALW)*, Vancouver, Canada.

Chikashi Nobata, Joel Tetreault, Achint Thomas, Yashar Mehdad, and Yi Chang. 2016. Abusive Language Detection in Online User Content. In *Proceedings of the 25th International Conference on World Wide Web*, pages 145–153. International World Wide Web Conferences Steering Committee.

John T Nockleby. 2000. Hate speech. *Encyclopedia of the American constitution*, 3:1277–79.

Jeffrey Pennington, Richard Socher, and Christopher Manning. 2014. Glove: Global vectors for word representation. In *Proceedings of the 2014 conference on empirical methods in natural language processing (EMNLP)*, pages 1532–1543.

Anna Schmidt and Michael Wiegand. 2017. A Survey on Hate Speech Detection Using Natural Language Processing. In *Proceedings of the Fifth International Workshop on Natural Language Processing for Social Media. Association for Computational Linguistics*, pages 1–10, Valencia, Spain.

Huei-Po Su, Chen-Jie Huang, Hao-Tsung Chang, and Chuan-Jie Lin. 2017. Rephrasing Profanity in Chinese Text. In *Proceedings of the Workshop Workshop on Abusive Language Online (ALW)*, Vancouver, Canada.

Stéphan Tulkens, Lisa Hilte, Elise Lodewyckx, Ben Verhoeven, and Walter Daelemans. 2016. A Dictionary-based Approach to Racism Detection in Dutch Social Media. In *Proceedings of the Workshop Text Analytics for Cybersecurity and Online Safety (TA-COS)*, Portoroz, Slovenia.

Jun-Ming Xu, Kwang-Sung Jun, Xiaojin Zhu, and Amy Bellmore. 2012. Learning from bullying traces in social media. In *Proceedings of the 2012 conference of the North American chapter of the association for computational linguistics: Human language technologies*, pages 656–666. Association for Computational Linguistics.

Merging datasets for aggressive text identification

Paula Fortuna[1] **José Ferreira**[1,2] **Luiz Pires**[3] **Guilherme Routar**[2] **Sérgio Nunes**[1,2]

(1) INESC TEC and (2) FEUP, University of Porto and (3) FCUP, University of Porto
Rua Dr. Roberto Frias, s/n 4200-465 Porto PORTUGAL
`paula.fortuna@fe.up.pt, sergio.nunes@fe.up.pt`

Abstract

This paper presents the approach of the team "groutar" to the shared task on Aggression Identification, considering the test sets in English, both from Facebook and general Social Media. This experiment aims to test the effect of merging new datasets in the performance of classification models. We followed a standard machine learning approach with training, validation, and testing phases, and considered features such as part-of-speech, frequencies of insults, punctuation, sentiment, and capitalization. In terms of algorithms, we experimented with Boosted Logistic Regression, Multi-Layer Perceptron, Parallel Random Forest and eXtreme Gradient Boosting. One question appearing was how to merge datasets using different classification systems (e.g. aggression vs. toxicity). Other issue concerns the possibility to generalize models and apply them to data from different social networks. Regarding these, we merged two datasets, and the results showed that training with similar data is an advantage in the classification of social networks data. However, adding data from different platforms, allowed slightly better results in both Facebook and Social Media, indicating that more generalized models can be an advantage.

1 Introduction

In the last few years, we have witnessed a growing number of online platforms where users can post content. As the number of platforms has increased, so has the number of aggressive interactions, such as cyberbullying or hate speech. The goal of our work is to contribute to the automatic identification of this type of communication through the participation in the Shared Task on Aggression Identification in text (Kumar et al., 2018a).

The task consisted in developing a classifier that could make a 3-way classification between Overtly Aggressive (OAG), Covertly Aggressive (CAG) and Non-aggressive (NAG) text data. The organizers provided a dataset of 15,000 aggression-annotated Facebook posts for training and validating the classification systems. Each team was allowed to test up to three systems and to use additional data for training, as long as the data would be publicly available before submission of the system paper. Different competitions were available with variations in language and data sources. It was possible to classify aggression in English and Hindi and also using data from Facebook or other Social Media platform unknown at submission time.

In our approach, we focused on understanding the effects of merging new datasets for training models. We used the Toxicity dataset, from the Toxic comment classification challenge in Kaggle, as an additional source of data, and we proceeded with the conversion from toxicity to aggression. We built and compared two systems, one using only the original data for training, and the second using also toxic data. We extracted some classic features and studied different machine learning classification algorithms using a methodology of training, validation, and testing. Our approach focused on English and in both test sets provided, Facebook and Social Media.

In the next sections, we present the related work (Section 2), our method (Section 3), the results (Section 4), and finally our conclusions (Section 5).

Proceedings of the First Workshop on Trolling, Aggression and Cyberbullying, pages 128–139
Santa Fe, USA, August 25, 2018.

2   Related Work

Aggression by text is a complex phenomenon, and different knowledge fields try to study and tackle this problem. In this analysis of related work, we focus mainly on a computer science perspective on aggression identification, a recent emerging area. In the last years, the scientific study of automatic identification of aggressive text, from a Computer Science and Engineering point of view, is increasing. One important aspect to consider is that in this scientific community, several related terms are used to express different types of aggression. Some of those are hate (Tarasova, 2016), cyberbullying (Chen, 2011), abusive language (Nobata et al., 2016), profanity (Dictionary, 2017), toxicity (Jigsaw, 2017), flaming (Guermazi et al., 2007), extremism (Prentice et al., 2011; McNamee et al., 2010), radicalization (Agarwal and Sureka, 2015), and hate speech (Schmidt and Wiegand, 2017).

Despite the differences between those concepts, previous research can give us insight into how to approach the problem of identifying aggressive interactions. For instance, particular attention has been given to the automatic detection of hate speech. In one survey paper (Schmidt and Wiegand, 2017), the authors provide a short, comprehensive, structured and critical overview of the field of automatic hate speech detection in natural language processing. In other, the main focus is on definitions and rules for classification (Fortuna and Nunes, forthcoming), which is important for solving this complex task. One of the main conclusions of these works is that the automatic classification of hate speech and other related concepts rely frequently upon Machine Learning and classification approaches.

Regarding the automatic classification of messages, one first step is the gathering of training data. Several studies published datasets for aggression identification with different classification systems. For example, in one dataset the classes "Racism", "Sexism" and "Neither" were used to annotate tweets for English (Waseem and Hovy, 2016). In another dataset collected for the specific topic of hate speech against refugees, tweets in German were annotated using only the class "Hate Speech" (Ross et al., 2017). Another study presents a hate speech detection dataset in Twitter for English, using the classes "Hate", "Offensive" or "Neither" (Davidson et al., 2017). A third dataset not publicly available contains comments from Yahoo! Finance and News in English and uses the classes "Hate Speech", "Derogatory", "Profanity" and "Neither" (Nobata et al., 2016). Finally, one last dataset from a classification challenge in Kaggle identifies Toxicity (Jigsaw, 2018). The dataset contains Wikipedia comments marked as "toxic", "severe toxic", "obscene", "threat" and "identity hate", in a multi-class and multi-label approach. Based on the information from these datasets, we conclude that none considers the class "aggression", which would be useful for this work. Another difficulty is the multiplicity of different concepts and definitions. A recent work identifies this problem and proposes a typology that captures the similarities between concepts (Waseem et al., 2017). According to this typology, abuse follows into directed vs. generalized and explicit vs. implicit categories. This topology has implications on the following parts of a classification procedure.

After the data collection, one of the most important steps when using classification is the process of feature extraction (Schmidt and Wiegand, 2017). Different approaches are being used, ranging from Dictionaries (Liu and Forss, 2015; Dadvar et al., 2012; Dinakar et al., 2011), to Bag-of-words (Burnap and Williams, 2016; Kwok and Wang, 2013; Greevy and Smeaton, 2004), N-grams (Burnap and Williams, 2016; Nobata et al., 2016; Waseem and Hovy, 2016; Liu and Forss, 2014; Greevy and Smeaton, 2004; Badjatiya et al., 2017; Davidson et al., 2017), Part-of-speech (Greevy and Smeaton, 2004; Dinakar et al., 2011; Burnap and Williams, 2014), Lexical Syntactic Feature-based (LSF) (Chen, 2011), Rule based approaches (Haralambous and Lenca, 2014), Participant-vocabulary consistency (PVC) (Raisi and Huang, 2016), Template-based Strategies (Powers, 2011), Word Sense Disambiguation Techniques (Yarowsky, 1994), Sentiment analysis (Liu and Forss, 2014; Liu and Forss, 2015; Gitari et al., 2015; Agarwal and Sureka, 2017; Del Vigna et al., 2017; Schmidt and Wiegand, 2017; Davidson et al., 2017), perpetrator characteristics (Waseem and Hovy, 2016), Paragraph2vec (Djuric et al., 2015) and Deep learning (Yuan et al., 2016). There are also features and approaches more specific to the problem of hate speech detection, namely: othering language (Burnap and Williams, 2016; Dashti et al., 2015), declarations of superiority of the ingroup (Warner and Hirschberg, 2012), objectivity (Gitari et al., 2015) and subjectivity (Warner and Hirschberg, 2012) of hate speech language. Additionally, in the typology of hate, some considerations are made regarding the features to use (Waseem et al., 2017). In the case of direct abuse, mentions, proper nouns, named entities, and co-reference resolution can be helpful. In generalized abuse, researchers should consider identifying vocabulary specificities regarding the groups targeted. On the other hand, explicit abuse is often indicated by specific keywords. Hence, dictionary-based approaches may work well. Finally, implicit abuse identification works with character N-grams (Mehdad and Tetreault, 2016), word embeddings (Djuric et al., 2015) and perpetrator characteristics (Waseem and Hovy, 2016).

Regarding the classification algorithms, the more common are SVM (Del Vigna et al., 2017), Random forests (Burnap and Williams, 2014), Decision trees (Dinakar et al., 2011), Logistic regression (Davidson et al., 2017), Naive bayes (Liu and Forss, 2015) and Deep learning (Yuan et al., 2016).

In this challenge, we are not only interested in distinguishing between aggressive and non-aggressive text, but different degrees of aggression are also considered. A recent discussion on the challenges of identifying profanity vs. hate speech highlighted some issues in this topic (Malmasi and Zampieri, 2018). The results revealed that discriminating hate speech from profanity is not a simple task, and it may require features more complex than N-grams. From this conclusion, we can extrapolate that distinguishing overt and covert aggression will be difficult as well. Overcoming this difficulty is a motivating factor for conducting this shared task.

Regarding the specificities of our approach, the main research question of our work concerns the effects of merging new datasets on the performance of models for aggression classification. Additionally, there are some open issues that motivate our work. One question is if it is possible the combination of datasets annotated with different classification systems (e.g. toxicity and aggression). This combination would allow the use of multiple datasets simultaneously. Another question is if it is possible to generalize models and apply them to data from different Internet sources. Finally, other question concerns the duration in time of the models, even when the same platform is used, due to the fast evolution of online language.

In the next sections, we aim to answer to some of these questions with our approach.

3   Methodology and Data

3.1   The datasets

The provided training datasets (Kumar et al., 2018b) contained Facebook text messages for English and Hindi. From those messages, 12,000 were for training and 3,000 for development (dev). This last was a dataset for testing before submitting final results. Regarding the test set, was the data available for final classification and final submission for ranking of solutions in the contest. Several scenarios were available for testing the final models. Besides different languages (English and Hindi), the teams could classify diverse message sources (Facebook and general Social Media). For the annotation of the datasets, there were three classes described solely as Overtly Aggressive (OAG), Covertly Aggressive (CAG) and Non-aggressive (NAG) and no additional information provided. This lack of deeper definitions opposes to previous recommendations (Ross et al., 2017), which pointed out the importance to clearly define concepts before addressing problems like hate speech identification.

Aiming to improve the available definitions, we tried to manually inspect some data, so that we could better understand the differences among the three types of messages. We concluded that it is not easy to distinguish the classes and that they overlap (Table **??**). For example, a text like "Nonsense" is marked as overtly aggressive (OAG), while "No respect for him now" is marked as non-aggressive (NAG).

Outside of the challenge, the definitions of the classes became available in the article presenting the dataset (Kumar et al., 2018b). According to these authors, overt aggression is any speech or text in which aggression is overtly expressed, either through the use of specific kind of lexical items, lexical features or certain syntactic structures, considered aggressive. On the other hand, covert aggression is any text in which aggression is not overtly expressed. It is an indirect attack against the victim and is often packaged as insincere polite expressions, through the use of conventionalised polite structures. For instance, cases of satire or rhetorical questions may be classified as covert aggression.

Considering the opportunities this task enabled, we decided to conduct our experiment only for English

Id	Text	Class
facebook_corpus_msr_326287	This is a false news Indian media is simply misguiding there nation and creating hatred.. Media should be v careful while spreading the news.. SHAME.:(	NAG
facebook_corpus_msr_1805657	No respect for him now	NAG
facebook_corpus_msr_401603	Now time has come to take firm action against pakistan, pl do not seat idle.....public anger....	NAG
facebook_corpus_msr_382223	Unfortunately this is wat indian govt is capable of doing!!!!...i dint vote for modiji to see such crap..	CAG
facebook_corpus_msr_470981	I visited 5 atm but I cont able to withdraw from money..not working..	CAG
facebook_corpus_msr_492174	I wanna meet the girl who said the iPhone is user friendly!!!	CAG
facebook_corpus_msr_1853672	What the hell is happening	OAG
facebook_corpus_msr_2032108	#salute you my friend	OAG
facebook_corpus_msr_2241597	Nonsense	OAG

Table 1: Examples of messages extracted from the provided dataset.

and to test the effect of adding a new dataset in our classification both in messages from Facebook and general Social Media. Despite our intention, we did not find an alternative dataset that would have classified text for aggression. We decided then to use a Toxicity dataset, already mentioned in Section 3.1. The Toxicity dataset consists of 170,355 messages marked as toxic, severe toxic, obscene, threat and identity hate, in a multi-class and multi-label approach (Jigsaw, 2018).

When we try to match the Aggression dataset with the Toxicity dataset, we are in the presence of two unequal classification systems. Therefore, we conducted a procedure for converting the classes of the Toxicity dataset into aggression (Figure 1).

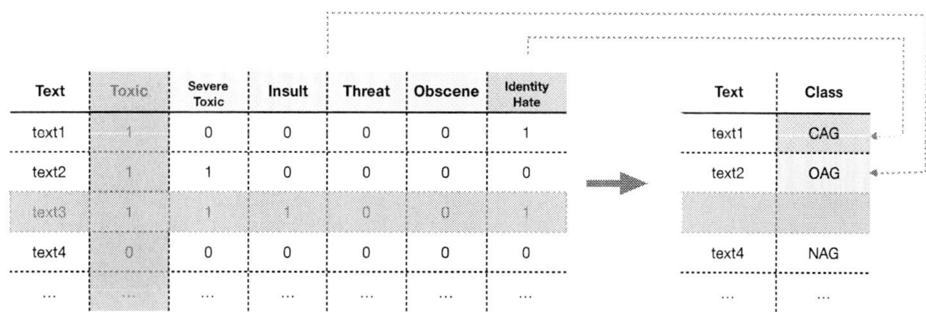

Figure 1: Procedure conducted for transforming the Toxicity dataset into Aggressive communication dataset.

The steps followed are:

- Regarding the toxic column, we decided to ignore it because it correlates strongly with the others.

- The columns "severe toxic", 'insult' ,"obscene" and "threat" would correspond to "overtly aggressive" (OAG).

- The column "identity hate" would correspond to "covertly aggressive" (CAG).

- We excluded the instances that would score in both OAG and CAG dimensions because that is not possible in our original dataset.

In this procedure, we decided to only keep "identity hate" in the covertly aggressive (CAG) class. Following previous studies (Malmasi and Zampieri, 2018), "profanity vs. hate speech" are considered and both identified and handled as different classes. In the case of the Toxicity dataset, we think that

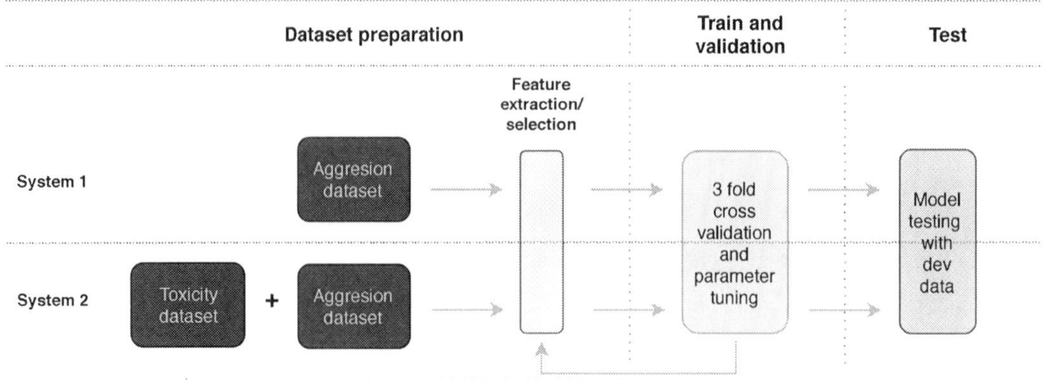

Figure 2: Conducted method for comparison of Systems 1 and 2 using training, validation, and test.

"severe toxic", "insult" ,"obscene" and "threat" are more similar to "profanity" than to "hate speech", and the four should be grouped together as overtly aggressive (OAG).

3.2 Method

In order to test the effect of adding a new dataset to our classification procedure, we compared two different systems (Figure 2). In the first, we build a model using only the training set provided in the contest. For that, we extracted some classic features and studied different machine learning classification methods. In the second, we applied the same procedure, but we fed the model not only with the provided data but also with the Toxicity dataset.

3.2.1 Dataset Preparation and Feature Extraction

Regarding the features, we used the NLTK 3.3 library (Bird et al., 2009) for extracting:

- Parts of speech (POS).

- Sentiment analysis.

- Combination of POS and sentiment analysis.

- Capitalized words.

- Punctuation patterns.

- Frequencies of insults.

The procedure consisted in tokenization and extraction of parts of speech (POS) with Penn Treebank style. Regarding sentiment, we considered Vader (Valence aware Dictionary and sentiment reasoner), a lexicon and rule-based sentiment analysis tool specialized in social media (Hutto and Gilbert, 2014). It produces four sentiment metrics, namely: positive, negative, neutral and compound. Additionally, to these metrics, we extracted the counts of negative words, and the counts of negative adjectives, combining both POS and sentiment analysis. We also measured the frequencies of capitalized words in a message and marked with a boolean full capitalized messages. Punctuation patterns were obtained as explained in Table **??**. Finally, we mapped the frequencies of insults, using a dictionary[1] with 350 words. The total number of features in each group is presented in Table **??**.

---

[1] http://www.insult.wiki/wiki/Insult_List

Individual features	Expression	Description
ellipsis	\.{2,}	ellipsis occurrence counts
ellipsis_reps	—	sum of the summed length of all ellipsis patterns
simple_qm	^?$	counts of single question mark
simple_exc	^!$	counts of single exclamation mark
reps_qm	^(\?+)$	counts of question marks with repetition
reps_exc	^(!+)$	counts of exclamation marks with repetition
mixed	(\?—\!){1,}	counts of patterns with both question and exclamation marks
num_punct	—	counts of punctuation patterns
max_punct	—	size of largest punctuation pattern

Table 2: Extracted features based on punctuation and regular expression used.

Feature group	Total features
Insult words	350
POS	36
Punctuation	9
Sentiment	5
Capitalization	2
POS + sentiment	2

Table 3: The total number of features by group.

3.2.2 Train and validation

In this phase, we used the R caret package (Kuhn, 2008) and the functions train, trainControl, predict and confusionMatrix. We opted by three-fold cross-validation with parameter tuning of length three. Regarding the classification algorithms, we used Boosted Logistic Regression (LogitBoost), Multi-Layer Perceptron (mlp), Parallel Random Forest (parRF) and eXtreme Gradient Boosting (xgbTree).

3.2.3 Test

For testing our model we conducted four different runs. We developed two systems (aggression data vs. aggression + toxicity data) that were tested in two different scenarios (Facebook data vs. Social Media). Based on the results of the train and validation phases, we submitted the following systems (Table **??**), for English data: training with the provided dataset, classification algorithm with parallel random forests and testing in Facebook data (Fb_ag_rf); training with the provided dataset plus the dataset classified on toxicity, classification algorithm with parallel random forests and testing in Facebook data (Fb_ag_tox_rf); training with the provided dataset, classification algorithm with parallel random forests and testing in Social Media data (Sm_ag_rf); training with the provided dataset plus the dataset classified on toxicity, classification algorithm with parallel random forests and testing in Social Media data (Sm_ag_tox_rf).

System id	Data for testing	Data for training	Classification Algorithm
Fb_ag_rf	Facebook	Aggression	Random forests
Fb_ag_tox_rf	Facebook	Aggression + Toxicity	Random forests
Sm_ag_rf	Social Media	Aggression	Random forests
Sm_ag_tox_rf	Social Media	Aggression + Toxicity	Random forests

Table 4: Systems considered in the submission, each corresponding to one run.

4 Results

4.1 Train and validation results

After training our models using cross-validation, and tuning them in the default parameters, we tested them in the development dataset. This section provides the results in this phase, which were used to decide on which classification algorithm to keep for the final submission. We concluded (Figure 3) that the models built using only the default dataset (marked as "without toxic dataset" in the figure) perform better than the ones using also the Toxicity dataset (marked as "with toxic dataset").

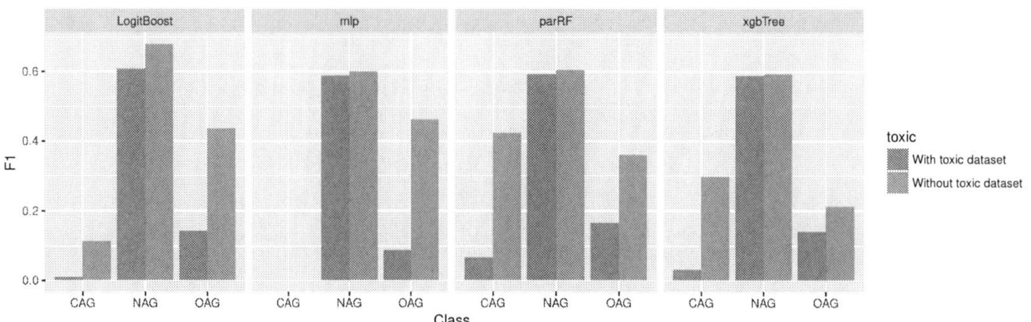

Figure 3: Results of different algorithms on the dev test set.

This is an expected result when using the development data for testing due to the source of its messages. In this case, the origin is Facebook, which is the same as in the training set. On the other side, the Toxicity dataset comes from a different platform (Wikipedia) and these extra messages can cause noise. Despite this result, we think that it worths to test the system built with the Toxicity dataset because on the final submission some test sets include unknown data. Regarding the classification algorithms, we decided to keep the parRF because it was the best performing algorithm if we take into account the results of the three classes.

4.2 Final test results

In this section, we present the results after submitting our classifications in the shared task platform. In Table 5, we can observe the results with the Facebook test set. With a mixed training dataset (Fb_ag_tox_rf system), we have a model with a slightly better performance than when using only the provided dataset for training (Fb_ag_rf system). In this case, we would expect the same results as in the development dataset because in both cases data originates in Facebook. Hence the model trained without Toxicity should have performed better. Regarding this unexpected result, one possible explanation would be if the moments for the collection of both dev and test set would not match, and therefore some differences existing due to that.

	CAG	NAG	OAG	avg
random baseline	-	-	-	0.3535
Fb_ag_rf	0.2135	0.6379	0.3439	0.5259
Fb_ag_tox_rf	**0.2217**	**0.6403**	**0.3439**	**0.5288**

Table 5: Results for the English (Facebook) task, comparing the use of aggressive data (FB_ag_rf) with the use of aggressive data plus Toxicity dataset (FB_ag_tox_rf) for training using Random Forests for classification.

We verified the same pattern described from the Facebook test set on the Social Media data (Table 6). Using a mixed dataset for training lead to models with a better performance. In this case, this is an expected result because the Social Media messages are from another source than Facebook and therefore a more generic model is likely to perform better.

	CAG	NAG	OAG	avg
random baseline	–	–	–	0.3477
EN-TW task, groutar 00	0.314	0.4863	0.2469	0.3609
EN-TW task, groutar 01	**0.3151**	**0.4889**	**0.2505**	**0.3633**

Table 6: Results for the English (Social Media) task, comparing the use of aggressive data (Sm_ag_rf) with the use of aggressive data plus Toxicity dataset (Sm_ag_tox_rf) for training using Random Forests for classification.

If we compare both (Table 5 and Table 6), we achieved an overall better performance when classifying Facebook than Social Media messages. This is also an expected result because we trained with messages from this social network and the added Toxicity dataset originates in Wikipedia. On the other hand, this pattern does not apply if we consider only the covertly aggressive messages (CAG). In this case, the classification worked better in the Social Media messages. This supports the idea that different social media platforms have different expressions of behavior and the covertly aggressive messages were easier to target on Twitter.

We also present here the confusion matrix for the Facebook test set and the Social Media (Figures 4 and 5). We concluded that, when adding the Toxicity dataset, the results are slightly better in identifying covertly aggressive messages (CAG) on Facebook, overtly aggressive messages (OAG) on Social Media and non-aggressive messages (NAG) in both.

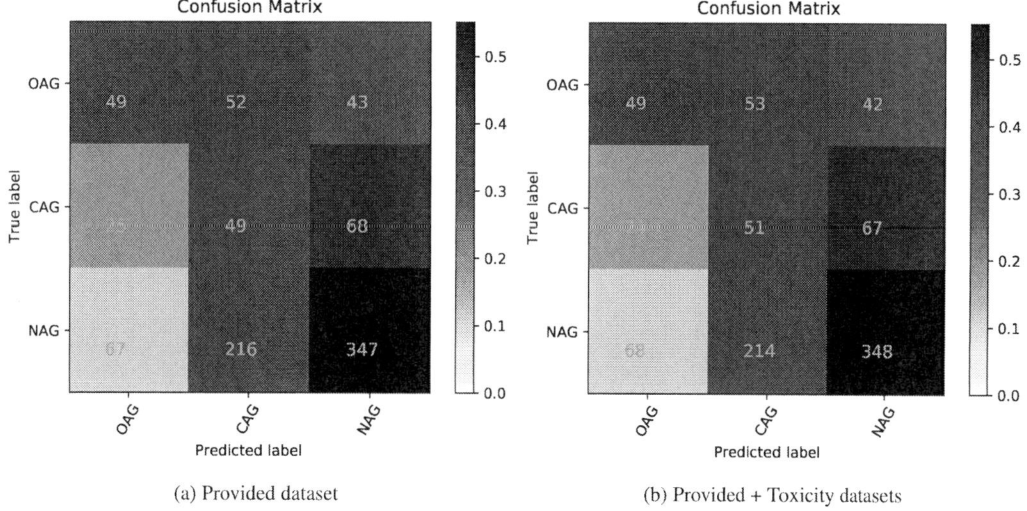

(a) Provided dataset   (b) Provided + Toxicity datasets

Figure 4: Confusion matrix for the two developed systems, using the Facebook test set and Random Forest classification algorithm.

5 Conclusion

Throughout our approach to this shared task, our goal was to discuss some open issues in aggressive text identification. Namely, the main motivation of our work was measuring the effects of merging new datasets on the performance of models for aggression classification. It can be difficult to combine distinct datasets due to the differences in the classification systems used. We conducted an experiment where we combined a toxicity dataset with the original aggression dataset used in this shared task. Our expectation was that, by adding external data from a different context, we could improve the performance of the system.

In the procedure of adding different datasets to the data from the shared task, we faced one problem.

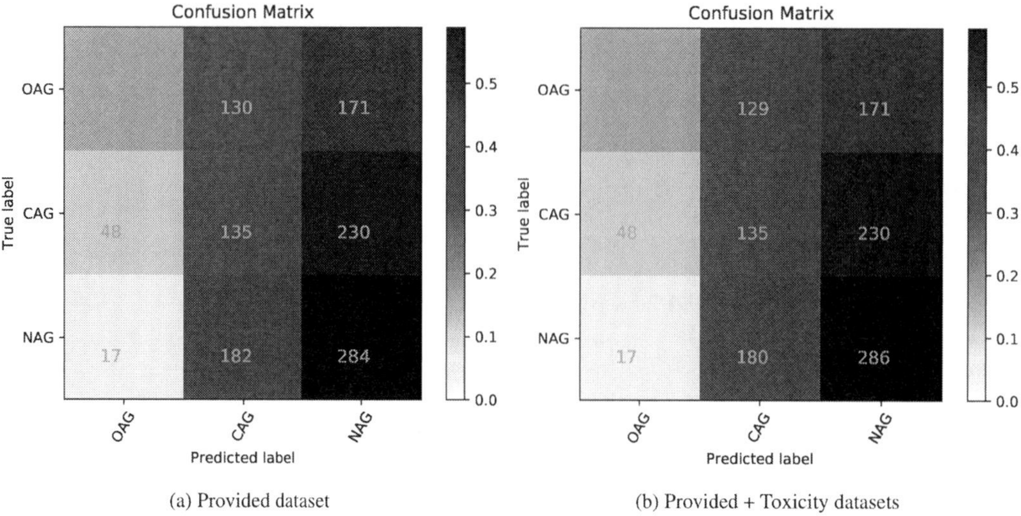

(a) Provided dataset   (b) Provided + Toxicity datasets

Figure 5: Confusion matrix for the two developed systems, using the Social media test set and Random Forest classification algorithm.

We found no alternative dataset with text classified for aggression and therefore we had to merge datasets using different classes (aggression vs. toxicity). This required a conversion procedure where we corresponded identity hate with covertly aggressive discourse, and severe toxic, insult, obscene and threat, were mapped to overtly aggressive discourse.

Another goal of our work was focused on evaluating if we can build models that are general enough to be useful across different social networks. From our experiments, on average we achieved a better performance in classifying messages from the same social network that we used for training (Facebook) when comparing to other social media. This confirms that training with similar data is an advantage in the classification of social networks data. However, on the other hand, adding data for training from a different platform, allowed us to slightly increase performance, indicating that more generalized models can be an advantage.

Regarding the features, we used POS tags, sentiment analysis, insult frequencies, capitalization, and punctuation counts. According to the literature, this kind of features are more related with explicit abuse detection (Waseem et al., 2017). However, we did not find any evident advantage in using them for detecting overtly aggressive discourse (OAG) in comparison with covertly aggressive (CAG). In our experiment, the results of classifying OAG and CAG were equivalent. This can be due to the simplicity of the extracted features, or possibly to some weaknesses in the data, as we explain in the next paragraph.

In the exploration of the dataset, we faced unclear definitions of the classification system used in the annotation. Also, the definitions provided a posteriori seemed to be superficial. We manually inspected some messages and concluded that it was difficult to identify the differences between the classes because messages with similar degrees of aggression were found in the three classes. Additionally, we also found lack of clear definitions in the toxicity dataset. This problem should be tackled in future research because the identification of aggression is complex and ambiguous even for humans and requires clear guidelines. Finally, we also noticed a higher percentage of aggressive messages in this dataset in comparison to previous studies in other related phenomenon (Davidson et al., 2017), which questions the quality of the annotation.

Acknowledgements

This work was partially funded by FourEyes, a Research Line within project "TEC4Growth Pervasive Intelligence, Enhancers and Proofs of Concept with Industrial Impact/NORTE-01- 0145-FEDER-000020", financed by the North Portugal Regional Operational Programme (NORTE 2020), under the PORTUGAL

2020 Partnership Agreement, and through the European Regional Development Fund (ERDF).

References

Swati Agarwal and Ashish Sureka. 2015. Using knn and svm based one-class classifier for detecting online radicalization on twitter. In *International Conference on Distributed Computing and Internet Technology*, pages 431–442. Springer.

Swati Agarwal and Ashish Sureka. 2017. Characterizing linguistic attributes for automatic classification of intent based racist/radicalized posts on tumblr micro-blogging website. *arXiv preprint arXiv:1701.04931*.

Pinkesh Badjatiya, Shashank Gupta, Manish Gupta, and Vasudeva Varma. 2017. Deep learning for hate speech detection in tweets. In *Proceedings of the 26th International Conference on World Wide Web Companion*, pages 759–760. International World Wide Web Conferences Steering Committee.

Steven Bird, Ewan Klein, and Edward Loper. 2009. *Natural Language Processing with Python*, volume 43.

Peter Burnap and Matthew L. Williams. 2014. Hate speech, machine classification and statistical modelling of information flows on twitter: Interpretation and communication for policy decision making. In *Proceedings of Internet, Policy & Politics*, pages 1–18.

Pete Burnap and Matthew L. Williams. 2016. Us and them: identifying cyber hate on twitter across multiple protected characteristics. *EPJ Data Science*, 5(1):11.

Ying Chen. 2011. *Detecting Offensive Language in Social Medias for Protection of Adolescent Online Safety*. Ph.D. thesis, The Pennsylvania State University.

Maral Dadvar, Franciska de Jong, Roeland Ordelman, and Dolf Trieschnigg. 2012. Improved cyberbullying detection using gender information. In *Proceedings of the Twelfth Dutch-Belgian Information Retrieval Workshop*, pages 23–25. University of Ghent.

Ali A. Dashti, Ali A. Al-Kandari, and Hamed H. Al-Abdullah. 2015. The influence of sectarian and tribal discourse in newspapers readers' online comments about freedom of expression, censorship and national unity in kuwait. *Telematics and Informatics*, 32(2):245–253.

Thomas Davidson, Dana Warmsley, Michael Macy, and Ingmar Weber. 2017. Automated Hate Speech Detection and the Problem of Offensive Language. In *Proceedings of ICWSM*.

Fabio Del Vigna, Andrea Cimino, Felice Dell'Orletta, Marinella Petrocchi, and Maurizio Tesconi. 2017. Hate me, hate me not: Hate speech detection on facebook. In *Proceedings of the First Italian Conference on Cybersecurity*, pages 86–95.

Cambridge Dictionary. 2017. Profanity. Available in `https://dictionary.cambridge.org/dictionary/english/profanity`, accessed last time in June 2017.

Karthik Dinakar, Roi Reichart, and Henry Lieberman. 2011. Modeling the detection of textual cyberbullying. *The Social Mobile Web*, 11(02).

Nemanja Djuric, Jing Zhou, Robin Morris, Mihajlo Grbovic, Vladan Radosavljevic, and Narayan Bhamidipati. 2015. Hate speech detection with comment embeddings. In *Proceedings of the 24th International Conference on World Wide Web*, pages 29–30. ACM2.

Paula Fortuna and Sérgio Nunes. forthcoming. A survey on automatic detection of hate speech in text. *ACM computing surveys (CSUR)*.

Njagi Dennis Gitari, Zhang Zuping, Hanyurwimfura Damien, and Jun Long. 2015. A lexicon-based approach for hate speech detection. *International Journal of Multimedia and Ubiquitous Engineering*, 10(4):215–230.

Edel Greevy and Alan F. Smeaton. 2004. Classifying racist texts using a support vector machine. In *Proceedings of the 27th annual international ACM SIGIR conference on Research and development in information retrieval*, pages 468–469. ACM.

Radhouane Guermazi, Mohamed Hammami, and Abdelmajid Ben Hamadou. 2007. Using a semi-automatic keyword dictionary for improving violent web site filtering. In *Signal-Image Technologies and Internet-Based System, 2007. SITIS'07. Third International IEEE Conference on*, pages 337–344. IEEE.

Yannis Haralambous and Philippe Lenca. 2014. Text classification using association rules, dependency pruning and hyperonymization. *arXiv preprint arXiv:1407.7357.*

CJ J. Hutto and Eric Gilbert. 2014. Vader: A parsimonious rule-based model for sentiment analysis of social media text. *Eighth International AAAI Conference on Weblogs and . . .*, pages 216–225.

Jigsaw. 2017. Perspective api. Available in `https://www.perspectiveapi.com/`, accessed last time in June 2017.

Jigsaw. 2018. Toxic comment classification challenge identify and classify toxic online comments. Available in `https://www.kaggle.com/c/jigsaw-toxic-comment-classification-challenge`, accessed last time in 23 May 2018.

Max et al. Kuhn. 2008. Caret package. *Journal of statistical software*, 28(5):1–26.

Ritesh Kumar, Atul Kr. Ojha, Shervin Malmasi, and Marcos Zampieri. 2018a. Benchmarking Aggression Identification in Social Media. In *Proceedings of the First Workshop on Trolling, Aggression and Cyberbulling (TRAC)*, Santa Fe, USA.

Ritesh Kumar, Aishwarya N. Reganti, Akshit Bhatia, and Tushar Maheshwari. 2018b. Aggression-annotated Corpus of Hindi-English Code-mixed Data. In *Proceedings of the 11th Language Resources and Evaluation Conference (LREC)*, Miyazaki, Japan.

Irene Kwok and Yuzhou Wang. 2013. Locate the hate: Detecting tweets against blacks. In *Association for the Advancement of Artificial Intelligence*.

Shuhua Liu and Thomas Forss. 2014. Combining n-gram based similarity analysis with sentiment analysis in web content classification. In *International Joint Conference on Knowledge Discovery, Knowledge Engineering and Knowledge Management*, pages 530–537.

Shuhua Liu and Thomas Forss. 2015. New classification models for detecting hate and violence web content. In *Knowledge Discovery, Knowledge Engineering and Knowledge Management (IC3K), 2015 7th International Joint Conference on*, volume 1, pages 487–495. IEEE.

Shervin Malmasi and Marcos Zampieri. 2018. Challenges in Discriminating Profanity from Hate Speech. *Journal of Experimental & Theoretical Artificial Intelligence*, 30:1–16.

Lacy G McNamee, Brittany L Peterson, and Jorge Peña. 2010. A call to educate, participate, invoke and indict: Understanding the communication of online hate groups. *Communication Monographs*, 77(2):257–280.

Yashar Mehdad and Joel Tetreault. 2016. Do characters abuse more than words? In *Proceedings of the SIGdial 2016 Conference: The 17th Annual Meeting of the Special Interest Group on Discourse and Dialogue*, pages 299–303.

Chikashi Nobata, Joel Tetreault, Achint Thomas, Yashar Mehdad, and Yi Chang. 2016. Abusive language detection in online user content. In *Proceedings of the 25th International Conference on World Wide Web*, pages 145–153. International World Wide Web Conferences Steering Committee.

David Martin Powers. 2011. Evaluation: from precision, recall and f-measure to roc, informedness, markedness and correlation. *International Journal of Machine Learning Technology*, 2(1):37–63.

Sheryl Prentice, Paul J Taylor, Paul Rayson, Andrew Hoskins, and Ben O'Loughlin. 2011. Analyzing the semantic content and persuasive composition of extremist media: A case study of texts produced during the gaza conflict. *Information Systems Frontiers*, 13(1):61–73.

Elaheh Raisi and Bert Huang. 2016. Cyberbullying identification using participant-vocabulary consistency. *arXiv preprint arXiv:1606.08084.*

Bjorn Ross, Michael Rist, Guillermo Carbonell, Benjamin Cabrera, Nils Kurowsky, and Michael Wojatzki. 2017. Measuring the reliability of hate speech annotations: The case of the european refugee crisis. *arXiv preprint arXiv:1701.08118.*

Anna Schmidt and Michael Wiegand. 2017. A survey on hate speech detection using natural language processing. *SocialNLP 2017*, page 1.

Natalya Tarasova. 2016. Classification of hate tweets and their reasons using svm. Master's thesis, Uppsala Universitet.

William Warner and Julia Hirschberg. 2012. Detecting hate speech on the world wide web. In *Proceedings of the Second Workshop on Language in Social Media*, pages 19–26. Association for Computational Linguistics.

Zeerak Waseem and Dirk Hovy. 2016. Hateful symbols or hateful people? predictive features for hate speech detection on twitter. In *Proceedings of NAACL-HLT*, pages 88–93.

Zeerak Waseem, Thomas Davidson, Dana Warmsley, and Ingmar Weber. 2017. Understanding Abuse: A Typology of Abusive Language Detection Subtasks. In *Proceedings of the First Workshop on Abusive Langauge Online*.

David Yarowsky. 1994. Decision lists for lexical ambiguity resolution: Application to accent restoration in spanish and french. In *Proceedings of the 32nd annual meeting on Association for Computational Linguistics*, pages 88–95. Association for Computational Linguistics.

Shuhan Yuan, Xintao Wu, and Yang Xiang. 2016. A two phase deep learning model for identifying discrimination from tweets. In *International Conference on Extending Database Technology*, pages 696–697.

Cyberbullying Detection Task:
The EBSI-LIA-UNAM system (ELU) at COLING'18 TRAC-1

Ignacio Arroyo-Fernández	**Dominic Forest**	**Juan-Manuel Torres-Moreno**
Universidad Nacional	Université de Montréal	LIA - UAPV (France) &
Autónoma de México	EBSI	Polytechnique Montréal

Mauricio Carrasco-Ruiz	**Thomas Legeleux**	**Karen Joannette**
Universidad Nacional	Université de Montréal	Université de Montréal
Autónoma de México	EBSI	EBSI

Abstract

The phenomenon of cyberbullying has growing in worrying proportions with the development of social networks. Forums and chat rooms are spaces where serious damage can now be done to others, while the tools for avoiding on-line spills are still limited. This study aims to assess the ability that both classical and state-of-the-art vector space modeling methods provide to well known learning machines to identify aggression levels in social network cyberbullying (i.e. social network posts manually labeled as Overtly Aggressive, Covertly Aggressive and Non-aggressive). To this end, an exploratory stage was performed first in order to find relevant settings to test, i.e. by using training and development samples, we trained multiple learning machines using multiple vector space modeling methods and discarded the less informative configurations. Finally, we selected the two best settings and their voting combination to form three competing systems. These systems were submitted to the competition of the TRACK-1 task of the Workshop on Trolling, Aggression and Cyberbullying. Our voting combination system resulted second place in predicting Aggression levels on a test set of untagged social network posts.

1 Introduction

The introduction of the Internet and its democratization in the public sphere has fostered the emergence of many sociological phenomena. It opens the possibility of forming friendly relations and information sharing from online networking platforms. These platforms, which are often the subject of strong ownership by young users, introduce a paradigm shift in interpersonal relationships since they are now interactive spaces where it is hard to put regulation rules in place. Thus, each time more we see the appearing of aggressive behaviors that were confined to the physical space until recently. These aggressions can take different forms: insults, intimidation, humiliation, exclusion, etc. All them have for common point to take place in a space where it is possible to cause serious moral damage without suffering the consequences, in particular because of the possibility of evolving in a completely anonymous way. This phenomenon, referred to as cyberbullying, or Internet harassment, is defined as *"the use of information and communication technologies to repeatedly, intentionally, and aggressively engage in behavior with respect to an individual or a group with the intention of causing harm to others"* – Belsey (2013).

Several solutions have been proposed, often based on a behavioral and pedagogical approach (ignore the attacker, confront him or even denounce him). However, it becomes necessary to think about relevant algorithmic strategies to better protect Internet users from cyberbullying. Such strategies would allow the establishment of an automated system to detect cyberbullying in social media. This assist moderators to identify the most serious cases, and thus to contribute to a safer virtual space for both the youngest and the adults.

In this paper we propose an approach based on multiple classical text mining pipelines. The aim of this is to explore the actual difficulties linguistic and extralinguistic phenomena may imply to effectively

Proceedings of the First Workshop on Trolling, Aggression and Cyberbullying, pages 140–149
Santa Fe, USA, August 25, 2018.

identify aggression levels of cyberbullying in social network posts manually labeled as Overtly Aggressive (OAG), Covertly Aggressive (CAG) and Non-aggressive (NAG). Our exploratory approach has two main stages. First, we tested multiple vector space modeling methods along with multiple well known learning machines (classifiers) for predicting each of aggression levels individually. The vector space modeling techniques included TF–IDF vectors, Latent Semantic Analysis (LSA, of varied dimensionalities) of TF–IDF vectors. Both TF–IDF and LSA were computed for character and word $n-$gram features. In addition, we used word embedding-based representations of posts. Learning machines that were evaluated along with the aforementioned vector space modeling methods include Naïve Bayes, Linear Perceptron, Support Vector Machine (SVM) and Passive-Aggressive classifier. Once this first stage gives us several preliminary results, we selected the two configurations giving the best accuracies as competing systems for the first two runs. As a third run, we combined these two systems, which incorporates a random class generator based on class frequencies of the training and development sets. This class generator draws one of the three classes in the case of disagreement of the combined systems. This approach resulted in 2nd place of the Facebook competition dataset with 0.6315 of weighted F1 score. In the Social Media dataset, our best system resulted in 4th place with 0.5716 of weighted F1 score.

This paper is organized as follows: the section 2 shows the state of-the-art, section 3 describes the methodology and the COLING'18 TRAC-1 dataset used, section 4 shows the results and finally the section 5 conclude our paper.

2   State of the Art

There already exist software designed to combat the phenomenon of cyberbullying, e.g. Bsecure[1], CyberPatrol[2], Eblaster[3] or IamBigBrother[4]. The main drawback of these systems is that they are based on keyword filtering, which is a limitation because no statistical features of texts are taken into account. Further, these keyword filtering methods require manual maintenance.

To overcome the limitations of keyword filtering systems, (Yin et al., 2009) is one of the former attempts to detect cyberbullying by using statistical features: word frequency, analysis of *feelings* (use of pronouns in the second person, insults, etc.) and context. (Dinakar et al., 2011) built a system that can detect bullying elements in commentaries of YouTube videos. These were classified according to different representative categories (sexuality, intelligence, race and physical attributes). The classification revealed weaknesses and an increase in false positive cases. Researchers emphasized the importance of using common sense to understand users' goals, emotions, and relationships, thereby disambiguating and contextualizing language.

In (Berry and Kogan, 2010) the authors were also interested in a word search method based on a bag of words (BoW) system incorporating sentiment and contextual analysis. They build a decision tree that predicted intimidating messages with an accuracy rate of 93%. The researchers also have developed the Chatcoder software to detect malicious activities on-line (Kontostathis et al., 2012)[5].

In another study it was tested a system that allows users of a website to control the messages posted on their web pages: it customized vocabulary filtering criteria using a machine learning method that automatically labeled the contents. This approach had limitations because it was unable to measure relationships between terms beyond a certain semantic level (Davdar et al., 2012).

(Nahar et al., 2014) provided a concrete method for detecting on-line harassment by measuring the score of sent and received messages (and thus their degree of involvement in a conversation) using the Hyper link-Induced Topic Research algorithm (HITS). The authors also proposed a graphical model that identifies the aggressors and their most active victims.

Other studies have attempted to go further by seeking to take into account more specific characteristics. (Davdar et al., 2012) tried to establish a system based on language features characterizing the author's

---

[1]http://www.bsecuregroup.com/
[2]https://www.cyberpatrol.com/
[3]https://www.veriato.com/
[4]http://www.parentalsoftware.org/bigbrother.html
[5]http://www.chatcoder.com/

genre of comments on MySpace. Their results revealed an improvement in the detection of bullying when this information is taken into account.

As we can see, recent work defines the means to respond to the cyberbullying phenomenon that is becoming more and more widespread as the use of the web does. This paper addresses such a phenomenon and discusses a number of approaches to address it.

3 Methodology and Data

The methodology employed in this study has two main parts. First, we explored the hypothesis that different levels of aggression have different difficulty levels of identification. This hypothesis implies that the classifiers behave differently for different levels of aggression, so we decided to explore each level separately in an OVR (One-Versus-Rest) approach. Furthermore, we hypothesized that Covered Aggressions (CAG) are harder to identify than the other ones. This is because of the undirected way things can be expressed by users. A high pragmatic component is present in the form of sarcasm, which requires to decode extra-linguistic information. Thus, during this first stage, a number of learning algorithms were trained along with different text representations of their input vector space modeling.

Given that this first stage was mainly an exploratory one, assessing the actual difficulties of identifying each level of aggression also involves exploring well-known text representation methods. This can be achieved, on one hand, by using classical methods such as TF-IDF (Spärk-Jones, 1972; Torres-Moreno, 2014), Bag of Words (BoW, simple word counts) and Singular Value Decomposition (SVD). And, on the other hand, we used an easy-to-use word embedding-based method allowing to observe whether Aggression Identification demands more representation ability than what is provided by traditional methods.

Exploring separately the difficulty of identification of each aggression level aims to be highly illustrative of the properties of the Aggression Identification task. Also, it aims to select the machine learning algorithms and the text representation methods that best perform in most of the exploratory experiments.

The second stage was to compete in three runs. To this end, we first used the two combinations of machine learning algorithms with text representations that best performed during the exploratory stage (out of the four that we tested). These combinations were submitted as two independent systems representing one run each. In addition, we combined these two systems as a fusion system (multi-agent system) that was submitted as our third run.

3.1 Dataset

The TRAC-1 dataset (Kumar et al., 2018) has been used in order to train our systems. The available dataset is composed of samples with a variable class distribution according to the task. It is divided into two subsets: a training set and a development set. The training set contains 12014 instances. 4241 of them are labeled as Covertly Aggressive (CAG), 5055 of them are labeled as Non-aggressive (NAG), and 2708 of them are labeled as Overtly Aggressive (OAG). The development dataset is constituted by 3003 samples. 1058 of them are labeled as CAG, 1233 of them are labeled as NAG and 711 of them are labeled as OAG. See that there is a class imbalance mainly affecting the distribution of the OAG class.

3.2 Methods

3.2.1 Classical Vector Space Modeling using TF-IDF

Term Frequency-Inverse Document Frequency (TF-IDF) is a document representation method originally used in Information Retrieval (Spärk-Jones, 1972; Torres-Moreno, 2014). This method represents a document d_i by building its associated sparse vector $x_i = (x_1, \ldots, x_n)^\top \in \mathbb{R}^n$. Each of its components $j = 1, \ldots, n$ is a weight associated to a word w_j in the vocabulary of a collection of documents $D = \{d_i\}_{i=1}^m$. In general, this weight can be seen as the information amount gained from D as w_j is observed in d_i. Each component $x_j \in \mathbb{R}$ of the TF–IDF representation x_i of a document d_i is given by equation (1):

$$x_j = \frac{f_{ij}}{1 + \log_2 m + \log_2 m_j} \tag{1}$$

where m is the total number of documents in the collection, m_j is the number of documents that share the word w_j, and f_{ij} is the frequency of occurrence of w_j within d_i. It has been showed that when the documents are small, a binary version of f_{ij} behaves better than raw frequencies (Salton et al., 1983), so f_{ij} can be defined as $f_{ij} = 1$ if $w_j \in d_i$ and $f_{ij} = 0$ otherwise. Furthermore, in our experiments we computed TF-IDF sparse representations both for character-based and for word-based $n-$grams.

3.2.2 Word Embedding-Based Method

In the NLP literature there are reported a number of text embedding methods at the sentence level. Among the State of the Art methods there is an easy to use one which uses a combination of word embeddings weighted with TF-IDF (*Word Information Series for Sentence Embedding*, WISSE). The word embeddings used were FastText of 300 dimensions (Joulin et al., 2016), which have been reported to performe well in sentence representations for Semantic Textual Similarity tasks (Cer et al., 2017; Arroyo-Fernández et al., 2017). WISSE simply represents a document d_i as in equation (2):

$$x_i = \sum_{w_j \in d_i} \varphi_j x_j,$$ (2)

where $x_i \in \mathbb{R}^n$ is the document/sentence representation of d_i and $x_j \in \mathbb{R}^n$ is the word embedding of w_j. φ_j is the TF–IDF weight of w_j. This weight represents the information amount provided by x_j to x_i given that w_j is observed in d_i and in D (the whole set of FB and SM posts).

3.2.3 Support Vector Machines

Let $\mathcal{X} = \{x_1, \ldots, x_n\}$ be a set of samples, $\mathcal{Y} = \{y_1, \ldots, y_n : y_i \in \{\text{CAG}, \text{NAG}, \text{OAG}\}\}$ a set of labels and $\mathcal{D} = \{(x_i, y_i) : x_i \in \mathcal{X}, y_i \in \mathcal{Y}\}$ a dataset of training examples. A Support Vector Machine (SVM) builds a model $f(x)$ such that given a new arbitrary point x it returns the category $y_i \in \mathcal{Y}$ the point belongs to (Cortes and Vapnik, 1995). The model is given by equation (3):

$$f(x) = \sum_{i=1}^{\ell} \alpha_i k(x_i, x) + b$$ (3)

where $k(\cdot, \cdot)$ is a kernel function acting as an inner product allowing to capture non-linear relationships among data points. The linear case can be considered by setting $k(x_i, x) = \langle x_i, x \rangle$. The so called dual coefficients α_i are associated to each training point in $\mathcal{X}$ and they indicate how important is each training point in representing $\mathcal{D}$. The coefficients are trained by means of linear programming with ℓ_1 regularization. Thus, after the training, most these coefficients result very small or zero. The remaining non-zero coefficients are associated to the so called support vectors, which are used to model the data.

For Aggression identification the SVM model is a representation of the Internet posts mapped so that they can be divided by a clear gap that is as wide as possible so that each division indicates a category.

3.2.4 Passive-Aggressive Classifier

Let $\mathcal{X} = \{x_1, \ldots, x_n\}$ be a set of samples, $\mathcal{Y} = \{y_1, \ldots, y_n : y_i \in \{\text{CAG}, \text{NAG}, \text{OAG}\}\}$ a set of labels and $\mathcal{D} = \{(x_i, y_i) : x_i \in \mathcal{X}, y_i \in \mathcal{Y}\}$ a dataset of training examples. A Passive-Aggressive learning algorithm (PA) updates a vector of weights w_i that parametrize a linear decision boundary $f(x_i) = \langle w_i, x_i \rangle$ if this vector causes an error in the training for a sample $x_i \in \mathcal{X}$. This modification is said to be aggressive. In case there is no error, the vector of weights is unchanged, i.e. $w_{i+1} = w_i$, and then the algorithm is said to be passive (Crammer et al., 2006). The update rule is given by equation (4).

$$w_{i+1} = w_i + \tau_i y_i x_i$$ (4)

where y_i is the training label of the $i-$th training example $(x_i, y_i) \in \mathcal{D}$ and w_{i+1} is the updated version of w_i. It's similar to the delta rule originally proposed for training one-layer neural networks (Haykin, 2009). The parameter τ_i is given by equation (5):

$$\tau_i - \min\left\{C, \frac{L_i(w_i, x_i)}{\|x_i\|^2}\right\}$$ (5)

where C is a manually set parameter that regulates *aggressiveness* (which is commonly termed as *momentum* in neural networks literature). L_i is the hinge loss $L_i(w_i, x_i) = \max\{0, 1 - y_i\langle w_i, x_i\rangle\}$, which indicates whether an error occurred and its magnitude. The version of PA explained here is the simplest one, and it allows to see a general portrait of this kind of algorithms. Nonetheless, a number of different versions of them are shown in detail in (Crammer et al., 2006).

3.2.5 Classifier Fusion Using Class Distribution

Our third run was a fusion of the two classifiers having the best performance on the validation dataset. The fusion is quite simple: for each sample, if the classifiers - Passive-Aggressive and SVM - are in agreement, the predicted class is assigned to the document. Otherwise, if the classifiers are in disagreement, a third classifier (based on the most statistically probable label from the class distribution of the training set) decides the final output by using a simple vote.

4 Results and Discussion

4.1 Results of the Exploratory Stage (training and development datasets)

In the Figures 1-3 we show results (in terms of accuracy) of four approaches, i.e. Naïve Bayes (NB), Perceptron, SVM and Passive-Aggressive (PA), in identifying independently each of the three levels of aggression (OAG, CAG, NAG) in a OVR fashion. To model the input vector space of these algorithms we used two baseline representation methods, i.e. Hashing (Bag of Words, BoW) and TF-IDF, and one state-of-the-art word embedding-based method, i.e. WISSE. One of the main things we observed during the exploratory stage was how the amount of training samples influenced the accuracy of the classifiers. Therefore we plotted the accuracy as a function of the amount of training samples (from the whole training set). The accuracy was measured on the development dataset.

The results show that NB, PA and SVM classifiers perform in similar ways. However, the Perceptron showed to be a bit unstable and performed the worst. In most cases, the classifiers attained relatively stable performance after 5000 training samples. In this sense, with respect to NAG and CAG, identifying OAG aggressions represented much less complexity as a classification problem ($2000 - 3000$ TF-IDF-transformed samples were required by classifiers to stabilize their performance). On the other hand, identifying CAG resulted in a much more complex task for the classifiers. Perceptron was again the worst while Naïve Bayes and linear SVM performed better, but barely surpassed 65% accuracy. Detecting NAG aggressions required much more samples to allow the classifiers to be relatively stable. Furthermore, it was hard for the classifiers to reach $73 - 74\%$ of accuracy. Overall TF-IDF representations allowed the classifiers to be much more stable than Hashing did.

Two additional experiments were conducted for exploring baseline representations on CAG detection in more detail. First, we used Singular Value Decomposition (SVD) for dimensionality reduction on the word-based TF-IDF representations of the posts. Although a number of dimensionalities were tested ($50, 100, 200, 300, 400$), this modification neither showed improvements with respect to sparse TF-IDF representations. Nonetheless, training time increased considerably as the implementations are better prepared for sparse presentations. Secondly, we segmented documents into character n-grams before represent them by means of TF-IDF. Surprisingly the classification accuracy was much better ($+10\%$) in general. This time, the Passive-Aggressive and linear SVM classifiers attained about 70% of accuracy in CAG identification by segmenting the input posts into a range of $[1 - 5]$ character-based n-grams. To observe this performance, more than 9000 samples were needed (See Figures 1-3). Other n-gram ranges did not perform better (e.g. $2 - 5, 3 - 5, 1 - 6, 2 - 6$, etc.).

We also used word embedding-based representations to represent the posts as sentence embeddings. Even when these embeddings showed state-of-the-art performance in STS, their performance in Aggression Identification was not better than the baseline methods presented above (see Figures 4 and 5). The behavior of classifiers with sentence embeddings showed much more unstable and the performance diminished by 5% in general with respect to the character-based TF-IDF sparse representations. Although the sparse representations are high dimensional (thousands of dimensions), 5% or less of their entries are nonzero. Most state-of-the-art implementations of the classifiers are prepared to deal efficiently with this

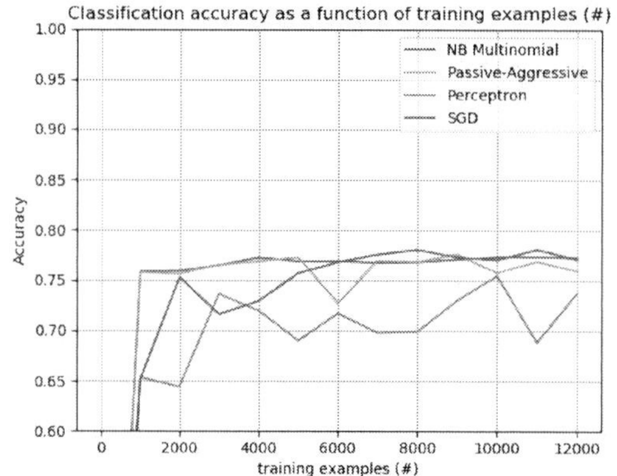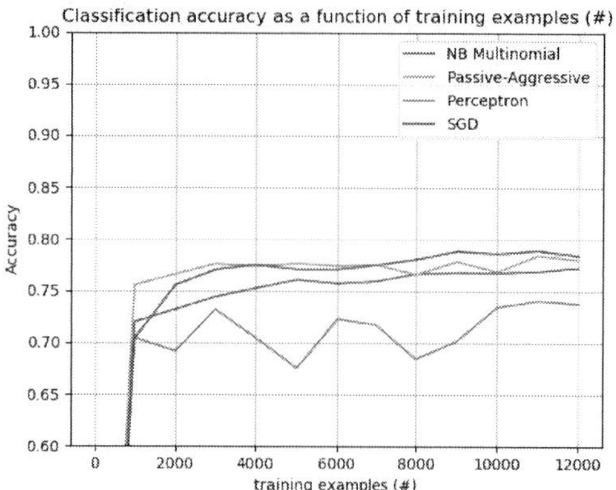

Figure 1: One versus rest accuracy of four learning machines in predicting Overtly Aggressive (OAG) Facebook posts (development dataset). The left hand side plot are accuracies of classifiers on (hashing) Bag of words vectors. The right hand side are plots of accuracies of same classifiers on TF–IDF vectors.

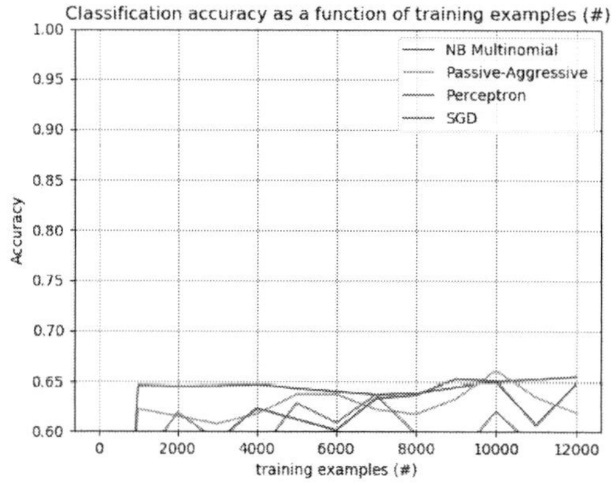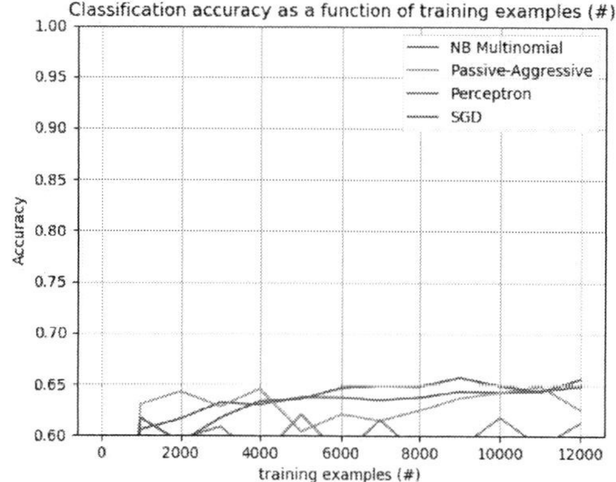

Figure 2: One versus rest accuracy of four learning machines in predicting Covertly Aggressive (CAG) Facebook posts (development dataset). The left hand side plot are accuracies of classifiers on (hashing) Bag of words vectors. The right hand side are plots of accuracies of same classifiers on TF–IDF vectors.

issue. Therefore, the classifier ends by learning from 100 or less nonzero entries by sample. Conversely, sentence embeddings based on word embeddings are dense representations of 300 dimensions, which adds complexity to the learning problem (varying dimensions of the embeddings did not offered improvements and the learning instability held). Furthermore, the original purpose of sentence embeddings is to represent an approximation of each word semantics, and then of the whole sentence semantics. This may result in much more complex patterns represented by sentence embeddings than what is needed for aggression identification.

This additional complexity in their input space can lead to over-fitting of the classifiers.

4.2 Results of the Competition Stage (test dataset)

The Aggression Identification competition required participants to apply their systems on a test dataset. This dataset consists of two files. The first one having a class distribution similar to the training set, and the second one with a so-called "surprise" configuration.

Three runs were conducted on the TRAC-1 test dataset, that was splitted into two files: Facebook and Social Media. There are 916 samples on the Facebook set, and 1257 samples on the Social Media set

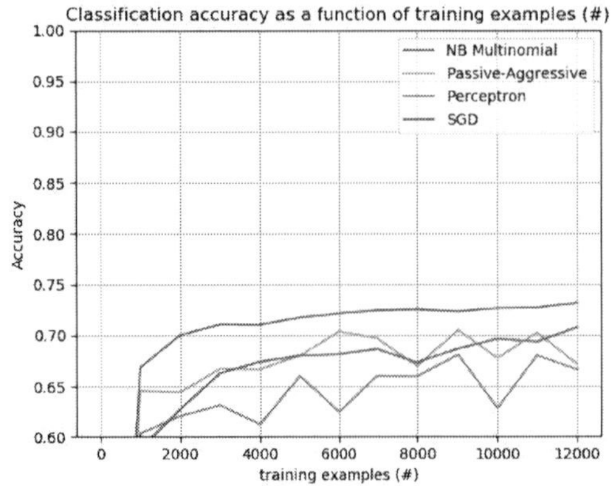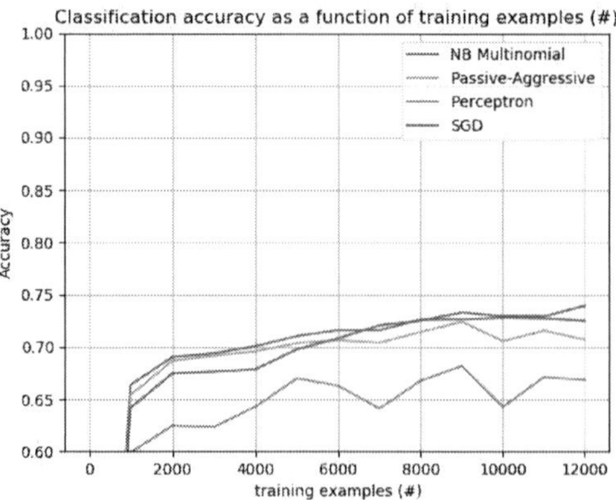

Figure 3: One versus rest accuracy of four learning machines in predicting Non-aggressive (NAG) Facebook posts (development dataset). The left hand side plot are accuracies of classifiers on (hashing) Bag of words vectors. The right hand side are plots of accuracies of same classifiers on TF–IDF vectors.

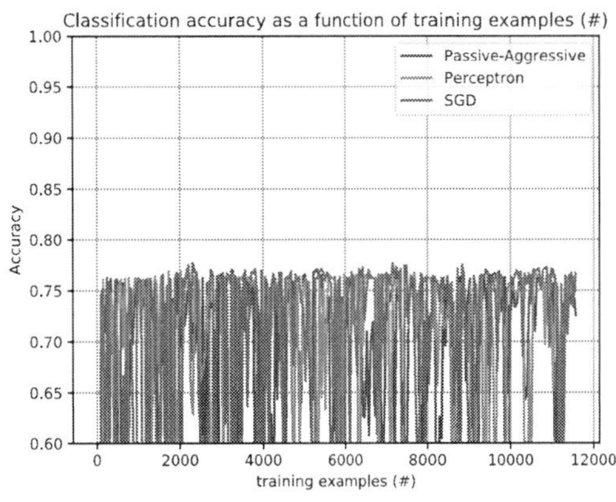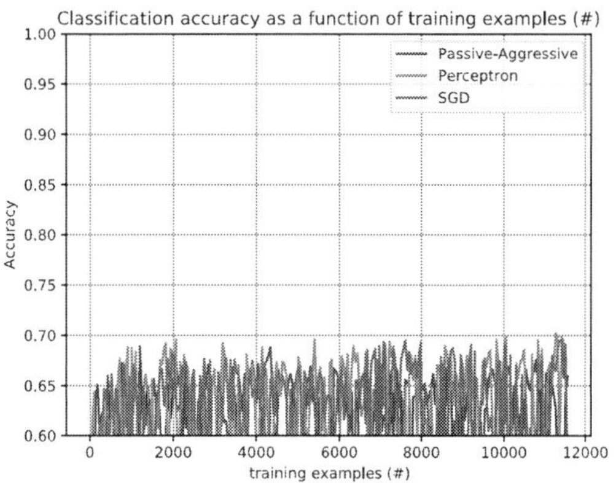

Figure 4: One versus rest accuracies of PA, Perceptron y SVM classifiers on Overtly Aggressive (left) and Non-aggressive (right) Facebook posts (development dataset). The input embeddings were WISSE of 300 dimensions.

(Kumar et al., 2018). During the exploratory stage we selected the two classifiers that performed the best in most experiments conducted, i.e. the Passive-Aggressive (PA) and the SVM classifiers. Therefore, our run 1 was executed by using a PA classifier whose hyperparameters were the best ones found via 3-fold cross-validation on the training dataset; the run 2 was executed by a SVM classifier whose hyperparameters were the best ones found with same method than for PA. And the run 3 was the fusion of both coupled with a probabilistic distribution of the classes. The PA and SVM implementations we used are the provided ones by (Pedregosa et al., 2011) (for the SVM we used the SGD version, Stochastic Gradient Descent). Furthermore, we selected the vector representation that best performed during the exploration stage, i.e. character based n-gram TF-IDF sparse representations with $n \in \{1, 5\}$. Because their low performance during the exploratory stage, we decided do not use the word embedding-based representations during the competition stage.

Tables 1 and 2 shows our rank position on the English Facebook (2nd place) and Social Media (4th place) tasks respectively.

The Figures 6 and 7 shows the confusion matrix (True label vs. Predicted label) measured on the English Facebook and Social Media files respectively. The confusion matrix in the case of Facebook

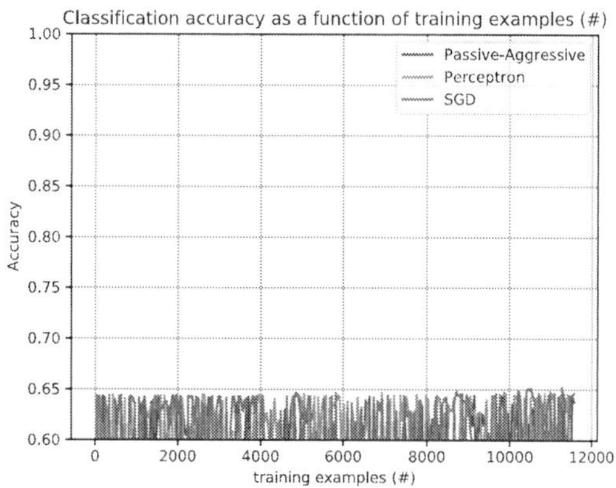

Figure 5: One versus rest accuracies of PA, Perceptron y SVM classifiers on Covertly Aggressive (CAG) Facebook posts (development dataset). The input embeddings were WISSE of 300 dimensions.

Rank	System	F1 (weighted)
1	saroyehun	0.6425
2	**EBSI-LIA-UNAM**	**0.6315**
3	DA-LD-Hildesheim	0.6178
4	TakeLab	0.6161
5	sreeIN	0.6037
...	...	...
30	bhanodaig	0.3572
	Random Baseline	*0.3535*

Table 1: Results for the English (Facebook) task. Our model EBSI-LIA-UNAM (ELU) is placed in 2nd rank.

Rank	System	F1 (weighted)
1	vista.ue	0.6008
2	Julian	0.5994
3	saroyehun	0.5920
4	**EBSI-LIA-UNAM**	**0.5716**
5	uOttawa	0.5690
...	...	...
	Random Baseline	*0.3477*
...	...	...
30	bhanodaig	0.1960

Table 2: Results for the English (Social Media) task. Our model EBSI-LIA-UNAM (ELU) is placed in 4th rank.

data, shows that the OAG and CAG classes are the most difficult to classify (with 52% error rate for OAG, 53% error rate for CAG). For the Social Media file, the CAG and OAG classes were the most difficult to categorize (with 53% error rate for OAG, 64% error rate for CAG). In both sets, the NAG class was detected correctly (33% and 11% error rate).

5 Conclusion

The methodology that we adopted allowed us to observe in broad strokes the complexity of the problem in question. On the one hand, word embeddings are possibly trained to represent much more complex or

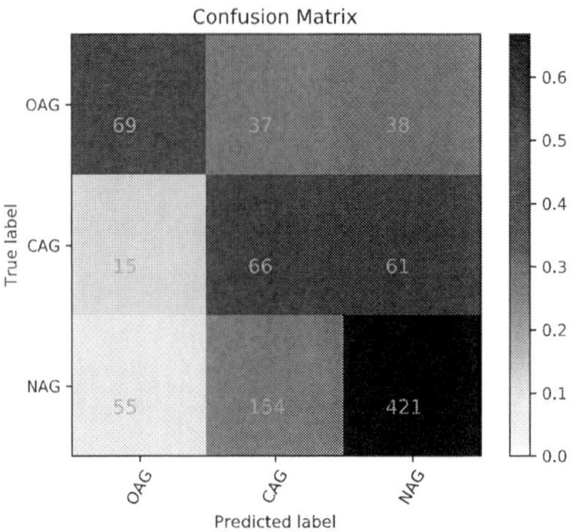

Figure 6: EN-Facebook task, EBSI-LIA-UNAM Run 03.

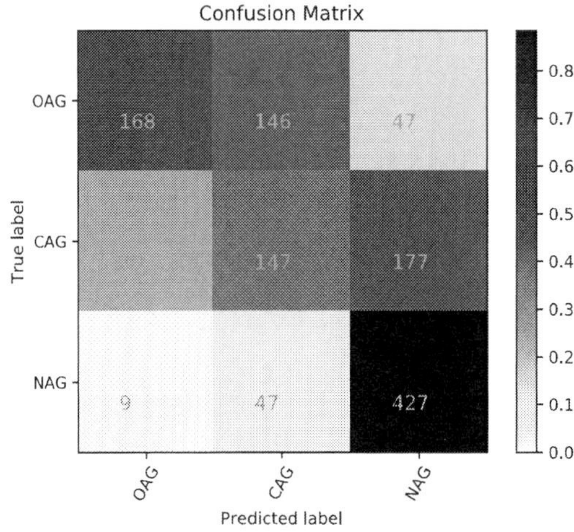

Figure 7: EN-Social Media task, EBSI-LIA-UNAM Run 03.

detailed patterns in the text (e.g., distributional semantics), which leads to over-fitting that is reflected in the instability of the predictions of the classifiers. Probably the word embedding approach is not the best option for this task. Indeed, text representations with classical methods show much better adaptation to this problem, and are much less complex to interpret than word embeddings. Finally, the datasets provided for the task allow for taking into account only linguistic evidence, we think better results require additional data contextualizing other aspects of aggressions in cyberbullying. For example, sarcasm, a pragmatic phenomenon, requires extra-linguistic knowledge to be processed properly. We would have liked to include a sentiment analysis resource in our experimentation. Finally, further processing of the data might have provided us with additional information. For example, it might have been possible to use the degree of severity associated with certain forms to refine our analysis, or to try to specify whether an insulting sentence implies a response that also contains intimidation.

The use of the Levenshtein algorithm could have allowed a more precise identification of insults. This algorithm takes into account changes in character strings, which is particularly suitable for discussions on social networks where non-homogeneous language is used (Baetens, 2013).

References

Ignacio Arroyo-Fernández, Carlos-Francisco Méndez-Cruz, Gerardo Sierra, Juan-Manuel Torres-Moreno, and Grigori Sidorov. 2017. Unsupervised Sentence Representations as Word Information Series: Revisiting TF-IDF. *arXiv preprint arXiv:1710.06524*.

M. Baetens. 2013. La détection automatique de cas de cyber harcèlement textuel dans les médias sociaux. Master's thesis, Université d'Anvers, Belgium.

B. Belsey. 2013. Cyberbullying research center. Technical report, https://cyberbullying.org/.

Michael W. Berry and Jacob Kogan, editors. 2010. *Text Mining: Applications and Theory*. Wiley, Chichester, UK.

Daniel M. Cer, Mona T. Diab, Eneko Agirre, Iñigo Lopez-Gazpio, and Lucia Specia. 2017. Semeval-2017 task 1: Semantic textual similarity multilingual and crosslingual focused evaluation. In Steven Bethard, Marine Carpuat, Marianna Apidianaki, Saif M. Mohammad, Daniel M. Cer, and David Jurgens, editors, *SemEval@ACL*, pages 1–14. Association for Computational Linguistics.

Corinna Cortes and Vladimir Vapnik. 1995. Support-vector networks. *Machine Learning*, 20(3):273–297.

Koby Crammer, Ofer Dekel, Joseph Keshet, Shai Shalev-Shwartz, and Yoram Singer. 2006. Online passive-aggressive algorithms. *Journal of Machine Learning Research*, 7:551–585, December.

Maral Davdar, Franciska de Jong, Roeland Ordelman, and Dolf Triechnigg. 2012. Improved cyberbullying detection using gender information. In *Dutch-Belgian Information Retrieval Workshop DIR 2012*, pages 23–25.

Karthik Dinakar, Roi Reichart, and Henry Lieberman. 2011. Modeling the detection of textual cyberbullying. In *The Social Mobile Web*, volume WS-11-02 of *AAAI Workshops*. AAAI.

Simon S. Haykin. 2009. *Neural networks and learning machines*. Pearson Education, Upper Saddle River, NJ, third edition.

Armand Joulin, Edouard Grave, Piotr Bojanowski, Matthijs Douze, Hérve Jégou, and Tomas Mikolov. 2016. Fasttext.zip: Compressing text classification models. arxiv:1612.03651 - ICLR 2017.

April Kontostathis, Andy Garron, Kelly Reynolds, Will West, and Lynne Edwards. 2012. Identifying predators using chatcoder 2.0. In *CLEF (Online Working Notes/Labs/Workshop)*.

Ritesh Kumar, Aishwarya N. Reganti, Akshit Bhatia, and Tushar Maheshwari. 2018. Aggression-annotated Corpus of Hindi-English Code-mixed Data. In *Proceedings of the 11th Language Resources and Evaluation Conference (LREC)*, Miyazaki, Japan.

Vinita Nahar, Xue Li, Hao Lan Zhang, and Chaoyi Pang. 2014. Detecting cyberbullying in social networks using multi-agent system. *Web Intelligence and Agent Systems*, 12(4):375–388.

F. Pedregosa, G. Varoquaux, A. Gramfort, V. Michel, B. Thirion, O. Grisel, M. Blondel, P. Prettenhofer, R. Weiss, V. Dubourg, J. Vanderplas, A. Passos, D. Cournapeau, M. Brucher, M. Perrot, and E. Duchesnay. 2011. Scikit-learn: Machine learning in Python. *Journal of Machine Learning Research*, 12:2825–2830.

Gerard Salton, Edward A Fox, and Harry Wu. 1983. Extended boolean information retrieval. *Communications of the ACM*, 26(11):1022–1036.

Karen Spärk-Jones. 1972. A statistical interpretation of term specificity and its application in retrieval. *Journal of Documentation*, 28(5):111–121.

Juan-Manuel Torres-Moreno. 2014. *Automatic Text Summarization*. ISTE Ltd, John Wiley & Sons, Inc., London.

Dawei Yin, Brian D. Davison, Zhenzhen Xue, Liangjie Hong, April Kontostathis, and Lynne Edwards. 2009. Detection of harassment on web 2.0. In *1st Content Analysis in Web 2.0 Workshop, CAW 2.0*, Madrid, Spain.

Aggression Identification Using Deep Learning and Data Augmentation

Julian Risch
Hasso Plattner Institute
University of Potsdam
Prof.-Dr.-Helmert-Str. 2-3
14482 Potsdam, Germany
`julian.risch@hpi.de`

Ralf Krestel
Hasso Plattner Institute
University of Potsdam
Prof.-Dr.-Helmert-Str. 2-3
14482 Potsdam, Germany
`ralf.krestel@hpi.de`

Abstract

Social media platforms allow users to share and discuss their opinions online. However, a minority of user posts is aggressive, thereby hinders respectful discussion, and — at an extreme level — is liable to prosecution. The automatic identification of such harmful posts is important, because it can support the costly manual moderation of online discussions. Further, the automation allows unprecedented analyses of discussion datasets that contain millions of posts.

This system description paper presents our submission to the First Shared Task on Aggression Identification. We propose to augment the provided dataset to increase the number of labeled comments from 15,000 to 60,000. Thereby, we introduce linguistic variety into the dataset. As a consequence of the larger amount of training data, we are able to train a special deep neural net, which generalizes especially well to unseen data. To further boost the performance, we combine this neural net with three logistic regression classifiers trained on character and word n-grams, and hand-picked syntactic features. This ensemble is more robust than the individual single models. Our team named "Julian" achieves an F1-score of 60% on both English datasets, 63% on the Hindi Facebook dataset, and 38% on the Hindi Twitter dataset.

1 Introduction

Social media platforms, such as Facebook, YouTube, Twitter, and Instagram, enable millions to publicly share user-generated content. Regardless of different content types, such as text, photos, videos, and events, a crucial point of these platforms is that users can discuss content. The opportunity to articulate opinions and ideas online is a valuable good: It is part of the freedom of expression, which is declared in the Universal Declaration of Human Rights. However, aggressive and/or hateful posts can disrupt otherwise respectful discussions. Such posts are called "toxic", because they poison a conversation so that other users abandon it. Toxicity is manifold and comprises, for example, obscene language, insults, threats, and identity hate. Such statements are not covered by the freedom of expression, because they harm others. The boundaries of the freedom of expression are a controversial topic. In moderated online discussions, it is the task of human moderators to identify toxic comments and potentially delete them.

An automatic identification of toxic posts could support (or even to some extent replace) the costly manual moderation of online discussions. For example, it could draw the attention of moderators to posts that have been automatically identified as toxic. Another advantage of the automatic identification of toxic posts is that it allows the analysis of much larger datasets. For example, classifiers that were trained on a rather small hand-labeled dataset have been successfully used to machine-label and analyze datasets with tens of millions of posts (Wulczyn et al., 2017).

The First Shared Task on Aggression Identification (Kumar et al., 2018a) deals with the classification of the aggression level of user posts at different social media platforms. It is part of the First Workshop on Trolling, Aggression and Cyberbullying at the 27th International Conference of Computational Linguistics (COLING 2018). The task is a three-way classification problem with the three classes "overtly aggressive" (OAG), "covertly aggressive" (CAG), and "non-aggressive" (NAG). The training data consists

Proceedings of the First Workshop on Trolling, Aggression and Cyberbullying, pages 150–158
Santa Fe, USA, August 25, 2018.

of 15,000 aggression-annotated Facebook posts each in Hindi and English. Weighted macro-averaged F1-scores serve as the evaluation metric: The individual F1-score of each class is weighted by the proportion of the concerned class in the test set and the final F1-score is the average of these individual F-scores of each class.

In this system description paper, we introduce our implemented system as submitted for the shared task. Our approach is based on a recurrent neural network, more specifically, a bi-directional gated recurrent unit (GRU) layer with max pooling and average pooling. However, the relatively small size of the training dataset is a strong limitation for deep learning approaches. Therefore, we propose to augment the training dataset: We use machine translation to translate each English comment into a foreign language, e.g. French, and translate it back into English afterwards. The result of these translations is another English comment that typically uses slightly different words compared to the initial comment. Examples for these translations are given in Section 3.1 and the augmented dataset together with our implementation is published online[1].

Our contributions can be summarized as providing a:

1. data augmentation method that triples the dataset size,

2. neural network architecture based on a GRU layer for the task of Aggression Identification,

3. comparison of our results at the different subtasks and an error analysis of our approach.

Section 2 gives an overview of related work. Section 3 explains our approach and goes into detail about the proposed data augmentation method and the neural network architecture. We lists our results at the different subtasks in Section 4 and discuss how the proposed approach generalizes to unseen data. Finally, we conclude and outline possible paths for future work in Section 5.

2   Related Work

While the shared task focuses on aggression identification, related work considers the broader field of hate speech, offensive, and abusive language identification. First approaches to the problem of classifying insulting messages use a decision tree and go back to Spertus (1997). A hand-written set of rules with syntactic and semantic text features are the basis of this model. For a slightly different task, harassment detection in the web, Yin et al. (2009) introduce contextual features, which consider a user's previous and succeeding posts as a context. The survey by Schmidt and Wiegand (2017) points out that bag-of-word models are good features for hate speech detection, although they ignore word order and sentence syntax. Further, the authors propose to generalize from particular words to clusters of words. To capture the semantic similarity of words our approach uses the fastText model by Bojanowski et al. (2017). According to the survey by Schmidt et al., positive, negative, and neutral words are promising features for hate speech detection. Polarity classifiers for short texts, such as SentiStrength (Thelwall et al., 2010), are suited to extract such words of polarity and we make use of a polarity classifier in our approach.

Previous work agrees that word n-grams are well-performing features for hate speech detection (Nobata et al., 2016; Badjatiya et al., 2017; Warner and Hirschberg, 2012; Davidson et al., 2017; Schmidt and Wiegand, 2017). Davidson et al. (2017) compared logistic regression, naive Bayes, decision trees, random forests, and support vector machines, and conclude that logistic regression and support vector machines are the best performing classifiers for hate speech detection. Based on these insights, we include word n-grams and logistic regression in our approach. Further, a combination of different models, as in the multi-level approach by Razavi et al. (2010), can make use of each model's strengths. Therefore, we combine four different models in an ensemble.

One of the main limitation for research progress in the field of toxic comment classification is the low amount of available accurately labeled data (Kennedy et al., 2017). Wulczyn et al. (2017) address this issue by training a classifier on a small set of human-labeled comments in order to afterwards generate a larger machine-labeled dataset. Recently, Kaggle's Toxic Comment Classification[2] made available more

---

[1] `https://hpi.de/naumann/projects/repeatability/text%2Dmining.html`
[2] `https://www.kaggle.com/c/jigsaw-toxic-comment-classification-challenge/`

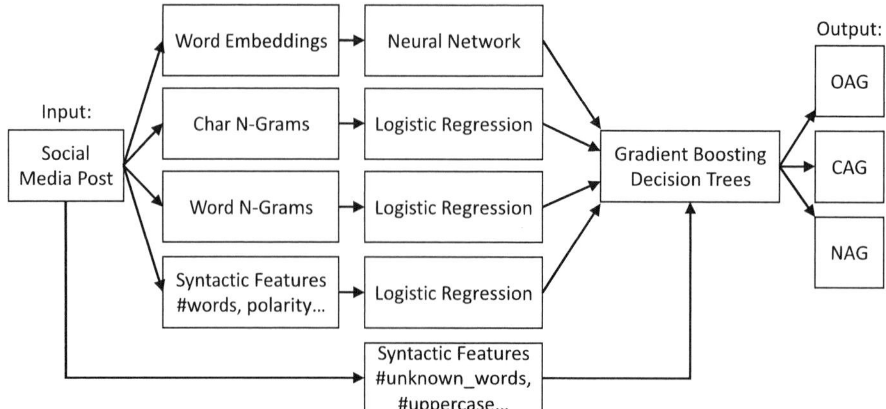

Figure 1: Given a social media post, we apply four different models and combine their predictions in an ensemble to identify the aggression level of the post (OAG, CAG, NAG).

than 150,000 English, hand-labeled comments. Other shared tasks provide non-English hand-labeled data, such as German tweets[3]. Besides this positive recent development of data sharing, fine-grained labeling becomes a topic of broader interest, for example in the work of Van Hee et al. (2015). A discussion on the challenges of identifying profanity vs. hate speech is given by Malmasi and Zampieri (2018). The results demonstrate that it can be hard to distinguish between overt and covert aggression in social media. The finer-grained labeling coincides with the demand for explanations of a classifier's decision. A human moderator that decides whether to delete an automatically identified toxic comment might want to know a fine-grained reason, such as whether the comment contains an insult, a threat, or identity hate.

3 Methodology and Data

Our approach is based on two main ideas: (1) increasing the amount of available training data by data augmentation in Section 3.1 and (2) leveraging the larger amount of training data with a deep learning approach in Section 3.3. In addition to that, we propose three other models besides the deep learning approach. Figure 1 is a system overview that shows how the four models are combined in an ensemble. We publish the augmented dataset and the implementation of our approach in python with Keras and Tensorflow online[4].

3.1 Data Augmentation Based on Machine Translation

The training dataset consists of 15,000 posts for the English task and 15,000 posts for the Hindi task. The data collection methods that were used to compile the dataset are described in Kumar et al. (2018b). We refer to the dataset with published training data as Facebook dataset, because it contains Facebook posts. The other dataset, which has been provided only as a test dataset without training labels, is referred to as Twitter dataset, because it contains tweets.

In the following, we present our data augmentation method, which is based on the following insight: Machine translating a user comment into a foreign language and then translating it back to the initial language preserves its meaning but results in different wording. This change in wording is essential for our approach: If the translation did not change the wording, it could not augment our dataset, because the dataset already contains the exact same comment. However, because the wording is different, the translated comment adds to our dataset. Only if the meaning is preserved, we can assume that the label (non-aggressive, covertly aggressive, overtly aggressive) of the initial comment also holds for the translated comment. Thanks to the recent advances of neural machine translation and its continuously

[3]https://projects.cai.fbi.h%2Dda.de/iggsa/germeval/
[4]https://hpi.de/naumann/projects/repeatability/text%2Dmining.html

improving accuracy, we can assume that machine translation preserves the meaning of posts. We give two examples for the data augmentation. The first example shows that different translations use different words, such as "health", "wealth", "(economic) growth", and "prosperity".

1. Initial English post: "Happy Diwali.!!let's wish the next one year health,wealth n growth to our Indian economy."

2. English to French to English: "Happy Diwali., Wish the next year health, wealth and growth to our Indian economy."

3. English to German to English: "Happy Diwali, let us wish the next year health, prosperity and growth of our Indian economy."

4. English to Spanish to English: "Happy Diwali We wish the health, economic growth and health of our next year!"

The second example is a rather short post and all its translations are similar. However, for example, the abbreviation "'u" for the word "you" is resolved.

1. Initial English post: "AAP dont need the monsters like u"

2. English to French to English: "AAP does not need monsters like you"

3. English to German to English: "AAP does not need the monsters like you"

4. English to Spanish to English: "AAP does not need monsters like you"

We applied this data augmentation method also to the Hindi dataset. Therefore, each Hindi post was machine-translated into English and afterwards translated back to Hindi. For Hindi, this method did not work as well. Often already the intermediate step of translating to English failed in preserving the meaning of the initial Hindi post. As a consequence, the meaning of the translated posts did not match with the initial labels and the translated posts could not be used for training. We assume that the quality of machine translations from Hindi to other languages is comparably worse due to a lower amount of training data.

3.2 Data Pre-Processing

We propose a special tokenization method for hashtags and user mentions. Many hashtags in the dataset are concatenations of multiple words. For example, the meaning of "#realsurgicalstrike", "#death-toPakistan", and "#saysiamaproudchutiyawhodoentknowshitabouthistory" can only be understood if the words are split correctly. In some cases, the full post contains only a hashtag, such as the post "#THANKYOUTAKER" which is labeled as covertly aggressive. We propose to split the strings after "#" and "@" symbols into their original words with a dynamic programming approach. Our assumption is that the best splitting is the one that maximizes the product of each word's individual probability of occurrence. For example, the splitting "real surgical strike" is to prefer over the splitting "real surgicals trike", because the probability of "surgical" is higher than the probability of "surgicals" and the probability of "trike" is higher than the probability of "trike". A word's probability of occurrence can be inferred from a large corpus of natural language, such as Wikipedia. Another splitting strategy would be to split at capitalized letters, but we did not explore this idea.

Our deep learning approach uses 300-dimensional, pre-trained word embeddings by fastText (Bojanowski et al., 2017). More specifically, we use the common crawl embeddings[5] for the English tasks and the Hindi Wikipedia embeddings[6] for the Hindi tasks (Grave et al., 2018). In comparison to other embedding methods, fastText embeddings do not suffer from out-of-vocabulary problems. A word that has never been seen during training time is represented by embeddings of character n-grams.

---

[5] https://fasttext.cc/docs/en/english%2Dvectors.html
[6] https://fasttext.cc/docs/en/crawl%2Dvectors.html

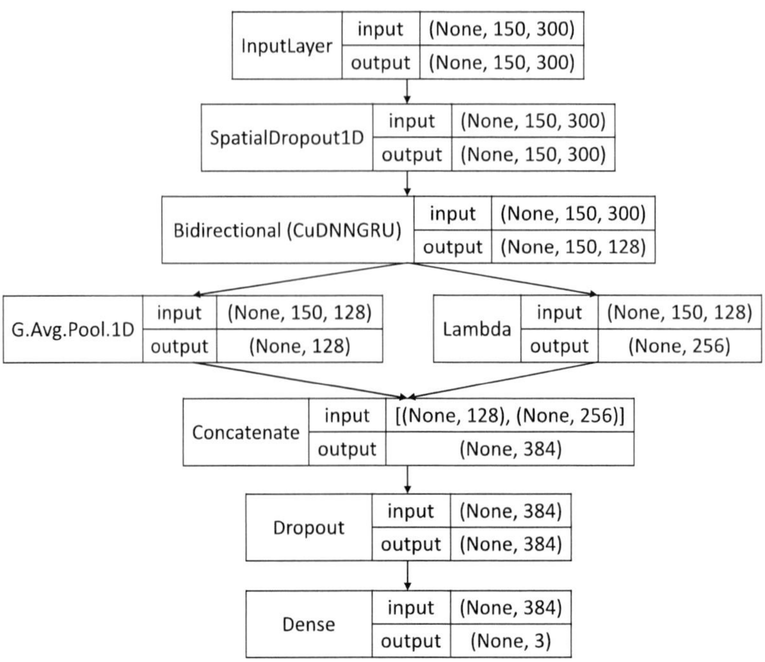

Figure 2: The neural network uses GRUs, average pooling, and k-maximum pooling (Lambda layer).

3.3   GRUs for Aggression Identification

We propose a recurrent neural network based on GRUs. The network architecture is visualized in Figure 2. We use pre-trained, fixed fastText embeddings, obtained as described in the previous Section 3.2. We pad all posts to sequences of 150 words. The word embeddings are input to a spatial dropout, which blocks the embeddings of 10% randomly chosen input words. A bi-directional layer of 64 GRUs processes the remaining 90% of input. The next layer performs global average pooling and global k-maximum pooling independently on the sequence of the outputs of all GRUs. A k-maximum pooling with $k = 2$ extracts not only the largest, but also the second-largest element of the previous layer. A Lambda layer implements this non-standard pooling technique. The average, the maximum, and the second-largest element are concatenated into one vector and a dropout of 10% is added to prevent overfitting. Finally, a dense layer with softmax activation outputs 3 class probabilities. The model is trained for 2 epochs with a batch size of 32. We observe that the data augmentation slightly reduces the number of epochs until overfitting starts.

3.4   Tf-idf on Character and Word N-Grams

We extract character n-grams of length 2 to 6 and limit the set to the 50,000 most frequent character n-grams. We extract word n-grams of length 1 to 2 and filter English stopwords, but also all words that occur in more than 50% of all documents or in less than 2 documents. We normalize the frequency of occurrence of all n-grams using tf-idf. As the classifier, we choose logistic regression for both, word and character n-grams. Based on the extracted n-grams, we train logistic regression models according to the one-vs.-rest strategy: We train one classifier per aggression level. For each aggression level, all posts of that level are positive and all other posts are negative training examples.

3.5   Hand-Picked Features

A set of hand-picked features captures various properties, such as punctuation and capitalization, but also emoticons. Overall, a combination of 35 extracted features serves as input to three logistic regressions, which are trained according to the one-vs.-rest strategy for each level of aggression. 25 of these features capture emoticons with regular expressions for sad, happy, and neutral faces. The remaining 10 features capture, for example, the number of words, the proportion of uppercase characters to lowercase characters, the number of negation words, and also the polarity of the post. We apply the VADER sentiment analyzer to extract polarity scores (Gilbert, 2014).

3.6 Ensembling

Word embeddings, word n-grams, character n-grams, and hand-picked features capture different properties of user posts and therefore have different strengths and weaknesses. For example, word n-grams suffer from out-of-vocabulary problems, which makes them sensitive to obfuscated words. The dataset contains posts that make extensive use of obfuscation, such as "Son of a B****", "***k them!!!!". Word embeddings and word n-grams cannot capture the meaning of these obfuscated posts, but character n-grams or the number of asterisks and exclamation marks as hand-picked features can.

For the four models, we analyze the pairwise Pearson correlation of their predictions as listed in Table 1. The word n-gram and the character n-gram models have the highest correlation. In contrast, the recurrent neural network and the word n-gram model have a rather low correlation. Their low correlation motivates to combine their predictions, because we can assume that they complement each other well. If they both have a similarly high F1-score, their combination outperforms the single models.

Class	RNN-Word	RNN-Char	RNN-Hand	Word-Char	Word-Hand	Char-Hand
OAG	0.7271	0.7489	0.4548	0.8417	0.4132	0.4229
NAG	0.8070	0.8241	0.4163	0.8844	0.3961	0.4213
CAG	0.6240	0.6516	0.1779	0.7687	0.1499	0.2102

Table 1: Pearson correlation of the different models and classes (RNN: recurrent neural network, Word: word n-grams, Char: character n-grams, Hand: hand-picked features).

The different strengths and weaknesses of the proposed four models motivate their combination in an ensemble. For each of the four models, we run 10-fold cross-validation and create out-of-fold predictions. For each of the 10 runs, we also make predictions for the test set and average all 10 predictions per model. We use the out-of-fold predictions to learn, what combination of the single models performs best. Instead of a simple weighted average of the different models, we propose a stacking approach: Given a comment, we extract features and based on these features, decide how to weight the different models' predictions for this particular comment.

For each comment, we extract: (1) the length (number of characters), (2) the relative number of uppercase characters (number of uppercase characters divided by the total number of characters), (3) the relative number of non-alpha characters (number of non-alpha characters divided by the total number of characters), and (4) the relative number of exclamation marks (number of exclamation marks divided by the total number of characters). For english-language comments, we also extract the relative number of how many words in the comment have a GloVe embedding (Pennington et al., 2014). Although we use fasttext embeddings, which do not suffer from out-of-vocabulary problems, we include this feature to measure how many uncommon words are used in the comment. Based on the extracted features, we train a stacker on the out-of-fold predictions and combine all approaches in an ensemble. The stacker uses gradient boosting trees. More precisely, we use 75 trees with a depth of 3, a bagging fraction of 0.8 and a feature fraction of 0.45.

4   Results

Table 2 lists our cross-validation results. The RNN, word n-grams and character n-grams perform equally well on the English data. The data augmentation makes only a small difference overall. However, it improves the F1-score of the RNN from 57.2% to 58.5%. On the Hindi data, character n-grams clearly outperform all other models. We assume that the performance of the RNN could be improved with better word embeddings, such as embeddings trained on Hindi social media posts. The hand-picked feature selection is superior to the random baseline but inferior to all other models for both languages.

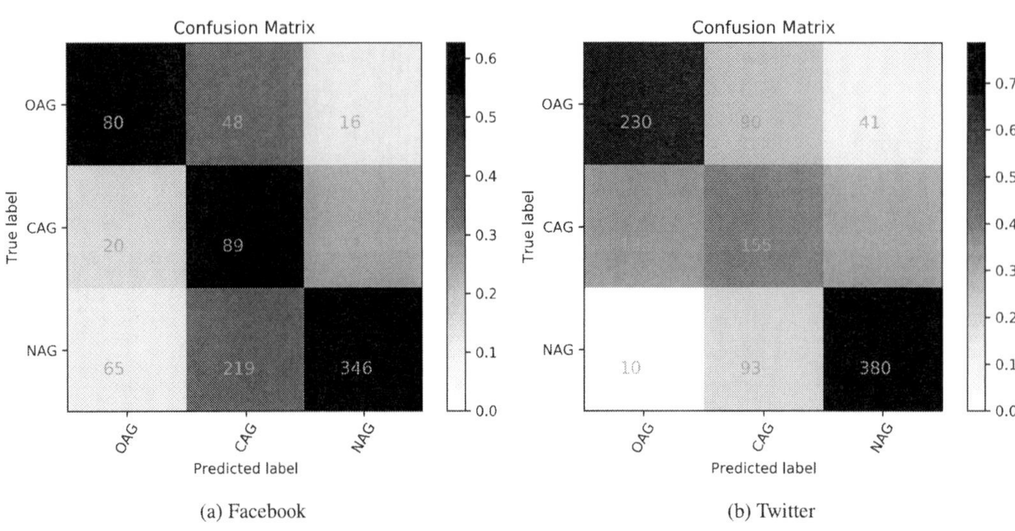

(a) Facebook   (b) Twitter

Figure 3: Confusion matrices for the ensemble appproach on the English test datasets.

Table 3 lists our test set results. Our results on both English test sets are the most stable results across all participating teams: We achieve an F1-score of 60.0% on both datasets, the Facebook dataset and the Twitter dataset. These results show that our approach does not suffer from overfitting to the training dataset and generalizes well to other datasets. Our approach achieves rank 6 out of 30 on the Facebook dataset with an F1-score of 60.0% (F1-score of the top team: 64.2%). On the Twitter dataset, it achieves rank 2 out of 30 with an F1-score of 60.0% (F1-score of the top team: 60.1%).

Our results on the Hindi test sets differ for the Facebook dataset and the Twitter dataset: Our approach achieves rank 4 out of 15 on the Facebook dataset with an F1-score of 63.1% (F1-score of the top team: 64.5%). On the Twitter dataset, it achieves rank 8 out of 15 with an F1-score of 38.3% (F1-score of the top team: 49.9%). The F1-scores of each team differ between the Facebook dataset and the Twitter dataset by 13.1% on average. Therefore, we assume that the differences in classification performance are inherent to the datasets.

System	F1 En FB	F1 En FB augm.	F1 Hi FB
Random Baseline	0.3324	0.3395	0.3425
RNN	0.5722	0.5846	0.5413
Word N-Grams	0.5764	0.5766	0.5883
Char N-Grams	0.5803	0.5791	0.6103
Feature Selection	0.3966	0.3871	0.3701
Ensemble	**0.6060**	**0.6084**	**0.6292**

Table 2: F1-scores with 10-fold cross-validation on English Facebook dataset (En FB) and Hindi Facebook dataset (Hi FB). F1-score of the RNN approach is improved on the augmented (augm.) dataset.

System	F1 En FB	F1 En SM	F1 Hi FB	F1 Hi SM
Random Baseline	0.3535	0.3477	0.3571	0.3206
Ensemble	**0.6011**	**0.5995**	**0.6311**	**0.3835**

Table 3: F1-scores on the test set. The ensemble achieves higher F1-scores on the test set than the single models in the cross-validation.

Figure 3 shows the confusion matrix of the ensemble submission for the English test datasets. Fig-

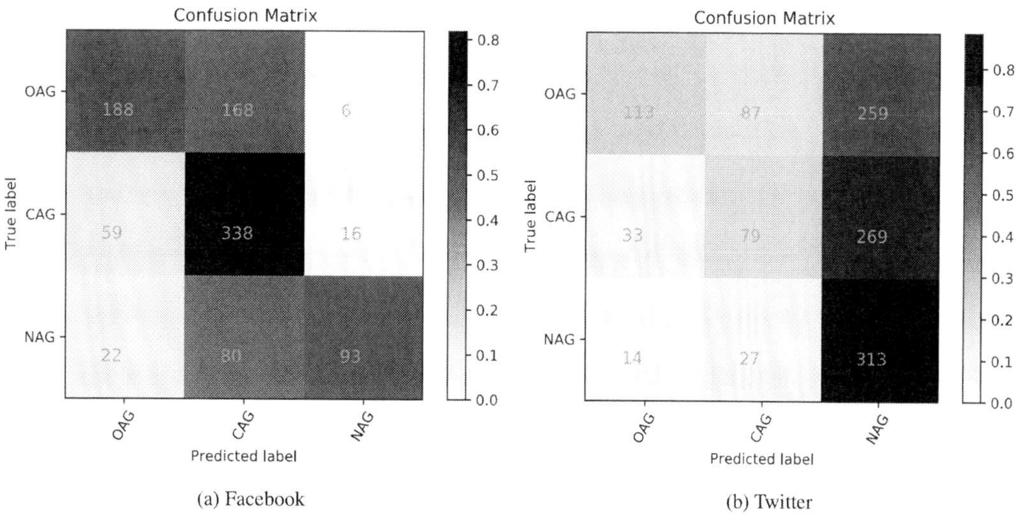

(a) Facebook   (b) Twitter

Figure 4: Confusion matrices for the ensemble approach on the Hindi test datasets.

ure 3b shows that the classifier works equally well for all three classes: overtly aggressive, covertly aggressive, and non-aggressive. As to expect, the non-aggressive class is more often confused with the covertly aggressive class than the overtly aggressive class. Similarly, the overtly aggressive class is more often confused with the covertly aggressive class than the non-aggressive class. While on the English Twitter dataset the classifier works well for non-aggressive posts and for overtly aggressive posts, it is only slightly better than a random baseline for covertly aggressive posts. Covertly aggressive posts are often misclassified as either non-aggressive or overtly aggressive. Figure 4a and 4b show the confusion matrices of the ensemble submission for the Hindi test datasets. It is hard for the classifier to distinguish overtly aggressive from covertly aggressive Facebook posts and covertly aggressive from non-aggressive ones. For the Twitter dataset, the majority of the posts is misclassified as non-aggressive.

5   Conclusion

In this paper we considered the problem of aggression identification in social media posts. We presented our submitted system for the First Shared Task on Aggression Identification (Kumar et al., 2018a) as part of the First Workshop on Trolling, Aggression and Cyberbullying at the 27th International Conference of Computational Linguistics (COLING 2018). Our approach leverages machine translation to augment the training dataset and includes a GRU-based deep neural network for the classification. A combination of four models makes our approach more robust and improves its ability to generalize to unseen data.

Across all participating teams, our approach achieves the most stable results: On the English dataset, we achieve rank 6 out of 30 on the Facebook dataset with an F1-score of 60.0% and rank 2 out of 30 with an F1-score of 60.0% (F1-score of the top team: 60.1%). The results confirm the assumption that an ensemble of different models is robust against changes of the dataset. In future, our approach could be extended by augmenting also the test dataset. Further, we are confident that better suited word embeddings would improve classification performance and that more labeled training data would give the opportunity to train more complex neural network architectures.

References

Pinkesh Badjatiya, Shashank Gupta, Manish Gupta, and Vasudeva Varma. 2017. Deep learning for hate speech detection in tweets. In *Proceedings of the International Conference on World Wide Web (WWW)*, pages 759–760. International World Wide Web Conferences Steering Committee.

Piotr Bojanowski, Edouard Grave, Armand Joulin, and Tomas Mikolov. 2017. Enriching word vectors with subword information. *Transactions of the Association for Computational Linguistics (TACL)*, 5:135–146.

Thomas Davidson, Dana Warmsley, Michael Macy, and Ingmar Weber. 2017. Automated hate speech detection and the problem of offensive language. In *Proceedings of the International Conference on Web and Social Media (ICWSM)*, pages 512–515.

CJ Hutto Eric Gilbert. 2014. VADER: A parsimonious rule-based model for sentiment analysis of social media text. In *Proceedings of the International Conference on Web and Social Media (ICWSM)*, pages 216–225.

Edouard Grave, Piotr Bojanowski, Prakhar Gupta, Armand Joulin, and Tomas Mikolov. 2018. Learning word vectors for 157 languages. In *Proceedings of the International Conference on Language Resources and Evaluation (LREC)*.

George Kennedy, Andrew McCollough, Edward Dixon, Alexei Bastidas, John Ryan, Chris Loo, and Saurav Sahay. 2017. Technology solutions to combat online harassment. In *Proceedings of the Workshop on Abusive Language Online*, pages 73–77. ACL.

Ritesh Kumar, Atul Kr. Ojha, Shervin Malmasi, and Marcos Zampieri. 2018a. Benchmarking Aggression Identification in Social Media. In *Proceedings of the Workshop on Trolling, Aggression and Cyberbulling (TRAC)*.

Ritesh Kumar, Aishwarya N. Reganti, Akshit Bhatia, and Tushar Maheshwari. 2018b. Aggression-annotated Corpus of Hindi-English Code-mixed Data. In *Proceedings of the Language Resources and Evaluation Conference (LREC)*.

Shervin Malmasi and Marcos Zampieri. 2018. Challenges in Discriminating Profanity from Hate Speech. *Journal of Experimental & Theoretical Artificial Intelligence*, 30:1–16.

Chikashi Nobata, Joel Tetreault, Achint Thomas, Yashar Mehdad, and Yi Chang. 2016. Abusive Language Detection in Online User Content. In *Proceedings of the International Conference on World Wide Web (WWW)*, pages 145–153. International World Wide Web Conferences Steering Committee.

Jeffrey Pennington, Richard Socher, and Christopher D. Manning. 2014. GloVe: Global vectors for word representation. In *Proceedings of the Conference on Empirical Methods in Natural Language Processing (EMNLP)*, pages 1532–1543. ACL.

Amir H. Razavi, Diana Inkpen, Sasha Uritsky, and Stan Matwin. 2010. Offensive language detection using multi-level classification. In *Proceedings of the Canadian Conference on Advances in Artificial Intelligence (Canadian AI)*, pages 16–27. Springer-Verlag.

Anna Schmidt and Michael Wiegand. 2017. A Survey on Hate Speech Detection Using Natural Language Processing. In *Proceedings of the International Workshop on Natural Language Processing for Social Media (SocialNLP)*, pages 1–10. ACL.

Ellen Spertus. 1997. Smokey: Automatic recognition of hostile messages. In *Proceedings of the National Conference on Artificial Intelligence and Conference on Innovative Applications of Artificial Intelligence (AAAI /IAAI)*, pages 1058–1065. AAAI.

Mike Thelwall, Kevan Buckley, Georgios Paltoglou, Di Cai, and Arvid Kappas. 2010. Sentiment strength detection in short informal text. *Journal of the Association for Information Science and Technology*, 61(12):2544–2558.

Cynthia Van Hee, Els Lefever, Ben Verhoeven, Julie Mennes, Bart Desmet, Guy De Pauw, Walter Daelemans, and Véronique Hoste. 2015. Detection and fine-grained classification of cyberbullying events. In *Proceedings of the International Conference Recent Advances in Natural Language Processing (RANLP)*, pages 672–680.

William Warner and Julia Hirschberg. 2012. Detecting hate speech on the world wide web. In *Proceedings of the Workshop on Language in Social Media (LSM)*, pages 19–26. ACL.

Ellery Wulczyn, Nithum Thain, and Lucas Dixon. 2017. Ex machina: Personal attacks seen at scale. In *Proceedings of the International Conference on World Wide Web (WWW)*, pages 1391–1399. International World Wide Web Conferences Steering Committee.

Dawei Yin, Zhenzhen Xue, Liangjie Hong, Brian D Davison, April Kontostathis, and Lynne Edwards. 2009. Detection of harassment on web 2.0. *Proceedings of the Content Analysis in the WEB*, 2:1–7.

Cyber-aggression Detection using Cross Segment-and-Concatenate Multi-Task Learning from Text

Ahmed Husseini Orabi, Mahmoud Husseini Orabi,
Diana Inkpen, Qianjia Huang
University of Ottawa
{ahuss045, mhuss092, diana.inkpen,
qhuan035}@uottawa.ca

David Van Bruwaene
SafeToNet Canada

dvanbruwaene@safe-
tonet.com

Abstract

In this paper, we propose a novel deep-learning architecture for text classification, named cross segment-and-concatenate multi-task learning (CSC-MTL). We use CSC-MTL to improve the performance of cyber-aggression detection from text. Our approach provides a robust shared feature representation for multi-task learning by detecting contrasts and similarities among polarity and neutral classes. We participated in the cyber-aggression shared task under the team name uOttawa. We report 59.74% F1 performance for the Facebook test set and 56.9% for the Twitter test set, for detecting aggression from text.

1 Introduction

Deep neural networks provide multiple structures that help learn abstract features from text, which is beneficial for NLP. However, deep neural networks are more likely to have overfitting issues more than traditional approaches. Multi-task learning (MTL) (Caruana, 1993) provides a solution to overcome such a limitation, due to its ability to provide transferable learning models (Baxter, 1997; Mou et al., 2016). We are interested in the use of MTL in NLP applications, particularly for detecting cyber-aggression in text — the trolling, aggression, and cyberbullying shared task.

Cyberbullying and cyber-aggression (Smith et al., 2008) have become a growing social problem. They have several definitions (Grigg, 2010; Smith et al., 2008; Tokunaga, 2010) due to their different forms and impacts on internet users. As opposed to traditional bullying and aggression, they can occur at any time, and they do not have restricted places; i.e. schools. Cyber-aggression basically describes the behavior of sending intentional offensive, derogatory, or harmful content (Grigg, 2010) to an individual or a group of people. Cyberbullying, as opposed to cyber-aggression, involves repetitions rather than intention. On the other hand, trolling has different definitions, some of which describe the behavior of disrupting or provoking people by posing inflammatory, malicious, or off-topic comments (Mihaylov & Nakov, 2015).

The trolling, aggression, and cyberbullying shared task (Bhatia & Maheshwari, 2018; Kumar, Ojha, Malmasi, & Zampieri, 2018) was used to determine the severity of cyber-aggression (Table 1) of Twitter and Facebook posts published by users. This task is challenging as it is new, and there is no prior data available for comparison. The leaderboard results have been anonymized during the compaction. The development sets are relatively small compared to the testing set. Thus, the models must be able to generalize, specially that the testing sets have a larger size as compared to the training sets.

In this paper, our contributions can be summarized as below.

- **Cross segment-and-concatenate multi-task learning (CSC-MTL):** we propose a novel approach that enables robust shared feature representation of multi-tasks by highlighting contrasts among polarity and neutral classes. We report the performance of our approach on binary and categorical problems and show that it leads to improved performance for both.
- **Multi-Convolutional Neural Network with Pooling (MultiCNNPooling) model:** we develop and evaluate the performance of our proposed method with MultiCNNPooling model for cyber-aggression intensity ordinal classification.

Proceedings of the First Workshop on Trolling, Aggression and Cyberbullying, pages 159–165
Santa Fe, USA, August 25, 2018.

Table 1: Number of text messages in cyber-aggression shared task 2018.

Category	Train	Dev	Test		Total
			Facebook	Twitter	
Covertly aggressive	4240	1057	142	413	5852
Overtly aggressive	2708	711	144	361	3924
Non-aggressive	5051	1233	630	483	7397

2   Data Preprocessing

We use a social media processing tool to prepare the text and provide a fast and reliable tokenization. It helps process social media posts such as emoticons, emojis, hash tags, and user mentions, as well as tokenization and sentence encoding. This involves the steps below:

- The NGram tokenizer is used with a supplied vocabulary. Sentences are tokenized into tokens, which are used afterwards to encode text as a sequence of indices to be fed to the network.
- Accents and non-Latin characters are cleaned from text.
- Emoticons and emojis are identified and then replaced with meaningful text. For instance, replace :(by "sad".
- Hashtags and URLs are recognized and then replaced with unique text; i.e., <hashtag_start>depressed<hashtag_end> instead of #depressed.
- User reference mentions are identified and replaced with person entities; i.e., <person>.

3   Cross Segment-and-Concatenate MTL (CSC-MTL)

Multi-task learning aims to exploit the shared representations across multiple classification tasks, in order to improve learning efficiency and prediction accuracy. The main underlying mechanism of MTL promotes task regularization over model overfitting regularization, which helps to penalize all complexity systematically.

There are two basic ways to share hidden layers within MTL in deep learning, 1) we train each task independently and then freeze all models before starting joint-learning training (Caruana, 1993). Freezing prevents shared layers from being modified, which helps alleviate model overfitting, and 2) we use a regularized loss function such as the l_2 -norm loss function (Ng, 2004) to constrain shared layers. This enables simultaneous training of multiple tasks, and helps avoid performance degradation. For instance, the overall cost function is $c = lc_1 + (1 - l)c_2$ where l denotes the learning rate, and c_1 and c_2 refer to the simultaneous tasks being trained.

Our novel approach uses a cross segment-and-concatenate (CSC) layer to enable multitask learning. This layer finds the abstract representation of tasks by identifying and segmenting polarity classes on each. Sentiment analysis tasks provide good examples. They include positive, neutral, and negative classes; e.g. positive and negative sentiments are the polarity classes. CSC is used as a shared weight layer that can be easily integrated with multiple network models. CSC-MTL helps enforce constraints to regularize learning and solve problems such as class imbalance.

We demonstrate the effectiveness of our approach used on the cyber-aggression detection from text shared task.

3.1   Cross Segment-and-Concatenate (CSC) Layer

Consider an example (Figure 1) of multiple tasks $X = \{ x_1, x_2 \}$, which report on different classification problems. They are fed the same input of a sequence (S) of tokens, such as words. The first step is to segment each task using class binarization in a one-vs-all (OVA) manner and then manually identify the polarity and neutrality of the tasks' classes.

For an n-class problem, neutrality is defined as the negative classes, which in the case of a binary class problem, neutrality is defined as concatenation of $p_{x_1} || p_{x_2}$ representations, where p denotes the shared weight feature of a polarity class, and the operator $||$ refers to the concentration. After that, we train each binarized class independently. Second, we provide a cross-concatenation layer to supervise and constrain the shared representation among tasks in a way that signifies the distinctive features between each polarity group and their neutral classes (Figure 1).

For two tasks x_1 and x_2, we define polarity $\{p_{x_1}, p_{x_2}\}$ and neutrality $\{n_{x_1}, n_{x_2}\}$ classes. Based on which, we learn the linear combinations $\{l_1 = p_{x_1}||p_{x_2}p_{x_1}, l_2 = p_{x_2}||p_{x_1}p_{x_2}\}$ of polarity classes. Then, we parameterize $\{l_1, l_2\}$ and concatenate them into neutrality classes $\{l_1 \mid\mid n_{x_1}, l_2 \mid\mid n_{x_2}\}$ in order to learn the polarity shared representation as compared to neutrality classes. l_{CSC} refers to the output of CSC, which is used to feed the next layers.

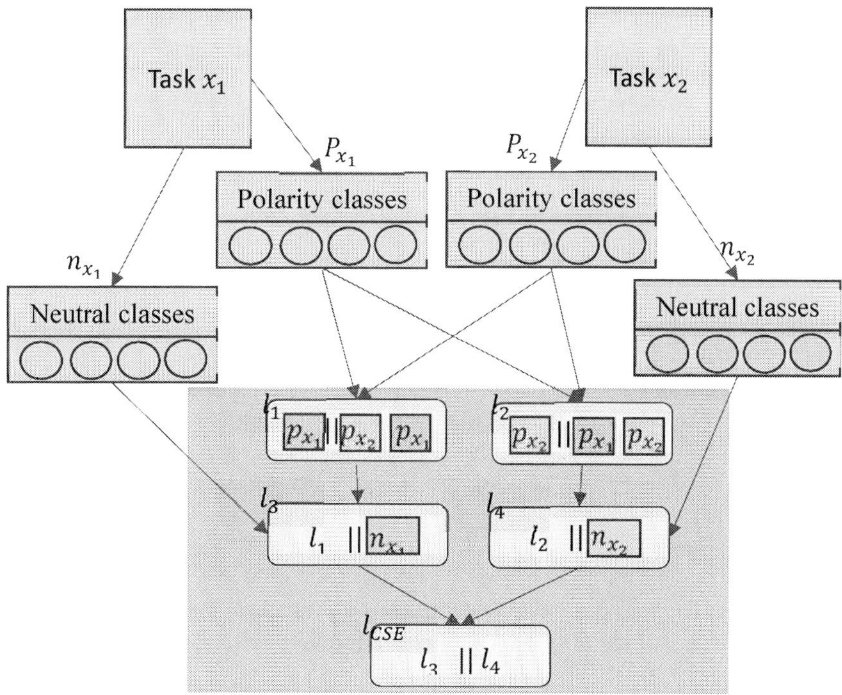

Figure 1: Shared representation learnt by linear combinations of tasks x_1 and x_2.

3.2 CSC Design

We evaluate our novel approach, CSC-MTL, using MultiCNNPooling model (explained in the next section). We perform, 1) *emotion analysis:* a categorical problem of analyzing emotions from text, so it will be binarized into 9 tasks (anger, fear, joy, sadness, surprise, anticipation, trust, disgust, and neutral), and 2) *cyber-aggression detection:* a problem involving two tasks, cyber-aggression and emotion analysis, which are used to detect aggression from text.

Emotion analysis: a categorical problem to detect emotion in text. We represent emotions using Plutchik's wheel of emotions (Plutchik, 2001), which provides emotional granularity by defining 8 primary bipolar emotions. Using this construct, we define our emotional polarity classes as the set of pairs {joy, sadness}, {anger, fear}, {trust, disgust}, and {surprise, anticipation}. We represent the neutral class as the singleton set {*neutral*} (no emotion).

Cyber-aggression detection: a categorical problem to detect aggression for given text. Polarity classes are defined as the set containing *covertly, overtly* and the *emotion CSC* inputs, while neutral classes contain one class, *non-aggressive*.

3.3 Model Description

A network input is a sequence s of tokens—such as words—where $S = [s_1, s_2, ..., s_t]$ and t denotes the timestep. S_i is a one-hot encoding of input tokens that have a fixed length (T), such that a sequence that exceeds this length is truncated in the pre-mode. For instance, a sentence such as "this is an example", which has a fixed length, thirteen, will be truncated to "is an example".

Word encoding: A word dictionary of fixed terms W is used to encode a sequence. It contains three constants that determine the start and end of the sequence in addition to the out of vocabulary (OOV) words. We normalize the variable text length using padding for short sequences and truncation for long sequences.

Word embedding: It is used to project words into a low-dimensional vector representation x_i, where $x_i \in R^W$ and W is the word weight embedding matrix. We use GloVe (Pennington, Socher, & Manning, 2014) pre-trained word embeddings. GloVe is pre-trained over social media posts, such as Twitter. For pre-trained embedding, we have an additional hyperparameter that is used to either freeze its weight matrix or allow for further training. We used cyber-aggression, and emotion corpora (Section 4.1) to build word embeddings of dimension 200; the resulting dictionary size is 60237 words.

Convolutional Neural Network (CNN): a convolution operation applies a sliding w-gram operation on a given input sequence $\{e_1, e_2, .., e_t\}$ with a length d. It results in a concatenated embedding vector $x_{i-f+1}, ..., x_i$ of dimension of a filter length f. Thus, it generates $p_i \in \Re^d$ using weights $W \in \Re^{d \times wd}$ for a bias $b \in \Re^d$ and $p_i = \tanh(W_{x_i+b})$

3.4   Models

We describe our CNN-based neural network model (Figure 2) for single task training, which are used to evaluate the performance of our CSC-MTL approach. We build this model on top of the word-embeddings described in the previous section. The word embedding layer is followed by a dropout. Each model is followed by a vanilla layer that is fully-connected, has 200 hidden units, and uses a Rectified Linear Unit (ReLU) activation. Then, we apply a final dropout. The output layer is a fully-connected layer with one hidden unit, and it uses a sigmoid activation to produce an output. Each CSC input is followed by a gaussian noise layer of the value 0.3.

MultiCNNPooling (Figure 2): consists of 3 convolutions. Each convolution has 64 features, as well as filters of the lengths 3, 4, and 5. After that, we apply a max-pooling operation to extract the abstract information $\widehat{w_i^f} = \max(C_i^f)$. Finally, feature representations are concatenated into a single representation. Convolutional operations is helpful with max-pooling pooling to extract word features (Kalchbrenner, Grefenstette, & Blunsom, 2014).

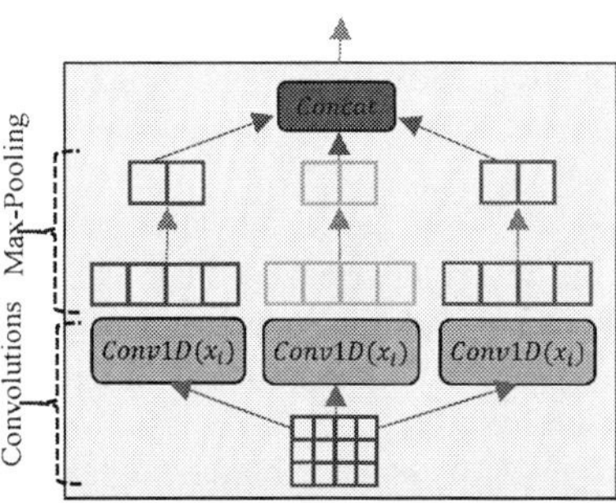

Figure 2: MultiCNNPooling network model.

3.5   Training

We use mini-batch gradient descent with a batch of the size 32 with back-propagation to reduce the loss error between the actual and predicted classes. For model training, Adam optimizer (Kingma & Ba, 2014) is used with a learning rate of 0.01. We also clip the gradient norm (Pascanu, Mikolov, & Bengio, 2012) at 7 to alleviate the risk of exploding gradient, in particular with recurrent model training.

Regularization: We apply dropout on neurons and recurrent connections to protect them from co-adaptation (Srivastava, Hinton, Krizhevsky, Sutskever, & Salakhutdinov, 2014). We additionally perform weight decay regularization using L2 penalty (Cortes, Mohri, & Rostamizadeh, 2012). We set the gaussian noise level to 0.3 for each CSC input.

Hyperparameters: We use an embedding layer of a dimension size 200. We set a dropout of 0.2. Finally, we use L2 regularization of 0.0002 at the loss function.

4 Datasets

We use two datasets to perform the cyber-aggression shared task to validate our CSC-MTL approach with MultiCNNPooling structure on detecting aggression from text.

4.1 Emotion Analysis Dataset

For emotion analysis from text, we prepared a dataset from three datasets, CrowdFlower text emotion[1], blogs (Ghazi, Inkpen, & Szpakowicz, 2015), and tweets (Buechel & Hahn, 2017). The total number of instances of our dataset is 67,091. The final dataset consists of 8,638 neutral, 16,252 joy, 10,290 sadness, 5,219 anger, 11,971 fear, 4,601 trust, 2,398 disgust, 6,196 surprise, and 1,526 anticipation instances.

4.2 Cyber-aggression Shared Task Dataset

The trolling, aggression, and cyberbullying shared task consists of 17,173 interchanged messages. These messages are categorized intro three different classes, covertly aggressive, overtly aggressive, and non-aggressive, which are labeled 5852, 3924, 7397 times respectively. Facebook and Twitter are used as unseen datasets to test the generalization ability of our approach.

5 Evaluation and Results

Our model ranks 5/30 and 8/30 on the Twitter and the Facebook test set, respectively. We evaluate the performance of a categorical problem, cyber-aggression (Section 4.2) from text, using our CSC-MTL model. We perform a stratified split on the cyber-aggression training set, so that the development set is used as a held-out dataset. The split ratio is 80%, and it is used for training, while 20% is used for the validation set. Then, we use these trained models to evaluate on the unseen Facebook and Twitter test sets.

Dataset		Accuracy	F1 (weighted)
Twitter	Baseline	-	34.77%
	Our model	**59.35%**	**56.9%**
Facebook	Baseline	-	35.35%
	Our model	**55.68%**	**59.74%**

Table 2: Results for English Facebook and Twitter test sets

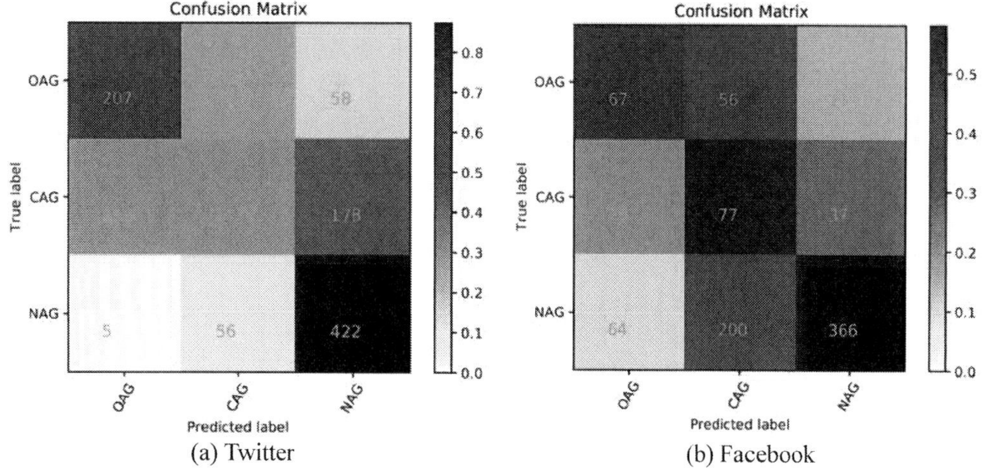

(a) Twitter   (b) Facebook

Figure 3: Confusion matrix on the Twitter and on the Facebook test set.

---

[1] https://www.crowdflower.com/wp-content/uploads/2016/07/text_emotion.csv

Table 1 reports good standing results of our model for the generalization ability test. This indicates that regularization and hyperparameter tuning managed to control the overfitting issue. The MultiCNN model with static pretrained GloVe embedding reported a higher F1 as compared to the baseline. Figure 3 shows the confusion matrix for both tasks. The generalization ability test (Table 2) shows that our model reports competitive performance with the Facebook set (59.74%) over the Twitter set (56.9%).

6 Conclusion

In this paper, we presented a novel approach, named cross segment-and-concatenate multi-task learning (CSC-MTL). We used our approach for cyber-aggression detection from text. Our experiment showed that our CNN-based model with CSC settings had promising results for cyber-aggression detection. MultiCNN with our CSC-MTL reported a competitive F1 score for both the Twitter and Facebook test sets.

In future work, we will further test our approach on different NLP tasks. We will need to perform a systematic evaluation of our method with different hyper-parameters, as well as to test on common neural network structures such as recurrent neural network (RNN).

Acknowledgements

This research is funded by Natural Sciences and Engineering Research Council of Canada (NSERC), Ontario Centres of Excellence (OCE) and SafeToNet.

References

Jonathan Baxter. 1997. A Bayesian/Information Theoretic Model of Learning to Learn via Multiple Task Sampling. *Machine Learning, 28*(1), 7–39. https://doi.org/10.1023/A:1007327622663

Sven Buechel, Udo Hahn. 2017. EmoBank: Studying the Impact of Annotation Perspective and Representation Format on Dimensional Emotion Analysis. In *Proceedings of the 15th Conference of the European Chapter of the Association for Computational Linguistics: Volume 2, Short Papers* (pp. 578–585). Stroudsburg, PA, USA: Association for Computational Linguistics. https://doi.org/10.18653/v1/E17-2092

Richard A. Caruana. 1993. Multitask Learning: A Knowledge-Based Source of Inductive Bias. In *Machine Learning Proceedings 1993* (pp. 41–48). Elsevier. https://doi.org/10.1016/B978-1-55860-307-3.50012-5

Corinna Cortes, Mehryar Mohri, Afshin Rostamizadeh. 2012. L2 Regularization for Learning Kernels. Retrieved from http://arxiv.org/abs/1205.2653

Diman Ghazi, Diana Inkpen, Stan Szpakowicz. 2015. Detecting Emotion Stimuli in Emotion-Bearing Sentences. In *Gelbukh A. (eds) Computational Linguistics and Intelligent Text Processing. CICLing 2015* (pp. 152–165). https://doi.org/10.1007/978-3-319-18117-2_12

Nal Kalchbrenner, Edward Grefenstette, Phil Blunsom. 2014. A Convolutional Neural Network for Modelling Sentences. In *Proceedings of the 52nd Annual Meeting of the Association for Computational Linguistics (Volume 1: Long Papers)* (pp. 655–665). Stroudsburg, PA, USA: Association for Computational Linguistics. https://doi.org/10.3115/v1/P14-1062

Diederik P. Kingma, Jimmy Ba. 2014. Adam: A Method for Stochastic Optimization. Retrieved from http://arxiv.org/abs/1412.6980

Ritesh Kumar Aishwarya N Reganti Akshit Bhatia, Tushar Maheshwari. 2018. Aggression-annotated Corpus of Hindi-English Code-mixed Data. In N. C. (Conference chair), K. Choukri, C. Cieri, T. Declerck, S. Goggi, K. Hasida, … T. Tokunaga (Eds.), *Proceedings of the Eleventh International Conference on Language Resources and Evaluation (LREC 2018)*. Paris, France: European Language Resources Association (ELRA).

Ritesh Kumar, Atul Kr. Ojha, Shervin Malmasi, Marcos Zampieri. 2018. Benchmarking Aggression Identification in Social Media. In *Proceedings of the First Workshop on Trolling, Aggression and Cyberbulling (TRAC)*.

Todor Mihaylov, Preslav Nakov. 2015. Hunting for Troll Comments in News Community. In *The 19th Conference on Computational Natural Language Learning. Proceedings of the Conference. Beijing, China* (pp. 310–314).

Lili Mou, Zhao Meng, Rui Yan, Ge Li, Yan Xu, Lu Zhang, Zhi Jin. 2016. How Transferable are Neural Networks in NLP Applications? Retrieved from https://arxiv.org/abs/1603.06111

Andrew Y. Ng. 2004. Feature selection, L 1 vs. L 2 regularization, and rotational invariance. In *Twenty-first international conference on Machine learning - ICML '04* (p. 78). New York, New York, USA: ACM Press. https://doi.org/10.1145/1015330.1015435

Razvan Pascanu, Tomas Mikolov, Yoshua Bengio. 2012. On the difficulty of training Recurrent Neural Networks. Retrieved from http://arxiv.org/abs/1211.5063

Jeffrey Pennington, Richard Socher, Christopher Manning. 2014. Glove: Global Vectors for Word Representation. In *Proceedings of the 2014 Conference on Empirical Methods in Natural Language Processing (EMNLP)* (pp. 1532–1543). Stroudsburg, PA, USA: Association for Computational Linguistics. https://doi.org/10.3115/v1/D14-1162

Robert Plutchik. 2001. The nature of emotions: Human emotions have deep evolutionary roots. *American Scientist*, 89(4), 344–350. https://doi.org/10.1511/2001.4.344

Peter K. Smith, Jess Mahdavi, Manuel Carvalho, Sonja Fisher, Shanette Russell, Neil Tippett. 2008. Cyberbullying: its nature and impact in secondary school pupils. *Journal of Child Psychology and Psychiatry*, 49(4), 376–385. https://doi.org/10.1111/j.1469-7610.2007.01846.x

Nitish Srivastava, Geoffrey Hinton, Alex Krizhevsky, Ilya Sutskever, Ruslan Salakhutdinov. 2014. Dropout: a simple way to prevent neural networks from overfitting. *The Journal of Machine Learning Research*, 15(1), 1929–1958.

Robert S. Tokunaga. 2010. Following you home from school: A critical review and synthesis of research on cyberbullying victimization. *Computers in Human Behavior*, 26(3), 277–287. https://doi.org/10.1016/j.chb.2009.11.014

Dorothy Wunmi Grigg. 2010. Cyber-Aggression: Definition and Concept of Cyberbullying. *Australian Journal of Guidance and Counselling*, 20(02), 143–156. https://doi.org/10.1375/ajgc.20.2.143

Delete or not Delete?
Semi-Automatic Comment Moderation for the Newsroom

Julian Risch
Hasso Plattner Institute
University of Potsdam
Prof.-Dr.-Helmert-Str. 2-3
14482 Potsdam, Germany
julian.risch@hpi.de

Ralf Krestel
Hasso Plattner Institute
University of Potsdam
Prof.-Dr.-Helmert-Str. 2-3
14482 Potsdam, Germany
ralf.krestel@hpi.de

Abstract

Comment sections of online news providers have enabled millions to share and discuss their opinions on news topics. Today, moderators ensure respectful and informative discussions by deleting not only insults, defamation, and hate speech, but also unverifiable facts. This process has to be transparent and comprehensive in order to keep the community engaged. Further, news providers have to make sure to not give the impression of censorship or dissemination of fake news. Yet manual moderation is very expensive and becomes more and more unfeasible with the increasing amount of comments. Hence, we propose a semi-automatic, holistic approach, which includes comment features but also their context, such as information about users and articles. For evaluation, we present experiments on a novel corpus of 3 million news comments annotated by a team of professional moderators.

1 Comment Moderation at Online News Providers

Comment sections of online news providers have enabled millions of readers to share and discuss their opinions on news topics publicly. While most people use such platforms to have constructive debates, a tiny minority of individuals or interest groups misuse freedom of speech: by injecting abusive and disruptive comments into online discussions, they spread hate and fear. Furthermore, malicious users misuse the discussion platform to disseminate misinformation with the intent to mislead and provoke readers: fake news. The moderation of online discussions is a huge effort for providers — and the only known way to prevent such attacks, to watch the compliance of users ("netiquette"), and to keep up good discussions.

The definition of inappropriate content is by no means clear and differs between different venues. Many platforms have individual guidelines that users must adhere to and that moderators employ for content assessment. Even with these guidelines there is no precise boundary between appropriate and inappropriate comments. Not only obviously unlawful content, such as ethnic or racial slurs needs to be removed, but the range is wider: personal attacks against other users and the editors, profanity, spam, or off-topic conversations need to be detected and moderated. In addition, legal liability is an issue for news providers and forces them to take action. Given the difficulty of the task, human moderators are needed to manually check and possibly remove comments. Further, it is crucial for moderators to not give the impression of censorship. This is especially the case if opposite positions on emotionally charged issues are involved. Therefore, moderators have to make a difficult choice for each and every comment: *delete or not delete*. With the increasing amount of comments also the costs for moderation increase and manually checking and editing of user-submitted content becomes more and more unfeasible. As a consequence, many large online media sites worldwide were forced to close their discussion areas or downsize them significantly (prominent examples of the last years are Bloomberg, the Internet Movie Database, and the US-American National Public Radio).

Based on a collaboration with a large online news provider, we propose a semi-automatic approach for comment moderation in order to assist human moderators. To this end, it is important to deeply understand the moderation process in the newsroom: moderators take notice of a potentially violating comment

Proceedings of the First Workshop on Trolling, Aggression and Cyberbullying, pages 166–176
Santa Fe, USA, August 25, 2018.

if an attentive user flags the comment as offensive. Besides that, moderators follow discussions in the comment sections preventively and check comments of newly registered users by default. In the event of an inappropriate comment, the moderator can either partly edit or completely delete the comment. Deletion is inevitable if a comment loses its original statement without the violating parts. To ensure a transparent process, moderators leave a message that explains the specific reason for moderation. Users who repeatedly post inappropriate comments can be banned temporarily or permanently. Moderators can close down an article's comment section entirely, if not only a single comment but the majority of comments is inappropriate or the discussion gets off the subject. Although this means can only be the last resort, selected articles are published even without a comment section at all. This shows how severe the problem of moderating inappropriate comments has become for news sites and, unfortunately, how individuals or interest groups successfully attack freedom of speech.

The guidelines of the collaborating news provider list the following attributes for inappropriate comments: (1) insults, discrimination, and defamation, (2) unverifiable suspicions and insinuations that do not rely on plausible arguments or credible sources, (3) advertisements and other commercial content, (4) personally identifiable information of others, (5) copyright reserved texts, (6) quotations without sources, and (7) web links to content that violate these terms of use. All these properties hinder a respectful discussion with other users. On the contrary, a good comment is respectfully worded, argues conclusively, and cannot be misunderstood. It refers to the news article or the subject of discussion.

In order to meet the requirements of the broad definition of inappropriate comments, this paper explores a large set of features. In a holistic approach, we combine information about comments, corresponding articles, and users in a logistic regression model. While we could have used a deep learning approach, such black-box models do not fulfill the requirement of comprehensible classification results. Moderators and readers both need to know the reasons for a classification result. As an advantage of our model, we can give insights into how each feature influences the classification and which features make a comment inappropriate in a specific context.

2 Related Work

The idea to automatically classify insulting messages with a rule-based system goes back to Spertus (1997). A decision tree is trained on a hand-written set of rules with syntactic and semantic text features serving as a basis. Despite the fact that surface-level features, such as bag-of-words, for the most part ignore sentence syntax and even word order, they have strong predictive power (Schmidt and Wiegand, 2017).

Davidson et al. (2017) compared several different classifiers for hate speech detection. Out of logistic regression, naive Bayes, decision trees, random forests, and support vector machines (SVMs), the authors conclude that logistic regression and SVMs perform best. We can confirm this observation with our experiments. In a multi-level approach, Razavi et al. (2010) combine several classifiers with an underlying dictionary of abusive and insulting phrases.

However, small datasets and different labeling schemes currently limit research progress in the field of harassment detection in social media and comment streams (Kennedy et al., 2017). Wulczyn et al. (2017) address this issue by providing machine-labeled data. To this end, a classifier is first trained on a small set of human-labeled comments and afterwards used to generate a larger machine-labeled dataset.

More recently, approaches focus on capturing the semantics of sentences. Methods from word sense disambiguation (Warner and Hirschberg, 2012) and subjectivity detection (Gitari et al., 2015) are explored to detect hate speech. With the rise of distributed dense vector representations, hate speech detection is tackled using deep learning methods. Djuric et al. (2015) propose to learn distributed low-dimensional representations of comments in order to use them as a feature for logistic regression. Nobata et al. (2016) give a comprehensive overview of the various types of abusive language and distinguish three main classes: *profanity*, inappropriate language and swear words; *derogatory speech*, personal attacks; and *hate speech*, directed towards a particular ethnic or religious group. According to the authors, intentional obfuscation, fluency and grammatical correctness of hate speech, make its detection a difficult challenge. The paper explores a variety of features, such as n-grams, linguistic features (length of comment or average word length), syntactic features (part-of-speech tags), and distributional semantics features. We build on their set of features and extend their approach for the similar, broader task of comment moderation.

Several authors suggest to distinguish separate subclasses of hate speech based on attributes of the attacked groups, such as race, religion or ethnic origin (Warner and Hirschberg, 2012; Gitari et al., 2015). Warner and Hirschberg (2012) observe that hate speech aimed against a specific group often exhibits a high frequency of stereotypical words. Therefore, they create individual language models for each attacked group and determine features, such as word unigrams, separately.

However, word-based models are prone to out-of-vocabulary issues. To this end, Schmidt and Wiegand (2017) propose to generalize exact words to more abstract concepts. They first create clusters of words and then use cluster IDs as features. According to the authors, indicators for appropriate or inappropriate comments are the number of positive verbs, positive adjectives and politeness rules (e.g., "no thanks", "please", "would you"). Polarity classifier for short texts, such as SentiStrength (Thelwall et al., 2010), can be used to count the number of positive, negative, and neutral words in a comment. Our approach makes use of such a polarity classifier and uses sentiment scores as an input feature.

Similar to our approach, Pavlopoulos et al. (2017a) propose a semi-automatic system to assist human moderation teams rather than to replace them. The system tries to classify comments as abusive or non-abusive and if the classification is uncertain a human moderator makes the final decision. Other work of the same authors examines how deep learning with attention layers can be used to moderate user comments and applies a recurrent neural network architecture (Pavlopoulos et al., 2017c; Pavlopoulos et al., 2017b). This approach allows a machine, such as a deep neural network, to delete a comment if its classification is certain enough. In our scenario, a machine that deletes comments automatically but cannot give an comprehensible explanation for its decision is unthinkable.

Park and Fung (2017) compare one step and two step classification. They apply a convolutional neural network as a multi-class classifier in order to detect abusive language. Similar research is conducted by Gambäck and Sikdar (2017), who detect abusive language and also distinguish finer-grained subclasses. Their experiments show a comparable performance for both methods. Finer-grained subclasses can help to give reasons why a comment is classified as abusive.

Napoles et al. (2017b) focus on the complementary task and find "engaging, respectful, and informative conversations". Similarly, Kolhatkar and Taboada (2017) propose to identify constructive comments. Their metric of *constructiveness* (relevant remarks, specific points, and appropriate evidence) is set in contrast to *toxicity* (hate speech, verbal abuse, offensiveness).

Most prior work in the domain of comment classification focuses on English-language datasets. Further, the existing body of work often tackles only a subset of hate speech, such as attacks based on ethnic origin or a specific domain, such as Twitter (Park and Fung, 2017; Badjatiya et al., 2017). In this work, we combine these different approaches and apply them to holistic comment moderation. Our exemplary scenario deals with comment sections at a large German online news provider.

3   Dataset

Our dataset consists of all comments published at a large German online news provider between January 1st, 2016 and March 31st, 2017. In total, there are about 3 million comments by 60k users associated with 26k articles out of which 100k are marked as inappropriate. Each comment is annotated with several moderation flags, which have been manually curated by professional moderators working at the news provider. Based on these flags, we create the binary ground truth for each comment, representing whether the comment is inappropriate or not.

Figure 1 visualizes that the amount of inappropriate comments varies over time, especially due to special or unforeseen high-impact events. The share of inappropriate comments varies between roughly 2% and 10%. We indicate events possibly causing the temporary changes with labels in the figure. For example, terror attacks typically result in emotional and controversial debates, which are prone to include provocative inappropriate remarks. It is worth noting, though, that the general increase in comments following those events might change the way moderators work. Under stress, moderators might choose

Figure 1: The share of inappropriate comments (black) aggregated with a 4-day centered moving average stands out at the date of specific news events. The trend of the total number of comments is shown downscaled for comparison (light gray).

to follow stricter moderation policies. This decision – wittingly or unwittingly – might result in a higher share of flagged comments, even though they do not seem to be objectively worse than similar comments at a different point in time.

Figure 1 also shows that events that gain the most attention are related to social, political or security issues. This circumstance is also mirrored in the news categories with the highest share of inappropriate comments: the categories related to society and politics have a share of 4.1% and 3.4%, respectively, while also containing the majority of all comments (70%). In contrast, the share in all other categories combined is only 2.1%, being lowest in the business category (1.7%). Furthermore, posts are not distributed uniformly among the users: only about 6% of the users posted more than 200 comments, the vast majority of roughly 48% of users have posted only once or twice. As to expect in a real-world dataset that was not meant for academic research purposes, it is far from lab conditions. For example, surprisingly, a single user posted 11,082 comments. 120 of these comments were flagged as inappropriate.

In addition to the platform's guidelines as described in Section 1, we observe that links to foreign language content have been removed by moderators. As not all users can be expected to understand foreign languages, such content hinders them in joining the discussion. Furthermore, moderators remove duplicate comments from the news site, which they do by flagging a duplicate just in the same way as they would do for insults or hate speech. Duplicate detection and hate speech detection are quite different tasks that ask for different approaches. For this reason, we filter exact duplicates in a pre-processing step and resolve data inconsistencies with data cleansing techniques. We aim to detect abusive and disruptive comments that have been moderated because of insults, discrimination, and defamation, but also unverifiable suspicions, which do not rely on plausible arguments or credible sources. These comments hinder a respectful discussion directly. We do not focus on comments flagged because of copyright infringements, web links to inappropriate content, or personally identifiable information.

4 A Holistic, Semi-Automatic Approach to Comment Moderation

We define three different categories of features to classify a given comment:

- Comment features aim to model linguistic, syntactic and semantic properties of the comment's text. Further, comment metadata, such as publication date belong to this feature set.

- User features introduce information about the individuals behind comments and their behavior, in particular the timespan between consecutive posts, previous inappropriate posts, and topics of interest.

- Article features relate to the news article referenced by a comment, for example its category, publication date or article author.

We propose a logistic regression model, implemented with the scikit-learn Python framework[1]. The logistic regression model is trained in a supervised fashion on training data with binary labels. For a given comment with information about the associated user and article, the model predicts a probability of appropriateness. In order to decide about a binary label of appropriateness, we choose a probability threshold that is tailored to achieve a high recall: we want to minimize our false-negative rate.

The set of presumably appropriate comments can be published instantly without any manual contribution. In contrast to that, the set of presumably inappropriate comments is presented to a human moderator for assessment. In practice, a high recall corresponds to the situation where moderators get to see mostly all actually inappropriate comments. The downside of a lower precision is that moderators also need to check a few actually appropriate comments. In a real-world scenario, this trade-off ensures that moderators can be (almost) certain that no inappropriate comment slips through their inspection.

4.1 Comment Features

Comment features are derived from a comment's text or describe a comment's nesting level in the overall thread structure of a discussion.

Linguistic Features Our linguistic features include character-level and word-level features. Neither normalization, such as stemming or lemmatization, nor any other preprocessing is applied. As the most basic feature, we consider a comment's number of characters and number of words. The combination of these two features describes the average word length of a comment. In our dataset, inappropriate comments are on average shorter (48 words) than appropriate comments (61 words). Our other text features focus mostly on extensive use of punctuation or capitalization of whole words. We assume that extensive use of punctuation or capitalization of whole words indicates an aggressive tone.

Comments with web links to external pages frequently violate user guidelines. For example, the linked page's content might contain insults or advertisements. We count occurrences of "http" to capture web links, but do not distinguish between internal and external links. Interestingly, inappropriate comments contain on average less negation words (0.92), such as "not" or "never", than appropriate comments (1.28). In summary, our set of linguistic features for a comment includes: (1) the number of characters, words, and distinct words, (2) the number of question marks, exclamation marks, periods, colons, quotation marks and uses of "http", as well as (3) the ratio of uppercase to lowercase letters.

Syntax Features While the syntax of a comment might not inappropriate itself, it can still serve as an indicator of inappropriateness. For example, the extensive use of personal pronouns might indicate personal attacks against others. Similarly, comments with many adjectives might indicate extensive descriptions or name-calling of other users or of organizations. To capture such behavior, we apply part-of-speech tagging and count the number of adjectives, determiners, personal pronouns, and adverbs in each comment.

Topic Features Off-topic comments that are not related to the article's topic are also considered inappropriate. To measure the topical similarity of an article and a user comment, we apply topic modeling. On a set of roughly 25,000 news articles, we learn a topic model with latent Dirichlet allocation. The topical similarity is then used as a feature in our classifier. Further, we compare the tf-idf vector of the comment with the tf-idf vector of its corresponding article and of inappropriate comments posted at this article. One feature is the cosine similarity of these vectors. Another, similar feature is the Kullback-Leibler divergence of the word frequency distributions of a comment and an article.

Word N-Grams The word cloud in Figure 2b illustrates German unigrams that are most frequently used in inappropriate comments in our dataset. Besides unigrams, we include 2-grams and 3-grams and thereby consider the context in which a word is used. The word cloud shows, for example, that mentioning German chancellor Merkel is already a strong indicator of an inappropriate comment. However, this

---

[1] `http://scikit-learn.org/`

indication might change depending on the preceding word: a comment containing "Thank you Merkel" is twice as likely to be inappropriate than a comment containing "Mama Merkel".

Character N-Grams   A German-language-specific challenge are arbitrarily long and rare compound nouns. Coining new words extensively increases sparsity of the data: such words typically occur only once in an entire corpus and are called "hapax legomena" by linguists. At test time, this phenomenon leads to frequent out-of-vocabulary problems. Character n-grams do not suffer from such problems, because they are able to capture substrings in compound nouns. Related work shows that character n-grams can be successfully applied to detect abusive language in English-language content (Nobata et al., 2016; Schmidt and Wiegand, 2017). Obfuscated words and unusual spellings typically pose problems for word-based approaches due to a potential of high sparsity, but can be countered with character-based techniques. For this reason, we add character n-grams ranging from length 3 to 5 to our feature set, targeting also the German-specific challenge of compound nouns in particular.

Word2vec   To capture the semantic meaning of words, we apply word embeddings. In particular, we use a standard Word2vec approach and model each word as a 100 dimensional vector. The embedding of an article or a user comment is simply the average embedding of all its words.

Structural Features   Typical interfaces of discussion sections allow users to post their comments as a reply to another comment. Thereby, a discussion thread can form a tree structure. In our dataset, comments that are direct replies to an article have a higher probability of being inappropriate (4.0%) compared to those that are replies to other comments starting at a depth of 3 (2.5%). Thus, the depth of a comment in the tree, which is the nesting level, is used as a feature.

4.2   User Features

Our dataset also provides information about the user (author) of each posted comment. We define two categories of features based on user information: time-based as well as history-based features. We model four time-based features: the time in seconds since the user last posted an appropriate or an inappropriate comment on the same or any other article. These values are an indicator of heated debates or possible reactions to a previous comment being deleted by the editors, which is frequent in the dataset. For example, if a comment is posted within 10 minutes after an inappropriate comment by the same user on the same article, it has a 19% chance of being inappropriate compared to the global average chance of around 3%.

The history-based features are statistics of a user's comments prior to posting a particular comment. In particular, we count the number of appropriate and inappropriate comments in the same category as the article and globally. Note that since our dataset is limited to the timespan between January 2016 and March 2017, we do not have access to historical information before that time. Therefore, our extracted history-based feature values are only a narrow excerpt of a user's full history. A user who posted only few comments in our dataset might have been much more active in the time before the beginning of our dataset.

4.3   Article Features

Each comment in our dataset is posted in the context of a news article. An article that was just published a few hours ago still has lots of potential for discussion, whereas articles older than a few weeks rarely get new constructive comments. As described in Section 3, the category of the article also influences its probability to receive inappropriate comments. Controversial categories revolving around politics lead to more inappropriate comments than categories about more mundane topics, such as sports. Based on these observations, we define the following features: (1) time since the article's publication, (2) time since the last comment on the article, (3) time since the last inappropriate comment on the article, and (4) category of the article.

Related work has shown that word n-grams are at the top of the best-performing features for hate speech detection (Nobata et al., 2016; Badjatiya et al., 2017; Warner and Hirschberg, 2012; Davidson et al., 2017; Schmidt and Wiegand, 2017). For this reason, we consider word n-grams as a baseline approach that all other features compete against. Nevertheless, we combine all single features into our holistic approach as a large feature set for the logistic regression. To the best of our knowledge, especially the context of comments, such as information about commenting users and referenced articles, has not been applied so far and extends the state-of-the-art. Our approach could also be used for the sub-task of hate speech detection or related tasks. The broad set of reasons for inappropriateness (as described, for example, in platform guidelines) motivates our large feature set, which might be unnecessary large and might include useless features in other scenarios. Further, other tasks could map probabilities of the linear regression to binary labels differently. If these tasks do not require explanations for automatic decisions, one might refrain from linear models at all in favor of recent deep learning approaches (Napoles et al., 2017a; Badjatiya et al., 2017).

5   Evaluation

We split our dataset time-wise into training and test set in order to train only on past data and evaluate on future data. Stratified sampling is employed to overcome effects of the imbalanced class distribution. The cutoff timestamp is chosen such that 10,000 inappropriate comments remain in the test set. Randomly sampled 10,000 appropriate comments from the remaining comments after the cutoff timestamp are added to the test set. Thereby, a balanced class distribution is obtained in the test set. All comments posted before that timestamp serve as training data. The regression model outputs probabilities of a comment being inappropriate, but not a binary label. In order to be able to compare with our ground truth labels, we map these probabilities to binary labels. To this end, all comments with a predicted probability above a given threshold are marked as inappropriate and all comments with a probability below that threshold are marked as appropriate.

With regard to use cases other than our real-world example, there could be scenarios with two thresholds: one for almost certainly appropriate comments and one for almost certainly inappropriate ones. Only comments between those two thresholds are left for manual assessment. A disadvantage is that the decision to delete a comment could still be made completely automatic if the model is certain enough, which is unthinkable in our scenario.

5.1   Results

Table 2a summarizes the results of our experiments. As can be seen in the table, we choose the threshold in a way that at least 75% of the inappropriate comments are correctly classified, which corresponds to a recall of 75%. The reasoning for this is that it is acceptable to present more comments than necessary to the moderators, but it is important that clearly inappropriate comments do not slip through. On the one hand, if the threshold is set for a higher recall, then the precision decreases until moderators do not profit from machine support but have to check almost all comments. On the other hand, if the threshold is set for a lower recall, more and more actually inappropriate comments are falsely classified as appropriate. As a consequence, inappropriate comments are inadvertently published without intervention.

There are two different error types that can be distinguished. First, our classifier misses to flag an actually inappropriate comment as inappropriate (false negative). Second, our classifier claims to have flagged an inappropriate comment but the ground truth label considers the comment to be appropriate (false positive).

After manual inspection for the first error type it turns out that false negatives are often not clearly inappropriate or further context is needed for the classification. This might be due to the fact that the moderation flags provided in our ground truth dataset have been created by different moderators who interpret the user guidelines differently and therefore make different decisions. Further, different discussions with different preceding comments might ask for more or less intervention by moderators.

As each comment in our dataset has been flagged by at most one moderator, there is no way to evaluate the inter-rater reliability of these flags. Thus, similar comments posted at different times can be flagged differently, which is a tough challenge for classification algorithms. Even a more sophisticated classifier or more features might not help in situations where a team of moderators disagrees at the classification of a particular comment. These hard decisions are another reason why we propose a semi-automatic

Method	Recall	Precision	F_1-Measure
Linguistic	0.773	0.552	0.644
Syntax & Topic	0.757	0.541	0.631
Word N-Grams	0.782	0.559	0.652
Char N-Grams	0.778	**0.649**	0.708
Word2vec	0.756	0.630	0.687
Article	0.753	0.538	0.627
User	0.826	0.516	0.636
Combined	**0.861**	0.615	**0.717**

(a) Overview

(b) Indicative Words for Inappropriate Comments

Figure 2: Classification results and word cloud of indicative words.

approach that integrates machine learning into the manual process of comment moderation.

In the following, we discuss the performance of selected features on our dataset. The analysis of single features is interesting because it helps to understand the result of an otherwise nontransparent automatic classification result. For the support of human moderators, these features can serve as indicators for inappropriate content and can provide explanations for suggested automatic decisions.

5.2 Discussion

Comment features The F1-score of character n-grams is exceeded only by the combined approach feature. Further, it achieves the best overall precision, as listed in Table 2a. One reason for the strong performance on character n-grams might be the complexity of the German language. Word-based models are prone to out-of-vocabulary issues and the German language allows to create very long compound words, which are used infrequently. Character n-grams are more robust than word-level features regarding compound words, neologisms and typos. Some extreme examples for compound nouns in our dataset are "Landesrundfunkanstaltsselbstbedienungsläden" loosely translated as "self-service stores of public service broadcasters" or "Stottertrottelkorbflechterautobahnlastkraftwagenfahrer" loosely translated as "stuttering douchebag who weaves baskets and drives trucks on highways". These nouns are unique in our dataset and also will almost certainly never be used again in any other comment. Even though character n-grams do not capture whole words, they still capture the meaning of a comment well according to our results.

As word embeddings perform comparably well and achieve the second-best F1-score, we further evaluate our approach of calculating a comment embedding by averaging the individual Word2vec embeddings. Therefore, we analyze words that are embedded in the neighborhood of the averaged word vectors. Exemplary results[2] are shown in Table 1. The examples demonstrate that the comment embedding is an adequate way of determining the broader topic of a comment.

Article Features Article features describe the context a posted comment. The classification of a comment as inappropriate only based on the article's category or the time since the article's publication obviously cannot lead to satisfying results. Article features are not a good stand-alone indicator of appropriateness. For example, in order to achieve a recall above 75%, entire categories would need to be considered as inappropriate. Article features seem to be more of a supportive evidence rather than stand-alone features.

User Features An extensive user history is available only for a small subset of all users. A reason for that is the limited time span of the considered dataset. Since the available data covers roughly a year, the observed overall number of comments posted by a user can be only a narrow excerpt of reality. In our dataset, every user initially starts at a comment count of 0, and only later on our model learns

---

[2]All examples in this paper are translations from German into English.

Table 1: Words in Vicinity of the Comment Embedding

Comment	Undermining democracy: correct, if a court of arbitration is part of a treaty that is an effect of that treaty. Thanks for the tip. DT negotiates, at least according to him, with "America First" in mind. The existing treaties, especially NAFTA, were primarily disadvantageous to Joe Sixpack AND Juan Prez in both Mexico AND the USA.. If Mexico does not like DT's suggestions they can mutually cancel the treaty with the USA and both profit. To rephrase it, it can only get better for the lower middle class and below.
Nearby Words	free trade agreement, trade agreement, trade treaty, treaty, free trade contract
Comment	The Kurdish population is being blackmailed by the PKK and hauled off into the mountains. If the Kurds in the FRG are for the PKK, then they should live there.
Nearby Words	Kurd, PKK, Kurdish area, Turkey, terrorist

to distinguish different users, for example based on the frequency of their comments We expect the features to perform better with a complete user history. Nevertheless, several features show promising results. The number of inappropriate comments by the user in the same article category and in total in the past strongly correlate with a new comment by the user being inappropriate. The time since the last inappropriate comment by the user also weakly correlates with a new comment by the user being inappropriate.

6   Conclusions and Future Work

In this paper, we studied the task of comment moderation. In contrast to the sub-task of hate speech detection, moderation needs to consider several other types of inappropriate comments, such as insults and defamation, but also unverifiable suspicions, which do not rely on plausible arguments or credible sources. Moderators ensure respectful, engaging, and informative discussions by editing or deleting inappropriate comments that do not facilitate constructive debates or even contain unlawful statements. This costly manual task puts a strain on the moderators, forcing more and more news sites to close down their comment sections. In order to meet this challenge, we propose a semi-automatic approach for assisting humans at comment moderation. Our holistic approach combines information about comments, users, and articles in a logistic regression model.

Despite the recent success of deep learning for natural language processing, the lack of comprehensibility of neural nets motivates the application of other models. For example, decision trees and regression models can give reasons for their final prediction results. A particular feature with a particularly large value or a combination of several features might be such a reason. In practice, moderators and users need to understand the automatic decision process underlying a trained machine learning model and in particular *why* a comment is classified inappropriate. For the application in a newsroom and the integration into the moderation process, it is important that classification results are comprehensible.

In future work, we plan to extend the explanatory aspect alongside the classification of comments. Explanations could, for example, include details about the user's comment history or highlight relevant words in the posted text. Such explanations would help moderators to understand the reasons for an automatic decision and explanations make the system and its decisions also more trustworthy. However, provided these explanations, malicious users will certainly use their criminal energy trying to fool automatic moderation approaches.

Acknowledgments

We thank our students Carl Ambroselli, Yannick Bäumer, Andreas Burmeister, Jan Ladleif, and Tim Naumann for their help with this project. We also thank Andreas Loos for his valuable feedback.

References

Pinkesh Badjatiya, Shashank Gupta, Manish Gupta, and Vasudeva Varma. 2017. Deep learning for hate speech detection in tweets. In *Proceedings of the International Conference on World Wide Web (WWW Companion)*, pages 759–760. International World Wide Web Conferences Steering Committee.

Thomas Davidson, Dana Warmsley, Michael Macy, and Ingmar Weber. 2017. Automated hate speech detection and the problem of offensive language. In *Proceedings of the International Conference on Web and Social Media (ICWSM)*, pages 512–515.

Nemanja Djuric, Jing Zhou, Robin Morris, Mihajlo Grbovic, Vladan Radosavljevic, and Narayan Bhamidipati. 2015. Hate speech detection with comment embeddings. In *Proceedings of the International Conference on World Wide Web (WWW)*, pages 29–30. ACM.

Björn Gambäck and Utpal Kumar Sikdar. 2017. Using convolutional neural networks to classify hate-speech. In *Proceedings of the Workshop on Abusive Language Online*, pages 85–90. ACL.

Njagi Dennis Gitari, Zhang Zuping, Hanyurwimfura Damien, and Jun Long. 2015. A lexicon-based approach for hate speech detection. *International Journal of Multimedia and Ubiquitous Engineering*, 10(4):215–230.

George Kennedy, Andrew McCollough, Edward Dixon, Alexei Bastidas, John Ryan, Chris Loo, and Saurav Sahay. 2017. Technology solutions to combat online harassment. In *Proceedings of the Workshop on Abusive Language Online*, pages 73–77. ACL.

Varada Kolhatkar and Maite Taboada. 2017. Constructive language in news comments. In *Proceedings of the Workshop on Abusive Language Online*, pages 11–17. ACL.

Courtney Napoles, Aasish Pappu, and Joel R Tetreault. 2017a. Automatically identifying good conversations online (yes, they do exist!). In *Proceedings of the International Conference on Web and Social Media (ICWSM)*, pages 628–631.

Courtney Napoles, Joel Tetreault, Aasish Pappu, Enrica Rosato, and Brian Provenzale. 2017b. Finding good conversations online: The yahoo news annotated comments corpus. In *Proceedings of the Linguistic Annotation Workshop*, pages 13–23.

Chikashi Nobata, Joel Tetreault, Achint Thomas, Yashar Mehdad, and Yi Chang. 2016. Abusive language detection in online user content. In *Proceedings of the International Conference on World Wide Web (WWW)*, pages 145–153.

Ji Ho Park and Pascale Fung. 2017. One-step and two-step classification for abusive language detection on twitter. In *Proceedings of the Workshop on Abusive Language Online*, pages 41–45. ACL.

John Pavlopoulos, Prodromos Malakasiotis, and Ion Androutsopoulos. 2017a. Deep learning for user comment moderation. In *Proceedings of the Workshop on Abusive Language Online*, pages 25–35. ACL.

John Pavlopoulos, Prodromos Malakasiotis, and Ion Androutsopoulos. 2017b. Deeper attention to abusive user content moderation. In *Proceedings of the Conference on Empirical Methods in Natural Language Processing (EMNLP)*, pages 1136–1146.

John Pavlopoulos, Prodromos Malakasiotis, Juli Bakagianni, and Ion Androutsopoulos. 2017c. Improved abusive comment moderation with user embeddings. In *Proceedings of the EMNLP Workshop: Natural Language Processing meets Journalism*, pages 51–55. Association for Computational Linguistics.

Amir H. Razavi, Diana Inkpen, Sasha Uritsky, and Stan Matwin. 2010. Offensive language detection using multi-level classification. In *Proceedings of the Canadian Conference on Advances in Artificial Intelligence (AI)*, pages 16–27. Springer-Verlag.

Anna Schmidt and Michael Wiegand. 2017. A survey on hate speech detection using natural language processing. In *Proceedings of the International Workshop on Natural Language Processing for Social Media*, pages 1–10.

Ellen Spertus. 1997. Smokey: Automatic recognition of hostile messages. In *Proceedings of the National Conference on Artificial Intelligence and Conference on Innovative Applications of Artificial Intelligence (AAAI/IAAI)*, pages 1058–1065. AAAI.

Mike Thelwall, Kevan Buckley, Georgios Paltoglou, Di Cai, and Arvid Kappas. 2010. Sentiment strength detection in short informal text. *Journal of the Association for Information Science and Technology*, 61(12):2544–2558.

William Warner and Julia Hirschberg. 2012. Detecting hate speech on the world wide web. In *Proceedings of the Workshop on Language in Social Media (LSM)*, pages 19–26. ACL.

Ellery Wulczyn, Nithum Thain, and Lucas Dixon. 2017. Ex machina: Personal attacks seen at scale. In *Proceedings of the International Conference on World Wide Web (WWW)*, pages 1391–1399. International World Wide Web Conferences Steering Committee.

Textual Aggression Detection through Deep Learning

Antonela Tommasel[*]
ISISTAN
UNICEN - CONICET
Tandil, Buenos Aires
Argentina

Juan Manuel Rodriguez
ISISTAN
UNICEN - CONICET
Tandil, Buenos Aires
Argentina

Daniela Godoy
ISISTAN
UNICEN - CONICET
Tandil, Buenos Aires
Argentina

Abstract

Cyberbullying and cyberaggression are serious and widespread issues increasingly affecting Internet users. With the widespread of social media networks, bullying, once limited to particular places, can now occur anytime and anywhere. Cyberaggression refers to aggressive online behaviour that aims at harming other individuals, and involves rude, insulting, offensive, teasing or demoralising comments through online social media. Considering the dangerous consequences that cyberaggression has on its victims and its rapid spread amongst internet users (specially kids and teens), it is crucial to understand how cyberbullying occurs to prevent it from escalating. Given the massive information overload on the Web, there is an imperious need to develop intelligent techniques to automatically detect harmful content, which would allow the large-scale social media monitoring and early detection of undesired situations. This paper presents the *Isistanitos*'s approach for detecting aggressive content in multiple social media sites. The approach is based on combining Support Vector Machines and Recurrent Neural Network models for analysing a wide-range of character, word, word embeddings, sentiment and irony features. Results confirmed the difficulty of the task (particularly for detecting covert aggressions), showing the limitations of traditionally used features.

1   Introduction

In recent years, social networking and micro-blogging sites have seen their popularity increased, attracting an increasing number of users, who share their personal information and interact with others. Additionally, social media sites allow users to publish content or photos and to comment or tag content published by other users. As social media usage grows, other undesirable phenomena and behaviours appear. Even when most of the time, Internet use is safe, online communications through social media involve risks. In this context, users might have to deal with threatening situations like cyberaggression or cyberbullying, amongst other undesirable phenomena (Whittaker and Kowalski, 2015).

With the widespread of social media networks, bullying, once limited to particular places or times of the day (e.g. schools), can now occur anytime and anywhere (Chatzakou et al., 2017). Cyberaggression refers to aggressive online behaviour that aims at harming other individuals (Hosseinmardi et al., 2015), and involves rude, insulting, offensive, teasing or demoralising comments through online social media (Chavan and S S, 2015). Aggressions could target educational qualifications, gender, family or personal habits, amongst other possibilities.

Given the dangerous consequences that cyberaggression has on its victims, and its rapid spread amongst internet users (specially kids and teens), it is crucial to understand how it occurs to prevent it from escalating. This has important applications on the detection of cyberextremism, cybercrime and cyberhate propaganda (Agarwal and Sureka, 2015). Nonetheless, several challenges hinder the successful detection of abusive behaviour (Chatzakou et al., 2017; Nobata et al., 2016). First, the lack of grammar correctness and syntactic structure of social media posts hinders the usage of natural language processing tools. Second, the limited context provided by each individual post, causing that an individual post

---

Proceedings of the First Workshop on Trolling, Aggression and Cyberbullying, pages 177–187
Santa Fe, USA, August 25, 2018.

might be deemed as normal text, whilst the same post inserted into a series of consecutive posts might be deemed as aggressive. Third, the fact that aggression could occur in multiple forms, besides the obvious abusive language, for example it could be disguised as irony and sarcasm. Fourth, it is difficult to track all racial and minority insults, which might be unacceptable to one group, but acceptable to another one.

This article reports the solution proposed by *Isistanitos* to the shared task of aggression detection (Kumar et al., 2018a). To that end, several combinations of feature sets and algorithms were evaluated. The remainder of this article is organised as follows. Section 2 describes related work regarding the detection of both aggressive content and bullying accounts. Section 3 describes the dataset used, the selected features and the proposed model for detecting aggressive content in social media. Section 4 analyses the obtained results. Finally, Section 5 presents the conclusions derived from the study, and outlines future lines of research.

2   Related Work

Research into cyberaggression detection has increased in recent years due to its proliferation across social media, and its detrimental effect on people (Salawu et al., 2017). Cyberaggression or cyberbullying detection can comprise four different tasks (Salawu et al., 2017): identification of the individual aggressive messages in a social media data stream, assessment of the severity of the aggression, identification of the roles of the involved individuals, and the classification of events that occur as a consequence of an aggression incident.

Nobata et al. (2016) aimed at detecting hate speech on 2 million online comments from Yahoo! Finance and News. Four types of features were considered: n-grams, linguistic, syntactic, and embedded semantic features. Comments were pre-processed by normalising numbers, replacing unknown words with the same token, replacing repeated punctuation. Results showed that combining all features achieved the best F-Measure results. Similarly, Chavan and S S (2015) aimed at distinguishing between bullying and non-bullying comments. The selected features included TF-IDF weighted n-grams, the presence of pronouns and skip-grams. Only the 3,000 highest ranked features according to χ^2 were selected. Experimental evaluation was based on approximately 6.5k comments from an unspecified site. Posts were pre-processed by removing non-words characters, hyphens and punctuation. Additionally, a spell-checker was applied to correct potential spelling mistakes. Results showed that the best performance was achieved when considering pronouns and skip-grams.

Unlike the binary classification studied in (Nobata et al., 2016; Chavan and S S, 2015), Van Hee et al. (2015) explored the fine-grained classification of cyberbullying events into 7 categories (non-aggressive, threat/blackmail, insult, curse, defamation, sexual talk, defence and encouragement to the harasser). The authors considered two types of lexical features: bag-of-words features (including unigrams, bigrams and character trigrams) and polarity features (including the number of positive, negative and neutral lexicon words averaged over text length, and the overall post polarity). The evaluation showed a high discrepancy of results amongst the diverse classes, which was allegedly due to the extent to which posts in each category are lexicalised.

In summary, most works have been based on content, sentiment, user, network-based features or a combination of them. Content-based features include the extractable lexical items of documents (e.g. aggressive or hate words), such as keywords, profanity, pronouns, part-of-speech tagging and punctuation symbols. Sentiment features refer to certain keywords, phrases or symbols that indicate the sentiment of emotion polarity of the content. User-based features represent those characteristics on users' profiles that can be used to judge the role played by such user in a series of online communications (e.g. age, gender or sexual orientation). Finally, network-based features refer to metrics that can be extracted from the social networks (e.g. the number of friends, number of followers, frequency of posting and how many times posts were shared).

3   Methodology and Data

To automatically detect aggression in social network posts, the proposed approach combines several feature extraction techniques with two well-known classification techniques. This section describes the dataset used (Section 3.1), the features selected for characterising aggressive content (Section 3.2) and the predictive model defined (Section 3.3).

3.1 Dataset

The used dataset was presented in (Kumar et al., 2018b). The original version comprised both Hindi and English posts related to pages and hashtags that are commonly discussed amongst Indians in *Facebook* and *Twitter*. Particularly, more than 40 *Facebook* pages were analysed. Selected pages include news sites, Web-based forums, political parties, student groups, and support and opposition groups revolving Indian University current events. In the case of *Twitter*, several popular hashtags amongst Indians were selected, including Indian vs. Pakistan cricket matches, election results, and beef ban. Since posts were not curated during the recollection, the dataset includes posts in English, Hindi, and other Indian languages, as well as mixed-language posts. Post were manually tagged into one of three aggression levels:

Overt Aggressive (OAG) comprises posts in which the aggression is clearly expressed by certain lexical features or syntactic structures that can be always considered aggressive.

Covert Aggressive (CAG) comprises posts in which the aggression is observed by the intent, but not by their lexical or syntactic structure. Posts in this category might present common polite expressions used in an insincere manner (e.g. irony or sarcasm).

Non Aggressive (NAG) comprises posts that convey no aggression at all. This category also includes posts written in languages different than English and Hindi.

For the purpose of the Shared Task, the proposed approach was designed only for English posts. The shared task organisers provided both training and validation English sets. Nonetheless, both sets also included several posts written in other languages, which made even more difficult the already challenging task of automatically detecting aggression.

3.2 Features for Characterising Aggression

Aggression is characterised by considering four different sets of features. The first feature set (referenced as *GloVe* features) describes each post as a sequence of vectors, where each vector represents a word within the modelled post. The vector representation of words is built using GloVe (Pennington et al., 2014)[1], a log-bilineal model with a least-squares objective that aims at estimating the probability of a word given its context. The model was trained using the social media dataset presented in (Zubiaga et al., 2015). Vector dimensionality was set to 300 as such value was reported to achieve high quality results (Mikolov et al., 2013; Pennington et al., 2014). According to the average post length in the training set, each post was represented by 23 vectors. For those posts having less than 23 words, zero-vectors were added. Those words that are not defined in the GloVe model are also represented as zero-vectors.

The second feature set (referenced as *Sentiment* features) also describes each post as a sequence of vectors, where each vector represents the sentiments conveyed by a word according to the SentiWordNet corpus (Baccianella et al., 2010). In this regard, SentiWordNet defines three sentiment scores for synsets in *WordNet*, namely positivity, negativity, and objectivity. Considering that a particular word might have associated several *WordNet* synsets, its associated vector will contain the average and standard deviation of each score, i.e., the vector will be constituted as $(Pos_{avg}, Neg_{avg}, Obj_{avg}, Pos_{std}, Neg_{std}, Obj_{std})$. The number of vectors representing a post was set to the average number of words that were associated to a *WordNet* synset, i.e. 10. The same strategies as for the *GloVe* features were adopted for dealing with shorter post and words without associated synsets.

The third feature set (referenced as *Composed* features) represents posts as a concatenation of a TF-IDF model, a sentiment analysis model, and several punctuation related features. First, the TF-IDF model is built considering the stems of the words in the training dataset, obtained by means of the Porter Stemmer (Porter, 1980). Then, the TF-IDF models are normalized using L-2 norm. The sentiment analysis model includes four features describing the force of negative, positive and neutral sentiments,

---

[1] GloVe implementation: `https://nlp.stanford.edu/projects/glove/`

Post Id	Text	Tokens
2018626	Puppies are way more important	'pup', 'upp', 'ppi', 'pie', 'ies', 'es ', 's a', ' ar', 'are', 're ', 'e w', ' wa', 'way', 'ay ', 'y m', ' mo', 'mor', 'ore', 're ', 'e i', ' im', 'imp', 'mpo', 'por', 'ort', 'rta', 'tan', 'pupp', 'uppi', 'ppie', 'pies', 'ies ', 'es a', 's ar', ' are', 'are ', 're w', 'e wa', ' way', 'way ', 'ay m', 'y mo', ' mor', 'more', 'ore ', 're i', 'e im', ' imp', 'impo', 'mpor', 'port', 'orta', 'rtan', 'puppi', 'uppie', 'ppies', 'pies ', 'ies a', 'es ar', 's are', ' are ', 'are w', 're wa', 'e way', ' way ', 'way m', 'ay mo', 'y mor', ' more', 'more ', 'ore i', 're im', 'e imp', ' impo', 'impor', 'mport', 'porta', 'ortan', 'puppi', 'are', 'way', 'more', 'import'

Table 1: N-gram TF-IDF features

and a composed score. These scores are obtained according to the Vader model (Hutto and Gilbert, 2014), which reported a F-Measure of 0.96 on *Twitter*. Additional features are added to account for the negative, positive and neutral sentiment score conveyed by emojis, according to (Kralj Novak et al., 2015). Interestingly, only 5.75% of the training posts had emojis, hence in case posts do not have any emoji, features are set to zero. Finally, punctuation related features analyse whether posts have two consecutive dots or commas, question marks, admiration marks, non-printable characters (such as emojis or non-latin characters), and quote marks ("").

Finally, the fourth feature set (referenced as *N-gram TF-IDF* features) represents posts as a normalised TF-IDF model that considers not only the word stems, but also all the possible 3-grams, 4-grams, and 5-grams within the post. Adding n-grams to the word stems aims at capturing different misspellings of words, which are fairly common within the considered dataset. Table 1 presents an example of the tokenisation used for this feature set, in which the last five tokens are stems of the post words, whilst the remaining tokens are n-grams.

3.3 Predictive Model

The prediction model comprises two probabilistic sub-models, a neural network and a Support Vector Machines (SVM). The final prediction is obtained by averaging the class-probabilities predicted by the sub-models and selecting the more probable class. The neural network considers the *GloVe*, *Sentiment*, and *Composed* features, whilst the SVM considers the *N-gram TF-IDF* features.

Figure 1 outlines the architecture of the neural network, which was implemented using Keras[2]. Unless specified otherwise, the hyper-parameters of each layer were set to their default value. The three input layers correspond, from left to right, to the *GloVe*, *Sentiment*, and *Composed* features. The first layer, which was applied to all the input layers, is a Gaussian Noise layer that introduces a noise of mean zero and average standard deviation defined as:

$$G_{stdev} = \frac{1}{NF} \sum_{i=1}^{NF} \sum_{j=1}^{NI} \left(X_{j,i} - \overline{X_i} \right)$$

where NF represents the number of features, NI the numbers of instances, $X_{j,i}$ is the value of the i-feature for the j-instance, and $\bar{X_i}$ is the average value of the i-feature. From left to right, the average standard deviations for the *GloVe*, *Sentiment*, and *Composed* features were approximately 0.15, 0.18, and 0.01. There were two reasons for using Gaussian Noise instead of a more traditional Dropout. Firstly, *GloVe* and *Sentiment* features could be seen as vectors representing concepts. Hence, adding Gaussian Noise can be seen as slightly changing the concept of a word hence working as data augmentation (Zhang and Yang, 2018), while Dropout introduces more drastic changes to the vector. Secondly, the *Composed* feature vectors are very sparse. For example, approximately 99.86% of the elements in the matrices representing both the Kumar's training and validation datasets are zeros. Hence, Dropout would have had almost no impact in this representation. Then, *GloVe* and *Sentiment* features were processes by LSTM layers (Hochreiter and Schmidhuber, 1997), which are well-known for their capabilities for processing sequences. The last LSTM layers were set to return the last predicted value instead of a sequence. On

---

[2]François Chollet et al. 2015. Keras. `https://keras.io`.

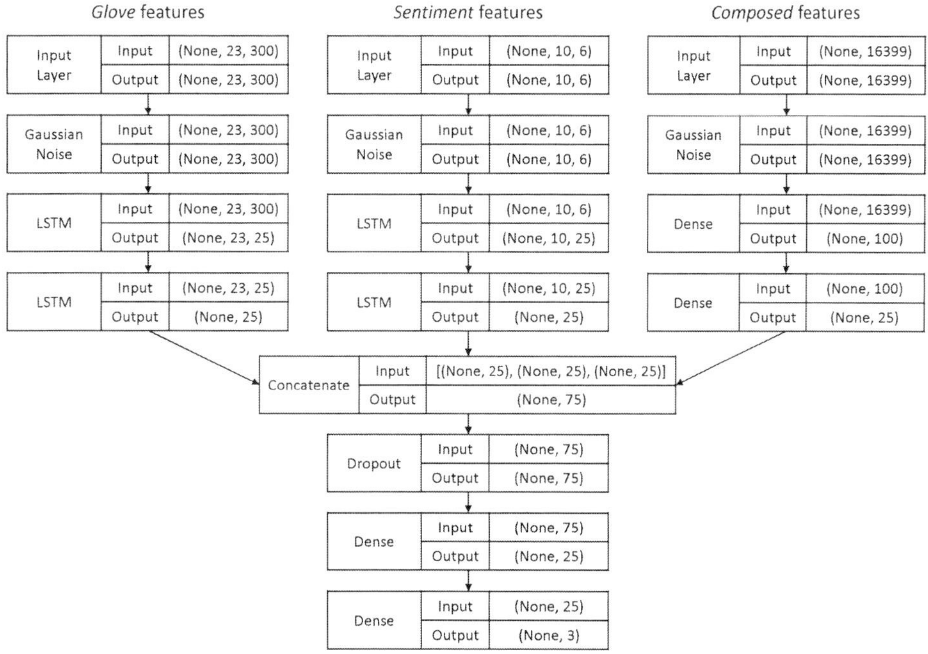

Figure 1: Neural Network

the other hand, the *Composed* features were processed by dense layers. The first dense layer used a $relu$ activation, whereas the second one a $tanh$ activation function. The goal was to constrain the elements in the output vector to values between -1 and 1, which is also a constrain imposed by LSTM layers. Thereby, after concatenating the resulting outputs, no normalisation was needed. Then, to reduce a possible overfitting, a Dropout layer was applied, which set 50% of the elements to zero. Finally, to get the predictions, another $relu$ and $softmax$ activated dense layer were applied. The neural network training considered a cross entropy loss function and weighted the classes using the "balanced" approach of scikit-learn[3]. Optimisation was based on a stochastic gradient descent with a learning rate of 0.01 and a momentum of 0.1. The network was trained for 600 epochs. The selected neural network model corresponded to the one achieving the highest classification performance over the validation dataset.

Finally, the SVM considered the *N-gram TF-IDF* features and was trained using the scikit-learn implementation[4]. Parametrisation included a RBF (Radial Basis Function) kernel, in which C was set to 1 and gamma was set to 0.4, according to the experimental evaluation performed over the training and validation sets. The SVM model was trained using *N-gram TF-IDF*, which considers both word stems (i.e. word level features) and n-grams (i.e. character level features) because it obtained better results that using only n-grams or stems.

4 Results

This section describes the results obtained during the design phase of the proposed model (Section 4.1), as well as the results reported by the Shared Task on Aggression Identification organisers (Section 4.2).

4.1 Design phase results

This section outlines several experiments that were performed during the design phase to assess different feature extraction techniques and classifiers. Such techniques and classifiers were evaluated by not only

---

[3] scikit-learn class weight: http://scikit-learn.org/stable/modules/generated/sklearn.utils.class_weight.compute_class_weight.html

[4] scikit-learn C-Support Vector Classification: http://scikit-learn.org/stable/modules/generated/sklearn.svm.SVC.html

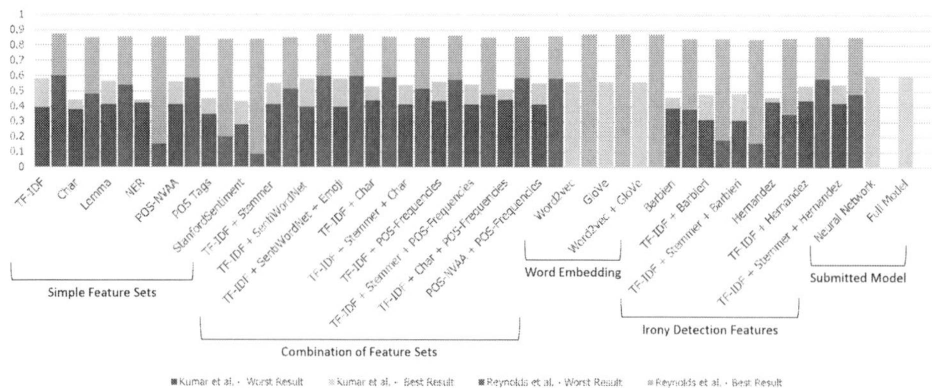

Figure 2: Design phase results

TF-IDF	Tokenisation, stopword removal and TF-IDF weighting.	*Stanford Sentiment*	Overall sentiment of the post and sentiment of each detected syntactic structure.
Char	The defined char-based features.	*word2vec*	Matrix representation based on word2vec.
Lemma	Only the lemma of the tokenised terms are kept.	*GloVe*	Matrix representation based on GloVe.
NER	Only the recognised types of entities are kept..	*Barbieri*	Irony detection features based on (Barbieri and Saggion, 2014).
POS-NVAA	Only noun, verbs, adjectives and adverbs are kept.	*Hernandez*	Irony detection features based on (Farías et al., 2016).
POS Tags	Instead of considering the actual terms, it considers their POS tags.	*TF-IDF + SentiWordNet*	TF-IDF + sentiment polarity of the post extracted with SentiWordnet.
POS-NVAA + POS-Frequencies	POS-NVAA + frequency of the different POS tags.		

TF-IDF + SentiWordNet + Emoji	*TF-IDF + Hernandez*	*TF-IDF + Stemmer + Barbieri*	TF-IDF + Stemmer
TF-IDF + Stemmer + Hernandez	*TF-IDF + Barbieri*	word2vec + GloVe	*TF-IDF + Char*
TF-IDF + Stemmer + Char	*TF-IDF + POS Tags*	*TF-IDF + Stemmer + POS Tags*	*TF-IDF + Char + POS Tags*

Table 2: Feature Extraction

considering the dataset provided by Kumar et al. (2018b), but also the one provided by Reynolds et al. (2011). The latter dataset consists of approximately $3,000$ questions and answers collected from *FormSpring.me*[5]. In this social media site, users can post questions and answer other users' questions with the option of anonymity. Posts were manually labelled into three categories: strongly aggressive, weakly aggressive and non-aggressive. According to the authors, the best classification achieved an overall accuracy of 81%, when considering features related to the number of curse words and their intensity. For Kumar et al.'s dataset, the training partition was used for training, while the validation partition was used for testing. As the Reynolds et al. dataset was not separated into training and test set, it was randomly split 70% training and 30% test sets. The worst and best results obtained using the described feature sets and classifiers are presented in Figure 2, as well as the results obtained for the models submitted to the challenge.

Table 2 summarises the selected feature sets for characterising aggression. Those feature sets (excepting the word embedding based features, i.e., *Word2Vec* and *GloVe*) were assessed considering multiple classification techniques, such as Näive Bayes, SVM with polynomial kernel, SVM with RBF kernel,

---

[5] https://spring.me/

and fully connected shallow neural networks, i.e., a neural layer without hidden layers. Näive Bayes and SVM with polynomial kernel were consistently outperformed by the other techniques regardless the dataset and feature set under evaluation. Conversely, SVM with RBF kernel and fully connected shallow neural networks obtained the best results. Moreover, using a Batch Normalization layer improved the results of the neural network. Deeper dense neural networks were also tested, using up to 2 hidden layers. Nonetheless, they presented two drawbacks. First, the training phase required more than the available hardware resources. Second, in those cases in which the model could be trained, it overfitted the training set. Thereby, deeper neural networks were disregarded. *Word2Vec* and *Glove* features were tested using LSTM-based neural networks as these features are structured as a sequence of features rather than a set of features.

For all the evaluated combinations of feature sets and classification algorithms, results for Reynolds et al.'s dataset were higher than those of Kumar et al.'s dataset. Moreover, results varied at most 3% for Raynolds et al.'s dataset, whilst for Kumar et al.'s dataset variations reached the 34%. This difference could be caused by the fact that posts in Kumar et al.'s dataset were probably written by non native nor Occidental English speakers. Hence, it is likely to find many typos, misused slang, or unusual expressions. Nonetheless, the different feature sets behaved similarly under both datasets. For instance, *TF-IDF+SentiWordNet* outperformed every other feature set, whist *StanfordSentiment* and *POS tags* achieved the worst performance for Reynolds et al.'s and Kumar et al.'s datasets, respectively. Interestingly, different types of features showed the same behaviour for both datasets. For example, considering simple textual features achieved for both datasets higher results than POS tags, lemmatisation, and word embeddings. Moreover, adding more features, such as adding *Char* to *TD-IDF+POS-Frequency* or *Emojis* to *TF-IDF+SentiWordNet*, did not improve results, hinting that some features could introduce noise to post representation.

Finally, the statistical significance of results' differences was tested. Since the data was shown not to be normal, a Wilcoxon test analysis for related samples was performed over the results for the different feature sets, where samples corresponded to the results for each classification algorithm. The null hypothesis stated that no difference existed amongst the results of the different samples, i.e. classification algorithms performed similarly regardless the feature set. Hence, the alternative hypothesis stated that the differences amongst the results obtained for each feature set were significant and non-incidental. In the case of Kumar et al., for most pairs of feature sets no statistically significant differences were observed with a confidence of 0.01. Nonetheless, statistically significant differences were observed for *Barbieri* and *StanfordSentiment*, which were shown to be statistically lower than feature sets involving *TF-IDF*. On the other hand, in the case of Reynolds et al., no statistical differences were observed for the different feature sets. In brief, simple textual features, such as *TF-IDF*, seem to have the same descriptive capability than other more complex features for aggression detection using traditional classification techniques. However, further research is needed to confirm this hypothesis.

4.2   Challenge results

For the purpose of the First Shared Task on Aggression Identification, two sets of predictions were submitted for evaluation. The first set was generated considering the Neural Network described in Section 3.3, whilst the second one was generated using the full method described in that section, i.e., the average between the Neural Network and the SVM model. Table 3 presents the F-measure obtained for the shared task, for both the *Facebook* and *Twitter* classification tasks. The Random Baseline presented in this table was provided by the shared task organisation. Neural Network and Full Model are the results for *Isistanitos'* models. Additionally, the last rows, for both tables present the results for the best performing models for each task. Similarly as for the design phase evaluations, *Isistanitos'* predictions were better for the *Facebook* task. This situation highlights the differences amongst the different social media sites, and the effect that their particular characteristics have over the performed task.

Figure 3 depicts the confusion matrices for both *Facebook* and *Twitter* task. From the obtained results, it is possible to determine the class distribution in the test set. For the *Facebook* set, class distribution was 15.72%, 15.50% and 68.78%, for the OAG, CAG and NAG classes, respectively. It is worth noting

System	F1 (weighted)
Random Baseline	0.3535
Neural Network	0.5894
Full Model	**0.5948**
Best Performing (saroyehun)	0.6425

(a) *Facebook* Task

System	F1 (weighted)
Random Baseline	0.3477
Neural Network	0.5369
Full Model	**0.5480**
Best Performing (vista.ue)	0.6009

(b) *Twitter* Task

Table 3: Results for the English task

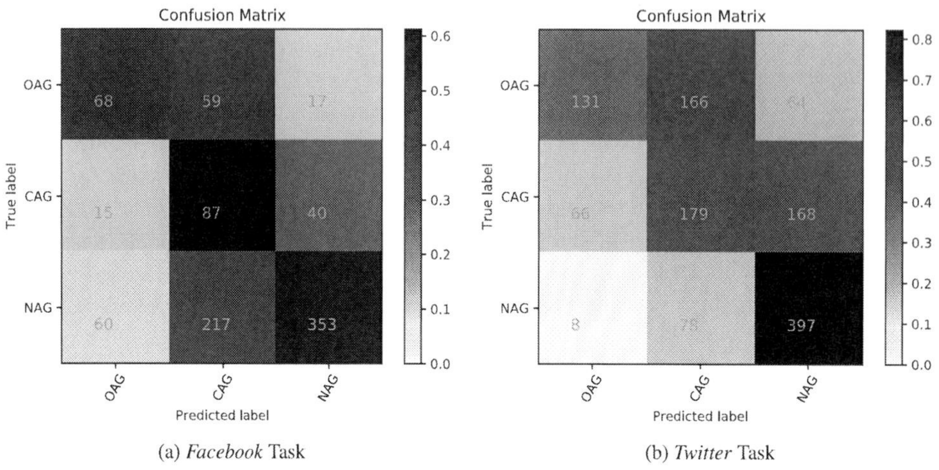

(a) *Facebook* Task

(b) *Twitter* Task

Figure 3: Confusion matrices

that this distribution differs from the one of the train set (22.57%, 35.34% and 42.09%, for the OAG, CAG and NAG classes, respectively), which could affect the predictive power of the trained models. On the other hand, for the *Twitter* set, the distribution was 28.72%, 32.86% and 38.42%, for the OAG, CAG and NAG classes, respectively.

Table 4 shows the confusion matrices of the best submitted predictions per class and task. In the depicted confusion matrices, one of the classes is considered the positive class and the other two are merged into the negative class, e.g. when analysing the NAG class, the posts actually belonging to that class are considering positive, whilst the posts belonging to CAG and OAG are regarded as negative. For the *Facebook* task, NAG had a high True Positive Rate (TPR) of 86.10%, but the True Negative Rate (TNR) was only of 45.26%. For the other two classes, the TNR was higher than 90%, but the TP was lower than 50%. Interestingly, the TPR for CAG was 23.97%, evidencing that the classifier had severe problems to detect posts with covert aggressions. In contrast, when analysing the *Twitter* task, the TNR of each class was higher than the corresponding TPR. Particularly, the TNRs were 86.31%, 71.94%, and 78.13% for NAG, CAG, and OAG respectively, whilst the TPRs were 63.12%, 42.32%, and 63.90%. Despite the different results observed for the *Facebook* and *Twitter* tasks, it can be concluded that detecting covert aggressions is more difficult and error prone that the detection of explicit aggressions.

It is worth noting that detecting CAG posts resulted particularly challenging as they are written without openly using aggressive vocabulary. Moreover, the intent of such posts might be given by their context. Since the CAG class was originally defined as "an indirect attack against the victim and is often packaged as (insincere) polite expressions", it might be necessary to know both reader and writer points of view to understand the real intention. As a result, detecting CAG posts might not be feasible if only the information regarding the individual posts is available.

The obtained results allowed inferring that the performance of the task is highly dependent on the particularities of the social network analysis. For example, Kumar et al.'s dataset was gathered from Indian *Facebook* and *Twitter* pages. In this sense, the dataset could encompass idiomatic expressions

		Actual *NAG* Class		Actual *CAG* Class		Actual *OAG* Class	
		Negative	Positive	Negative	Positive	Negative	Positive
Predicted	Negative	229	277	498	55	697	76
	Positive	57	353	75	68	75	68

(a) *Facebook* Task

		Actual *NAG* Class		Actual *CAG* Class		Actual *OAG* Class	
		Negative	Positive	Negative	Positive	Negative	Positive
Predicted	Negative	542	86	600	234	822	230
	Positive	232	397	244	179	74	131

(b) *Twitter* Task

Table 4: Error per class

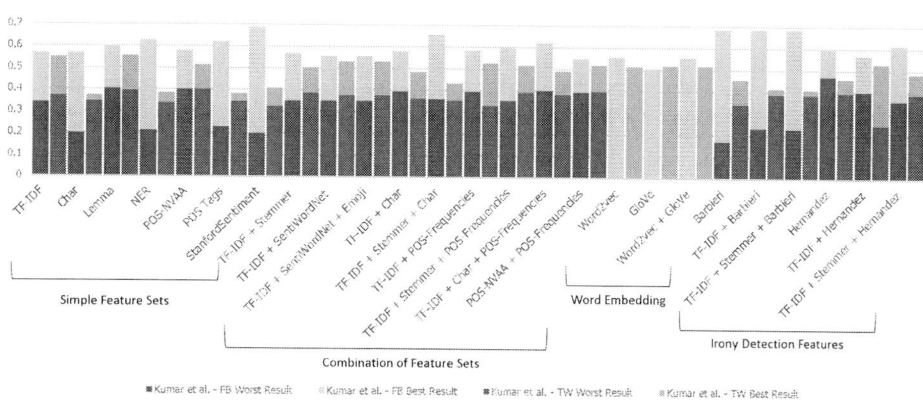

Figure 4: *Facebook/Twitter* gold standard results

that could differ from those used by Occidental users, or with those presenting a more colloquial usage of English. Additionally, given the cultural differences, the criteria for defining what an aggression is and what it is not could differ, hence it could also occur that posts might have a hidden sense that the English language might not be able to capture. In this context, the performance of certain techniques and corpus commonly used for English natural language processing could be reduced.

Finally, after Kumar et al.'s gold standard was publicly released, the evaluations described in section 4.1 were repeated. In this case, Kumar et al.'s training and validation sets were both used for training, thus increasing the size of the training set, and testing was performed using *Facebook* and *Twitter* testing sets. Figure 4 depicts the obtained results. When comparing these results with those obtained during the design phase (Figure 2) for the Kumar et al.'s dataset, the *Facebook* test set obtained better results in 66% of the cases, with differences up to 44%. This was expected as both Kumar et al.'s training and validation sets were purely gathered from *Facebook*. However, such improvements were not statistically significant. This might be due to the fact that feature sets performed differently for the validation dataset. The Pearson correlation between the results obtained during the design phase and those for the *Facebook* test set was -0.66 (p-value <0.01). This implies that the greater improvements were observed for those feature sets that performed poorly during the design phase. For example, *StanfordSentiment*, which achieved the worst performance in the validation dataset, presented the best results for the *Facebook* test set. On the other hand, *TF-IDF+SentiWordNet*, which obtained the best performance for the validation set, decreased its performance when considering the *Facebook* test set. In consequence, the negative correlation shows that it was particularly challenging to predict the performance of a feature set for the *Facebook* test set from the validation set.

Although the performance for the *Twitter* test set was slightly lower than the one observed for validation dataset, such differences were statistically insignificant. Conversely than for the *Facebook* test set, the correlation between the validation and test *Twitter* results was 0.9 (p-value <0.0001). Moreover, *TF-IDF+SentiWordNet* did not achieved the best results as for the *Facebook* test set, even achieving results a 7.58% lower than lemmatisation (the best performing feature set). Since the *Twitter* test set has a similar class distribution to the original Kumar et al.'s training and validations sets, the observed performance might be linked to the class distribution. Nonetheless, more research is required to confirm this hypothesis.

As in section 4.1, a Wilcoxon test was performed with the results for both *Facebook* and *Twitter* test set, defining the same hypotheses. When considering a confidence of 0.01, the null hypothesis could not be rejected for any pair of feature sets. With a confidence of 0.05, the null hypothesis could be rejected for some pair of features in both the *Facebook* (e.g. *Barbieri* and *POS-NVAA*, or *StanfordSentiment* and *TD-IDF*) and the *Twitter* (e.g. *StanfordSentiment* and *Barbieri*, or *TF-IDF* and *POS tags*) test set. Interestingly, the pair of feature sets showing statistically significant differences differed according to the considered dataset. Since the same trained model was used for evaluating both datasets, it cannot be stated that any feature set was inherently superior to another feature set. Hence, further studies are required to assess the descriptive power of features.

5 Conclusions

Aggression in social media is a common issue currently affecting users. Considering the current rate of posting, it is infeasible to manually curate social networks. Therefore, automatic approaches to detect aggression are required, which need to be able to adapt to new aggressive behaviour as cyberaggressors modify their behaviours to avoid detection. It is worth noting that other important applications of the detection of aggressive content are the detection of cyberextremism, cybercrime and cyberhate propaganda.

This paper was developed in the context of the Shared Task of Aggression Detection (Kumar et al., 2018a), which focused on detecting aggression on social media textual content. The proposed approach integrated several textual representations including traditional character, word, sentiment and irony features, and state-of-the-art approaches, such as word embeddings. Results suggested that automatically detecting aggression is a rather complex task, specially when the aggression is covert. Since the shared task was at a post level granularity, information that might be relevant for the task was unavailable. For example, user profile (point of views, common expression, and general behaviour) and post context were both unknown.

Regarding future work, the consideration of new information sources, such as user profiles or context information could be explored. Other neural network architectures, such as CNN or BiLSTM, could also be explored in this context. Another line of work is studying unsupervised machine learning algorithms for feature generation. Considering that the presented approach is English specific, unsupervised algorithms might help to extend the model to different languages without requiring a new corpus from which to extract features. Finally, it could be analysed the adaptation of the proposed model to changes in language usage to cope with the ever evolving nature of social media sites.

Acknowledgements

We acknowledge the financial support provided by ANPCyT through PICT-2017-1459.

References

Swati Agarwal and Ashish Sureka. 2015. Applying social media intelligence for predicting and identifying on-line radicalization and civil unrest oriented threats. *arXiv preprint arXiv:1511.06858.*

Stefano Baccianella, Andrea Esuli, and Fabrizio Sebastiani. 2010. Sentiwordnet 3.0: An enhanced lexical resource for sentiment analysis and opinion mining. In *Proceedings of the Seventh conference on International Language Resources and Evaluation (LREC'10).*

Francesco Barbieri and Horacio Saggion. 2014. Modelling irony in twitter. In *Proceedings of the Student Research Workshop at the 14th Conference of the European Chapter of the Association for Computational Linguistics,* pages 56–64.

Despoina Chatzakou, Nicolas Kourtellis, Jeremy Blackburn, Emiliano De Cristofaro, Gianluca Stringhini, and Athena Vakali. 2017. Mean birds: Detecting aggression and bullying on twitter. In *Proceedings of the 2017 ACM on Web Science Conference*, WebSci '17, pages 13–22, New York, NY, USA. ACM.

Vikas S Chavan and Shylaja S S. 2015. Machine learning approach for detection of cyber-aggressive comments by peers on social media network. In *2015 International Conference on Advances in Computing, Communications and Informatics (ICACCI)*, pages 2354–2358, Aug.

Delia Irazú Hernaǹdez Farías, Viviana Patti, and Paolo Rosso. 2016. Irony detection in twitter: The role of affective content. *ACM Trans. Internet Technol.*, 16(3):19:1–19:24, July.

Sepp Hochreiter and Jürgen Schmidhuber. 1997. Long short-term memory. *Neural computation*, 9(8):1735–1780.

Homa Hosseinmardi, Sabrina Arredondo Mattson, Rahat Ibn Rafiq, Richard Han, Qin Lv, and Shivakant Mishra. 2015. Analyzing labeled cyberbullying incidents on the instagram social network. In Tie-Yan Liu, Christie Napa Scollon, and Wenwu Zhu, editors, *Social Informatics*, pages 49–66, Cham. Springer International Publishing.

Clayton Hutto and Eric Gilbert. 2014. Vader: A parsimonious rule-based model for sentiment analysis of social media text. In *Eighth International Conference on Weblogs and Social Media (ICWSM-14). Available at (20/04/16) http://comp. social. gatech. edu/papers/icwsm14. vader. hutto. pdf.*

Petra Kralj Novak, Jasmina Smailović, Borut Sluban, and Igor Mozetič. 2015. Sentiment of emojis. *PLoS ONE*, 10(12):e0144296.

Ritesh Kumar, Atul Kr. Ojha, Shervin Malmasi, and Marcos Zampieri. 2018a. Benchmarking Aggression Identification in Social Media. In *Proceedings of the First Workshop on Trolling, Aggression and Cyberbulling (TRAC)*, Santa Fe, USA.

Ritesh Kumar, Aishwarya N. Reganti, Akshit Bhatia, and Tushar Maheshwari. 2018b. Aggression-annotated Corpus of Hindi-English Code-mixed Data. In *Proceedings of the 11th Language Resources and Evaluation Conference (LREC)*, Miyazaki, Japan.

Tomas Mikolov, Kai Chen, Greg Corrado, and Jeffrey Dean. 2013. Efficient estimation of word representations in vector space. *arXiv preprint arXiv:1301.3781.*

Chikashi Nobata, Joel Tetreault, Achint Thomas, Yashar Mehdad, and Yi Chang. 2016. Abusive language detection in online user content. In *Proceedings of the 25th International Conference on World Wide Web*, WWW '16, pages 145–153. International World Wide Web Conferences Steering Committee.

Jeffrey Pennington, Richard Socher, and Christopher D. Manning. 2014. Glove: Global vectors for word representation. In *Empirical Methods in Natural Language Processing (EMNLP)*, pages 1532–1543.

Martin Porter. 1980. An algorithm for suffix stripping. *Program*, 14(3):130–137.

Kelly Reynolds, April Kontostathis, and Lynne Edwards. 2011. Using machine learning to detect cyberbullying. In *2011 10th International Conference on Machine Learning and Applications and Workshops*, volume 2, pages 241–244, Dec.

Semiu Salawu, Yulan He, and Joanna Lumsden. 2017. Approaches to automated detection of cyberbullying: A survey. *IEEE Transactions on Affective Computing*, In press.

Cynthia Van Hee, Els Lefever, Ben Verhoeven, Julie Mennes, Bart Desmet, Guy De Pauw, Walter Daelemans, and Veronique Hoste. 2015. Automatic detection and prevention of cyberbullying. In Pascal Lorenz and Christian Bourret, editors, *International Conference on Human and Social Analytics, Proceedings*, pages 13–18. IARIA.

Elizabeth Whittaker and Robin M. Kowalski. 2015. Cyberbullying via social media. *Journal of School Violence*, 14(1):11–29.

Dongxu Zhang and Zhichao Yang. 2018. Word embedding perturbation for sentence classification. *CoRR*, abs/1804.08166.

Arkaitz Zubiaga, Damiano Spina, Raquel Martínez, and Víctor Fresno. 2015. Real-time classification of twitter trends. *Journal of the Association for Information Science and Technology*, 66(3):462–473, March.

Combining Shallow and Deep Learning for Aggressive Text Detection

Viktor Golem   Mladen Karan   Jan Šnajder
Faculty of Electrical Engineering and Computing, University of Zagreb
Text Analysis and Knowledge Engineering Lab
`{viktor.golem,mladen.karan,jan.snajder}@fer.hr`

Abstract

We describe the participation of team *TakeLab* in the aggression detection shared task at the TRAC1 workshop for English. Aggression manifests in a variety of ways. Unlike some forms of aggression that are impossible to prevent in day-to-day life, aggressive speech abounding on social networks could in principle be prevented or at least reduced by simply disabling users that post aggressively worded messages. The first step in achieving this is to detect such messages. The task, however, is far from being trivial, as what is considered as aggressive speech can be quite subjective, and the task is further complicated by the noisy nature of user-generated text on social networks. Our system learns to distinguish between open aggression, covert aggression, and non-aggression in social media texts. We tried different machine learning approaches, including traditional (shallow) machine learning models, deep learning models, and a combination of both. We achieved respectable results, ranking 4th and 8th out of 31 submissions on the Facebook and Twitter test sets, respectively.

1 Introduction

Violence has always been present in human society. As it evolved and technology improved over time, forms of violence changed as well. While only a few decades ago most of the physical and psychological abuse occurred face-to-face, today a lot of psychological violence gets through to the victim via the Internet, and in most cases, social networks. This kind of violence might even be worse, as it can take place at any time, regardless of the physical distance between the victim and the perpetrator. Moreover, social consequences that a person would endure for aggressive speech in real life are virtually absent on the Internet, lowering the inhibitions of potential perpetrators. Although it is next to impossible to prevent people from being rude in real-life conversations, violence through social networks might be alleviated by simply making it impossible to send or share offensive content.

The first step on that path is figuring out which among the millions of messages or posts are indeed aggressive. While it is always possible to rely on the users themselves, e.g., by allowing them to report offensive and inappropriate content, the most common and fastest way to detect aggressive posts is by using supervised machine learning. One option is to frame the task as a binary classification problem and learn a model that discerns between aggressive and non-aggressive speech. In this context, we can define aggressive speech as any kind of text which is offensive or inappropriate. A more ambitious alternative is to subcategorize the aggressive speech into specific types such as racism, sexism, homophobia, trolling, cyberbullying,[1] etc. A successful system employing either approach would obviously be of significant practical value, as it would facilitate detecting and intercepting the aggressive texts before they reach their intended victim, as well as allow implementation of disciplinary measures to discourage aggressive behaviour. This offers considerable motivation for pursuing this strand of research.

Building a system for aggressive text detection using machine learning was the goal at the TRAC1 shared task on aggression detection (Kumar et al., 2018). The goal was to build a system that can label messages from a given dataset as *openly aggressive*, *covertly aggressive*, or *not aggressive*. Open

---

[1] The difference between aggression and bullying is that aggression can be a one-off situation or remark that the perpetrator does not necessarily recognize as being wrong, whereas bullying is a malicious and targeted approach of repeated aggression where the perpetrator has an intent to harm the other person (Whitney and Smith, 1993).

Proceedings of the First Workshop on Trolling, Aggression and Cyberbullying, pages 188–198
Santa Fe, USA, August 25, 2018.

aggression in face-to-face conversation implies yelling, swearing, insulting and dominant attitude, while convert aggression refers to gossiping, inappropriate sarcasm and non-constructive criticism. The typology is arguably challenging when it comes to applying it to online communication, as some of the nuances required to recognize aggression are difficult to discern from text alone. The task turned out to be challenging for human annotators, even though they could refer to context of each message. Expectedly, the task turned out to be even more challenging for automated systems.

In this paper we describe our submissions to the shared task. We tackled the task using traditional (shallow) machine learning models, namely logistic regression and support vector machine (SVM), as well as deep learning models, namely convolutional neural networks (CNNs) and long short-term memory networks (LSTMs). To get the best of both worlds, we experimented with a combination of shallow and the deep learning models. We achieved respectable performance, ranking 4th and 8th out of 31 teams on the Facebook and Twitter test sets, respectively.

The rest of this paper is structured as follows. In Section 2 we give a brief overview of existing work on aggression detection and related tasks. Section 3 presents the data set, while the machine learning models we use are explained in Section 4. In Section 5 we present and discuss the results, followed by a conclusion and ideas for future improvements in Section 6.

2   Related Work

Aggressive speech i.e., abusive language on the web, comes in many flavours, including racism, sexism, homophobia, trolling, cyberbullying etc. Waseem et al. (2017) proposed a typology for various sub-types of abusive language. Similarly, an annotation schema for socially unacceptable discourse practices was proposed by Fišer et al. (2017). Focusing on microblogging, Founta et al. (2018) propose a characterization of abusive behaviour on Twitter. There is a considerable body of work dealing with detecting various types of abusive language; a good overview can be found in (Schmidt and Wiegand, 2017). While distinguishing between aggressive and non-aggressive speech is a already a challenging task, distinguishing between different subtypes of aggressive speech is of course even more difficult. This was observed for the case of open vs. covert aggression by Malmasi and Zampieri (2018), and served as primary motivation for this shared task (Kumar et al., 2018).

A separate issue, which further increases the difficulty of the task, is that there is no universally agreed-upon definition of aggressive speech – a situation which negatively affects the reliability of annotated data. A study by Ross et al. (2016) has shown that supplying hate-speech definitions to annotators can better align their view with the definition, but this does not positively affect annotation reliability. A related study by Waseem (2016) indicated that having expert knowledge during annotation can result in less annotation effort, but this does not necessarily lead to overall better prediction models.

Initial studies dealing with the detection of aggressive speech (or its many subtypes) rely on traditional text classification techniques, such as the naive Bayes classifier (Kwok and Wang, 2013; Chen et al., 2012; Dinakar et al., 2011), logistic regression (Waseem and Hovy, 2016; Davidson et al., 2017; Wulczyn et al., 2017; Burnap and Williams, 2015), or support vector machines (SVM) (Xu et al., 2012; Dadvar et al., 2013; Schofield and Davidson, 2017). For example, the work of Van Hee et al. (2015) focuses on classifying different subtypes of cyberbullying using an SVM. In a similar vein, Malmasi and Zampieri (2017) built a system to discern between hate speech and mere profanity using a combination of traditional models. Recent work also features dictionary based approaches for detecting abusive language in languages other than English (Tulkens et al., 2016; Mubarak et al., 2017). Other approaches focus on users instead of single texts, such as the work of Ribeiro et al. (2018), where the goal was to determine which social networks users resort to hate speech. They employed gradient boosting, adaptive boosting, and a semi-supervised learning method. Notable is also the work of Nobata et al. (2016), who employ a rich feature set and the regression model from Vowpal Wabbit (Langford et al., 2007), which outperformed even deep learning-based models.

In recent years deep learning-based approaches have become increasingly popular for this task. Pitsilis et al. (2018) worked on detecting offensive language in tweets using LSTM, while Gambäck and Sikdar (2017) used CNN for hate speech classification. A CNN model was also used by Zhang et al. (2018),

Text	Label
Well said sonu..you have courage to stand against dadagiri of Muslims	OAG
How does inflation react to all the after shocks of this demon...?	NAG
Not good job.....this guis creating a problem n our socacity	CAG
pakistani team a world racod 373 run in 20 over.	NAG
I visited 5 atm but I cont able to withdraw from money..not working..	CAG
Your nation is neither islamic nor humane	OAG

Table 1: An excerpt from the train set (OAG – openly aggressive, CAG – covertly aggressive, NAG – not aggressive).

but in a combination with a gated rectified unit (GRU) layer. The work of Potapova and Gordeev (2016) describes an approach to detect aggressive speech using CNN and random forest separately, but not their combination. Similarly, Gao and Huang (2017) explore a logistic regression model with a rich set of features and a bidirectional LSTM, without combining the models. Djuric et al. (2015) employ a logistic regression layer on top of representations learned on a huge hate-speech data set using paragraph2vec (Le and Mikolov, 2014). Several varieties of recurrent neural networks (RNN) as well as a CNN were also evaluated in (Pavlopoulos et al., 2017), yielding good results. A survey of related work indicates that, while both shallow and deep learning models have been extensively tested on this task, the approaches that build on their combination are few and far between.

Approaches most related to ours explore combinations of traditional and deep learning methods. Badjatiya et al. (2017) focus on detecting racism and sexism using a combination of models from different paradigms, specifically LSTM in combination with gradient boosting. Similarly, Park and Fung (2017) use logistic regression in combination with several variants of CNNs in a two step scenario. The first step distinguishes between abusive and non-abusive texts, while the second step distinguishes between different subtypes of abuse. The work most similar to ours is that of Mehdad and Tetreault (2016), where an SVM metaclassifier is trained on outputs of a variant of SVM- and an RNN-based model.

3 Dataset

The shared task dataset consists of 15,000 Facebook messages (train and validation portion combined), out of which 3,419 are labelled as openly aggressive, 5,297 as covertly aggressive, and 6,284 as not-aggressive. Table 1 lists some examples from the dataset. As mentioned in the introduction, data labeling was a challenging task as there is a certain degree of subjectivity present when determining the aggression type. From our experience, the most problematic are the openly vs. covertly aggressive cases, in particular the messages that contain no swear words, since swear words usually imply open aggression. Their absence, on the other hand, does not mean that the message is not openly aggressive. We also noticed that many of the texts had grammatical and typing errors, typical of user-generated content. Moreover, a smaller number of texts were not in English. Finally, an additional difficulty is posed by the fact that sometimes broader context is required to correctly classify a message. For example, the text from the third row of Table 1 need not necessarily be covertly aggressive; whether this is the case depends on what the speaker is referring to.

For the above reasons, performing this task manually is not trivial at all. This is also reflected in the final scores of machine learning algorithms, which are relatively low – the top performing systems on the shared task attained 0.64 and 0.60 weighted F1 measure on the Facebook and Twitter test sets, respectively.

4 Models

4.1 Experimental setup

The dataset provided by the task organizers had already been split into a train and development part. However, since it is not uncommon for the test data in such competitions to be unrepresentative of train data, we decided to use the official development set as held-out test data for all preliminary experiments to avoid overfitting our models and to obtain a realistic performance estimate.

We first evaluate our models using 5-fold cross-validation on the train data (the official train set). In each iteration of the cross-validation, models are fitted on four out of five folds, and they are used to label the remaining fifth fold, which is also considered a validation fold. Model hyperparameters (details below) are chosen (in each iteration separately) to maximize weighted F1-score on this validation fold, making the obtained cross-validation score an optimistic estimate of true model performance. This also produces five trained models, each trained on 4/5 of the train data. Labels on the held-out data, i.e., the official development set, are derived for each model by voting of these five models, which could be considered a type of bagging. The main motivation for this slightly atypical setup is ensuring that deep learning-based models have access to a validation fold in each iteration for regularization via early stopping.

For producing the official test set labels, we used an identical setup, but used the union of train and development sets as the train data and the official test set as the held-out test data.

4.2 Classification models

In order to classify the messages, we used three base models: logistic regression, CNN, and bidirectional LSTM (BiLSTM). Apart for lowercasing and tokenization, we did not perform any additional preprocessing.[2] We next describe our models.

The first model we considered was logistic regression. We explored three variants, each based on unigrams, bigrams, and character n-grams, respectively. For each of these variants we also include the following additional features:

- *Bad word occurrences* – boolean feature which indicates if the text contains a word from a list of inappropriate and likely offensive words, obtained from the web;[3]

- *POS tags* – number of occurrences for nouns, verbs, adverbs, adjectives, foreign words, and cardinal numbers (a total of six numerical features). We extract the counts using the POS tagger from NLTK (Loper and Bird, 2002);

- *Text length* in both characters and tokens (two numerical features);

- *Capitalization features* – the number of words that are capitalized and the number of words written in all caps (two numerical features);

- *Numerical tokens* – the number of tokens that represent a number;

- *Named entities* – the number of named entities; three numerical features corresponding to counts of named entities of type *person*, *organization* and *location*, respectively. We used the named entity recognizer (NER) from NLTK (Loper and Bird, 2002) to extract the named entities;

- *Sentiment polarity* – a single numerical feature indicating sentiment polarity of the text. We used the VADER (Gilbert, 2014) sentiment analysis system[4] to predict the sentiment.

Although the final result did not change much after adding all of these features, we did observe minor improvements. The only hyperparameter which was adjusted for this model is the inverse regularization strength C, for which the search interval was $\{2^-15, 2^-14, ..., 2^5\}$. The measure that was maximized was weighted F1-score on the validation fold of the train set. It is worth mentioning that we also tried a linear SVM instead of logistic regression and got very similar results with a somewhat longer training time.

---

[2] We did try to expand contractions (e.g., *can't → can not*) and remove non alphanumeric tokens, but this did not have a significant positive impact.

[3] https://www.cs.cmu.edu/~biglou/resources/bad-words.txt.

[4] Available online at https://github.com/cjhutto/vaderSentiment.

For deep learning models, we tried using a CNN and a BiLSTM network architectures. Inputs to both models were GloVe (Pennington et al., 2014) 300-dimensional word embeddings trained on 840 billion tokens from the Common Crawl or 200-dimensional word embeddings trained on 20 billion tweets.[5] Since the train and dev data are from Facebook, we believed the Twitter-based embeddings might fare better, as the messages from Facebook and tweets should be similar. For this reason, we tried both types of embeddings in our experiments, yielding two variants of each deep learning model. For the BiLSTM we used 100 units as the size of the hidden state and sigmoid transfer functions. The output of the BiLSTM layer is fed into a fully connected layer with three output neurons and a softmax transfer function. Both dropout and recurrent dropout hyperparameters were set to 0.2. Our CNN model used a single convolution layer containing 50 filters of width 3 and 30 filters of width 5, using the ReLU transfer function. This layer was followed by a max pooling layer and a dropout layer with a dropout rate of 0.5. Similarly as for the LSTM, the output of this layer was fed into a fully connected layer with three output neurons and a softmax transfer function. Both BiLSTM and CNN were trained by minimizing categorical cross-entropy using Adam (Kingma and Ba, 2015), with learning rate values of 0.001 and 0.0005, respectively.[6]

We have also tested voting combination of seven models: three logistic regressions, two LSTMs, and two CNNs. Logistic regressions differed in a way that sentences were vectorized (unigrams, bigrams, and character n-grams) and deep learning models used two different embedings we mentioned. Hard voting was used and ties were resolved by choosing the class that was most frequent in the train data.

Finally, we tried taking predictions of the seven models and feeding them into a metaclassifier. It is worth mentioning that we only used hard predictions for the voting classifier, as opposed to using probabilities of each class for the metaclassifier, although it does not seem that this had a significant impact on the final result. The metaclassifier we used was an SVM with an RBF kernel. Hyperparameters that were tuned were the inverse regularization strength C and the width of the kernel function γ. We optimized these using grid search in the range of $\{0.001, 0.01, 0.1, 1, 2, 4, 8\}$ for both hyperparameters.

5   Results

5.1   Preliminary evaluations

Before submitting the final results to the shared task organizers, we ran a number of preliminary evaluations. The results of our models using both 5-fold cross-validation on the train set as well as on the development set are given in Table 2. In general, results of BiLSTM and logistic regression are comparable, while the standalone models perform slightly worse. Among the standalone models, the best results were obtained with the BiLSTM, which is not surprising since this model is considered by many to be the state of the art. The second-best result was achieved by logistic regression with word bigrams as features, which is an interesting indicator that, although logistic regression is considered to be among the simplest traditional machine learning models, it can yield satisfactory results on this task. Results on the development set were slightly different, and this time logistic regression achieved the best results. Moreover, what we find the most interesting is the fact that both combinations of the models (voting and stacking with an SVM metaclassifier) yield somewhat better results than any of the seven standalone models, indicating that combining models is useful.

5.2   Test set results

For the final testing the task organizers made it possible to submit up to three models. We decided to trust the cross-validation scores more than those on the official development set and chosen (1) BiLSTM with Common Crawl embeddings, (2) logistic regression with bigrams, and (3) SVM trained on predictions of the seven models as our final submissions. Testing was conducted by the task organizers on two data sets – one from Facebook, same as the train data, and another one from Twitter. On the Twitter test set SVM had the best result among our models, as expected. Surprisingly enough, on the Facebook dataset the best results were obtained by the BiLSTM-common model; we investigate the reasons for this in

---

[5]Both pretrained GloVe embeddings are available online at https://nlp.stanford.edu/projects/glove/.

[6]All the hyperparameters were chosen to maximize weighted F1-score on the validation fold of the train data.

System	F1 cross-validation	F1 train/dev
Random Baseline	0.345	0.341
Logistic regression unigrams	0.560	0.567
Logistic regression char-ngrams	0.566	0.566
Logistic regression bigrams	0.570	0.583
BiLSTM-common	0.585	0.571
BiLSTM-twitter	0.575	0.561
CNN-common	0.570	0.561
CNN-twitter	0.562	0.580
Voting	0.591	0.595
SVM metaclassifier	**0.603**	**0.603**

Table 2: Results using cross-validation on the official train set (the first column) and on the official development set (the second column). The designations next to the deep learning models refer to the type of embeddings they were given as input.

System	F1 Facebook	F1 Twitter
Random baseline	0.354	0.347
saroyehun	**0.642**	0.592
EBSI-LIA-UNAM	0.632	0.572
DA-LD-Hildesheim	0.618	0.552
TakeLab	0.616	0.565
sreeIN	0.604	0.508
vista.ue	0.581	**0.601**
Julian	0.601	0.599
uOttawa	0.597	0.569

Table 3: Test set results of models which where in top 5 on either dataset. Our (TakeLab) model refers to the the BiLSTM-common model and the SVM metaclassifier model for the Facebook and Twitter test sets, respectively.

the error analysis section below. Table 3 shows the F1-scores of the five best models on each dataset. There is an overlap, since two models were in top 5 on both the first and the second dataset. We ranked fourth on the first dataset and eighth on the second dataset out of 31 competitors. We omit statistical significance tests that compare our system to other systems, as we do not have access to their labels, but instead refer to (Kumar et al., 2018) for additional comparison details.

5.3 Error analysis

We next analyse predictions of our best performing models on the test data, focusing on the erroneous predictions. Figure 1 shows confusion matrices of our best models (BiLSTM-common for the Facebook test set and logistic regression with bigrams for the Twitter test set). The matrices reveal that it was much easier for our model to differ between open aggression and non-aggression than between covert aggression and non-aggression, which is intuitive and in line with findings of Malmasi and Zampieri (2018). Distinguishing between open and covert aggression was also quite challenging, especially on the second dataset. We have also noticed that all labels were distributed more or less evenly over the second dataset, which was the case with our train data as well. On the other hand, most of the sentences from the first dataset were labelled non-aggressive, and our model had a tendency to predict covert aggression when the sentence should have been labelled non-aggressive. There is a chance that this imbalance caused the SVM to perform worse than expected.

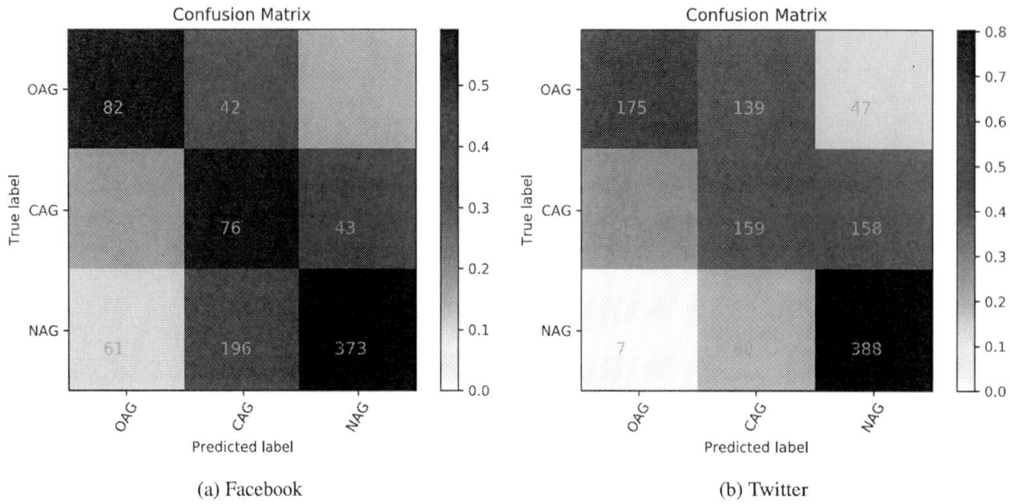

(a) Facebook   (b) Twitter

Figure 1: Confusion matrices of our best models. On the the Facebook (left) test set the matrix is for the BiLSTM-common model. On the Twitter test set (right) the matrix is for the SVM metaclassifier model.

Tweet	True label	Voting	Predictions
me and my mate swapnil patel watching bat swapnil patil!! too confused!! #indvsuae	N	C	C C N N C C N
wickets are falling faster than updates, lol #indvsuae	C	N	C C N N N N N
its like pikachu vs team rocket today .. #indvsuae	C	N	N N N N N N N
#shutdownjnu over democratic setup feeds these thugs	C	O	C C O O O O C
#ShutDownJNU ,it has never been an educational institution,must b handed over to Army to teach them proper lesson.	O	C	O O C C C C C
If glorifying a terrorist can be jusified under FoS, then you can say just any thing. #ShutDownJNU	C	O	O O O O O O O
Send Umar Khalid to Afzal before its too late. Don't let him become another Afzal Guru in real! #ShutdownJNU #MadarsaJNU	O	C	C C C C C C C

Table 4: Tweets, true labels, prediction of the voting classifier, and predictions of all the seven models, where O stands for open aggression, C stands for covert aggression and N for non-aggressive speech.

194

Table 4 shows several interesting misclassifications made by voting combination of our models, as well as predictions of every standalone model. [7] First three examples show misclassifications in which non-aggression was confused with covert aggression. In the first two examples we can see that some models were correct but the majority voted for the opposite class. Interestingly enough, none of the models predicted open aggression. The third example was classified as non-aggression by all models and we believe some human annotators would probably make the same decision. However, there are also situations where all of our models are in agreement but the label they have assigned is obviously incorrect. The remaining examples show cases where open and covert aggression were confused. Deciding between open and covert aggression would have probably been the most difficult for human annotators, so it is not surprising that this is challenging for machines too. Again, we can see that none of the models predicted non-aggression in this situation. Examples in which open aggression is mistaken for non-aggression are quite rare.

6 Conclusion and Future Work

In this paper we have proposed a machine learning model for the problem of detecting open and covert aggression speech using shallow machine learning models, deep learning, and their combination. Among standalone models, the best score was achieved by a bidirectional long short term memory network (BiLSTM). However, combining BiLSTMs with Convolutional Neural Networks (CNN), and variants of logistic regression via a support vector machine (SVM), that served as a metaclassifier, turned out to offer improvements in some cases. This speaks in favor of the idea that combining deep learning models with traditional ones through voting or stacking might result in the best performance. Even though the potential of deep learning itself is evident and deep learning models often do have exceptionally high standalone scores.

We have chosen logistic regression as the "representative" of traditional (shallow) models because it had good initial results and it was fast and easy to optimize, but our experiments were not sufficiently exhaustive to determine whether it really is the best traditional model for this task. However, the combination of traditional and deep learning paradigms did prove promising. Consequently, an immediate venue of future work would be adding other models into the voting ensemble and the SVM metaclassifier. Another possibility would be to explore approaches that combine tree kernels with word-embeddings derived from deep learning, such as the work described in (Plank and Moschitti, 2013; Kim et al., 2015). We feel another promising direction for future work would be addressing the highly noisy nature of the data. One option would be more rigorous preprocessing, such as using specialized tools for normalization of social media text (Han et al., 2013; Baldwin et al., 2015). Finally, the data set could be improved by adding additional context information, if possible, e.g., other social media posts collocated with the post in question, or posts by the same user at other points in time.

Acknowledgements

This research has been partly supported by the European Regional Development Fund under the grant KK.01.1.1.01.0009 (DATACROSS).

References

Pinkesh Badjatiya, Shashank Gupta, Manish Gupta, and Vasudeva Varma. 2017. Deep learning for hate speech detection in tweets. In *Proceedings of the 26th International Conference on World Wide Web Companion*, pages 759–760. International World Wide Web Conferences Steering Committee.

Timothy Baldwin, Marie-Catherine de Marneffe, Bo Han, Young-Bum Kim, Alan Ritter, and Wei Xu. 2015. Shared tasks of the 2015 workshop on noisy user-generated text: Twitter lexical normalization and named entity recognition. In *Proceedings of the Workshop on Noisy User-generated Text*, pages 126–135.

---

[7]The point of the prediction column is not to show what each standalone model has predicted, but to demonstrate what was the voting classifier's dilemma. For the sake of completeness, the order of predictions is: logreg-unigrams, logreg-bigrams, logreg-charngrams, BiLSTM-common, CNN-common, BiLSTM-tweet, CNN-tweet.

Pete Burnap and Matthew L Williams. 2015. Cyber hate speech on twitter: An application of machine classification and statistical modeling for policy and decision making. *Policy & Internet*, 7(2):223–242.

Ying Chen, Yilu Zhou, Sencun Zhu, and Heng Xu. 2012. Detecting offensive language in social media to protect adolescent online safety. In *Privacy, Security, Risk and Trust (PASSAT), 2012 International Conference on and 2012 International Confernece on Social Computing (SocialCom)*, pages 71–80. IEEE.

Maral Dadvar, Dolf Trieschnigg, Roeland Ordelman, and Franciska de Jong. 2013. Improving cyberbullying detection with user context. In *Advances in Information Retrieval*, pages 693–696. Springer.

Thomas Davidson, Dana Warmsley, Michael Macy, and Ingmar Weber. 2017. Automated Hate Speech Detection and the Problem of Offensive Language. In *Proceedings of ICWSM*.

Karthik Dinakar, Roi Reichart, and Henry Lieberman. 2011. Modeling the detection of textual cyberbullying. In *The Social Mobile Web*, pages 11–17.

Nemanja Djuric, Jing Zhou, Robin Morris, Mihajlo Grbovic, Vladan Radosavljevic, and Narayan Bhamidipati. 2015. Hate speech detection with comment embeddings. In *Proceedings of the 24th International Conference on World Wide Web Companion*, pages 29–30. International World Wide Web Conferences Steering Committee.

Darja Fišer, Tomaž Erjavec, and Nikola Ljubešić. 2017. Legal Framework, Dataset and Annotation Schema for Socially Unacceptable On-line Discourse Practices in Slovene. In *Proceedings of the Workshop Workshop on Abusive Language Online (ALW)*, Vancouver, Canada.

Antigoni-Maria Founta, Constantinos Djouvas, Despoina Chatzakou, Ilias Leontiadis, Jeremy Blackburn, Gianluca Stringhini, Athena Vakali, Michael Sirivianos, and Nicolas Kourtellis. 2018. Large Scale Crowdsourcing and Characterization of Twitter Abusive Behavior. *arXiv preprint arXiv:1802.00393*.

Björn Gambäck and Utpal Kumar Sikdar. 2017. Using Convolutional Neural Networks to Classify Hate-speech. In *Proceedings of the First Workshop on Abusive Language Online*, pages 85–90.

Lei Gao and Ruihong Huang. 2017. Detecting online hate speech using context aware models. *arXiv preprint arXiv:1710.07395*.

CJ Hutto Eric Gilbert. 2014. Vader: A parsimonious rule-based model for sentiment analysis of social media text. In *Eighth International Conference on Weblogs and Social Media (ICWSM-14)*. Available at (20/04/16) *http://comp. social. gatech. edu/papers/icwsm14. vader. hutto. pdf*.

Bo Han, Paul Cook, and Timothy Baldwin. 2013. Lexical normalization for social media text. *ACM Transactions on Intelligent Systems and Technology (TIST)*, 4(1):5.

Jonghoon Kim, François Rousseau, and Michalis Vazirgiannis. 2015. Convolutional sentence kernel from word embeddings for short text categorization. In *Proceedings of the 2015 Conference on Empirical Methods in Natural Language Processing*, pages 775–780.

Diederik P Kingma and Jimmy Ba. 2015. Adam: A method for stochastic optimization. pages 1–13.

Ritesh Kumar, Atul Kr. Ojha, Shervin Malmasi, and Marcos Zampieri. 2018. Benchmarking Aggression Identification in Social Media. In *Proceedings of the First Workshop on Trolling, Aggression and Cyberbulling (TRAC)*, Santa Fe, USA.

Irene Kwok and Yuzhou Wang. 2013. Locate the hate: Detecting Tweets Against Blacks. In *Twenty-Seventh AAAI Conference on Artificial Intelligence*.

John Langford, Lihong Li, and Alex Strehl. 2007. Vowpal wabbit online learning project.

Quoc Le and Tomas Mikolov. 2014. Distributed representations of sentences and documents. In *International Conference on Machine Learning*, pages 1188–1196.

Edward Loper and Steven Bird. 2002. Nltk: The natural language toolkit. In *Proceedings of the ACL-02 Workshop on Effective Tools and Methodologies for Teaching Natural Language Processing and Computational Linguistics - Volume 1*, ETMTNLP '02, pages 63–70, Stroudsburg, PA, USA. Association for Computational Linguistics.

Shervin Malmasi and Marcos Zampieri. 2017. Detecting Hate Speech in Social Media. In *Proceedings of the International Conference Recent Advances in Natural Language Processing (RANLP)*, pages 467–472.

Shervin Malmasi and Marcos Zampieri. 2018. Challenges in discriminating profanity from hate speech. *Journal of Experimental & Theoretical Artificial Intelligence*, 30(2):187–202.

Yashar Mehdad and Joel Tetreault. 2016. Do characters abuse more than words? In *Proceedings of the 17th Annual Meeting of the Special Interest Group on Discourse and Dialogue*, pages 299–303.

Hamdy Mubarak, Darwish Kareem, and Magdy Walid. 2017. Abusive Language Detection on Arabic Social Media. In *Proceedings of the Workshop on Abusive Language Online (ALW)*, Vancouver, Canada.

Chikashi Nobata, Joel Tetreault, Achint Thomas, Yashar Mehdad, and Yi Chang. 2016. Abusive Language Detection in Online User Content. In *Proceedings of the 25th International Conference on World Wide Web*, pages 145–153. International World Wide Web Conferences Steering Committee.

Ji Ho Park and Pascale Fung. 2017. One-step and two-step classification for abusive language detection on twitter. In *Proceedings of the First Workshop on Abusive Language Online*, pages 41–45.

John Pavlopoulos, Prodromos Malakasiotis, and Ion Androutsopoulos. 2017. Deep learning for user comment moderation. In *Proceedings of the First Workshop on Abusive Language Online*, pages 25–35.

Jeffrey Pennington, Richard Socher, and Christopher D. Manning. 2014. Glove: Global vectors for word representation. In *Empirical Methods in Natural Language Processing (EMNLP)*, pages 1532–1543.

Georgios K Pitsilis, Heri Ramampiaro, and Helge Langseth. 2018. Detecting offensive language in tweets using deep learning. *arXiv preprint arXiv:1801.04433*.

Barbara Plank and Alessandro Moschitti. 2013. Embedding semantic similarity in tree kernels for domain adaptation of relation extraction. In *Proceedings of the 51st Annual Meeting of the Association for Computational Linguistics (Volume 1: Long Papers)*, volume 1, pages 1498–1507.

Rodmonga Potapova and Denis Gordeev. 2016. Detecting state of aggression in sentences using cnn. *arXiv preprint arXiv:1604.06650*.

Manoel Horta Ribeiro, Pedro H Calais, Yuri A Santos, Virgílio AF Almeida, and Wagner Meira Jr. 2018. Characterizing and detecting hateful users on twitter. *arXiv preprint arXiv:1803.08977*.

Björn Ross, Michael Rist, Guillermo Carbonell, Benjamin Cabrera, Nils Kurowsky, and Michael Wojatzki. 2016. Measuring the Reliability of Hate Speech Annotations: The Case of the European Refugee Crisis. In *Proceedings of the Workshop on Natural Language Processing for Computer-Mediated Communication (NLP4CMC)*, Bochum, Germany.

Anna Schmidt and Michael Wiegand. 2017. A Survey on Hate Speech Detection Using Natural Language Processing. In *Proceedings of the Fifth International Workshop on Natural Language Processing for Social Media. Association for Computational Linguistics*, pages 1–10, Valencia, Spain.

Alexandra Schofield and Thomas Davidson. 2017. Identifying Hate Speech in Social Media. *XRDS: Crossroads, The ACM Magazine for Students*, 24(2):56–59.

Stéphan Tulkens, Lisa Hilte, Elise Lodewyckx, Ben Verhoeven, and Walter Daelemans. 2016. A Dictionary-based Approach to Racism Detection in Dutch Social Media. In *Proceedings of the Workshop Text Analytics for Cybersecurity and Online Safety (TA-COS)*, Portoroz, Slovenia.

Cynthia Van Hee, Els Lefever, Ben Verhoeven, Julie Mennes, Bart Desmet, Guy De Pauw, Walter Daelemans, and Véronique Hoste. 2015. Detection and fine-grained classification of cyberbullying events. In *International Conference Recent Advances in Natural Language Processing (RANLP)*, pages 672–680.

Zeerak Waseem and Dirk Hovy. 2016. Hateful symbols or hateful people? predictive features for hate speech detection on twitter. In *Proceedings of the NAACL student research workshop*, pages 88–93.

Zeerak Waseem, Thomas Davidson, Dana Warmsley, and Ingmar Weber. 2017. Understanding Abuse: A Typology of Abusive Language Detection Subtasks. In *Proceedings of the First Workshop on Abusive Langauge Online*.

Zeerak Waseem. 2016. Are you a racist or am i seeing things? annotator influence on hate speech detection on twitter. In *Proceedings of the first workshop on NLP and computational social science*, pages 138–142.

Irene Whitney and Peter K Smith. 1993. A survey of the nature and extent of bullying in junior/middle and secondary schools. *Educational research*, 35(1):3–25.

Ellery Wulczyn, Nithum Thain, and Lucas Dixon. 2017. Ex machina: Personal attacks seen at scale. In *Proceedings of the 26th International Conference on World Wide Web*, pages 1391–1399. International World Wide Web Conferences Steering Committee.

Jun-Ming Xu, Kwang-Sung Jun, Xiaojin Zhu, and Amy Bellmore. 2012. Learning from bullying traces in social media. In *Proceedings of the 2012 conference of the North American chapter of the association for computational linguistics: Human language technologies*, pages 656–666. Association for Computational Linguistics.

Ziqi Zhang, David Robinson, and Jonathan Tepper. 2018. Detecting Hate Speech on Twitter Using a Convolution-GRU Based Deep Neural Network. In *Lecture Notes in Computer Science*. Springer Verlag.

Filtering Aggression from the Multilingual Social Media Feed

Sandip Modha
DA-IICT, Gandhinagar
sjmodha@gmail.com

Prasenjit Majumder
DA-IICT, Gandhinagar
prasenjit.majumder@gmail.com

Thomas Mandl
University of Hildesheim, Hildesheim
mandl@uni-hildesheim.de

Abstract

This paper describes the participation of team DA-LD-Hildesheim from the Information Retrieval Lab(IRLAB) at DA-IICT Gandhinagar, India in collaboration with the University of Hildesheim, Germany and LDRP-ITR, Gandhinagar, India in a shared task on Aggression Identification workshop in COLING 2018. The objective of the shared task is to identify the level of aggression from the User-Generated contents within Social media written in English, Devnagiri Hindi and Romanized Hindi. Aggression levels are categorized into three predefined classes namely: 'Overtly Aggressive', 'Covertly Aggressive' and 'Non-aggressive'. The participating teams are required to develop a multi-class classifier which classifies User-generated content into these pre-defined classes. Instead of relying on a bag-of-words model, we have used pre-trained vectors for word embedding. We have performed experiments with standard machine learning classifiers. In addition, we have developed various deep learning models for the multi-class classification problem. Using the validation data, we found that validation accuracy of our deep learning models outperform all standard machine learning classifiers and voting based ensemble techniques and results on test data support these findings. We have also found that hyper-parameters of the deep neural network are the keys to improve the results.

1   Introduction

Social media become the popular platform for the common man to the celebrities to discuss or to give their opinions about any real-world events. In the last a few years, the growth of social media users was enormous. With this large user base, a massive amount of User-generated content is posted continuously on Social Media. Social media gives freedom of speech and anonymity to its users. However, often Social media users abuse this liberty to spread abuses and hate through the posts or comments. On many occasions, these User-generated contents are offensive or actively aggressive in nature. Many times, such contents written in a way that might defame or insult individuals or groups of people without actually using any explicit hate-related or abusive words. Genuine social media users may become the victim of such abusive or hate comments. Recently, many cases of suicide have been reported by mainstream media due to trolling or cyberbullying in social media.

Day by day, Anti-Social behavior like Abuse, trolling and cyberbullying is becoming more common than before on the Social media platform. It is high time for researcher, industry to develop a system which identifies problematic posts. Social media posts might contain words which can be considered as either highly or open aggressive or have hidden aggression. Sometimes posts do not have any aggression. Based on these, posts or comments are classified into three classes namely: 'Overtly Aggressive', 'Covertly Aggressive' and 'Non-aggressive' by the track organizers (Kumar et al., 2018a). Henceforth, in rest of paper, we will denote these classes by these abbreviations namely: OAG, CAG, NAG respectively. Table 1 shows the sample posts belonging to these classes.

Our approach for the shared task TRAC (Kumar et al., 2018a) is based on Machine Learning and Deep learning. Track organizers have provided training and validation data as per the schedule. Initially, we have implemented all standard machine learning classifier along with voting based ensemble technique and prepare baseline results on validation data. Thereafter, we have started to develop deep

Proceedings of the First Workshop on Trolling, Aggression and Cyberbullying, pages 199–207
Santa Fe, USA, August 25, 2018.

Id	Text	Class-label
1	Do you see further downside in bank nifty till expiry	NAG
2	Demonitisation like a medicine, it might be sour but slowly and steadily	CAG
3	Woman shame on u	OAG

Table 1: sample post for each class

learning model for the multi-class classification. Since Dataset was created from Facebook posts and comments, we have chosen fastText pre-trained vector for the word-embedding. Our deep learning models were based on Bidirectional LSTM, Convolution neural network. In section 3.2 we will discuss our approaches. It is important to note that we did not engage in any specific pre-processing on the text before they were fed into the deep neural net.

Results declared by track organizers show that our deep learning models perform top in the Social media Hindi dataset, third in English Facebook dataset, fifth in Facebook Hindi dataset. So, overall our models perform fairly well across all the datasets.

The rest of this paper is organized as follows. In section 2 we briefly discuss related work in this area. In section 3, we present the corpus statistics and methodology. In section 4, we present results and give the brief analysis. In section 5, we will give our final conclusions along with future works.

2 Related Work

Hate speech and sentiment analysis are the well studied are in the field of Natural Language Processing. Aggression identification shared task (Kumar et al., 2018a) is more specific than hate speech and sentiment analysis task. In (Xu et al., 2012) authors introduce cyberbullying to the NLP community. They have performed various binary classification on tweets text with bullying perspective to determine whether the user is cyberbully or not, from the sentiment perspective. They reported binary classification accuracy around 81%.

In (Kwok and Wang, 2013), authors have tried to classify tweets against black or not. They have collected two classes (racist and non-racists) of tweets and used the Naive Bayes classifier for binary classification. The average accuracy for the binary classification was around 76 %. (Djuric et al., 2015) also build a binary classifier to classify in between hate speech and clean user comments on a website. Authors have proposed to learn distributed low-dimensional representations of comments using word embedding model such as paragraph2vec model. Authors have created corpus comprises 56,280 comments containing hate speech and 895456 clean comments from Yahoo finance. They have reported AUC score around 0.8007 using CBOW paragraph2vec model against 0.7889 in the bag-of-words model using term frequency.

In (Burnap and Williams, 2015), authors explore cyber hate on Twitter. They have collected tweets for the specific domain in a two-week time window. Collection of 450,000 tweets was annotated as hateful or genuine. They have performed binary classification using SVM, BLR, RFDT, Voting base ensemble and hey achieved best F1-score of 0.77 in the voted ensemble. In (Malmasi and Zampieri, 2017), authors have used NLP based lexical approach to address the multi-class classification problem. They have used character N-gram, word N-gram and word skip-gram feature for the classification.

In (Schmidt and Wiegand, 2017), authors have described the key areas that have been explored to detect hate speech. They have surveyed different types of features used for hate speech classification. They have categorized features in Simple surface features, word generalization features, sentiment features, linguistic features, lexical resources features, Knowledge-based features, and Meta-Information features. Simple surface features include features like character level unigram/n-gram, word generalization features include features like the bag-of-words, clustering, word embedding, paragraph embedding. Linguistic features include PoS tag of tokens. list of bad words or hate words can be considered as lexical resources. Existing knowledge base like ConceptNET, Bullyspace can be used as features.

Another type of problematic post is classified in the shared task eRisk(Losada and Crestani, 2016) within the Cross-Language Evaluation Forum (CLEF). Here, risk situations regarding health and safety are of interest and the research is dedicated to identifying such situations from social media data. In the first classification task, posts which indicate depression of a user need to be found. To simulate the identification of such condition early, the shared task provides 10% of the user data for 10 weeks.

Most of the approaches discussed above are the lexical approaches. Our approach is based on pre-trained word embedding. We have developed deep learning models which implicitly learn features from the text. Some of the lexical features like the length of the post, number of unique words are added explicitly in our model but the system performance was degraded.

3 Methodology and Data

In this section, first, we describe the datasets used in the experiment in 3.1 and in section 3.2 we will discuss our approaches in details

3.1 Dataset

Track organizers provided 15,001 aggression-annotated Facebook Posts and Comments each in Hindi (Romanized and Devanagari script) and English for training and validation (Kumar et al., 2018b). Table 2 shows a detail description of the training and validation Dataset.

Class	English Corpus		Hindi Corpus	
	# Training	# Validation	# Training	# Validation
NAG	5052	1233	2275	538
CAG	4240	1057	4869	1246
OAG	2708	711	4856	1217
Total	12000	3001	12000	3001

Table 2: Class distribution in the Training Dataset

Table 2 shows that there is class-Imbalance in the training data. For English corpus posts from NAG class are the highest and OAG class is lowest. Similarly, for Hindi corpus, posts from OAG class are the highest and NAG class is lowest. We will discuss the effect of class Imbalance on results in the methodology section. Table 3 gives details of the test data corpus. It is worth to note that track organizers provided an open domain Facebook corpus for training and validation but for testing, in addition to Facebook English and Hindi corpus, a Twitter corpus dataset was provided from the completely different domain for both English and Hindi languages.

Test Dataset	# of posts
Facebook English Corpus	916
Twitter English Corpus	1257
Facebook mixed script Hindi Corpus	970
Twitter mixed script Hindi Corpus	1194

Table 3: Test Data Corpus statistics

3.2 Methodology

In this section, we describe our various runs in details. First, we have implemented all standard machine learning classifiers like Multinomial Naive Bayes, Logistic Regression, SGD, KNN, SVC, Decision Tree, Random forest, various voting based ensemble soft and hard classifier with different text representation schemes like count based and TF/IDF to prepare baseline results. On the Facebook English Validation dataset, we got the best-weighted F1 = 0.57 in Logistic Regression with TF/IDF text representation scheme. KNN classifier gives worst weighted F1 = 0.36 on English Validation data. However soft voting based Ensemble of Logistic Regression, Naive Bayes, and Random Forest gives best weighted F1 =0.58 with count-based text representation scheme. As discussed in section 3.1, there is a class imbalance in the training Dataset. We have performed the experiments with equal class labels of training data but weighted F1 decreased substantially on validation data. So, we concluded that there is no need to tackle the class imbalance for this dataset.

3.2.1 Word Embedding for Text representation

Initially, we have implemented both variants of Word2vec namely CBOW and Skip-gram for word-embedding, but the accuracy was around 50%. We obtained the pre-trained Glove vector with different dimensions, but the accuracy improved only marginally. Finally, we settled with fastText (Mikolov et al., 2018) which is an extension of Word2vec. The fastText consider each word as N-gram characters. A word vector for a word is computed from the sum of the n-gram characters. Word2vec and Glove consider each word as a single unit and provide a word vector for each word. Since Facebook users make a lot of mistakes in spelling, typos, fastText is more convenient than Glove and Word2vec. In the followings, the main advantages of fastText are given over other embedding techniques.

1. fastText can generate word embedding for a word which is not processed during the training from its N-gram character features. Word2vec and Glove can't generate word embedding for unseen word.

2. For the rare word, fastText generates better word embedding than Word2vec and Glove due to the n-gram character features

3.2.2 Model Architecture

Track organizers had provided four Datasets from the open domain of Facebook and Twitter for the testing. For each dataset, we have submitted three runs. In this subsection, we will discuss the architecture of our deep neural network models and machine learning models which we developed during the training phase and tested on validation data.

Bidirectional LSTM This is our first deep neural network model which we developed to submit our first run. There is two LSTM layer instead of one in Bidirectional LSTM. Bidirectional LSTM is the extension of the single LSTM. Model parameters are as follows: Maximum features 10000 words; length of the sequence is 500. We believe that embedding layer is the most critical layer for the model. fastText (Mikolov et al., 2018) pre-trained vector is used for word embedding with embed size is 300. We have designed simple bidirectional LSTM with two fully connected layers. We add dropout to the hidden layer to counter overfitting. There are 50 memory units in LSTM and hidden layer. Adam optimization algorithm is used to update the weight matrix. 3 epochs are sufficient for the model to get overfitted.

Single LSTM with higher dropout: This model is based on traditional LSTM model with higher dropout. The first layer is an embedding layer with Maximum features 10000, The length of the sequence is 1024(maximum length of comment in the dataset). We believe that embedding layer is the most critical layer for the model. fastText (Mikolov et al., 2018) pre-trained vectors are used for word embedding with embed size is 300. There are 64 memory units in LSTM layer plus one dense layer with 256 nodes. We add dropout around 0.5 to counter overfitting in the hidden layer. Adam optimization algorithm is used to update the weight matrix. 3 epochs are sufficient to get the best validation accuracy around 58.4 % on English corpus and 61.1 % on Hindi corpus.

Model based on Convolution Neural Network This model is based on Convolution Neural Network. The first layer is an embedding layer with maximum features 10000; the length of the sequence is 1024(maximum length of comment in the dataset). The fastText (Mikolov et al., 2018) pre-trained vectors are used for word embedding with embed size is 300. We have added a one-dimensional convolution layer with 100 filters of height 2 and stride 1 to target biagrams. In addition to this, Global Max Pooling layer added. Pooling layer fetches the maximum value from the filters which are feed to the dense layer. There are 256 nodes in the hidden layer without any dropout. Validation accuracy is around 58.9 % on English corpus and 62.4 % on Hindi corpus.

Model based on Convolution Neural Network with different Filter height This model is by and large same with previous CNN model except for different one-dimensional filters with height 2,3,4 to target bigrams, trigrams, and four-grams features. After convolution layer and max pool layer, model concatenate max pooled result from each of one-dimensional convolution layer, then build one output layer on top of them. We have implemented this model from (Zhang and Wallace, 2015). There are 256 nodes in the hidden layer with 0.2 dropouts. Validation accuracy is around 57.6 % on English corpus and 62.4 % on Hindi corpus.

Model based Bidirectional GRU and Convolution Neural Network This model is the hybrid model of Recurrent Neural Network and Convolution Neural network. The model contains one embedding layer with pre-trained weight matrix from fastText, max features is 10000 and embed size is 300 followed by bidirectional GRU layer with 128 units and one- dimensional convolution layer with 64 filters having filter height 2. Validation accuracy is around 59 % on English corpus.

Voting based ensemble model This model is voting based ensemble model of Bidirectional LSTM, Single LSTM, CNN, Logistic Regression, BIGRU with CNN, the soft ensemble of (random forest classifier, Naive Bayes classifier, Logistic Regression).

Model based on Logistic Regression During the training phase, we got best validation accuracy from using logistic regression among all standard classifier. TF/IDF gives better accuracy than count based text representation scheme. We have set logistic regression parameters like N-gram, minimum document frequency using grid search. We have done little pre-processing on corpus like Non-ASCII character removal. Stop words are not removed. Validation accuracy is around 57.8 % on English corpus and 59.18 % on Hindi corpus.

4   Results

In this section, we first present results on the validation dataset. Table 4 and 5 show results on the English and the Hindi validation data corpus respectively.

Classifier	Accuracy	Precision	Recall	F1 (weighted)	Text Repre. scheme
Naive Bayes	0.5734	0.58	0.58	0.57	count based
Logistic Regression	0.5768	0.56	0.56	0.56	TF/IDF
KNN	0.4415	0.42	0.44	0.38	Count based
Linear SVC	0.5631	0.56	0.56	0.56 0	TF/IDF
Decision Tree	0.4841	0.48	0.48	0.48	count base
SGD	0.5691	0.57	0.57	0.57	TF/IDF
Random Forest	0.5101	0.5	0.51	0.49	TF/IDF
Soft ensemble	0.5894	0.59	0.59	0.58	count based
Hard Ensemble	0.5751	0.57	0.58	0.57	count based
LSTM NN + fasttext	0.584	0.59	0.58	0.59	word embedding
Convolution NN + fasttext	0.589	0.58	0.59	0.58	word embedding
Convolution Ngram+fasttext	0.576	0.6	0.58	0.58	word embedding
BIGRU+FASTTEXT	0.59	na	na	na	word embedding
Bidirectional LSTM + fasttext	0.5928	0.59	0.58	0.58	word embedding

Table 4: Results on English (Facebook) validation data

As we look at the result on validation data, we obtained best weighted F1 score and validation accuracy for English dataset in the soft ensemble of Logistic Regression, Random Forest, and SGD and in the Bidirectional LSTM. For Hindi corpus, we got the best weighted F1 score and validation accuracy in Convolution Neural Network.

Classifier	Accuracy	Precision	Recall	F1 (weighted)	Text Repre. scheme
Naive Bayes	0.5718	0.59	0.57	0.56	TF/IDF
Logistic Regression	0.5991	0.62	0.6	0.59	TF/IDF
KNN	0.3318	0.43	0.33	0.34	Count based
Linear SVC	0.5784	0.58	0.58	0.58 0	TF/IDF
Decision Tree	0.5211	0.52	0.52	0.52	count base
SGD	0.5924	0.60	0.59	0.59	TF/IDF
Random Forest	0.5511	0.56	0.55	0.55	TF/IDF
Soft ensemble	0.5981	0.61	0.60	0.60	TF/IDF
Hard Ensemble	0.5944	0.60	0.59	0.59	TF/IDF
LSTM NN + fasttext	0.611	0.6454	0.6111	0.6042	word embedding
Convolution NN + fasttext	0.624	0.6278	0.6241	0.6244	word embedding
Convolution Ngram NN	0.624	0.63	0.62	0.62	word embedding

Table 5: Results on Hindi (Facebook) validation data

System	F1 (weighted)
Random Baseline	0.3535
BiDirectional LSTM with fastText-run-1	0.5959
LSTM with higher dropout-run2	**0.6178**
N-Gram CNN-run-3	0.5580
top team saroyehun	0.6424

Table 6: Results for the English (Facebook) dataset

Table 6, 7, 8 and 9 shows our models results on different test datasets which are created from Facebook and Twitter posts. Figure 1, 2, 3 and 4 show the confusion matrices for the each dataset. One can observe that weighted F1 score on the test data is better than the validation dataset. Posts in the datasets are related to different events. Without any given context, our model gives a weighted F1 score around 0.6178 for English Facebook dataset and 0.6081 for Hindi Facebook Dataset. The Hindi and English Social media test datasets were created from the Twitter with 3 or 4 domain like # JNUShutdown, #Cricket2015, #demonetization. We have trained models on Facebook comments or posts and tested on Twitter posts. It is worth to note that there are lexical differences between Twitter posts and Facebook posts. Twitter posts are 140 characters long and the majority contain user mentions, external URL, and Hashtags while most of Facebook posts are longer than Twitter posts does not have Hashtags or user mentions in the text. However, our model gives a weighted F1 score around 0.5520 for English Twitter dataset and for mixed script Hindi Twitter dataset, our model gives F1 weighted around 0.4992 in model based on Convolution Neural network.

4.1 Result Analysis

In this subsection, we will present result analysis. The results on validation data show that models based on LSTM and CNN marginally outperform (around 2 % to 3%) standard machine learning classifiers with respect to weighted F1- score and accuracy on Facebook English corpus and Hindi corpus. Table 10 shows tweets which belong to the CAG class are classified under the NAG class. Table 11 shows the tweets which belong to NAG class are classified under the OAG class.

The main reasons for the posts which are failed to classified under CAG class are the unavailability of the context and difference with the wisdom of the human assessor. Same reasons can be applied to the tweets which are classified in OAG but actually they belong to NAG class.

System	F1 (weighted)
Random Baseline	0.3477
BIGRU-CNN-withfasttext-run-1	0.5486
CNN-withfastText-run-2	**0.5520**
BiDirectional LSTM with fastText-run-3	0.5423
Top team vista.ue	0.6008

Table 7: Results for the English (Social Media(Twitter) Dataset

System	F1 (weighted)
Random Baseline	0.3571
CNN-withfastText-run-1	**0.6081**
N-Gram CNN-run-2	0.5965
logistic Regression with Tf/IDF -run-3	0.6034
top team na14	0.6450

Table 8: Results for the Hindi (Facebook) Dataset

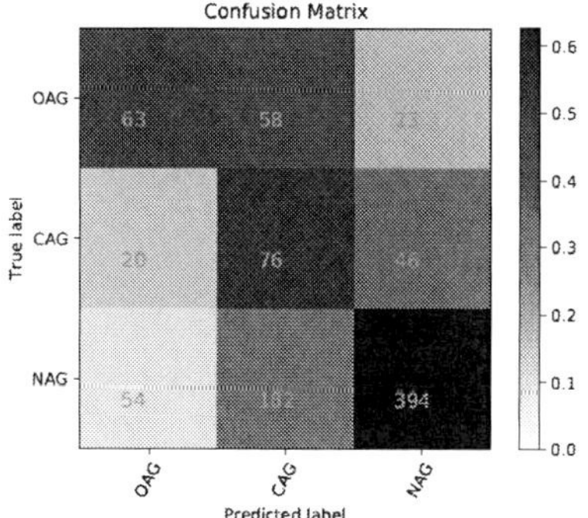

Figure 1: Confusion Matrix for EN-FB task

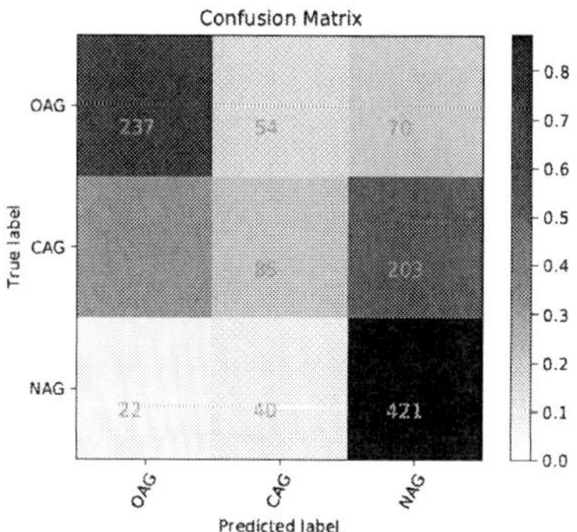

Figure 2: Confusion Matrix for EN-TW task

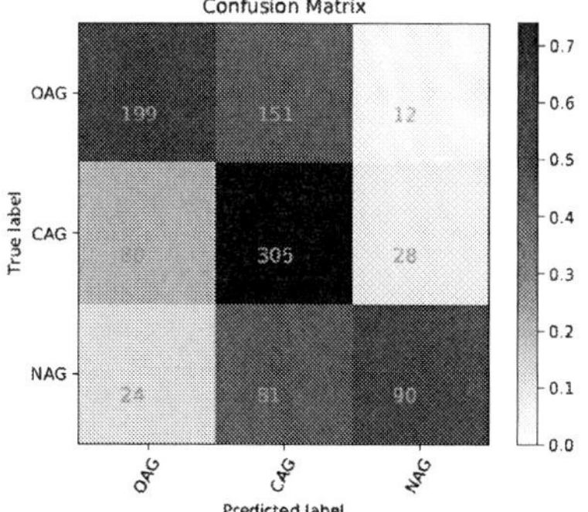

Figure 3: Confusion Matrix for HI-FB task

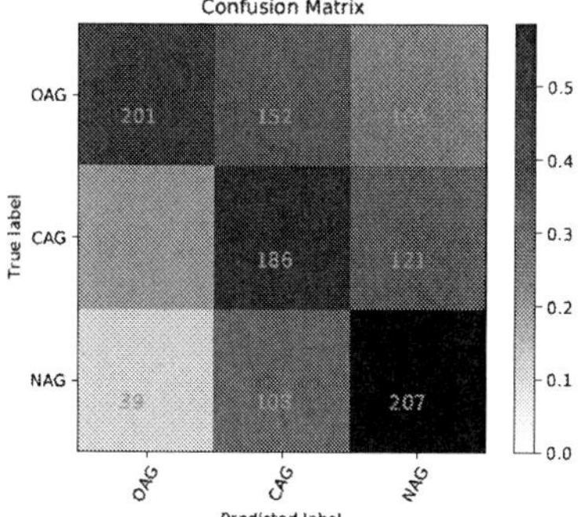

Figure 4: Confusion Matrix for HI-TW task

System	F1 (weighted)
Random Baseline	0.3206
CNN-withfastText-run-1	**0.4992**
LSTM with higher dropout-run2	0.4579
voting based ensemble	0.4797
top team DA-LD-Hildesheim	0.4992

Table 9: Results for the Hindi (Social Media(Twitter)) Dataset.

Post-id	Text	Actual Class	Predicted Class
facebook-467581	modi should learn from him how what to communicate common people not to corporate people.	CAG	NAG
facebook-442501	The name and the meaning has changed of RBI to reverse bank of India.	CAG	NAG

Table 10: Tweets which are hard to classify in CAG class

Post-id	Text	Actual Class	Predicted Class
facebook-408314,	Pakistan is a terrorist country and no body would like to play with Pakistan.	NAG	OAG
facebook-355578,	Gandhi Killer Ram (Nathu) Temple in India Big Shame 4India.	NAG	OAG
facebook-400906	You have to goes for this facts in U N O in USA and then you can claims for Kashmir.	NAG	OAG

Table 11: Tweets belongs to NAG but classified under OAG class

5 Conclusion

After performing exhaustive experiments, we conclude that Deep Neural Network with proper word embedding marginally outperforms all standard machine learning classifier and ensemble techniques. The critical parameters for the models are the batch size and learning rate. We also concluded that higher drop out will help to counter model overfitting and improvise a standard evaluation metric. CNN and LSTM are the better models for these datasets. On the English test corpus, we obtained a better F1 score for NAG class and poor F1-score for CAG class which supports the previous (Malmasi and Zampieri, 2017) findings. For the Facebook Hindi test corpus, the same seems not to be true. We obtained a better F1 score for CAG class than NAG class. In the future, we will focus on various pre-trained word embedding models and study how the word is represented by this model. we have planned to develop deeper Neural nets and identify optimal parameters using grid search. It is also to be noted that the model leads to poor result on test data created from the different source than the training corpus source.

Acknowledgements

We would like to acknowledge undergraduate students of LDRP-ITR Mr.Daksh Patel, Mr.Aditya Patel, Mr.Yash Madhani, Mr.Kishan Thakkar, and Miss. Krishna Tank for their support in post hoc analysis and they have prepared bad-word files for both the English and Hindi languages(Romanized and Devanagari). In the future, we would like to incorporate these lexical resources features in our models.

References

Pete Burnap and Matthew L Williams. 2015. Cyber hate speech on twitter: An application of machine classification and statistical modeling for policy and decision making. *Policy & Internet*, 7(2):223–242.

Nemanja Djuric, Jing Zhou, Robin Morris, Mihajlo Grbovic, Vladan Radosavljevic, and Narayan Bhamidipati. 2015. Hate speech detection with comment embeddings. In *Proceedings of the 24th International Conference on World Wide Web Companion*, pages 29–30. International World Wide Web Conferences Steering Committee.

Ritesh Kumar, Atul Kr. Ojha, Shervin Malmasi, and Marcos Zampieri. 2018a. Benchmarking Aggression Identification in Social Media. In *Proceedings of the First Workshop on Trolling, Aggression and Cyberbulling (TRAC)* Santa Fe, USA.

Ritesh Kumar, Aishwarya N. Reganti, Akshit Bhatia, and Tushar Maheshwari. 2018b. Aggression-annotated Corpus of Hindi-English Code-mixed Data. In *Proceedings of the 11th Language Resources and Evaluation Conference (LREC)*, Miyazaki, Japan.

Irene Kwok and Yuzhou Wang. 2013. Locate the hate: Detecting Tweets Against Blacks. In *Twenty-Seventh AAAI Conference on Artificial Intelligence*

David E. Losada and Fabio Crestani. 2016. A test collection for research on depression and language use. In *Conference Labs of the Evaluation Forum*, pages 28–39. Springer.

Shervin Malmasi and Marcos Zampieri. 2017. Detecting Hate Speech in Social Media. In *Proceedings of the International Conference Recent Advances in Natural Language Processing (RANLP)*, pages 467–472.

Tomas Mikolov, Edouard Grave, Piotr Bojanowski, Christian Puhrsch, and Armand Joulin. 2018. Advances in pre-training distributed word representations. In *Proceedings of the International Conference on Language Resources and Evaluation (LREC 2018)*

Anna Schmidt and Michael Wiegand. 2017. A Survey on Hate Speech Detection Using Natural Language Processing. In *Proceedings of the Fifth International Workshop on Natural Language Processing for Social Media. Association for Computational Linguistics*, pages 1–10, Valencia, Spain.

Jun-Ming Xu, Kwang-Sung Jun, Xiaojin Zhu, and Amy Bellmore. 2012. Learning from bullying traces in social *Proceedings of the 2012 conference of the North American chapter of the association for computational linguistics: Human language technologies*, pages 656–666. Association for Computational Linguistics.

Ye Zhang and Byron Wallace. 2015. A sensitivity analysis of (and practitioners' guide to) convolutional neural networks for sentence classification. *arXiv preprint arXiv:1510.03820*

Author Index